Jesus, Resurrected

Jesus, Resurrected

Risk Analysis and Recovery of Nine Post-Crucifixion
Encounters with Jesus in the Contemporary Setting of
First-Century Palestine and Haunted Galilee

ROGER S. BUSSE

Foreword by Stephen J. Patterson

RESOURCE *Publications* · Eugene, Oregon

JESUS, RESURRECTED
Risk Analysis and Recovery of Nine Post-Crucifixion Encounters with Jesus in the Contemporary Setting of First-Century Palestine and Haunted Galilee

Copyright © 2017 Roger S. Busse. All rights reserved. Except for brief quotations in critical publications or reviews, no part of this book may be reproduced in any manner without prior written permission from the publisher. Write: Permissions, Wipf and Stock Publishers, 199 W. 8th Ave., Suite 3, Eugene, OR 97401.

Resource Publications
An Imprint of Wipf and Stock Publishers
199 W. 8th Ave., Suite 3
Eugene, OR 97401

www.wipfandstock.com

PAPERBACK ISBN: 978-1-5326-1122-3
HARDCOVER ISBN: 978-1-5326-1124-7
EBOOK ISBN: 978-1-5326-1123-0

Manufactured in the U.S.A.   JANUARY 23, 2017

With love and gratitude to my wife, Tami, to my children, Josh, Kim, Hunter, and Sophia, and my family, this book is dedicated to my teachers, O. H. Tabor, DD, and Helmut Koester, Dr. theol.

A special thanks to Stephen J. Patterson for his encouragement, suggestions, and criticisms. I would also like to thank the editors and staff of Wipf and Stock, particularly Matthew Wimer. I would also like to express my sincere thanks to Kark Coppock, my copy editor for his excellent suggestions and corrections to the manuscript.

I remember the day my daughter Kim sent Ogden's book *Magic, Witchcraft, and Ghosts* to me. I am indebted to her for this contribution and for the years of research that resulted. In our final discussions, Helmut Koester remained interested in this subject and was so generous to me. He was a friend for thirty years, and a demanding mentor. I am indebted to him for opening my mind to questions and issues still to be investigated in the origins of Christianity.

Contents

Foreword by Stephen J. Patterson | ix

1. Troubling Beginnings: Entry into an Alien World | 1
2. Demons, Ghosts of the Retributive Dead, and Satan | 14
3. Confronting Satan, Demons, and the Dead in Galilee | 22
4. Destroying the "Evildoer": Practices Used to Neutralize Dark Magicians | 47
5. Hunting Jesus' Followers: The Urgency to Neutralize Jesus' Exorcists | 60
6. Post-Crucifixion Encounters with the Dead in the First Century | 66
7. Recovering the Risk Context of Post-Crucifixion Events in Mark | 75
8. The Risk Context of Post-Crucifixion Encounters in Matthew | 106
9. Luke and the Refinement of the Post-Crucifixion Tradition | 141
10. Post-Crucifixion Encounters as Sign (*Semeion*) in John | 172
11. The Noncanonical Sources | 201
12. The Perilous Risk Context of Paul's Encounter | 212
13. Risk Analysis and the Recovery of Reliable Events in Their Contemporary Setting | 223
14. Other Risk Implications: The Messianic Secret and House Churches | 252

Bibliography | 255

Foreword

In the winter of 2014 I met Roger Busse for one of our regular late afternoon chats over beer (me) and wine (him). Roger is a banker who went to Harvard Divinity School. I didn't meet him there, but later in Oregon, where we both had settled. Roger's business is banking and risk analysis, but his passion is the critical study of the Bible and, especially, the study of Christian origins. We shared a mentor in Helmut Koester at Harvard, so we always had plenty to talk about. On this afternoon Roger had a new book to discuss: Daniel Ogden's *Magic, Witchcraft, and Ghosts in the Greek and Roman World* (Oxford, 2009). If I recall correctly, his daughter had seen it and thought he might add it to his library on the world of Christian origins. Ogden, of course, is well known to Classicists for his scholarship on ancient magic, especially his 2001 book, *Greek and Roman Necromancy* (Princeton). But to ordinary biblical scholars he was as yet not widely known. As it happened, one of my students had just turned up his work on necromancy in researching ancient ways of understanding the resurrection of the dead. So when Roger brought my attention to *Magic, Witchcraft, and Ghosts*, I was all ears. As usual, he had a hundred questions about how Ogden's materials might impact the way we understand a myriad of texts, including the stories of Jesus' entombment and subsequent resurrection, about Jesus and his disciples exorcising demons, and especially those stories in which Jesus himself raises the dead. Would ancients have understood Jesus as a necromancer and an exorcist?

This all brought to mind the work, now a generation past and largely ignored, of Morton Smith on the Secret Gospel of Mark. The Secret Gospel itself became so controversial that Smith's scholarship, which was devoted primarily to filling in the ancient world of magic, in which such a text would make sense, was scarcely noticed. But, as if the publication of the Secret

Gospel (*Clement of Alexandria and a Secret Gospel of Mark*, Harvard, 1973) had not already generated enough controversy, Smith went on to publish a second book entitled *Jesus the Magician* (Harper, 1978), in which he argued that ancients, particularly the enemies of Jesus, would have understood Jesus and his followers within the broad categories of magic, witchcraft, and the "dark arts." Most of Smith's evidence was drawn directly from the Greek Magical Papyri, which were not yet widely available in translation. All of this took nearly everyone by surprise and evoked broad dismay, even though much of it sounded quite plausible. So Smith, finally, did not have much impact on the study of Jesus and his approach was not adopted by anyone else. Until now.

The present work is the result of Busse's own interest in these seemingly esoteric matters, which, however, seem to have very significant heuristic value. In many ways it is a simple account, which assumes the historicity of too many things—a matter of perennial dissent in our afternoon conversation. Smith's was too. But these assumptions at least allow for a very straightforward historical exercise. Busse's question is: how would ancients, particularly Jesus' enemies, have understood what Jesus was doing, the mechanisms, the techniques, the outcomes. And why, he asks, would people have risked associating themselves with a person accused of being engaged in such shadowy, disreputable activity. The result is an engaging and enlightening read of the Jesus tradition that is sure to surprise, and perhaps even delight the reader whose mind is open to new ideas and able to handle the subtleties of cross-cultural exploration. And it was all made possible by Ogden's recent book. Now that this material is easily accessed and digested, more will see the relevance of it and continue down this path.

Stephen J. Patterson
George H. Atkinson Professor of Religious and Ethical Studies
Willamette University

1

Troubling Beginnings

Entry into an Alien World

Why Would Anyone Name a Crucified Dark Magician "Master?"

> The resurrection and the appearances of Jesus are best explained as a catalyst which prompted reactions that resulted in the missionary activity and founding of the churches, but also in the crystallization of the tradition about Jesus and his ministry.[1]

Are the post-crucifixion encounters with Jesus adequately typified as a "catalyst"? Can this rather benign word account for the perilous risk of naming a peasant Galilean Jewish exorcist "master," or especially "my teacher"; particularly when this man was publicly accused by the Jerusalem religious elite of being possessed by Beelzebul, prince of demons,[2] and then was convicted and crucified by the powerful Roman elite as an "evildoer," i.e., a contemporary term used for dark magicians?[3] To name Jesus "master" or "teacher" was punishable by death under Roman law in first-century Palestine.[4] How can we explain why they would take such risks?

---

1. Koester, *History*, 84–85.

2. Mark 3:22. A full discussion of the accusation of possession by Beelzebul is provided in this study.

3. John 18:28–32. Contemporary use of this term is provided below.

4. Specific references to the prohibition and punishment for the crime of magic under Roman law, including punishment by death, are provided in subsequent chapters. The prohibition is found even in the earliest form of Roman law, including the *Twelve Tables*, II.7, VII.3 and 14. For a comprehensive reconstruction of the *Twelve Tables*, see the Constitution Society (http://www.constitution.org/sps/sps01_1.htm), as well as

Certainly, Koester's statement fails to capture the deadly, contextual risks of those who ultimately did embrace itinerant "missionary activity" on behalf of a crucified criminal, boldly invoking his name to take control of satanic demons despite being tracked by the same enemies, spies and informants of the Roman authorities that had captured Jesus. No wonder these men and women met secretly in homes for years. They did so because they lived in a social and cultural milieu that feared those who controlled demons, encounters with the evil dead and dangerous retributive ghosts. Contemporary examples show that authorities sought out and quickly killed dark magicians and "evildoers" considered possessed by Satan and, therefore, threatening to those in power—the very accusation brought against Jesus by the Jerusalem elite.[5] Why would Jesus' peasant exorcists not flee and hide?

To be clear, Jesus' activity was understood by his enemies as the *darkest of magic*,[6] particularly in his forbidden practice of necromancy, the manipulation and raising of the dead.[7] John 11:1–44 records Jesus publicly practicing a form of necromancy in Bethany. It was this event that led authorities in Jerusalem to capture and destroy him, exactly because he blatantly performed the most terrifying form of illegal dark magic.[8] Only this explains the quick

---

Ogden, *Magic*, 277–99, and Plessis, *Borkowski's Textbook on Roman Law*, 5–6, 29–30.

5. See, e.g., Luke 11:20, and especially John 18:28, 30. Jesus is portrayed not just as a criminal, but instead, as an "evildoer," a term in the ancient world equivalent to an illegal, dangerous dark magician. Pilate certainly knew Jesus' reputation as an exorcist and necromancer. It is he alone who ordered his crucifixion, a form of death known to neutralize retribution by the dead against their executioners (see below). Also see Smith, *Jesus the Magician*, 41, 109, 175. Smith states: "'Doer of Evil' = Magician: Codex Theodosianus IX.16.4; Codex *Justinianus* IX.18.7, citing Constantius; compare 1 Peter 4:15 and Tertullian, *Scorpiace* 12.3. Selwin, *1 Peter*, understood 4.15 correctly and cited Tacitus' use of *malefica*, Annals II.69."

6. Luke 11:20; see also Hull, *Hellenistic Magic*, 61–62, 68–72.

7. Ogden, *Magic*, 192–205.

8. John 11:1–44, the raising of the Lazarus. Here Jesus practices necromancy, the darkest of magic in the ancient world (Ogden, *Magic*, 146, 149–52). It is this event, witnessed by Jesus' enemies, which led to the urgent plot to kill him, i.e., John 11:53. This is also the most convincing reason why a plot to ritually kill Jesus by crucifixion was sought out, i.e., that Jesus was practicing the most heinous kind of magic under the influence of Satan and was extremely dangerous to the ruling elite whom he had publicly denounced as "vipers," i.e., the demonic possessed, and announced their end. As will be demonstrated in later chapters, crucifixion extinguished the possibility of retribution by the evil dead by placing a divine curse on the deceased. Necromancy was punishable by death under Roman law. As such, for the Roman-sympathizing Jerusalem aristocracy to allow its practice by a peasant exorcist would also make them susceptible to execution. Raymond Brown incorrectly understands the Lazarus event as a theological motif (Brown, *John*, 428–29); Bultmann similarly sees this as a motif of

action of his enemies to find, brutalize and ritually execute him; i.e., assuredly as a magician possessed and under control of Beelzebul, the angel of Satan.[9] Consequently, the risks of embracing Jesus as master become almost incomprehensible in their contextual setting after the crucifixion. Why would a Galilean peasant-exorcist—one who had watched his master labeled "Satanic," captured, brutally beaten and hobbled, tortured and intentionally executed under a divine curse (intended to annihilate him body and soul)—suddenly embrace the perilous risk of announcing encounters with this demonized Jew? Particularly after having literally cursed and denied him before these same enemies after his capture![10] In a world that acknowledged and expected encounters with ghosts, demons and spirits, what would make *any* experience with the convicted wicked dead justify acceptance of such risks, or inspire a willingness to suffer the same fate? But, this is exactly what happened, so risk-related questions are fascinating and truly abound. They demand an explanation and evaluation in this contemporary setting.

Yet, even before these post-crucifixion encounters with Jesus were said to have taken place, there were other events that raise even more fundamental questions. In fact, they must be answered first to reach a reasonable comprehension of the contemporary risk setting of first-century Palestine and the risk response of Jesus' followers post-crucifixion within that context. Only such an inquiry can make any encounter comprehensible or recoverable in their original setting.

What is noteworthy is that these questions all address risk, or more specifically, actions taken to either avoid or accept perilous risks. For example, why was Jesus crucified by Romans, versus stabbed, beheaded or stoned like other Jewish antagonists?[11] Indeed, why would his enemies demand that he be crucified? Why was a penniless Galilean peasant-exorcist sealed in an expensive new hand-hewn stone tomb and his body guarded, as opposed to his corpse being thrown into the city dump for the dogs or birds like other crucified criminals?[12] Even earlier, why would he put his family at risk,

---

preparing the way to the cross (Bultmann, *John*, 409–12). Instead in the contemporary setting, Jesus' practice of necromancy and other actions of manipulating the dead to be discussed were terrifying and dangerous, and called for his immediate capture and execution under law, as accurately recorded in John 11:57.

9. Luke 11:14–23.

10. Mark 14:71.

11. Horsley, "Popular Messianic Movements," 471–95, and, e.g., Josephus, *Antiquities*, 17:273–75, how Gratus ultimately caught Simon and cut off his head.

12. Josephus, *Antiquities*, 4:8.6, speaks of those condemned for blasphemy to be buried dishonorably. The valley of Gehenna is thought by some to have maintained a

dispossessing them and depriving them of subsistence support, and instead move to the shores of Galilee to practice exorcism among subsistence-living peasants? Why would Jesus publicly make radically dangerous claims, such as speaking with Satan or being possessed by the "finger of God"? Why did he employ practices during his exorcisms (e.g., spittle, mud, necromancy) that were clearly considered dark and then teach others to do the same? Corollary questions about his followers then rise after the crucifixion: Why would anyone go to a guarded tomb at night during the deadly haunting hour, knowing that demons and the evil dead roamed there and looked for victims to attack?

Finding answers to these and many other risk questions requires that we enter a world completely alien to our own. In *To Be Near the Fire: Demonic Possession, Risk Analysis and Jesus' War on Satan*,[13] risk analysis proved to be effective in evaluating and recovering Jesus' practice of exorcisms and his assault on demonic imperialism and pollution of the temple in its contemporary setting.[14] Employing risk analysis in order to assess

---

fire into which refuse and the bodies of dead criminals (and animals) and evil ones were thrown (see also Matt 5:29).

13. Busse, *To Be Near the Fire* (2014). I am very grateful to professor Paul Slovic for his insights and advice, along with the invaluable critique, input and encouragement of Dr. Stephen J. Patterson, George H. Atkinson Professor of Religious and Ethical Studies, Willamette University.

14. Risk analysis definition in *To Be Near the Fire*: Qualitative risk analysis generally follows a standard evaluative pattern that is iterative. To begin, there is a perception of "perilous risk" (danger of immanent serious, material harm) that is thought to be real and threatening to the stability or survival of an entity under analysis. Qualitative risk analyzes the scope and vulnerability of the entity to those threats, and evaluates the effectiveness of the measures employed to cancel them out. If there is success, these countermeasures are usually patterned, replicated or embellished by the entity, thereby attracting other adherents and standard practices. However, when countermeasures fail, devastation, catastrophe, or even physical harm or death can occur. Further, where there are two conflicting entities, additional criteria apply that are particularly applicable. When two entities in a common historical context perceive the other as a perilous risk, the countermeasures they employ to cancel the other out almost always isolate verifiable historical conflict, such as the Beelzebul controversy between Jesus and his enemies. In almost every case, the core risk issues are uncovered, and often they provide a basis for assessment of the factual nature as to the escalation of a conflict and the countermeasures employed (i.e., actions, sayings or events). Many times, obscure and distracting or irrelevant issues are identified and can be set aside (e.g., later embellishment and exaggeration of the original conflict). The goal of the two conflicting entities is victory over the other (including annihilation), rarely negotiated settlement (only when perilous risk assures mutual annihilation). In failure, the entity or its followers may shift to a different strategy, usually more clandestine, in order to survive. However, if after defeat an entity embraces heightened perilous risk, an overt form of embracing increased perilous risk, then the historical conflict is reengaged in a very interesting and provocative way. The risk motivation for this can be recovered in its contextual

perilous situations, including whether responses adequately counter and neutralize such risks, we can often recover the original form of conflict and events. *To Be Near the Fire* demonstrated the value of risk analysis in recovering historical conflict and related events in first-century Palestine.

Why use risk analysis in addressing these new questions? During forty years employing risk analysis, I carefully identified the factors leading to actual or potential risk, its impact and scope, and whether the countermeasures employed satisfactorily neutralized that risk.[15] Since response to perilous risk is a universal human event,[16] risk analysis can enter into conflict both ancient and contemporary when context can be recovered. Indeed, I came to realize that if the original context of the New Testament could be adequately recovered—particularly the worldview in which Jesus performed exorcisms, spoke with demons and Satan, and was accused of being possessed by Beelzebul—then risk analysis could provide new independent insights into events within these traditions. Combining my professional experience and training,[17] risk analysis proved fruitful, particularly in providing important findings about Jesus' risk response to encounters with demons and the dead. As such, this study extends the methods and conclusions of risk analysis in *Fire* to new risk questions and encounters with Jesus, post-crucifixion.

Is our starting point valid? No scholar disputes that Jesus was an exorcist—an illegal practice and susceptible to accusations of possession and being the agent of Beelzebul or Satan. The techniques he employed in his exorcisms demonstrate why he was accused of dark magic, and why in the Hellenistic and Roman world they were considered magic.[18] Shockingly, Jesus admitted to conversations with not only Satan, but also with multiple demons, many of who were tacitly malevolent or evil spirits of the dead. To many, particularly his enemies, this made Jesus dangerous and a threat. In

---

setting using risk analysis and other tests. This study sets out to employ this methodology and assess findings. Similar to conclusions rendered in the scientific analysis of "affect heuristic," confirmed in the research of Slovic et al., "Risk as Analysis," 311–22; see also Slovic and Weber, "Perception of Risk Posed by Extreme Events," 1–21.

15. Risk positions included: SVP, Portfolio Risk Administration; SVP and Manager, Credit Administration; and SVP and Manager of Credit Risk Assessment, US Bancorp, 1994–2003, and Chief Credit Officer, Pacific Continental Bank. Author of *Essentials of Commercial Lending*, US Bancorp's analytical lending text from 1997 to 2006, and *Business Profiles*, 1995 to 2003; Certified Management Consultant (IMC, USA), 2006 to present.

16. The works of Paul Slovic and others noted above.

17. BA, Reed College, MTS, Harvard Divinity School. My advisor and friend for thirty years was Professor Helmut Koester.

18. Hull, *Hellenistic Magic*, 68–72.

Fire, I began to address why Jesus would take such risks for Galilean peasants. The Beelzebul controversy in Luke 11:20, and other related sayings that most scholars regard as reliable, provided the central event and controversy where the conflict between two forces that saw the other as a perilous risk could be carefully evaluated. These results allowed us to continue to build reliable findings and assess new risk-related questions as to practices, sayings and events.

One Person's "Darkness" Is Another's "Light"

Let me be transparent about the risks of this endeavor. One person's "light" can be threatening to another and seen as "darkness." Using terms like "magician," "possession," "charismatic," "trance," "Beelzebul," or "exorcist," all words found in the New Testament, can be seen positively or negatively in a contextual setting; but for those helped or those harmed (or threatened), peril and risk perspective are everything. If you were a powerless Galilean peasant living a subsistent existence, starving and threatened by landlords or overseers, and had family ill or suffering, of course you would turn to the local exorcists for help and protection, because you knew demons, including curses and the malevolent dead, were at work against you. You were powerless without such help. However, if you felt threatened by someone who could control demons (such as the Jerusalem elite, who feared retributive attack by Jesus because the had accused them of being satanic and "vipers"), you would take action to neutralize that risk, particularly if he turned and headed toward you, the temple city and family. If you drank water and became sick, you knew that demons and spirits inhabited the waters and were attacking, whether capriciously or in retaliation for wrongs committed as an offense to God. We can actually explore these events when there is risk, response to that risk, and conflict, even centuries later. That's what was demonstrated in *Fire*, and with some remarkable results that I would call "reliable," perhaps even "historical," within the contemporary context and social setting of a world completely foreign to ours.

As noted, in *Fire* we began with a controversy even the most critical scholars accept as authentic—the Beelzebul controversy. For Jesus' enemies, his exorcisms and the practices he used (particularly some of those described in the canonical gospels that have contemporary parallels) were magic, satanic and forbidden. This was abundantly clear to them. But for Jesus, his authority to exorcise and control demons, or command the fish of Galilee, was by a divine spirit that possessed him, or was made accessible to him, which he named the "finger of God." To the peasant exorcists he trained, those who called him "master," this claim made him a holy man, a shaman-like figure and a *charismatic*, possessed by a divine spirit. So, "light" and "darkness" were revealed in the risk each presumed evidenced in Jesus' exorcisms. This risk conflict is most reliably reflected in the Beelzebul controversy—a lightening rod event.[19] Jesus and his enemies perceived the other as a perilous risk that must be neutralized by any means. Once this risk conflict was accurately recovered, we were able to correlate and contextualize other things Jesus and his followers said and did, as well as why and how he was captured and brutally murdered. It is clear that for Jesus all was at risk, and if he failed, the kingdom of Satan would prevail. Jesus therefore would employ contemporary techniques to defeat demons that were at his disposal and efficacious, such as spittle and mud;[20] but these were techniques that in his world were often considered magic, particularly among the Romans and Jerusalem elite who feared him. No wonder that the terse reports of Jesus' exorcisms in Mark were softened and recast in later gospels like Matthew, or dropped altogether in Luke and John. As the Jesus movement spread into the Roman world, house-by-house, the oral tradition gradually tempered the implications and accusations of his opponents, i.e., that Jesus was practicing the darkest of magic.[21]

So, Who Would Name a Crucified Dark Magician Their Master? An Example: Paul of Tarsus

We have the original conflict that opened so many new insights using risk analysis (i.e., the Beelzebul controversy), but it demands we go even further into the risk conflict between Jesus and demonic forces to answer some of the most troubling questions and even answer the most problematic of all issues—were post-crucifixion encounters with Jesus "an idle tale"?[22]

To set the historical context for this analysis, contemporary encounters with the dead from the first- and second-century period must be analyzed and evaluated first. This is what the next chapter addresses. Based on presentation of various encounters, we can evaluate difficult questions within this otherworldly risk context, using the gospels and other noncanonical sources and their relation to these contemporary accounts. Indeed, the spectrum of expected encounters with ghosts, spirits, demons and the untimely dead in the first century was surprisingly broad, and *was a cultural reality and an*

19. Mark 3:19b–35; Luke 11:14–28; Matt 12:22–50.
20. Frayer-Griggs, "Spittle, Clay and Creation"; Smith, *Jesus the Magician*, 128.
21. Smith, *Jesus the Magician*, 128–41.
22. Luke 24:11.

expectation. It is clear that those who witnessed or encountered the dead were not limited only to dark magicians, necromancers, *goetes* (sorcerers), charismatics or exorcists. All classes did, including, obviously, the agrarian peasants of Galilee whom Jesus trained as exorcists. But did these Galilean peasant-exorcists expect to encounter a crucified Jewish criminal, even if it were their master?[23] Why not just deny the encounter if it was common and would create perilous risk for them? Indeed, would not the admission of an encounter with the man who had been crucified as a dark magician,[24] an "evildoer,"[25] accused of being possessed by Satan[26] (i.e., the very man who had trained them to expel demons and control evil spirits), create deadly heightened perilous risk? We can examine these challenging questions in a new light and assess implications about these encounters and reports.

To that point, the experiences of a young, violent and ambitious Pharisee, Saul of Tarsus—a paid and commissioned "hit man" of the Roman-sympathizing Jerusalem elite[27]—are also evaluated from a risk perspective. The same opponents that captured, tortured and killed Jesus also authorized Saul to commit atrocities against Jesus' followers, or in his own words, annihilate (*eporthoun*) them.[28] Scholars universally accept that Saul is the earliest and only direct witness claiming to have seen and have been possessed by Jesus, i.e., "revealed" in him (*en emoi*).[29] His authentic letters (usually engendered

---

23. See Craffert, *Life of a Galilean Shaman*, 395–403.

24. Many of Jesus' practices when driving out demons reflected magical practices, including the use of spittle and touching of the tongue (Mark 7:33), spittle to make clay (John 9:6), and special words (Mark 5:40–41); see also Smith, *Jesus the Magician*, 128–29.

25. To be discussed in more depth in future chapters, a term used to describe a dark magician, see John 18:30, not simply a "criminal."

26. Mark 3:22, the essence of the charge against Jesus by his opponents, he is possessed by Satan, creating perilous risk for Jesus and his fellow exorcists; most scholars accepts this charge as authentic, and that his family wanted to seize him because he had become "mad."

27. The high priestly families, the Herodian aristocracy and rich elite aligned with Rome were *de facto* Roman patrons. There are multiple attestations to this view of the elite in Josephus, pagan historians and New Testament sources that will be cited in forthcoming discussions. See also Hanson and Oakman, "Social Impact," 146–54. Saul carried "letters" of authority from these same Roman supported elite in Jerusalem. Such letters carried the power and presence of those who signed them, and, as will be later noted in this study, the authority to disable even evil from attack through a blessing, a curse, a spell, or other magical words of power. Paul's letter to the Galatians is filled with such powerful protective blessings and curses, confirmed by Betz, "Letter to the Galatians," 352–53.

28. Gal 1:13.

29. Gal 1:16.

by a risk response to opponents infiltrating and trying to disband his *ecclesiae* [churches]) describe his own multiple ecstatic experiences. Remarkably, these experiences include spirit[30] and soul[31] transportation, possession,[32] attack by angels of Satan, ecstatic language,[33] and trances.[34] They also include his encounter with an executed man he once hated, which he depicts as having seen, specifically not in a vision, séance or trance familiar to his world,[35] nor in an ethereal encounter with a *Bi(ai)othanatori*,[36] but with his own eyes (*opthe*), as a visible, in some way a substantial manifestation.[37] It was this event that created perilous risk, so dramatic for Saul, that he changed his name, abandoned his claim to privilege in his religious heritage (calling it "refuse"),[38] and adopted a starving, hunted, poor and wandering life. He became a self-proclaimed *apostolos* of that risen criminal.[39] This ecstatic event, in a world filled with capricious gods, ghosts, angels, demons and spirits, and a religious law that Saul once embraced but now claimed condemned one to death,[40] defined for the new man, Paul, the radical countermeasure to death, and the only "way" to achieve eternal life. To refuse was to condemn oneself to a divine curse and annihilation—"woe to me," Paul says if he refused.[41]

30. 1 Cor 5:4.

31. 2 Cor 2:12; Paul describes his being lifted up to the place of redeemed humans in "heaven."

32. 1 Cor 14:1–25.

33. 1 Cor 14:18.

34. 1 Cor 12:2.

35. For the historical context and variety of ecstatic expressions, see Smith, *Jesus the Magician*, 75–80; for a broader definition of "trance," see also Lewis, *Ecstatic Religion*, 29–31, and then descriptions that correspond to Hellenistic and Roman settings such as in 39–57.

36. A ghost, "those dead by violence." See Ogden, *Magic*, 146, 149–52.

37. The word "appeared" (*ophthe*) literally means that "he was seen" with the eyes, i.e., not as an indistinct vision but was literally seen with the eyes of the individual, often in some form of materiality, and in historical time. For discussion, see Conzelmann, *1 Corinthians*, 256–57, esp. 257n74. Paul does not describe a human flesh and blood body or a recognizing of Jesus by his wounds. His encounter was overwhelming and shocking primarily because he encountered a crucified, and so divinely cursed, Jewish criminal who was thought annihilated. Traditions of bodily encounter (such as touching wounds and handling a "flesh and blood" Jesus) were unknown to Paul, but more, were unnecessary.

38. Phil 3:8.

39. Gal 2:20; 2 Cor 11:23–27.

40. 1 Cor 15:56.

41. 1 Cor 9:16.

By Paul's own admission after this event he, like Jesus, came to radically reject the Jerusalem elite he considered evil and deceived. Remarkably, Paul's rejection of the Jerusalem elite ultimately extended to certain leaders (the "pillars") of the Jerusalem *ecclesia*, declaring that Satan and his demons had taken control.[42] His "apology" letter to the Galatian *ecclesiae* reviling the infiltration of Yacob, the brother of Jesus, whose spies attempted to disband his assemblies in that province, is literally a "magical letter" in that it contains a conditional curse and blessing *immediately* when read.[43] Those Galatian Christians who continued to reject Paul's charismatic "gospel" when the letter was read were infected with a deadly curse. In a startling implication, this curse extended to Yacob, the brother of Jesus! And this wasn't his only use of such power. Paul cursed a man in 1 Cor 5:3: "I have already judged . . . and give him over to Satan for the destruction of the flesh." By Paul's giving the man to Satan, he was practicing what was considered the "blackest of magic" in the ancient world.[44]

As an itinerant in conflict with demonic powers and Satan, Paul expected to be attacked and states he was.[45] Yet both he and Jesus embraced this terrifying risk, and total annihilation, the curse leading to the death of both body and soul, for the sake of the most powerful permeating substance ever encountered, the *euangelion*, "gospel" of God. Once received and accepted, one was united with God, whether in the charismatic rite of baptism in water (*into which* evil was expelled and absorbed), or by baptism by possession of Spirit (which expelled evil), or both. For both, a material change overcame that person's being and soul, the practice of *agape* becoming protection. A new person began to emerge, like a plant from a seed. This was the work of God, not Satan, the divine, not magic or sorcery for these men. All powers were to bow to this authority,[46] literally for Paul meaning every demon, the prince of demons, evil spirits, malevolent ghosts and even Satan, who was "falling like lightening."[47]

---

42. Gal 6:13–15; Schweitzer asserts that Paul's accusation of possession and curse is leveled against Cephas, James and John, who were the "Super Apostles." See Schweitzer, *Mysticism of Paul the Apostle*, 156–57.

43. Betz, *Galatians*, 14–25.

44. Morton, *Magic*, 110.

45. Paul, 2 Cor 12:6–9; Jesus, Luke 4:9, and other ecstatic experiences in the desert wilderness of Judea.

46. Phil 2:9–11.

47. Luke 10:18.

Why Did Paul Reject Jesus as a Dark Magician Only to Accept Him as "Master" and "Lord"? Euangelion as Metamorphosis

We can even extend this new risk understanding within this first-century context to words that have become powerless in today's setting. Here's an example. According to Jesus and Paul, transformation into a new being was made immediately possible in *euangelion*, or "Gospel"; a word not as we may understand it today, that is, as a noun, but as a powerful supernatural verb, saturated with life-giving power that overwhelmed body and soul, and supplanted one's risk of death or the capricious control of evil beings in that context.[48] "Gospel" literally altered the possibility of one's physical nature, from death to life, made impotent all evil powers,[49] all beginning with the raising of Jesus, the "first fruits."[50] Encounter with Gospel was an event that was shattering, irreversible and undeniably risky to reject.[51] It created a cataclysmic shift in what perilous risk now represented to each that encountered it.[52] If Gospel was rejected, one was not just intellectually doomed, but cursed, permanently blemished; one's eternal soul was annihilated, and nothing could be done. This terrifying risk of rejecting Gospel for Paul, regardless if it came as the result of the crucifixion of an accused sorcerer and magician under Roman law, brought on such a weighty curse (a material blight or stain that was irremovable, invoking inescapable penalty), one's complete and ultimate being was immediately to be considered void, useless, at an end, and was blanketed with death and consumed by evil.[53]

Only an analysis of the perilous risks that led this young, violent Jewish zealot[54] to radically change—even publicly admit he was both "in" (one with), as well as possessed by the Spirit of Jesus for the sake of Gospel—is capable of recovering the original historical context.[55] More, Paul's risk responses can be accurately analyzed: What could have led Paul to invoke the name of Jesus for protection against demons and spirits, or to combine the name of Jesus with "Lord (*kurios*) and *Christos* (Messiah)," or use these to

48. See Craffert, *Life of a Galilean Shaman*, for a complete analysis of the "alien" world of first-century Palestine.

49. Rom 8:38.

50. 1 Cor 15:20.

51. 1 Cor 15:31.

52. Rom 7:24.

53. 1 Cor 15:8.

54. Gal 1:14; a man who not only publicly participated in, but led others to murder Jesus' exorcists, and violently attack and imprison sympathizers!

55. Gal 1:16.

assert the overwhelming supernatural power of his letters, usually written to repel opponents he announced were of Satan? By implication, why would Paul publicly reject the assertion that Beelzebul, the prince of demons, had possessed Jesus (as he, Saul, most certainly had claimed in concert with the Jerusalem elite),[56] instead announcing that it was the Spirit of God that possessed him![57] Paul was a later witness. There were several others who preceded him, which he lists. What experiences led them to embrace perilous risk in their contemporary setting, and particularly, why in Galilee?

The Value of Risk Analysis for Investigation

Risk analysis has no agenda, seeks no biases, but objectively looks at contextual settings, seeking their original conflict and mitigations. Like archaeology, which examines a site using careful methods of analysis and allows that site and its artifacts to suggest various findings, facts or conclusions, so too risk analysis of contextual settings, where human conflict and perilous risks are experienced, can do the same. Risk analysis allows the human response to perilous risk in any setting to come forth on its own and within that contextual reality or worldview, even one foreign to our own. And so, what is "light" or "dark" is important only from the standpoint of how individuals respond to their understanding of each, and from their own contextual setting. In my view, risk analysis should be free of theological bias for these reasons, and because it attempts to always evaluate risk events as drawn from its given context, once that context is recovered, it can be shocking or even troubling. Whether Paul or Jesus, or the Romans and their sympathizers that brutalized and killed Jesus, response to risk, particularly when there is conflict between two enemies that perceive the other as a perilous risk, can be reliably recovered. Risk analysis therefore allows us to enter worldviews that are alien and assess them with some rather remarkable precision, even first-century Palestine. The outcome of applying risk analysis to "sacred" and "protected" traditions or sources can be very controversial, and

---

56. Mark 3:22; Jesus was under control of Beelzebul, prince of demons: "Take that away, and all that remains is a collection of unrelated complaints, most of them not very serious; introduce it, and then these complaints can be seen as component elements of a comprehensive structure." Jesus was working for Satan according to the view of his opponents. Smith, *Jesus the Magician*, 31–32.

57. The contrast between two kinds of spirits, Beelzebul and the Holy Spirit that possesses Jesus, is clear in Mark, particularly implicit in Mark 3:20. See Robinson, *Problem of History*, 36. As Robinson points out, "The rarity of this identification in Mark [i.e., the Holy Spirit as empowering Jesus' actions] shows the importance the present issue has for him."

I realize even disturbing. Yet, being open to assessing traditions by recovering context and the human response to perilous risk can deepen insights, and perhaps even faith, by placing us within that worldview. The outcome, however, is what it is.

The First Task of Risks Analysis: Recovering a Contextual Setting

Our first task is to assess the world of the first century with regard to the backdrop we've already reliably recovered in *Fire*; namely, the world of demons, the evil dead and Satan, evidenced in the Beelzebul controversy between Jesus and his deadly enemies. To begin, the study must first carefully examine the context of expectations surrounding encounters with the dead, ghosts and spirits in the Roman and Hellenistic world.

With regard to the New Testament, we will primarily rely on Mark and Q, but also look to traditions found in Matthew, Luke and, as noted, John. We must also supplement the New Testament with independent historical sources—Jewish, Roman and pagan, as well as noncanonical gospels and documents, and current research on exorcism, magic and ecstatic religion within various cultures, particularly patterns of shamanism and ecstatic behavior. Only in this way can we recover the contextual risks and original form of any encounter, i.e., the original risk setting. We will also look to Paul's undisputed letters.[58] It is to this first effort, contextual analysis, which we now turn.

---

58. Accepted by New Testament scholars as: most of Romans, 1 Corinthians (with some editorial modifications), the seven or more letters that comprise 2 Corinthians, Galatians, 1 Thessalonians, Philemon, and Philippians.

2

Demons, Ghosts of the Retributive Dead and Satan

Recovering the Contextual *Sitz im Leben* of the First-Century Palestine with Risk Analysis

There is something quite disturbing as we begin this contextual study. We enter a very strange, disconcerting and different world—one filled with phantasms, malevolent and retaliatory ghosts, spirits and demons, some of which were under the control of Satan and his fallen angels, such as Beelzebul. According to traditions in just Mark and Luke, Jesus conversed with and expelled demons, including evil spirits and phantasms of the malevolent, retributive dead.[1] Virtually all peoples were susceptible to the capricious nature of dark forces,[2] particularly the poor. These forces could also be conjured and used to attack, possess, harm or even kill victims. Some confronted these powers, including exorcists such as Jesus. Exorcists, magicians and sorcerers were often embraced by peasants, the poor and the disenfranchised as protectors. They were feared and hunted by the powerful and wealthy as dangerous enemies who could turn dark forces against them and destroy their lives, families and fortunes.[3] To recover the historical context in which the conflict between Jesus and his enemies took place over demonic possession, spirits of the dead and satanic powers, careful analysis of contemporary sources is required. As such, Hellenistic, Roman and Palestinian encounters with demons and retaliatory ghosts and exorcists begin the contextual analysis that will allow recovery of the *sitz im leben*

---

1. Hull, *Hellenistic Magic*, 67–68.
2. Lewis, *Ecstatic Religion*, 32–33. Mark 3:20–30, Luke 11:14–28.
3. Ibid., 32–33.

(the life setting) of the first century. A recovered context provides a basis on which to compare and evaluate these events with the encounters of others, such as Jesus (i.e., as found in New Testament and noncanonical sources). How similar are these encounters? Do they mirror contemporary sources?

The Risk Context of the Dead: Ghosts (Phantasms), Demons and Retaliatory Spirits

To begin, it is immediately evident from even a cursory reading of all primary sources that the world of first-century Palestine is completely alien to our own. In fact, it is difficult to recover its otherworldly context given our biases. What can be said is that recreating this context requires a new perspective of reality that is grossly foreign and even disturbing. Ghosts (*phantasms*), or ghostly spirits of the dead (see definitions below), sometime also identified as "demons," were accepted as aggressively active and harmful. Malevolent ghosts and demons were known to be the cause of almost every malady, deformation, bad fortune and death.[4] Consequently, they were feared, and even thought to be the cause of high mortality rates among infants. Only dark magicians, witches, or *goetes* (sorcerers) were thought to consult, conjure, or use them to attack and even kill enemies. Multiple pagan and Jewish accounts show that they were assumed to be active and prevalent throughout the ancient world, including in first-century Palestine.[5] In Judaism, Satan was known to employ demons (fallen angels and spirits of the dead), and Beelzebul, the prince of demons (a fallen angel), a.k.a., the "strong man," was active in manipulating forces in his war with God, viciously attacking all enemies and deceiving and destroy God's people.[6] Other chief demons wandered and on special days were expected to attack the innocent.[7]

Often the malevolent dead, these demons, attempted to take control of their victims so that they harmed themselves. In the most extreme cases, demons killed their victims by suffocating, stabbing, strangulation, inciting suicide or committing violent acts that led to death, or else possessed others

---

4. From Kayfa's mother-in-law's fever (Luke 4:38–40) to being mute (Matt 4:10), even death (Mark 5:36–43).

5. See Rousseau, "Exorcism," 88–93, as well as Penny, "Beelzebul," 620–50, and Dimant and Rappaport, *Dead Sea Scrolls*. Generally exorcism and protection against demons is emphasized: e.g., 4Q510–11, 4Q560 and 11Q11. For a discussion of exorcism, Jesus and Dead Sea Scroll psalms, see Evans, "Jesus and Psalm 91," 541–55.

6. Luke 11:14–28; see Josephus, *Antiquities* IX, 2, b 1.

7. The female demon in particular, Lilith, in *Songs of the Sage* (4Q510–11).

to destroy their victims.[8] There was physical evidence of their presence in the form of a foul smell, vapor or wind, a shadow or a phantasm with ethereal appearance, or a *soma* (body) with physical presence sufficient in materiality to touch, strike, wrestle or punch a victim. When present, they refused to leave, continuing to afflict and cause suffering until the exorcist arrives.

> But you don't need to take my word for it. Everyone knows the Syrian from Palestine who is such an expert at this. He takes anyone who falls down at the sign of the moon, twists their eyes and foams at the mouth and sets them on the their feet again and sends them out sound in mind, delivering them from their affliction for a large fee. Whenever he stands over them as they lie afflicted and asks from whence they have come into the body, the sick man himself makes no response, but the demon answers, speaking in Greek or the language of its country of origin, and explains how and when it entered the person. The Syrian adjures it to leave, and if it does not obey he drives it out with threats. I saw one leaving; it was black and smoky in color.[9]

As such, the context of these malevolent spirits and demons must be explored. Fortunately, we have contemporary descriptions of various forms of ghosts and demons that are remarkably similar to descriptions found in the New Testament gospels and sources.

The demons that were controlled and expelled by Jesus and his exorcists were not necessarily portrayed as ghosts of the dead in the New Testament. They were sometimes considered malevolent spirits or fallen angels,[10] and yet, although the origin of demons is obscure in the gospels, Luke 11:24 and 4:33 confirm that the majority were termed "unclean spirits" or "demons," i.e., that they were the foul or wicked dead employed by Satan or his minions. Other ancient sources confirm that demons were active spirits of the wicked dead,[11] and in most cases acted malevolently, seeking retribution by possessing and harming their victims. Jesus is able to identify them by name.[12] While they most often appeared in dreams,[13] they were active day to day, found near tombs.[14] Sometimes they appeared in deformed and

---

8. Ogden, *Magic*, 158, Cicero *On Divination* 1.57 (44 BCE).
9. Ogden, *Magic*, 50, quoting Lucian, *Philopseudes*, 16 (170 CE).
10. *Testament of Solomon* 6:1–4.
11. Josephus, *War*, 6.3.
12. Luke 8:30, "Legion," i.e., the name taken by a group of demons.
13. Ogden, *Magic*, 146–47.
14. Ibid., 148–49, Virgil, *Aeneid* 6.

decaying forms. Often their attack was by possessing the victim and bringing on malady, madness or illness.

Apuleius, *De deo Socratis* 15 (later 2nd century CE), provides a rare "taxonomy of ghosts," which are also identified as demons:

> Another variety of "demons" consists of the human soul that abandons its body when it has finished with its services in life. I note that in the old Latin language these used to be termed *lemures*. Now, to some of these *lemures* was allotted the care of their descendants. These occupy houses with a propitious and peaceful attitude, and they are called *Lares* of the family. But others, because of their misdeeds in life are punished with a kind of exile, namely with the denial of a home and with undirected wanderings. They can only be harmless terrors to good men, but they are dangerous to bad men. People usually call these *larvae*. When it is unclear what category of ghost one is dealing with, whether it is one of the *Lares* or the *larvae*, the term one uses the term *Di manes*.[15]

Di Manes, or demons, particularly malevolent ghosts, were feared and could attack, particularly after midnight or near cemeteries or tombs.[16] Attacks were often capricious, attempting rape and harm on the unsuspecting, thereby evidencing some form of materiality to their victims.[17] Many of what were considered the restless dead (i.e., the beheaded or mutilated, soldiers or criminals who had been killed or murdered) were excluded from Hades and wandered desolated places.[18] Because they wandered and sought retribution, they would seek innocent victims, particularly the poor and frail. Witches, sorcerers and dark magicians could conjure these restless dead as demons and send them to bring illness, and as noted, even commit murder.[19] Upper classes feared these individuals, and laws were brought forward to execute them if caught. Indeed, demons and evil spirits sought to possess victims regardless of status. When exorcised by a command, ritual technique, song or incantation, a material substance was often seen, usually smoky (i.e., the sign of a departing demon or ghost), or departure was evidenced by the overturning of cups or even pails of water.[20] Exorcists sometimes went into a trance, rolled their eyes (looking up to heaven?), and

15. Ibid., 149.
16. Ibid., 147.
17. Ibid., 314, Xenophon of Ephesus, *Ephesiaca*, 5.9.7–9.
18. Deserts, lakes, rivers and even springs.
19. Ibid., 152, 154.
20. Eleazar the exorcists, Josephus, *Antiquities*, 8.45–48.

spoke in undecipherable sentences or words. Witnesses were spellbound and terrified. Josephus himself witnessed an illegal exorcism with the emperor Vespasian present, where incantations of Solomon (who was considered also a powerful Jewish exorcist, passing on specific and efficacious rituals and spells) were employed. The demon was drawn out of the victim using a magical ring placed at the nose and expelled, while the exorcist repeated Solomonic incantations (some of which are found in ancient texts). In this case, the exorcism was allowed. Other contemporary exorcists would force the demon or spirit to confess its identify and origin and then expel it by force, or sometimes negotiate its departure (e.g., such as sending the demon into desolate places,[21] or into a herd of swine to reenter haunted waters in Galilee).[22] Spittle was sometimes used, but as a magical fluid, imbued with the authority of the exorcist, not unlike the practice of Jesus.[23] Indeed, when read in a contemporary risk setting, many of the gospel accounts of Jesus' exorcisms can be seen to reflect these same practices in their original form and context.

Consequently, the numerous reports of encounters included all segments and strata in Roman and Hellenistic society. They were active in cities, rural areas and provinces, including Palestine and Egypt. Jesus announced that demonic forces were attempting to overtake the kingdom of God,[24] and that Satan was employing all means to succeed, whether demons, fallen angels or occupying pagan rulers and their sympathizers. Their attacks included destroying the messengers of God—most notably for Jesus, John the Baptizer.

The Restless Dead and Demonic Activity

Malevolently active ghosts, whether conjured by magic or sorcery or not, were often termed "restless."[25] This restlessness was defined by their encounter with the living and can be categorized into groups, although these categories often overlapped.[26] They are as follows in Greek:

- *Aoroi*—those dead before their time who seek revenge by haunting the living

21. Talmud, "Treatise Berachoth," fol. 3, a; and Tobit 8:3; Luke 11:24.
22. See Lucian's *Philopseudes* 16, as quoted by Ogden, *Magic*, 50–51.
23. Smith, *Jesus the Magician*, 128.
24. Busse, *To Be Near the Fire*, 22–43.
25. Ogden, *Magic*, 146–78.
26. Ibid., 146.

DEMONS, GHOSTS OF THE RETRIBUTIVE DEAD AND SATAN 19

- *Bi(ai)othanatoi*—those violently killed in war, including executed criminals, with murder victims and those committing suicide the most active and angry
- *Agamoi*—those dead before being married, which includes particularly bitter female ghosts seeking revenge
- *Ataphoi*—those who died and were not buried or given funeral rites

All of these were encountered as reported in ancient literature, sometimes provoked by enemies and dark magicians, or by the restless demons themselves. There are multiple examples were the restless dead could also be known as a "demon" of the dead. Protection was often obtained from charismatics, magicians, or by witchcraft or sorcery. To begin, we will focus our emphasis on the *Bi(ai)othanatoi*, those violently killed, including criminals like Jesus.

Tertullian,[27] one of the Christian "fathers" writing about 200 CE, provides a remarkable account of encounters with the "restless dead and dead by violence." This account is clearly an attack on popular magicians and sorcerers known to evoke the ghosts of the dead, and even provides a list of famous ones, including one Simon and Elymas, the Jewish sorcerer reportedly blinded by Paul.[28] The passage from *De Anima* (56–57) contends that the appearance of these ghosts, or demons, evoked by these magicians and sorcerers are actually not the dead souls of those criminals (as commonly thought by all), but demons that existed with the soul that became detached at death, and may have even had a part in bringing on the untimely death of the man or women—that is, demon possession and attack. They can appear with a sort of body, i.e., having some form of material body, although Tertullian makes clear that this is an incorporeal manifestation of spiritual substance, but not flesh and blood. He acknowledges that these manifestations appear, and more, seem to be material. In other words, a demon may appear to be the dead person evoked, but actually is not, as all souls of the dead in his view are transported to Hades to await judgment, which again is contrary to other evidence in other Hellenistic and Roman sources. When conjured and controlled, the dark magician grabs the demon and makes it do what is required, most likely for monetary gain related to evil intentions. These demons can be retaliatory, be sent for evil purposes, or simply be acting independently through capricious attacks. Tertullian states that these demons can be exorcised and made to rightly identify their true

---

27. Quintus Septimius Florens Tertullianus, 160–225 CE, of the Roman province of Carthage; the Christian writer and father of Latin theology, and later a Montanist.

28. Acts 13:6–12.

identity as the *demon of the dead*. He warns that caution must be exercised, as some so-called magicians are actually frauds; as for example, a *Pythonicus* (in this case a ventriloquists) feigns the voice of the dead. Lastly, the dead that appear in dreams are also demons, not the soul of the dead criminal or murder victim. By negative affirmation then, Tertullian confirms both the contemporary belief in the existence, as well as encounters with, those violently killed.

Consequently, what is striking is that Tertullian unquestionably accepts the existence of ghosts and demons as part of the evil, threatening world in which he lives—a world completely different to our understanding, but certainly is reflective of Jesus' worldview and setting. For Tertullian then, these demons can be exorcised and exposed for what they are, that is, *not* the resurrected dead.

> So too the nature of magic is apparent to us. It is of course a second idolatry, in which demons pretend that they are dead people, just as in the case of idolatry proper, demons pretend that they are gods.... But demons work under the cover of these souls, particularly those demons that were within them when they were still alive and had driven them to death of this sort.[29]

Some magicians and sorcerers have evoked these ghosts for personal gain and control, and even make their appearances seem to have a corporeal body, or at least a body of some substance that is visible.

> Even so, the demon, after attempting to trick the spectators, is overwhelmed ... an apparition is made manifest, and a body is attached to it.[30]

For Tertullian, resurrection is only when the living soul is restored to the body and fully animated in a material, flesh and blood form—clearly a later interpretation associated with the gospels of Luke, Matthew and John, i.e., 80 to 110 CE. Any other manifestation is trickery.

Perhaps not surprisingly, Tertullian never associates Jesus, a crucified criminal, with an appearance as a demon ghost, the dead by violence, nor places him in this category. Tertullian is the original Latin proponent of the "trinity," i.e., three of one substance, so the very thought of Jesus being separate from God is impossible. As such, Tertullian could not imagine Jesus' appearance to be that of a simple ghost, and interprets the New Testament accounts from this perspective. Indeed, by 160 CE, the birth of Tertullian, the appearance of Jesus was never understood to be that of a

---

29. Ogden, *Magic*, 149, 150.
30. Ibid., 150.

ghost, apparition, or incorporeal spirit—such entities were demons and clearly understood to be so. Tertullian defined Jesus' appearances as resurrection—God restored Jesus' soul to his body.

> In these cases [of actual resurrection] it is evitable, because of the solid, physical, and fulfilled truth of the resurrected body that the shape of truth is such as to make you judge every incorporeal manifestation of the dead to be mere trickery.[31]

In this same passage, he lists all of the well-known magicians and sorcerers who were capable to evoking or controlling demons of the dead. As such, Tertullian accepts these rites as prevalent and capable of convincing participants that they have experienced the actual dead, creating a deception that turns away believers. As a Montanist, one who embraced a charismatic form of nascent Christianity, this is a striking passage. While we cannot associate Tertullian's charismatic experiences with those of Jesus' band of exorcists, and he never claims to have conducted an exorcism himself or to have risked his life in doing so, he stands in a minority tradition in the Roman world. He practices not only an illegal religion that was still under murderous persecution, but rejects current beliefs and practices as deception and evil, thereby attempting to separate ghostly appearances known to him and his world from the resurrection appearances of Jesus. This was risky and dangerous. His writings, which were the most public and perilous of all forms of communication in the ancient world (because they were irrefutable evidence) were contrary to the norms accepted by society as to demons, ghosts and apparitions, the conjuring of the dead, and a rejection of the fame of those who claimed to control the supernatural by magic and sorcery. Tertullian thereby embraced heightened perilous risk.

Ultimately, Tertullian was both feared and despised by much of contemporary society in Carthage; he and his fellow Christians were called charlatans, "evildoers," deserving conviction and execution in the most horrible fashion. Yet, Tertullian was a radical and embraced corporeal resurrection because not to do so was to be overwhelmed by evil, possession and death—the most perilous risk of his time. However, the difference between Tertullian and the terrified band of exorcists who had witnessed their leader brutally murdered by crucifixion is striking: Tertullian had reflective context in the form of redacted and well-developed written gospel accounts. The peasant exorcists of Galilee had only their contemporary understanding and expectations. It is this we must now attempt to recover more fully.

---

31. Ibid., 151.

3

Confronting Satan, Demons and the Dead in Galilee

Rediscovering Jesus' Contemporary Risk Setting

To Be Near the Fire recovered core evidence that Jesus' ecstatic practices were much like those of other contemporary exorcists, particularly in his aggressive encounters with demons and phantasms.[1] Yet, Jesus' activity and the description of these encounters included parallels to magical practices considered dark, and described deadly confrontations with evil, satanic adversaries familiar in the Hellenistic world. Demons, many of which were retributive ghosts of the dead, manifested themselves near tombs,[2] spoke through their victims, and viscously attacked and possessed the innocent, just as described in contemporary encounters of the Graeco-Roman world. *Fire* also demonstrated that this young exorcist, Jesus, the son of Mary,[3] embraced perilous risk and conducted a very public, antagonistic and dangerous war against Satan and demonic pollution of the land, including verbal attacks against those he considered under Satan's control. This included the

---

1. Busse, *To Be Near the Fire*, 31–53 (Palestinian Judaism and demonic possession), 58–60 (the Beelzebul controversy), 70–88 (Jesus' attack on Satan and demonic imperialism).

2. See Mark 5:1–20 for a demon that possessed a man near the tombs.

3. *Yeshua*, "son of Mary" (Mark 6:3), is the earliest attestation of Jesus to any familial affiliation, even though she is mentioned only twice in Mark. It is significant within the highly important kinship affiliation system of sustenance and support in first-century Palestine (see Freyne, "Herodian Economics in Galilee," 42–43) that Jesus is thrown out of his village in Nazareth and is rejected by his brothers and sisters and that Joseph disappears from all later narratives. Jesus is called "mad," possessed by a demon, and so is alienated. Jesus fails to provide support for his kin, rejecting them (Mark 3:35), and instead, supports a band of exorcist from various fishing villages along Galilee. See also Neyrey, "Loss of Wealth," 139–49.

Jerusalem aristocracy and religious elite, who were tacitly Roman sympathizers.[4] Consequently, Jesus was distinct from his contemporaries in what he said these exorcisms represented, the fall of Satan and inbreaking of the kingdom of God,[5] as well as the multiplicity of the encounters with the dead and demons.[6]

The Nature of Jesus' Attack on Demons, Satan and the Retributive Dead in Galilee

Jesus went about exorcising the demons of Satan, and also the retributive spirits of the dead,[7] from synagogue assemblies throughout the land after the ritual mutilation by beheading of John the Baptist. Many of these accounts reflect practices similar to other contemporary exorcists noted. In fact, Jesus is even thought by the religious elite to employ techniques of other exorcists who invoked Solomonic authority and incantations, all of which were widely known (in all strata of society) and considered highly effective.[8] Of course, Jesus claimed that his Spirit was superior to Solomon's power. Exorcism took many forms and had many techniques. Indeed, John's charismatic baptismal rites "cleansed," or better said, drove out evil into the water[9] and protected those heeding his call from possession and attack, returning them to the divine protection.

---

4. Busse, *To Be Near the Fire*, 9–11, 20–26, 29–30; Hanson and Oakman, *Palestine in the Time of Jesus*, 146–54.

5. Luke 10:18; 11:20; 17:20–21.

6. Busse, *To Be Near the Fire*, 40.

7. The reliability of the exorcism tradition as originating in the context of Jesus' historical activity is now uncontested; see the excellent analysis of Evans, "Jesus and the Jewish Miracle Stories," 214–43, as it predates any messianic claim and is controversial (why would the church creates so many controversial stories about Jesus, many of which in Mark are later dropped or softened?). Evans demonstrates their historicity, and their distinctiveness from any contemporary Jewish charismatic. The tradition also cannot be simply associated with Jesus as a "holy man" (see Vermes, *Jesus the Jew*) or a magician (see Smith, see below), but is complex and must be associated with his mission to drive Satan and demonic imperialism from the land.

8. Josephus, *Antiquities*, 8.2.5, and Eleazar before Vespasian; Jesus states, "One greater than Solomon is here" (Luke 11:31).

9. See below on the expulsion of demons into waters to entrap or destroy them evidenced in the activity of Jesus. This was a contemporary practice, particularly in sacred waters and springs that were thought visited or protected by angels. Bar-Ilan, "Exorcism by Rabbis": "Some springs have a complete family of spirits living in each; it is understood that hot springs, as in Tiberias (Galilee), are heated by spirits (acting on the basis of the commands of King Solomon). It can be generalized that there is hardly a source of water in the land of Israel without a spirit (one or more)." Bar-Ilan cites as

According to the gospels, Jesus claimed to be himself possessed, but by a divine Spirit, which he called the "finger of God."[10] He was empowered by this Spirit to control and exorcise all demons and retributive spirits of the dead, even drive the curse of death away, using various rituals, methods, words or commands.[11] His claim was similar to other exorcists who took on or were possessed by spirits, making them able to control (expel or send away) or absorb (trap) less powerful demons. Like other contemporary accounts, these were not calm encounters, but violent confrontations with various demons under Satan's control—shouting, orders, crying out—where demons shouted back at Jesus in front of terrified witnesses.[12] "Jesus is not conversing with demons; he is disposing of them."[13] Jesus resisted, and had survived numerous attempts of satanic possession and attack (including satanic invitations to kill himself), admitting to conversations with Satan, terrifying even to other exorcists.[14] Consequently, Jesus' social role was different than other charismatics, such as Hainina ben Dosa. It is what Jesus said his exorcisms of demons and retributive spirits signified, combined with the number and magnitude of them that appeared seditious to the elite that made him a dangerous, perilous risk.[15] His reputation as a dark, dangerous magician and antagonism against the Roman elite in Jerusalem, *left little choice but to destroy him, body and soul, to prevent retribution.* Jesus' public statements and mission spoke to their decision. To rescue Palestine from demonic control after the murder of John the Baptist, Jesus likely claimed the spirit of John (just as his accuser, Herod Antipas, had charged)[16] and began a deliberate and dangerous itinerant route of retributive attack against Satan to drive him and his demons from villages and towns. His method of

---

additional support the *Pesachim* 112 p. 1, two baraitot.

10. Luke 11:20.

11. But not like the Hellenistic accounts of necromancy discussed by Ogden.

12. Robinson, *Problem of History*, 36: "We do not find calm conversations, but shouts and orders. The demons 'shout' at Jesus: 1.23; 3.11; 5.7; 9.26. In 5.7 the demon 'adjures' Jesus. Jesus 'orders' the demons (1.27:9.25), or 'reproaches' them with an order (1.25; 3.12; 9.25). The only passage approaching normal conversation is 5.9–13, after the struggle is over and the authoritative word of exorcism has been uttered (v. 8). This conversation does not serve to place Jesus or the demons in 'normal' relations, but rather to accentuate the completeness of Jesus' victory, a trait which recurs normally in the Marcan narrative."

13. Ibid.

14. Busse, *To Be Near the Fire*, 60–69.

15. Freyne, *Jesus and the Gospels*, 233–34.

16. Mark 6:14. Herod assumes this, and Jesus was associated with having reclaimed the spirit of John. Taking up his conflict with Jerusalem was tacitly an aggressive attack using magic on Herod and his house.

attack was the exorcising of demons and casting out spirits brought against the villagers and then his fellow exorcists.[17] For Jesus, the collaboration of the Jerusalem religious elite with the Romans has fostered proliferation of demonic imperialism and pollution of the land.[18] The kingdom of Satan was emerging.

Accompanied by a band of exorcists he selected and trained, each with *their own technique* in exorcism,[19] Jesus assaulted demonic forces village by village in Galilee, then in certain towns of the Decapolis, as well as villages in Samaria and Judea. He encircled Jerusalem, intending to displace Satan and reestablish the kingdom of God and the temple.[20] If not, all was lost. The perilous risks were too high.[21] Consequently, his exorcisms were more than simply paid protection from evil (i.e., as for other exorcists, magicians and "healers"); they were aggressive acts of unseating Satan and bringing about the return of the kingdom and sovereignty of God.[22] Consequently, these were intense, hostile conflicts with demons, intended to take back what was lost.[23] When allowed,[24] Jesus entered villages and towns on the Sabbath, specifically the synagogue gatherings of the village and leaders. It is clear that Jesus and his trained exorcists wore distinctive clothing. Jesus wore an exorcist's mantle.

The Sabbath was the holy day *when demons were vulnerable*. He followed a ritual pattern of attack that was not dissimilar from other contemporary exorcists: Jesus shouted and called out the demons that were present, particularly those that had afflicted or harmed victims (all ages,

---

17. Busse, *To Be Near the Fire*, 60–69, and chs. 3 and 4.

18. Ibid., 22–40.

19. These will be explored more fully in the next chapters.

20. Josephus also believed the temple was destroyed because of corruption, see *Antiquities*, 20:8, 4–5.

21. Robinson, *Problem of History*, 42.

22. Evans, "From Public Ministry," 307–8.

23. "The hostility which Mark expresses in his descriptions of the conversations is confirmed by an examination of what was said. Bauerenfeind has shown (*Die Worte Der Demonen Markusevagelium*, 3) that the three sayings spoken by demons to Jesus (1.24; 3.11; 5.7) are all closely parallel to incantations of witchcraft in the magical papyri and elsewhere. Therefore the words could very well for Mark and his readers give the impression of a defensive magical incantation. This hostility is of course only accentuated by the reference in the demons' sayings to Jesus; destroying (1.24) or 'tormenting' (5.7) them, as well as by the opening challenge (1.24:5.7): 'What have you to do with us?' In 5.7 the demon appeals to God against Jesus in language commonly used *against* demons; *horkizo de ton theon*." Robinson, *Problem of History*, 37.

24. Mark 5:17. According to Matt 8:34, Jesus was forbidden from entering not just a village, but a "region."

male and female, mostly Jews); he then compelled the demon(s) or malevolent spirit(s) to reveal their name(s), i.e., to take control of the demon; conversing and sometimes negotiation with them, he commands silence; he then expelled the demon into nearby waters (e.g., sacred pools or springs controlled by angels or into the haunted waters of Galilee), or into the wilderness (the desolate places of evil). Jesus performed these exorcisms both privately (since failure was possible, using spittle and other familiar techniques known to contemporary charismatics, including magicians), as well as publicly (where he was identified as a son of God, or a holy one). He is accused of being possessed by Beelzebul, prince of demons, by his enemies.[25]

The actions of the demons and the untimely dead were violent, destructive, and "intended to cause injury or death."[26] The fact that demons forced their victims to kneel or fall to the ground before Jesus must not obscure the hostility of these confrontations.[27] Once the village is cleansed, Jesus demands that the synagogue leaders and elders, indeed the village assembly itself, reject Jerusalem and its elitism, the sign of Satan, and accept the disenfranchised, dispossessed, even those that had been demon possessed, the sign of God and the mercy he had shown them.[28] Jesus claimed that he is "master" of the Sabbath; more clearly, he is the master of all demons on the Sabbath.[29] This mercy afforded protection from a return by demons.[30] Therefore, Jesus' command of *agape* ensured freedom from re-possession, which could be sevenfold worse.[31] Jesus' insistence on *agape* was a central feature of his itinerant mission to free the people from demonic imperialism and satanic oppression. Jesus and *agape* are irrevocably intertwined in this battle with Satan, as *agape's* power was immune from demonic control, as its presence was evidence for possession of the Spirit of God. God, the true patron and king, their new *Abba*,[32] was soon to arrive and bring the kingdom,

---

25. Mark 3:22.

26. Robinson, *Problem of History*, 39.

27. Ibid., 37.

28. Luke 14 presents in full Jesus' demand on acceptance, particularly Luke 14:1–14.

29. Matt 12:8.

30. The outcome of the exorcisms is a return to normal life and acceptance; Robinson, *Problem of History*, 41.

31. Matt 12:45.

32. *Abba* (in Aramaic, *Ab baȼ*, accent on the later syllable), an intimate word (but not 'daddy': see Barr, "Abba Isn't Daddy," 28–47), was used to address one's own father, and was the unique and characteristic address of Jesus in his speech about and prayers to God, multiply-attested as having originated with Jesus. See Jeremias, *Prayers of Jesus*, 54–55. It is attested in all strata of the tradition—Q, Mark, Matthew and Luke, John and Paul; Paul's use of the term *Abbaȼ* in Gal 4:6 and Rom 8:15, i.e., an Aramaic word in the Greek-speaking world of his itinerant activity, is decisive proof that this was the

and with it the general resurrection of the dead, with vindication of the just. For Jesus, all was at risk, and if he did not act all would be lost to Satan.

For the exorcists that followed Jesus, both *men and women*, Jesus seemed invincible to demonic attack, as he was successfully fomenting the return of God's rule in villages and demonic expulsions. However, Jesus was betrayed, quickly captured at night outside the city and killed within hours. He was brutalized to hobble him and then crucified under a divine curse the next morning, all under Roman law, and at the insistence of his enemies. He was accused as an "evildoer,"[33] i.e., as a dark magician opposing the Romans, and so was a Jewish rebel who made claim to be a "son of a God," rejecting the temple and Roman authority. Herod and the elite, even perhaps Pilate, certainly believed Jesus could control and absorb the spirits of the dead and attack, as Pilate's wife was attacked in a dream.[34] Jesus was to be utterly destroyed so he could not seek retribution, or be made available to others like him. Certainly, none of Jesus' exorcists anticipated these events, confirmed by how they fled and denied even knowing him when captured.

The Exorcists of Jesus and Confrontation with Demons

Jesus selected and trained a group of seven to twelve exorcists to assist in his effort to drive Satan out of the land, mostly drawn from the poor, tiny villages of Galilee.[35] Virtually all of these uneducated, peasant men and women were related to subsistence fishing, working under ever burdening taxation, with contracted minimum catch quotas in rural Galilee. Struggling daily for survival, and with confidence in Jesus' ability to control Satan's demons and evil spirits (having witnessed his exorcising demons from family members),[36] even the spirit of animals (directing fish into their nets to meet their catch quotas),[37] they chose relief from the relentless risks and economic hardship of Herodian and Roman oversight and taxation.[38] They joined in his war on Satan to drive demonic forces out of the land and reap

---

way in which the historical Jesus addresses God. Jesus authorized his exorcists to do the same in their ecstatic prayer, similar to the Lord's Prayer, as a unique address in ancient Judaism to God most certainly.

33. John 18:30.
34. Mark 6:14–29.
35. See setion below, The Meaning of "Fishers of Men."
36. Mark 1:29–31, Kayfa's mother-in-law.
37. Luke 5:4 is one of several examples of Jesus' charismatic direction and ability to control animals to assist his villagers.
38. Horsley, *Archaeology, History and Society*, 121–30.

the benefits of food for family, relief from oppression. They, like Jesus, became exorcists for the villagers, who then supported, housed and fed them. Their success led to a trance or vision of "Satan falling like lightening."[39] As Satan fell, so too would their pagan occupiers and their burden of brutal taxation. The kingdom of God was emerging, already in their midst.

When sent ahead by Jesus to villages, these men and women employed Jesus' name to attack, a name feared by demons, or used methods to exorcise and free the victim. Yet, they often had limited success.[40] By practicing exorcism, they took on perilous danger—the illegal practice of black magic, which carried with it the threat of execution under Roman law.[41] Moving into villages in the morning or after dark, they were easy to spot, and were often taken into small homes where they were needed. They wore distinctive clothing, lived an itinerant life and survived from the often paltry donations given for their exorcisms, carrying a single communal purse—but were often still starving, evidenced by their picking grain left after harvesting from the barren fields.[42] They were feared by the ruling elite as dangerous dark magicians (their magic and spells could be sent against them), and more, for the endearment of the poor and disenfranchised (who protected them), and those who detested the control of the urban pagan patrons.[43] They were welcomed by the dispossessed and outcasts, but particularly by the subsistence laborers, i.e., the impoverished strata. No one stood up for the desperate poor, the subsistence peasants,[44] nor offered protection against demonic illness, injury, starvation, death, unending poverty and social persecution—other than fringe charismatic rebels, like John the Baptist, Jesus and his fellow exorcists. But, as noted, when Jesus was quickly captured and executed in Jerusalem as an "evildoer"[45] it all ended, and with it, perilous

---

39. Luke 10:18.

40. Mark 9:18–20; certainly, this is not the only time they could not exorcise, otherwise the record would not have been remembered by later Christians who also failed to do so, but called on the spirit of the risen Lord Jesus for assistance and success.

41. Specific references are provided in the next section of our study: also see Ogden, *Magic*, 275–99.

42. Mark 2:23.

43. See Lewis, *Ecstatic Religion*, 32–33.

44. Patterson, *Lost Way*, 75.

45. John 18:30 may be the most historically reliable tradition in this case. Pilate's wife fears contact with Jesus due to an ecstatic dream. Dreams were considered wholly reliable as forewarnings of evil and danger, and so, this tradition fits the contemporary setting. Pilate thereafter interrogated Jesus as a dark magician, and attempted to turn him over to his accusers as such. Pilate acceded to their demands that he be crucified, so as to kill both body and soul and, as noted, prevent retaliation. Considered a dark magician and dangerous even after death, Jesus must be annihilated and his power vacated

risk of capture and death; the apparent failure of Jesus' mission made evident, they hid in terror of a similar fate and fled to Galilee. To their horror, Roman legal prohibitions (e.g., *Lex Cornelia de sicariis et veneficit*),[46] which included the penalty of death, and by crucifixion under a Jewish curse,[47] evil had prevailed. Satan had been victorious. They fled and hid among their own kind fearing retribution from demons they had expelled and the collaborators with Rome.

Jesus War on Satan Began in Galilee

Our contextual risk analysis is clear. The world in which Jesus operated and battled evil was at risk from being overtaken by Satan and his demons. Demons included the evil dead and retributive spirits and dark angels. Risking annihilation of both one's body and soul, Jesus intended to counter the perilous risk of satanic rule. There was no choice. But why go to Galilee? Why would an exorcist go there to fight Satan and demons? Specifically, what compelled him to be there?

Why Did Jesus Exorcise Demons in Galilee?

There is now a very obvious answer, but one that needs thorough examination. *Galilee was haunted* by phantasms, demons and evil spirits—the lake, its springs and streams, the nearby caves and adjacent villages. The evidence is overwhelming,[48] and explains why an exorcist would have been active and

---

by executing him under a divine curse, i.e., crucifixion (Deut 21:22–23).

46. Ogden, *Magic*, 288; this law was introduced by Sulla in 81 BCE.

47. Smith, *Jesus the Magician*, 75–76.

48. Van der Toom et al., *Dictionary of Demons*, 236: "They held power during dangerous situations and times: Chiefly at night, during sleep, during a wind storm or an eclipse, or heat of mid-day, and especially in child birth." These were poor peasants whose worlds were inundated with otherworldly forces out of their control. Multigenerational families huddled in small rooms with central small courtyards, cooking with simple stone ovens, living subsistence existences. In Galilee they were totally reliant on local resources—their primary diet was bread, olives and fish—and the whims of evil forces haunting Galilee could quickly force them into starvation. Dwellings made them susceptible to illness and diseases, as they were made of rough basalt stones, filled with mud and pebbles, covered with twig and mud roofs. Every day was a struggle for existence. That Beelzebul haunted the waters is confirmed by Hull: "Beelzebul has a demonic child who haunts the Red Sea (Test.Sol. 5.11) and has been trapped there against his will (Test.Sol. 25.7)." See Hull, *Hellenistic Magic*, 104. That Jesus is accused of being possessed by Beelzebul and is able to control the fish for the benefit of subsistence fishermen (to deceive them according to his enemies) presents an interesting

embraced by the peasants in the villages along its shore and would move there to practice their profession. This certainly explains why Jesus did not behave like other contemporary Jewish sons in helping to support his family or kin. He abandoned them, or perhaps better, they abandoned him. Indeed, when we begin our examination of perilous risk in the context of first-century Palestine, it first cannot pass our notice that Jesus left his kin and family behind in lower Galilee (Nazareth to be specific—a village of perhaps four hundred),[49] after having been almost killed by the villagers there.[50] He was accused by village leaders, the *rosh ha-knesset* or *archisynagogos*,[51] at the Sabbath assembly of being dangerous—in essence, either a fake or a dark magician,[52] and a blasphemer, claiming that he had the authority to communicate with and control demons through his being possessed by what he later identified as the "finger of God."[53] His family did not try and protect him, nor could they. Jesus had crossed the line and entered what most considered a dark and dangerous, even forbidden, world.

We do know this because of something irrefutable; i.e., a truly embarrassing tradition, one that the early church would like to have extinguished, but it was already well known. Jesus' broke with kin and family, one of the most serious risks to survival and social standing in the ancient world. The conflict between Jesus and his family was vehement and vocal on both sides.[54] Jesus barely escaped death in the tiny village of Nazareth where he lived with them, likely invoking a warning or curse, allowing him to walk away from a

---

correlation between possession of the waters Galilee, under the control of Jesus (and thus Beelzebul), and the Red Sea, by Beelzebul's son. Jesus' enemies must have understood this connection. Also see Bar-Ilan, *Exorcism by Rabbis*: "Some springs have a complete family of spirits living in each; it is understood that hot springs, as in Tiberias (Galilee), are heated by spirits (acting on the basis of the commands of King Solomon). It can be generalized that there is hardly a source of water in the land of Israel without a spirit (one or more)." Bar-Ilan cites as additional support the *Pesachim* 112 p. 1, two baraitot: "The Rabbis learned: One should not drink water from rivers or lakes at night. And if he drinks, he risks his life because of the hazard. What hazard? The hazard of demons." Also cited by Bar-Ilan, "Haunted Springs," 153–70.

49. Horsley, *Archaeology, History and Society*, 109.

50. Luke 4:29.

51. Horsely, *Galilee*, 149–50.

52. Mark 6:3–5. In Luke 4:14–30, the original conflict of rejection and attempt to kill Jesus as a charlatan and dark magician has been expanded into the rejection of the Jews for the Gentiles. Salvation is now for the Gentiles, i.e., the thrust of the Lucan theological program.

53. Luke 4:20–30 and 11:20.

54. Jesus' public rejection of his kin: Mark 3:35; Matt 12:46–50; Luke 8:21; his family's rejection of Jesus, Mark 3:21 and John 7:1–9 (certainly authentic given the negative implications of Jesus and his kin who rejected him).

terrified and angry mob (perhaps including family), who were ready to throw him off a cliff. He escaped to a place where he would be welcomed—the shores of Galilee. There he could provide his protection as an exorcist, expelling demons of all types, particularly those causing illness and death. Indeed, Jesus became the protector of other's kin, not his own. He was provided subsistence support (a meal, a roof and clothing) in Capernaum, and later, other villages of Galilee, only a few miles from Nazareth.[55] Jesus' protection of the desperately poor and possessed led to his identification of them as his true kin, even his children—a radical and unparalleled claim in the contemporary setting. As such, Jesus was indeed a mysterious, charismatic figure, operating among the heavily oppressed Jewish agrarian populace of first-century Galilee as their protector. At times he disappeared for days into the hills and caves of Galilee. Clearly, Jesus was so overwhelmed at times from those seeking his help, he had to flee to sleep and eat.

The Village Setting of Jesus' Activity

Jesus performed the majority of his ecstatic activities and exorcisms in these tiny villages adjacent to the freshwater lake there (13 miles long by 8.1 miles wide, with a depth of 121 feet), including Capernaum (the "village of Nahum," perhaps with one thousand villagers),[56] Magdala ("place of salted fish"), Chorazin and Bethsaida ("temple of the fish god"); in fact, places where he later recruited and trained other exorcists from the agrarian fisher-peasants there,[57] but villages he later cursed for rejecting him.[58] Archaeologists have not yet located Chorazin (perhaps Bethsaida), mentioned in the earliest gospel source Q,[59] as it was so small that no trace yet has been found.

> These small villages are not places of mythic importance, like Jerusalem or Sodom. Neither are they well-known cities in the Galilee, like Sepphoris, near Nazareth, or Scythopolis (Bethshean), to the south of the Sea of Galilee. Q never mentions these larger places. Instead its range is focused on these tiny villages.[60]

---

55. See Mark 2:1 and Luke 4:38, Jesus being a guest in Kayfa's' home after exorcising a demon causing the illness of Kayfa's' mother-in-law, Luke 4:39.
56. Horsley, *Galilee*, 114.
57. Mark 3:15; 9:1, 38.
58. Matt 11:20–24; Luke 10:13–15.
59. Patterson, *Lost Way*, 66–84.
60. Ibid., 66.

Because Jesus and his fellow exorcists—men and women who also initially vacated all of their kin relationships and responsibilities[61]—came from this agrarian setting,[62] we must come to understand the social and religious context of first-century Galilee in order to assess perilous risks and countermeasures that can be recovered and how they would react to encounters with the dead. To follow Jesus was to embrace perilous risks, to be "near the fire,"[63] but only as countermeasures to more dangerous risks that when aggregated, led these men to challenge the most feared force of their time, demons and imperial Rome. For this conflict,[64] they accepted the risk of starvation,[65] arrest and execution. It was on the shores of Galilee that Jesus was accused of being possessed by Beelzebul, and was called mad (*exeste*) by his own family, where they tried to seize and silence him.[66] That Q and the Synoptic Gospels record these village names and these accusations is a testament to the veracity as to where, with whom and how Jesus conducted his demonic activity and made his controversial statements. Thus, the essential need for the evaluation of Galilee, its social, religious and political setting and influence.

Oppression, Poverty and Subsistence Existence in Galilee during Jesus' Activity

What is certain is that the typical picture painted by many scholars, theologians and Christian writers—those who tend to portray these agrarian workers and fishers as living almost an idyllic life with bountiful surplus, and as if market forces and capitalism were the norm—is completely errant and foreign to Jesus' world and the context of oppression in first-century Galilee. Recent archaeology and updated studies have shown that nothing could be further from reality. For example, excavations in the village of Capernaum have revealed some first-century Roman ruins, but a much

---

61. Luke 14:26.
62. Luke 9:60.
63. *Gospel of Thomas*, saying 82.
64. Jesus statement, "I come to bring the sword," is a contemporary reference to the brass sword that drove demons and phantasms away. More will be discussed on this below.
65. Starving, they pick the remaining heads of grain in a harvested field on the Sabbath, Matt 12:1.
66. Matt 12:22–25, 46–47 (the rejection of his family standing nearby), and Mark 3:21.

larger peasant area, which dominated most of the original site.[67] These poor, simple structures, made with black basalt fieldstones and rubble-filled walls, and branch, grass and mud roofs, provided only the barest of subsistence living conditions.[68] These were not the houses of any middle class folk, but the poor, heavily taxed, struggling extended families (everyone worked)— the very villagers that embraced Jesus as an exorcist, a kind of village Shaman, or protector. In fact, the real social, political and economic situation for poor peasants and their families during the time of Jesus' activity in Galilee was a daily struggle for survival under harsh tenant/landlord relationships and ever-increasing taxation,[69] and uncontrolled demonic attack that brought poverty (demonic imperialism), illness, maladies and death. Production was funneled to the larger urban cities, including Sepphoris, "leaving nothing for the peasant producers themselves to live on."[70] It is only in this context that the prayer Jesus taught might be fully appreciated. It was a plea for one's daily bread, the forgiveness of debts (i.e., unpaid sums owed to landlords or licensed Roman agents for food, rent and supplies when production quotas were missed or bad production seasons occurred) in order to avoid being expelled from land (or use of boat), and protection from evil, particularly demonic activity.[71] These villagers were the *ptochos*, the truly destitute.[72] To provide context as to the social and political setting, we must understand the importance of Galilee economically to the rich elite, the Jewish client king Antipas (a patron of Rome), and the Roman Empire, represented by the brutal and corrupt prefect, Pontius Pilate.[73]

Galilean Villages and Oppression: Understanding Demonic Imperialism

There were primarily two fertile agrarian production regions during the first century in the western Roman provinces—the Nile Valley in Egypt, and the Galilee in Palestine. Both were exploited for the benefit of the empire; that

67. Horsley, *Galilee*, 115.

68. Ibid.

69. Patterson: "Ancient cities were parasitic. Each was assigned a *chora*, a large agricultural area surrounding it, upon which the city could draw for its basic food supply and income" (*Lost Way*, 69).

70. Horsley, *Galilee*, 45; Horsley references another excellent article: Reed, *Population of Capernaum*.

71. Patterson, *Lost Way*, 71.

72. Ibid., 202.

73. Busse, *To Be Near the Fire*, 8–30, on Roman imperialism.

is, for the benefit of the wealthy aristocracy and landowners, as well as local rulers empowered to levy and collect taxes, which included Herod Antipas, who built a new and opulent Roman city, Tiberius, on the shores of Galilee, and contrary to Jewish law, near an old necropolis (cemetery).[74] Sepphoris, another Hellenistic city with pagan temples, was constructed only a few miles north of Nazareth.

The population of both cities combined has been more recently estimated at ten to fifteen thousand,[75] and when compared to the tiny villages on Galilee and in the surrounding areas of its region, the size of this population demanded much, if not all of their resources. Sepphoris was Herod the Great's original stronghold until its leveling by the Romans after the rebellion of Judas.[76] Herod Antipas rebuilt the city, which Josephus called the "ornament of Galilee," indicating the immense funding and taxation required to rebuild it, placing tremendous burden on the villages for resources. There was little consideration for the agrarian peasants. They labored daily to meet quotas of production under contracts or overseers, leaving little if any food and money to sustain their families. Illness, starvation and destitution were only days away, all dependent on their success in the fields or on the dangerous waters, harvesting or processing olives, oil, salted fish or fish sauces for export—all for the benefit of the wealthy and empire in cities far from Galilee. A network of kin support was sometimes the only means of financial safety.

To assess this very different world, we must examine the details of life in Galilee based on independent sources available to us, as well as some of the earliest sources of the Jesus tradition. We will begin with the agrarian setting and context, then turn to these sources, including the most primitive gospel that can be recovered, Q, whose origin has been established to have been first-century Galilee.[77]

Galilean Subsistence Fishing and Haunted Waters— From Fishers to Exorcists

What was the social risk context of first-century Galilean fishermen? Why did they leave their fishing trade and leased boats, risk critically important

---

74. Josephus, *Antiquities*, 18:36–38.
75. Horsley, *Galilee*, 45.
76. Josephus, *Antiquities*, 17.271.
77. See Patterson's excellent presentation in *Lost Way*, 66–109, "The Galilean Gospel," which is a compelling and thorough analysis of the origin and original setting of Q in Galilee.

kin relationships, responsibilities and subsistence survival,[78] even arrest, to be trained as exorcists by a reclusive young ecstatic? A man disowned and thought to be "mad" by his own family, possessed by Satan, and expelled from a tiny nearby agrarian village of only four hundred persons, i.e., Nazareth.[79] Analysis of such questions is paramount in developing our understanding of risk and the countermeasures employed by Jesus' chosen band during their time with him, as well as after his execution.

Scholarship unanimously accepts that all of Jesus' closest followers became exorcists, but most important, originally at least seven came from agrarian, subsistence life as village fisherman under oppressive production quotas, or were related to that work and exposure to subsistence existence: brothers Simeon (Kayfa, the new "exorcist" name given to him by Jesus, translated from Aramaic,[80] the "rock") and Andreas ("warrior"); brothers Yecob and Yohannes (renamed by Jesus, Boanerges, "sons of power/thunder");[81] Toma ("my twin," from Bethsaida)[82] and Mattay (likely one of the Galilean licensed assessors of catch, i.e., a tax collector licensed under Antipas to collect agrarian production quotas for the elite).[83] Their reliance

78. See Hanson and Oakman, *Palestine*, 106-9, and further discussed below.

79. Mark 3:21; recent analysis has shown Nazareth to be a small village, see Horsley, *Archaeology and Society in Galilee*, 109.

80. Simeon, son of Yonah, was renamed "the rock" by Jesus after being trained as his leading exorcist. In Greek, "the rock" is Petros, but in Aramaic, Kayfa, the "s" being added to adjust the Aramaic ending "a" implying a feminine ending, thereby making it masculine. Consequently, Kephas, commonly used by scholars should be Kayfa, the original Aramaic, with the long "a." The other translation of Cephas improperly drops the hard "k" of Aramaic.

81. Mark 3:17.

82. This may have also been an exorcist name awarded by Jesus, i.e., the "twin" being Jesus' twin, or better said, the exorcist who shares the same authority and power as Jesus.

83. The tradition of Jesus awarding trained exorcists a new "exorcist" name, either to protect them from demonic attack, or to use in attacking demons and to signify their power and authority, is founded upon multiple attestations in the Synoptic, Johannine, and Pauline writings: Simeon *Kayfa* (the rock, i.e., leader of the exorcists and the rock on which Satan is broken); Mary the Magdalene (the fortress, overcoming and taking control of multiple demons—seven in all [Luke 8:2] indicating a multitude of demons that she overcame); Yecob (and Yohannes) *bane-reghesh* (in Greek, Boanerges, the thunderers, or the ones who drive out demons); Levi to *Mattay* (Sanhedrin 43a, Mattai, or Mittithyahu, "God's gift"); Toma *Didymus* (twin, i.e., equal to Jesus in authority); Simon *Kanna' im* (the Zealous, i.e., zealous to overtake satanic control; not a designation of a "Zealot," one of the "Fourth Philosophy" that led armed resistance against Rome during the Jewish rebellion, 60–70 CE; see Eiseman, *James the Brother of Jesus*, 132–35, and Morrison, *Turning Point in Mark*); Yacob, *Mikros* (the child, i.e., of *Abba¢*); Judas *Iscariot* (according to Joan Taylor, "the choker"; see Taylor, "Name Iskarioth." The "choker" would be one that expelled demons into the waters to trap or destroy them, or one who may have burned certain herbs that choked the demon out of the victim

on the lake of Galilee as fishers, and their decision to risk all and leave this agrarian life, must be carefully explored.

To begin, these tenant fishermen and their kin knew that demons and evil inhabited the land, and that the refuge of demons was under the waters of Galilee,[84] a fact even the earliest Jesus tradition supports.[85] Ghosts roamed over the lake, particularly at night, and for this reason, fishermen would have only continued to fish after dark if they were desperate. During the day, immediate changes in the weather and wind would were thought to be brought about by the forces of darkness that were real and dangerous, seeking to capture the souls of those drowned if possible.[86] As such, the waters were known to be the haunt of demons and malevolent ghosts by Jews of Palestine.[87] Mastery of the waters, whether through silencing or muzzling the wind and waves, was awed; it was considered an authority known to only few charismatics and ecstatics (and several rabbis)[88]—including Jesus[89]—and to dark magicians and witches in the Roman world.[90]

---

when inhaled, forcing it to flee [see also Cohen, *Primitive Mind*, 147, as well as a choking possession referenced by Josephus as understood by Avioz, *Josephus' Interpretation*, 63]); Saul to Paulus *Apostole*. This practice of renaming adherents likely originated with the charismatic baptizer John, i.e., *Yoannes ho Baptizon*, (who immersed in water to capture evil spirits and demons). This practice was continued by Jesus and then his followers. Paul identifies Jesus as Iesus *Christos*, Jesus *Christ*; in the Synoptics and Q, Jesus is renamed *Iesus bar enos* (Greek, *uios tou anthropou*), the son of man.

84. See Bar-Ilan, "Exorcism by Rabbis": "Some springs have a complete family of spirits living in each; it is understood that hot springs, as in Tiberias (Galilee), are heated by spirits (acting on the basis of the commands of King Solomon). It can be generalized that there is hardly a source of water in the land of Israel without a spirit (one or more)." Bar-Ilan cites as additional support the *Pesachim* 112 p. 1, two baraitot: "The Rabbis learned: One should not drink water from rivers or lakes at night. And if he drinks, he risks his life because of the hazard. What hazard? The hazard of demons." Also cited by Bar-Ilan, Canaan, "Haunted Springs," 153–70. The waters of Galilee were considered filled with demons and spirits, as were all the springs around Galilee.

85. Mark 6:45–56. A deadly encounter with a malevolent ghost was feared. Also, the tradition concerning the demon Legion that Jesus exorcised is additional testament to the demonic infection of Galilean waters. Legion requested to be cast into swine, then driven by their request to be drown into Galilee, that is, into a place of refuge for demons; from Q, Luke 8:26–39.

86. Craffert, *Life*, 226.

87. Ibid., 301–2; Jesus walking on water can also be seen as his mastery over the demons of the waters. Other Hellenistic traditions also exist, see Ogden, *Magic*, 175.

88. Evans, *Jesus and His Contemporaries*, 242–41, and the chapter "Jesus and Jewish Miracle Stories" as a whole.

89. We must reject our scientific assumptions or understanding of sudden waves or wind as detached from their world of demons, spirits or even God. This would be alien to Galileans.

90. Ogden, *Magic*, 125 (Tibullus's story of changing the course of rivers, 27 BCE); 25

When Jesus does muzzle the wind and waives, the words employed are the same as when he cast out demons.[91] Consequently, the first-century account of Jesus walking over these waters, certainly from oral tradition originating in Galilee, was *the* demonstration of this authority to trample over demonic powers of the lake, so feared by these fishers and villagers. This is one of the reasons it was remembered and recounted.

As such, Jesus' power and social role, particularly in confrontation with satanic demons, the retributive dead, and spirits of the lake, was markedly different than that ascribed to other contemporary charismatics, including Hainina be Dosa.[92] This context is critical in understanding the decision of the fishermen to embrace perilous risk—adopting a subsistence existence as an itinerant exorcist over the daily struggle to meet ever-increasing quota contracts so as to avoid starvation and homelessness. One would only do so if convinced that the authority of Jesus over the waters and dark forces provided safety and mitigation of perilous risk from demons *and* the risk of starvation. Clearly, this authority over demons, and Jesus' willingness to train these men and women to help others overcome evil and provide for themselves and kin, was persuasive. Villages all over Galilee, including Bethsaida, held fishermen willing to embrace power over the demonic waters (until it was no longer effective and they rejected him). This helps to explain why virtually all of Jesus' original followers were agrarian fishers, or were related to production of fish, both men and women.

Bethsaida, home to at least two of Jesus' exorcists, Yecob and Yohannes, was a small village on the northeastern shore of Galilee, only 2.5 miles from the village of Capernaum. Its name is most often translated, "the fishing village," but is more accurately translated as the "place of the fish god's temple (or house)."[93] This ancient village name is important, as it underscores the common view of the lake as spirited, controlled by gods and demons—dangerous, requiring homage and sacrifice to appease. Fish were one of the most important foods of agrarian life and subsistence existence, and so, were used in magical practices and incantations, and were associated with control over others. Uses of certain sacred fish were employed in rites to silence enemies or even harm others and were feared in ancient times.[94] Practices to appease malevolent spirits and ensure the benefits of

---

(the Telchines, able to induce clouds and rain, hailstones and snow, 1st century BCE); and 269 (a magic amulet provided to divert hailstones, 2nd century CE).

91. Ibid., 301.

92. Freyne, *Galilee, Jesus and the Gospels*, 234–35.

93. Hanson, "Galilean Fishing Economy."

94. Ogden, *Magic*, 129 (i.e., the "Drunken bawd-witches: An old woman passes on her skills to girls," where the witch uses magical ingredients, sewing them into a fish

safe catch were undoubtedly used, including in Bethsaida. It is of interest that Jesus places a curse on Bethsaida, along with other villages of Chorazin and Capernaum, for their rejection of him and their "unbelief,"[95] suggesting that the local villages were unwilling to abandon their practices to mitigate risks from the lake for the protection of Jesus and his band. But for Jesus and these men and women, rejection brought doom and the risk of satanic control that required they "kick the dust" off their feet,[96] not only to signal condemnation, but also to cast of any pollution. Yohannes and Yecob, the "sons of power" asked for permission to call down fire and destroy these villages![97]

Given this context, the risk-motivating factors of at least seven fishermen to abandon the dangerous waters of Galilee for an equally dangerous life of itinerant exorcism could be associated with the protection Jesus provided them. Galilean fishermen operated at risk of life, the risk of demonic control and possession; if forced to the bottom, the risk of becoming the "untimely dead," leading them to roam as dead spirits, or most terrifying of all, being available for conjuring by dark magicians for sinister attacks, even murder. This terror, and its mitigation by Jesus, is reflected in the stilling of the storm (Mark 4:35–44) and the appearance of Jesus at night on the lake (Mark 4:45–62). As the tradition recounts, they realized their deadly dilemma, being assailed by the evil forces within the lake that made claim on them. When Jesus arrives, the appearance (reported first as ghost) becomes instead a tradition recounting "soul projection," which would have been expected by the Galilean fishermen. Kayfa tries to reach Jesus, only to be pulled into the water (i.e., he was not simply sinking) by malevolent spirits.[98] Jesus is able to control the demonic waters and prevent him from capture—just as he rescues these fishermen from death and starvation. Only this understanding is contextually coherent with the world of the Galilean fishermen—those who experienced and expected these dark threats and perilous risks daily. Certainly, for these men, joining Jesus was a countermeasure to perilous risk. But was this countermeasure so pressing to have led them to abandon their life for itinerant exorcism, or instead, simply ask Jesus for protection? Likely not, as it is clear other risk factors must have been operative, including economic risk to influence a change. It is impor-

---

head, to "silence" enemies; written about 8 CE: Ovid, *Faust* 2.572–83); also 287 (relating to charges in court against Apuleius for using fish in incantations and magic, 2nd century CE).

95. Ibid., 167.
96. Mark 6:11.
97. Luke 9:54.
98. Craffert, *Life*, 226.

CONFRONTING SATAN, DEMONS AND THE DEAD IN GALILEE   39

tant to return to this concept knowing their struggle for food and fear of demonic attack and resulting illness, which could quickly starve a family.

Returning to our former analysis, Galilean fishermen were living subsistence lives under backbreaking quotas—a cycle of poverty controlled by overseers tantamount to slavery or sharecropping. Antipas and Rome licensed these overseers. Speculation among some scholars[99] that these fishers (including Kayfa, Yohannes and Yecob) were of "moderate means," presuming that they owned their boats and were fairly well off "middle class," is false. There was no such thing as a "middle class." Their cooperatives (*koinonoi*) with other family clans (the "Yonah-Zebedee" cooperative) demonstrate this. Such idealized views have been shown to be absurd by K. C. Hanson.[100] Galilean fishermen were of the desperately poor subsistence peasant class. They lived day to day under duress. This included not only physical hardship, but the onerous quota requirements of fulfilling tax lease payments to Roman licensed tax collectors working on behalf of the elite, as well as the scrutiny of "game wardens" that monitored catch for collection (and to ensure "sacred fish" were not harvested).

Indeed, cooperatives with other families were formed by necessity in order to survive and meet contracted fishing quotas, having been provided refurbished boats at additional fees as part of their cooperative lease.[101] The first-century Galilee boat shows that it was repaired for decades before being sunk.

> Peasants did not voluntarily supply labor for the elite, nor did they work willingly for wages. Most traditional peasants are devoted to self-sufficient household economy as the elites are to the welfare of their estates.[102]

Antipas rebuilt Sepphoris, a Hellenized city near Nazareth, and constructed Tiberius on Galilee in honor of the emperor, exacerbating the taxation and quotas on villagers at this time of Jesus' activity.[103] Economically, the fishing cooperatives were by necessity organized, certainly due to being burdened with multiple taxes—Roman, from Antipas, and the temple tax.[104] Taxation was so heavy[105] there was no surplus, as all production above subsistence

---

99. Including Jeremias in *Jerusalem in the Time of Jesus*.
100. Hanson, "Galilean Fishing Economy."
101. The recovered Galilee boat was a refurbished boat, repaired repeatedly, using as many as 40 different woods. Wachsmann, *Sea of Galilee Boat*.
102. Ibid., 119.
103. Freyne, "Herodian Economics in Galilee," 23–46.
104. Matt 17:24–27.
105. Hanson, "Galilean Fishing Economy," 115.

was confiscated and sent to the urban centers and the elite for consumption and profit. Escape from this cycle of poverty, much like agrarian tenant sharecrop farming in first-century Palestine, was virtually impossible.[106] Such tenant fishers and farmers were under the control of severe landowners who intended to bond them to dependence and economic destitution—slavery being a close analogy to their plight.

With fishing on Galilee also being seasonal, and susceptible to drought, poor inflow from the Jordan and poor catch, practices to appease spirits and gods were important, critical and prevalent, as quotas had to be achieved to feed families.[107] The protection of an exorcist like Jesus, one who controlled the demonic waters and who stood for the hopeless and economically helpless; one who denounced the elite of Jerusalem as possessed and their displacement by the empire of God immanent; was ultimately persuasive to these fishermen, particularly when he began his war to free the land of demonic control and retake Jerusalem's temple.[108]

Consequently, in the context of the Galilean fishing village harbors, filled with poor and illiterate people struggling for survival, there were cultural practices employed to mitigate risks from death, demonic possession and attacks by spirits and ghosts. These included not only prayer and supplication, but also sacrifice and divination, particularly among Hellenized Jews and Gentiles who looked for protection and safety on the waters and from forces below. Those who controlled such demons, provided protection, and could increase catch, were embraced, protected and fed.[109] Jesus' encounters with several fishermen, soon to be exorcists, where he was able to increase their catch (e.g., Luke 5:4–6; John 21:6; and Matt 17:27), confirmed that he held control over these dark forces and spirits and the fish that provided life.[110]

The Meaning of "Fishers of Men"

Struggling for survival, falling short on fishing quotas and contracted requirements, it is no wonder that certain men left fishing to learn control over demons and the lake, and agreed to be "fishers of men (*aleeis*

---

106. Freyne, *Galilee and the Gospels*, 161.

107. As noted, evidenced by the name Bethsaida, the "temple (or house) of the fish God."

108. The thesis of *To Be Near the Fire*.

109. Jesus is invited to remain with Kayfa and his family after driving a demon from his mother-in-law.

110. Craffert, *Life*, 302–3.

CONFRONTING SATAN, DEMONS AND THE DEAD IN GALILEE 41

anthropon)," i.e., trained *and paid* exorcists, able to pull humans, like fish, from the depths of evil and control of dangerous demons and deadly spirits. They also sought the authority to increase fish catch, exercising release from subsistence survival and hunger—not just for themselves, but also for other villages. Jesus, like a village Shaman,[111] offered them a way to escape poverty and control forces that threatened survival and expel demons, returning the land to God. Evidenced by Jesus' charismatic activity, Satan's power was waning, again appearing in visions to "fall like lightening."[112]

If they could be taught this charismatic gift, exorcise and control evil, especially the demons that controlled the waters, then they would be able to feed their extended families. For this, leaving nets behind to follow this Jesus was essential and urgent; particularly in the height of the fishing season when catch was not forthcoming and their quotas were dangerously short.[113] All was at risk! It was this event that drew them into the company of Jesus and, ultimately, his war on Satan. While their success as exorcists was varied,[114] and their fear of ghosts and spirits continued, only this context would mitigate the perilous risks associated with abandoning agrarian life to become charismatics and exorcists, and explain why they did so immediately.

Galilee's Influence on the Jesus Tradition

The striking influence of the Galilean fishing culture on the Jesus tradition, including its risks and harsh life, indicates its fundamental importance in any evaluation of charismatic experiences of Jesus' band of exorcists and his practices, either pre- or post-crucifixion.[115] Just as important, Jesus was immersed in this culture; he made Galilee, and especially the fishing village of Capernaum, his home base and found it to be the place he could actively practice his charismatic skills on behalf of the fishermen, where he was welcomed—and supported.[116] It was here that he formed his closest relationships, as noted, with those he renamed, trained and empowered (us-

---

111. Craffert provides a model and analysis of Jesus as Shamanic figures that has compelling features suggesting the peasant Galilean villagers may have considered him such. See, *Life*, 353–82.

112. Luke 10:18.

113. Luke 5:5, where they risk life by staying out all night on the lake to meet their required quotas!

114. Mark 9:30–37, Matt 17:19, Luke 9:37–56.

115. Hanson, "Galilean Fishing Economy," 115.

116. See Craffert, *Life*, 302–4.

ing his name) as exorcists—Kayfa, "the rock" (on which demonic power is broken); Yacob and Yohannes, "the sons of thunder/power (from which demons flee)," and "Magdalene" (the Fortress). The role of the Galilean fishing culture and social/kin network, as well as beliefs and fears, risks and struggles, have been completely undervalued in most scholarly works, as has risk analysis and evaluation of the "alien world" of spirits, ghosts, demons, magic and sorcery that dominated the fabric of everyday life. Without rendering an understanding of this context, one cannot undertake an analysis of the expectations of Galilean fishermen-turned-exorcists as to what they might have expected.[117]

Jesus and the Ghost Story of Galilee— A First Look and the Value of Risk Criteria

It is certain in the context of first-century Palestine that Jesus' fishermen-turned-exorcists encountered men and women possessed by demons of the dead and dark angels, heard the voices of demons speaking through their victims, witnessed the serious impact of curses, but also recognized and feared aggressive attacks of ghosts of the dead and evil spirits. Jesus was mistaken for a malevolent *phantasm* wandering atop the waters of Galilee at night.[118] This tradition could only have originated in Galilee and is reliable due to its controversial nature, as the disciples encountered what they thought was a "ghost Jesus." It is unlikely that this tradition was a product of the early church, as it could have led opponents to claim that Jesus' appearances were common ghost encounters. When traditions that are embedded in the Jesus Tradition can be identified as problematic to the early church (e.g., Jesus' baptism by John; his betrayal by one of the exorcists he had personally selected), they meet the test known as the "criterion of embarrassment."[119] The early followers would never have manufactured such traditions due to the controversies they fostered.[120] Consequently, this

---

117. See conclusion in ibid. K. C. Hanson provides an excellent critical bibliography as follows: Corcoran, "Roman Fishing Industry"; Freyne, "Urban-Rural Relations"; Freyne, "Geography, Politics, and Economics"; Freyne, "Herodian Economics"; Hanson and Oakman, *Palestine in the Time of Jesus*; Nun, *Sea of Galilee*; Nun, "Cast Your Net"; Nun, "Ports of Galilee"; Parásso, "Lease of Fishing Rights"; Oakman, *Jesus and the Economic Questions*; Oakman, "Archaeology of First-Century Galilee"; Raban, "Boat from Migdal Nunia"; Stern, *New Encyclopedia*, "Marine Archaeology," 957–65; Wuellner, *Meaning of "Fishers of Men."*

118. Mark 6:45–56.

119. Meier, *Marginal Jew*, 93.

120. Of course, it is possible that the tradition was retained because it was helpful

criterion can be very helpful in our analysis of traditions that may be seen as embarrassing, particularly relating to encounters with the risen Jesus, because it is a *risk-based criterion*. Retaining such traditions created a risk of criticism, conflict, or even violent response from enemies or authorities, including the patrons of Rome (Antipas and the Jerusalem aristocracy and elite) and the Romans themselves (the brutal Pontius Pilate).

Also helpful to our analysis is the "criterion of dissimilarity,"[121] i.e., where traditions about Jesus differ from the needs of the early church on the one hand and the context of first-century Judaism in Palestine on the other (as best as can be recovered). In these instances, what is distinctive about Jesus' actions or sayings may have a claim to authenticity.[122] Often, what this criterion identifies as unique to Jesus uncovers significant risk, even perilous risk, for both him and his fellow exorcists (e.g., Jesus' charge that the elite were possessed;[123] that he is possessed by the "finger of God";[124] that he claims to have the "finger of God" from the right hand of God [an authority equal with God]; or that the temple was doomed and that he would destroy, then rebuild it).[125] While limiting traditions to only what is unique to Jesus, thereby eliminating correlations with first-century Judaism, this criterion is another tool of our risk analysis.

By employing these two criteria along with qualitative risk analysis (which does allow for correlations with first-century Judaism), assessment of some critical risk-based questions, and later the post-crucifixion encounters with Jesus—all set in the context of first-century Galilee and Palestine—can commence from a new, unique risk perspective. As noted in *Fire*, perilous risk and countermeasures to neutralize that risk can reveal historical conflict between conflicting parties in a similar setting, even when these countermeasures fail.

---

to the early church. Perhaps this tradition embraced the charge by enemies that Jesus appeared as a *phantasm*, but then neutralized it by noting that he climbed into the boat. Yet, this does not diminish the problematic nature of the tradition, as it still accepts that Jesus was mistaken for a ghost.

121. Suggested by Bultmann, *History*, 205. A fuller application was presented by Perrin, *Rediscovering*, 40–59; also see Evans, *Contemporaries*, 215–20. This criterion is typically employed when analyzing sayings, but has been employed in analyzing traditions and events.

122. Bultmann, *History*, 162. Bultmann asserts that the saying in Luke 11:20 has the "highest claim to authenticity"; see Koester, *Trajectories*," 217, on the reliability of this saying as having come from Jesus' ministry, and Koester, *Ancient Christian Gospels*, 343–44, on the multiple attestations to the saying; Perrin, *Rediscovering*, 64–66.

123. Matt 23:33.
124. Luke 11:20.
125. Mark 14:58.

Summary on Galilee

Jesus dramatically shifted his activity as a local exorcist for the peasants to the aggressor against the demonic forces and influence of Satan, who had destroyed John the Baptist. Galilee would attract an exorcist because it was haunted, and many were needed to protect the villages and peasants there susceptible to the dark forces that surrounded the lake, filled its waters and springs, and had taken control of the land through pagan oppressors.

Excursus: Why Did Jesus Sleep in Gethsemane after Leaving Galilee?

When Jesus arrived in Jerusalem to face the forces of Satan that occupied the temple, and accused one of his own of being possessed by Satan, he did something very risk averse, coherent with the context of our foregoing analysis—he escaped the risk of demonic attack. To do this, there was a place of safety from attack—Gethsemane.

The cave in which Jesus is traditionally thought to have retreated each night just outside of Jerusalem was surrounded by a grove of olive trees. In that cave was an olive press, thus its name in Hebrew, *Gath Shemanim*, or in Greek, *Gethsemane*. This cave could easily have held Jesus and his band of exorcists, being thirty feet by forty feet, providing shelter. But why would Jesus stay in this particular cave and not in Jerusalem? Understanding the contemporary context in which Jesus lived provides the answer. Both the grove and press were places of safety for an exorcist—free from demons and attack, as olive oil (and magical oils) repulsed demons. Jesus and his exorcists were reported to have used olive oil to drive out demonic contagion that caused illness and maladies as a practice.[126] Indeed, Jesus was apparently anointed with oil on several occasions by those he healed.[127] In Gethsemane, surrounded by these trees,[128] Jesus would have been able to find rest and protection, and the ability to pray for escape from Satan's power, not unlike what is recorded in the gospel tradition the night he was captured.[129]

---

126. Mark 6:13.

127. See Mark 14:3–9 (parallel to Matt 26:6–13 and Luke 7:36–50), also John 12:1–8; the anointing with oil is often associated with Jesus' being anointed as Messiah by the early church. However, the original setting is one of protection from demons and evil spirits. They are offering even expensive oils (such as that perfumed with very expensive and rare nard) to ward off evil from the man who protects and heals them from demonic assault.

128. Hull, *Hellenistic*, 71. The use of olive branches in exorcism is well attested.

129. Luke 22:42.

Judas obviously knew the location of the cave having been there with Jesus, but more, he also understood it as the safest place and best opportunity to capture Jesus: It was free of demons that Judas believed Jesus could call upon and employ in his defense if needed. Jesus' powers, including his ability to call on legions of angels (just as Agrath could call on her legion of demons),[130] would be impotent, and he would be unable to resist capture—thus, Judas' bold move to identify Jesus with a kiss.[131] A kiss was a deliberate act in the ancient world to pass on magical contagion to neutralize the power of opponents, even kill. As such, Judas' kiss was not an act of love or contrition. It was additional protection to ensure he (and those with him) would not be harmed, something dark and intentional to mitigate the risk Jesus presented to his betrayer. Judas was infecting Jesus with dark magic and evil, and thus, likely a spell to disarm him. Indeed, Judas' betrayal was thought have resulted from possession of "the devil (a demon)" that night, as the tradition records "then Satan entered into Judas Iscariot."[132] Both the elite and Jesus' followers may have held the same view of Judas' possession that night.

As such, every effort would have been taken to mitigate the perilous risk of capturing Jesus and then binding his hands.[133] Binding was to prevent touching or movement of the hands that would conjure protection or attack using dark magic, as there was little concern Jesus would singularly attempt a physical attack against a well-armed mob. Indeed, the fear of those accompanying Judas to take Jesus, who in their view was an agent of Satan, is still vividly captured in John 18:6, "When Jesus said, 'I am he,' they drew back and fell to the ground." They presumed Jesus was powerless, but still were in terror that they were wrong. Jesus' exorcists also knew they were powerless in that grove. They fled, but not before one raised a sword and struck one of the mob. We must understand that if the person was a servant of the high priest, he or she may have been wearing a white robe. Awaking from sleep, one would presume being attack by a malevolent force. It is clear one of Jesus' exorcists carried a ritual sword, brass or iron, as these were thought to drive away and sometimes control phantasms and demons.

130. Matt 26:53, twelve legions of angels, which were the servants of God.

131. The mob that came with Judas was armed with swords, but why? Would Jesus' small band of eleven men be dangerous enough to warrant this? Brass swords were used to protect from demonic attack and ghosts in the ancient world. To ensure safety, these men were ready to ward off evil forces and spirits of the dead they feared Jesus might conjure and then use to attack them. Certainly, this is why in John 18:6 when Jesus steps forward and identifies himself to the mob, they quickly step back in fear.

132. Luke 22:3, John 6:70.

133. John 18:12.

Striking the servant would presume to protect Jesus since all else was of no use in Gethsemane. This risk context is coherent with the setting recovered in our earlier analysis.

The perilous risk arising from the success of dark forces having taken control of Jesus left the Galilean exorcists with no countermeasures other than to escape. In this risk context, the terror experienced by these opposing parties in the Gethsemane encounter is finally recovered in its risk context. It is abundantly clear why the Galileans could never return to Gethsemane, but flee and return to Galilee. With Jesus in hand and bound, cursed by Judas' disarming kiss, the next task of the elite was to ensure Jesus would be annihilated, unable to strike back from the dead. This then leads us to the question as to why Jesus was brutalized and then crucified.

4

Destroying the "Evildoer"
Practices Used to Neutralize Dark Magicians

Why Was Jesus Crucified, Sealed in a Stone Tomb and His Corpse Guarded?

Those who were an annoyance to Rome and to Roman sympathizers (e.g., Herod Antipas) were usually captured and immediately killed by soldiers, spies or temple guards. A few were executed publicly, but not usually—take John the Baptizer for example.[1] Local rulers and authorities could simply throw someone off a high wall, behead, stone or stab them. Jesus was obviously quickly killed, but not in any of these ways. Why then was he crucified? Why would another Jew, even a Roman sympathizer, want the crucifixion of another Jew? What kind of danger and threat were present? Why was he so brutalized before the crucifixion that he couldn't carry the crossbeam to his death like others? In this contemporary risk setting, why would brutalization and crucifixion be the preferred method for this particular man's death, and more, why did his enemies demand it?[2]

The Protective Power of Crucifixion from Retribution and the Evil Dead

As we have established, Jesus' band of exorcists had unique social and cultural context concerning activity of the dead in Jewish occupied Palestine and Galilee that is corroborated by independent sources. The Romans,

---

1. Mark 6:14–29.
2. The Jerusalem elite, who were sympathizers with Rome, and Pilate in Luke 23:21.

specifically Quirinus, had crucified, i.e., "killed by violence," hundreds if not thousands of Jews in Galilee during the lifetime of Jesus and the exorcists after the tax revolt of Judas of Gamala in 6 CE. The bodies of crucified Jewish "rebels" lined the road not far from Nazareth into Galilee.[3] This visage would have been familiar to the young Jesus and, perhaps, many of these same agrarian peasants-turned-exorcists. Certainly, Hellenistic Jews in Roman occupied Palestine expected to encounter ghosts of the untimely dead—angry and violent, looking for retribution.[4] However, there is no evidence of any encounters with these crucified Jews, nor fear of Romans that they would experience retribution. Indeed, crucifixion was ritual annihilation of Jews, body and soul. Evidence in the Dead Sea Scrolls, 4Q 169 3–4 II (Pesher Nahum) and 11QT LXIV, 7–13 (Temple Scroll), confirms the concept that the eight hundred Jews crucified by Alexander Jannaeus were subject to the curse.[5] Consequently, there was no expectation that any of these "criminals" would seek retribution—how could they, they had been annihilated. The Romans understood that they were safe from any retribution of the dead by employing crucifixion on Jewish rebels since it was death under a curse according to Jewish ritual law.[6] Indeed, crucifixion may have afforded Romans relief from retaliation, indicating that this brutal form of execution had magical powers to protect them. This implies that Jesus was intentionally crucified to prevent retaliation; a subject analyzed in more detail later in this study.

Short of crucifixion, there is contemporary evidence in Josephus and the New Testament concerning fear of a dead criminal's retribution. To be specific, terror that this charismatic and exorcist, executed as a criminal, would return from the dead and seek retribution against his killer, Herod Antipas. John the Baptist, about 29 to 30 CE, was ritually killed. He was beheaded, and likely armpitted,[7] which was thought to prevent retribution by forcing his ghost to be *hobbled* and wander aimlessly. John was a charismatic Jew that rejected the elite of Jerusalem and the temple, and whose baptismal rituals brought about the ecstatic vision or trance of the exorcist Jesus that drove him into confrontation with Satan. John publicly accused the Jerusalem elite of being possessed; they were demons, a "brood" of vipers,[8] that

---

3. Two thousand of them, see Josephus, *Antiquities*, 18:1.1–10, 23.
4. Craffert, *Life*, 131, 176–77.
5. See also Thatcher, "I Have Conquered," 147–48.
6. Deut 20:23, also referenced by Paul in Gal 3:13.
7. Ogden, *Magic*, 162: "Armpitting" was the mutilation of the corpse of the murdered to prevent return, retribution and attack. As horrible as it may seem to consider, this may also have been done to Jesus' body.
8. Matt 3:7.

is, Satan's minions. He rejected Jerusalem's authority, and considered the temple polluted. John demanded that Jews avoid the polluted temple; come miles away from Jerusalem to Aenon; accept his charismatic baptismal rites to exorcise demons and "sin," all of which drove away pollution and the possibility of satanic control or attack. These demons were expelled into the water.[9] The demonstration of freedom from evil and unity with God was to embrace the dispossessed and outcasts, and reject the minions of Rome, which included the priestly elite, Herod and the Romanized Jerusalem aristocracy. Beheading was reserved for Roman citizens, *or* those whose ghosts were feared, or whose death would engender divine retribution.

The mutilation of John's body to hobble the power of his ghost[10] confirms that Herod, a Roman Hellenist, believed the ghosts of the dead did return, particularly the ghost of the criminal. His statement confirms this: "[He] heard of him [Jesus control over demons] . . . and he said, John the Baptist was risen from the dead."[11] More, he believes that Jesus has made claim as a charismatic evildoer on John's spirit, to use against demons, and ultimately against Herod. This is striking evidence of the contemporary expectation of ghosts and their use against the powerful elite. For Herod, Jesus was empowered by John's spirit, *his retributive ghost*. He was terrified. Facing perilous risk and danger, Herod was powerless. He perceived that Jesus has taken hold of John's spirit.[12] Jesus, now considered a dark magician, was now Herod's deadly enemy, employing the spirit of John to "deceive" others, attack and destroy him.

In this tradition, "risen of the dead" was never understood as a form of corporeal resurrection, but a return from death by a ghost or spirit, particularly one that is manipulated by another charismatic, magician or *goetes* (sorcerer). Literally, in Herod's understanding, John's spirit, his ghost, was pulled from the dead pool of wandering souls through magical rites of conjuring to be employed by Jesus for retribution. This would allow Jesus and his fellow exorcists the opportunity to control other demons, and in his horror, attack Herod, his family and engender the power of his enemies to turn against him. This view of Herod's "fear" of the rabble is now revealed in a more dynamic perilous risk context, that is, the fear of manipulation of spirits and dark magical influence of his enemies to turn on him. When we think of "deception" today (in the form of lies or rumors about someone),

---

9. There is overwhelming evidence that this was a common belief in Palestine. Details will be provided below in our study.

10. Ogden, *Magic*, 162.

11. Mark 6:14, 15.

12. Smith, *Jesus the Magician*, 97.

Herod and those of his time thought instead of evil influence that was absolutely present and powerful, in the grasps of dark magicians, evildoers like Jesus who were in control of the popular, but now murdered and retributive, John. Clearly, this tradition about Herod Antipas is grounded in history, as it is coherent with the perilous risk and countermeasures to neutralize it.[13]

Given that Jesus' exorcists lived and operated in this contextual world, Jesus' crucifixion as an "evildoer" and criminal under Roman law was considered essential to end his retributive return.[14] That the "sleeping" dead, those that did not meet these special categories, could be raised was a common expectation, whether by Herod Antipas or the rabbis, so the belief was prevalent in ancient Judaism, except among the Sadducees.[15] With this death, those possibilities might be ended.

Was Anything Expected Post-Crucifixion by Jesus' Exorcists?

Did the Galilean exorcists (trained men *and* women that followed him to Jerusalem) expect to encounter Jesus in any form after his crucifixion? According to the Synoptic and Johannine traditions, the answer is a *resounding "no!"* Based on risk analysis of the various traditions previously discussed and the events in Gethsemane, the Galilean exorcists never expected Jesus to rise, and at first refused to accept that he had,[16] certainly believing he had been annihilated under a divine curse (i.e., to be hung on a tree, Deut 21:23). The Galilean women who followed Jesus to Jerusalem and to his death did not expect him to reappear.[17]

Within the context of first-century Palestine, Jesus' capture, his beating and bodily mutilation from being viciously and professionally scourged

---

13. This tradition makes doubtful that Herod was "glad to see Jesus," i.e., hoping to see him perform some miracle, as Herod was terrified of Jesus of Nazareth; see Luke 23:8.

14. Smith, *Jesus the Magician*, 75–76, from the jurist Paulus.

15. Mark 6:16; see also Dan 12:2 and Rabbinic literature, such as Sanhedrin 90b and 91b: "From the Torah: For it is written: 'And the Lord said to Moses, Behold you shall sleep with your fathers; and this people will rise up' [Deut 31:16]. From the Prophets: As it is written: 'Your dead men shall live, together with my dead bodies shall they arise. Awake and sing, you that dwell in the dust; for your dew is as the dew of herbs, and the earth shall cast out its dead.' [Ias 26:19]; From the Writings: As it is written, 'And the roof of your mouth, like the best wine of my beloved, like the best wine, that goes down sweetly, causing the lips of those who are asleep to speak' [Song of Songs 7:9]."

16. Luke 24:11, the disciples at the report of the women.

17. John 20:11–15, also reflected in Mark, Luke and Matthew.

(*verberatio*)[18] by the Roman *flagrum*, followed by his crucifixion (demanded by the elite to annihilate the "evildoer [a dark magician]" under a divine curse),[19] left little doubt that Jesus was dead in every sense to the Galileans—he was not even expected to wander like the ghosts of the "untimely dead."[20] None of his fellow exorcists even dared carry Jesus' body to burial of any kind for fear of being contaminated by the curse, or more immediate, fear of capture, scourging and a brutal death. Other than some of the women, none of the exorcists even knew where his body had been taken. They likely assumed it had simply been thrown into the city dump, a common practice. The stark human fear portrayed in these traditions, indeed, the perilous risks associated with any overt action or affiliation with Jesus after his betrayal by one of his own exorcists (when confronted, Kayfa, the "rock," leader of the exorcists, denied even knowing him!) are all certainly reliable.

With regard to perilous risk, it cannot be ignored that these men and women were recognizable *because they were Galileans*. They spoke "Galilean"; that is, Aramaic with a distinct accent that was ridiculed by Judeans who considered them country rubes.[21] They wore special clothing as required of exorcists by Jesus.[22] They were poor, uneducated, and with little means of bribing or paying their way to escape. As risk analysis will confirm, the Galileans fled Jerusalem and went into hiding because they stood out, and because they had been seen with Jesus. They faced perilous risk and death daily on that flight to kin, and feared retributive attack by demons they had expelled. There were no countermeasures available to them, so they hid in desperation and terror and clearly did not expect to see Jesus in any form.

Jesus' Enemies Were Terrified about Retribution

Crucifixion was expected to annihilate Jesus, body and soul. However, there remained a threat. He had warned his enemies that if they did kill him, particularly by crucifixion, or if others of his band were similarly murdered, they would not be destroyed, implying they would still be active and return to seek terrifying retribution. Jesus warned they would return in three days.

---

18. A "cat of nine" tail, or whip with multiple leather strips whose ends held metal strips or balls designed to lacerate the flesh, so that the victim was near death from pain and loss of blood; limited to slaves, non-Romans and criminals.

19. Deut 21:23, and see Gal 3:13.

20. See above on the discussion of the "untimely dead" and executed criminals.

21. Matt 26:73.

22. Mark 6:9.

To declare that he and his followers should "take up the cross" was to boldly reject the finality of ritual annihilation of crucifixion under a curse. As such, additional protective steps were needed to ensure that the end of this dark magician had been achieved. The only way to ensure he was no longer active was to entrap his body, and thus his spirit, to confirm he was no longer active and dangerous.

Why Was Jesus' Corpse Sealed in a Stone Tomb?

Jesus wasn't the first "evildoer" (or even feared individual) whose body was taken to prevent retributive attack.[23] There are multiple examples where those who expected retribution took a corpse (or remains of an enemy), placed it in a sealed container and then set it among magical amulets, spells and tablets to contain it. Based on the foregoing analysis, it is evident that the enemies of Jesus were still terrified he might return as one of the "untimely dead," those violently murdered or killed; a *biaeothanati*, able to curse, punish and harm, even kill his murderers, under the authority that empowered him.[24] They had accused Jesus of being possessed by the dark angel Beelzebul, prince of Satan's demons—a charge they leveled against him repeatedly and publicly. Might this possession and control of Jesus by Beelzebul make impotent the divine curse?[25] To ensure and prevent dark powers being unleashed on them, Jesus' body was intentionally taken for ritual disposal.

The Tomb as Entrapment of a Dark Magician

Given the context of first-century Palestine, where our analysis demonstrated that the threat of the retributive dead returning were feared by enemies (e.g., as it had for Herod Antipas),[26] we must explore this possibility from

---

23. For example, the laying of a ghost into a tomb or cenotaph with controlling spells (see Ogden, *Magic*, 164–65, 29–30). The use of spells, amulets and other means to seal the ghost into a tomb or grave are also mentioned and described below. As Ogden states: "The means by which the ghost is bound into its grave is not entirely clear: there is one reference to the use of stones, another to the use of bars, numerous ones referred to with the use of iron bands or chains, apparently knotted, and one reference, apparently to swords being driven down into the grave, no doubt to pin the ghost down."

24. Ogden, *Magic*, 152–53, 158; and as disputed by Tertullian in 200 CE reflected in Ogden, 149–50.

25. Busse, *To Be Near the Fire*, 54–58.

26. Herod Antipas was a Hellenized Jew and patron of Rome. As is evidenced in the tradition of Herod's fear of John's return, that is, his fear of Jesus claiming John's spirit

a risk perspective.²⁷ Such a countermeasure would presume that Jesus did publicly announce that if killed, he would rise in three days, and that the elite presumed this would lead to retaliation—that he would escape the tomb, visit and harm his murderers. In fact, according to Mark 8:31 and Matt 16:21, Jesus made such claims that he would rise, which his fellow Galilean exorcists completely misunderstood or ignored, but which his opponents, Romans and Hellenized Jews, very well understood as a threat.

To begin, critical scholars have long rejected the historicity of any such predictions as having come from the historical Jesus, assuming the early church, looking back on Jesus' ministry, inserted them.²⁸ However, risk analysis allows that such predictions are very possible, particularly if Jesus would have made such a prediction in the context of qualitative risk analysis; that is, as a warning and countermeasure to a threat of perilous risk, such as threats of capture and murder by opponents, particularly crucifixion. In this context, having witnessed the arrest and execution of his beloved mentor, John the Baptist, Jesus' "prediction" was instead intended to be a dire warning to his opponents—a countermeasure they would clearly understand. Jesus publicly states that if murdered he would return from the dead, i.e., as one of the "untimely dead," those violently murdered or killed; a *biaeothanati*, able to punish and harm, even kill his murderers, under the authority that empowered him.²⁹ As noted, this authority, they believed, was of Beelzebul, prince of the demons of Satan.³⁰ "In three days I will rise again"³¹ would be perceived as a perilous threat under the authority of Satan—the most dangerous and ominous of all. *Jesus in death was more dangerous than in life, if not extinguished correctly.* More, even if Jesus were unable to return by Satan's power, his opponents certainly feared that his Galilean exorcists, also considered dark magicians, would attempt to conjure and send the malevolent ghost of Jesus to attack them.³² For this reason, Jesus' exorcists were to be sought out, captured and silenced before

---

and power (see Busse, *To Be Near the Fire*, "Herod Antipas," 16–17), Herod would have been fully aware of the risks associated with retaliation from Jesus' ghost, particularly given the plentiful reports in the Greek and Roman world of malevolent ghosts of the untimely dead who were brought under control of sorcerers and magicians to attack their enemies.

27. Mark 6:14.
28. Bultmann, *Theology*, 29.
29. Ogden, *Magic*, 152–53, 158.
30. Busse, *To Be Near the Fire*, 54–58.
31. Luke 18:33.
32. Ogden, *Magic*, 152–53.

they escaped to Galilee,[33] which was the same commission and authority later given to the brutal young minion of the elite and participant in murder, Saul of Tarsus.[34] But, would Jesus' opponents, those who considered him possessed by Satan, have expected him to be capable of vacating his tomb to harm them if killed, necessitating that his body be isolated, watched, even guarded? The answer is *yes*.

The ability to rise and vacate a tomb, even if sealed, is believed to have occurred in the ancient world,[35] and certainly would be feared by Jesus' enemies among the Romanized-elite, including Herod Antipas. In some examples, escape was not for retribution alone, but to be with one that was loved. While rare, such events were recounted by reliable sources (ascribed to well-known individuals, or real persons) that circulated before and after Jesus' ministry. For example, Phlegon, a Hellenistic writer and freedman of Hadrian, provides an account of a deceased girl, Philinnion, doing just this—leaving her tomb (after six months!) and physically interacting with a loved one, Machetes. In this account, Philinnion is able to vacate her tomb (still apparently sealed), appear at a location of choice, physically manifest in bodily form, and even leave clothes and jewelry at sites visited. Her ability to do so, according to Phlegon, was allowed by "the gods." When her parents, Charito and Demostratus, alerted by a servant (a nurse) about her presence in the house, find her in the room sitting with Machetes, they grasped her in joy. But when touched, she laments and says she is unable to remain any longer, all to their despair. When the family tomb is checked, only an iron ring is present on the bier, one that belonged to her lover. Her body is later recovered (outside the tomb), and due to the terror in the city arising from these events, she is burned by the order of a local shaman-sorcerer. There are similarities in Phlegon's account that mirror aspects of the traditions associated with Jesus' empty tomb, such as his sudden appearances in locked rooms,[36] physical interaction with loved ones,[37] and his warning not to touch him.[38] It must be remembered that while Jesus' tomb was unsealed and his body found gone, this did not mean he walked out as is sometimes presumed, that is, as if he needed to be freed. The unsealing on the third day *confirmed* that Jesus was already gone and, for his opponents, active and

---

33. This is exactly where the women instructed them to flee (on behalf of Jesus) and where he would appear to them there per Mark 16:7.

34. Gal 1:13. Saul was present at the murder of Stephen, Act 7:54–60.

35. Even in the sense of physically touching, eating, sleeping or harming living victims.

36. John 20:19, Luke 24:36–49.

37. Matt 28:9.

38. John 20:17.

dangerous. Like the iron ring found on Philinnion's bier, the neatly folded cloth that had covered Jesus' face and the linens on the spot where his body had been left to decay confirm this.[39] Such an account is reliable in its contextual setting.

Phlegon's remarkable tradition, dating from about 140 CE,[40] recounts an event ascribed to the city of Amphipolis, Greece, during the reign of Philip II, 359 to 336 BCE. The tradition, however, was recounted because this type of event was considered real and possible in the Roman world, and is contemporaneous with the activity of Jesus and his followers. While Phlegon's tradition relates events of loving action, malevolent intent could also be ascribed to such activities, particularly for those killed by violence or by injustice, *particularly if the murdered victim had warned of return*—just as Jesus had most certainly done. From a qualitative risk perspective, this countermeasure of Jesus, that is, his warning to his opponents of a return from the dead, finds strong contextual validation. More, it satisfactorily meets the criterion of dissimilarity in this context, as Jesus' warning was distinct from the expectations of contemporary Judaism[41] and alien to the understanding of the church.[42] It also meets the criterion of embarrassment, as Jesus' followers, men and women, are portrayed as oblivious to his resurrection predictions, and thus, the warning to his opponents. Given this context, it is also highly probable that Jesus described the brutality he would

---

39. John 20:7.

40. Phlegon of Tralles, *Mirabilia I*, in Ogden, *Magic*, 159–60.

41. As established, it was the Galileans, Jesus' fellow exorcists, who rejected any such concept or expectation.

42. Jesus' predictions in the Synoptics are never expressed as a warning, but as a promise, yet still one that his disciples never understood. This portrayal of misunderstanding by Jesus' disciples employed by the early church is used to obscure the historical context of Jesus' true message to his opponents, i.e., it is a warning that if they kill him, even crucified, he would rise and retaliate against them. Peasant Galilean Jews understood the concept of malevolent and retributive ghosts, but Jesus' exorcists were unfamiliar with any such concept of a post-crucifixion return due to the curse placed on Jews executed by being "hung on a tree." Mark 8:28–30 confirms the markedly different perspectives about Jesus held by the elite and the peasant Galileans. When asked by Jesus, they report that some say he is Elijah or John the Baptist raised from the dead (clearly understood as being for retributive judgment on the enemies of God). His opponents claim he can conjure the spirits of the dead for malevolent purposes (conjured through dark magic). But their understanding is that he is not demonic. Jesus is the liberator from Satan, destined to free them from demonic imperialism. This is exactly what my *To Be Near the Fire* demonstrates. Jesus' fellow exorcists presume his control of demons and Satan heralds the inbreaking of the kingdom of God. Jesus, by the "finger of God," leads the expulsion of demons and the elimination of pagan pollution and Satanic control of the land. Consequently, Jesus' original warning to his enemies is completely foreign to the portrayal found in the Synoptics and the early church.

suffer, by whom and how he would be killed; amplifying the injustice he would suffer at the hands of his enemies—the strongest warning possible to them of their fate if he were to be murdered.[43]

Consequently, risk analysis supports a conclusion that Jesus did warn that he would rise again after three days if brutalized and killed. His opponents understood that Jesus' threat was a real, tangible, perilous risk.[44] They took Jesus' body, placed it in a tomb and guarded it to ensure his death, under a divine curse, which had ended the risk of retaliation by the dark magician who was empowered by Beelzebul and Satan. The sealed tomb was to entrap Jesus behind stone, to prevent any possible retaliation against his enemies. Risk and the recovered historical context therefore support the entombment of Jesus.

With the fear of retribution now contained in a sealed tomb, they need only check that there was no further activity after three days. Of course as noted, Jesus warned his enemies that if killed, even on a cross, he would return for them. For this reason, they took another extraordinary step to ensure he was no longer a perilous threat to them.

Why Was Jesus' Corpse Guarded?

Given this risk context, it is highly probable that Jesus' opponents also guarded the tomb. Only in this way could they verify Jesus had been annihilated. The best option, as noted, was a rock-hewn tomb with only one entrance that could be sealed. First-century Herodian tombs of this type were commonly sealed with a heavy round stone that could be rolled along a trench to cover the entry. The trench in front of the tomb allowed the stone to roll and drop into place, if for permanent placement, or more commonly, a small stone was used to keep the round stone in place once positioned, called a *dofek*, allowing for reentry.[45] In this case, the *dofek* could be removed and the stone rolled back with a lever, sometimes requiring great strength. This was commonly done to check the tomb after three days to ensure the individual was dead, or much later, to collect the bones and place them in an ossuary. Depending on the size, rolling the stone back could take two

---

43. Mark 8:31; 10:34.

44. Matt 27:63: While this is a unique tradition to Matthew and is later (perhaps 80 CE), this tradition explains the historical context of tomb resurrection well, and the context of sealing the tomb and hiding his body from his disciples so that it can be watched, verifying it had not left to do harm to the opponents. Even though killed under a curse, Jesus' opponents were also Hellenized Jews, and feared retribution.

45. See http://www.bible-archaeology.info/tombs.htm.

or more men on the lever. A few men would be present to move the stone into place; however, in this case these men were more properly described as ritual guards, perhaps special *kohen* (priests), who wore *white linen robes*.[46] It is also likely that they were armed with other protective garb and objects, such as protective amulets (see below), and also iron or brass swords, as swords were considered protection from evil spirits and malevolent ghosts, and when held up before the ghost, stopped an attack.[47]

It was this guard that was charged with checking the tomb periodically, particularly at dawn, which marked the end of night when dark spirits and evil roamed. In this case, confirmation was not meant as a positive check, i.e., the hopeful possibility a person had been accidently buried alive. Here, a body absent from the tomb meant immanent threat of harm, an active and retributive dead phantasm. As noted, the rising and retribution of the murdered and mutilated John the Baptist was already a fear of Herod Antipas.[48] Consequently, guarding and monitoring the tomb would be an appropriate and valid countermeasure to the perilous risk of Jesus' commitment and warning to return within three days if murdered. Jesus warned of retribution after three days at least three times, according to Mark and Luke.

The gravity and magnitude of this warning is now clear when set in this contemporary risk context. If Jesus' body was found to have vacated the tomb, the elite would be warned, and protection by amulets, magicians or sorcerers' spells would be needed immediately.[49] And so, despite the gospel's

46. White robes were protective garb used to prevent attack from evil and Satan. For example, the Talmud states that the high priest was to wear a white robe to appear like an angel. Lauterbach states: "The white garments were to deceive Satan, who, when seeing the high priest dressed in white, would mistake him for an angel and not seek to harm him" (*Rabbinic Essays*, 63). The special ritual power of white linen robes has been confirmed both in archaeology and in literature. Over 200 linens, many from bleached white robes, have been uncovered in caves near Qumran, are all linked to the Essenes and their ritual power as purists, standing against evil and their war against darkness. Jesus wore the mantle of an exorcist, as did those he sent into the villages. The power of ritual clothing was prevalent in early Christian literature, including Revelation, that was heavily influenced by Jewish apocalyptic and tradition. For example, in Rev 7:9–17, the Gentile righteous dead are given white robes indicating they are both angelic and priests, i.e., they are protected. White worn by the high priest, the priests, and the Essenes confirm that purity and protection were linked in the wearing of white linen robes.

47. See Ogden, *Magic*, 179, 181; pre-Tamudic literature speaks of Solomon's sword, transformed into the magic sword of Moses (Pesik 140a, Pesik R15, Testament of Solomon), where the sword is able to ward off evil at night, certainly including ghosts and spirits.

48. Mark 6:14.

49. *Eerdmans Dictionary of Early Judaism*, s.v. "amulets" (written by Gideon Bohak). In the Second Temple period, the use of amulets was widespread, both of textual and non-textual amulets. These were used to protect from disease, evil, demons, or the

portrayal of a good deed ascribed to Joseph of Arimathea, it is more likely that he was one of the elite who participated in this risk-plan to take and watch the body of the dark magician, Jesus.[50] The gospel tradition states that Joseph cautiously approached Pilate for the body of Jesus because he was a "secret disciple"[51]—yet it is clear that such a request would be an obvious admission of his support of a condemned and crucified "evildoer," and so to approach Pilate would be extremely dangerous, really unimaginable in this context.[52] Pilate agreed to crucify Jesus because he was considered a dark magician and dangerous. Instead, Joseph must have been acting on behalf of the elite to seize the body of Jesus, seal it in a tomb and guard it. Even the gospel tradition confirms that Joseph was a not just a member of the Sanhedrin, he was a "prominent" counselor (*euschemen bouleutes*). The Sanhedrin was an elite association whose membership included the ruling Jerusalem families, including the high priest, Caiaphas, among others approved and appointed by Roman authority—in this case by Pilate or his predecessor, Valerius Gratus (15 to 26 CE). Joseph explained the context of danger to Pilate, who must have understood the risk; even his wife had warned him "to have nothing to do with this *righteous* man."[53]

Joseph asks for the body of Jesus,[54] places it in a tomb, seals it up, and tells Pilate where Jesus is buried. By taking the body, Jesus' opponents could confirm if he and his retributive spirit had been successfully silenced (i.e., annihilated), and so, was unable to retaliate. Only this explains the risk context of these traditions in their contemporary setting. Certainly this new

---

dead and their spirits. "There are numerous *mishnaic* references to the use of knots, coins and such rarer items as the egg of a locust, the tooth of a fox, or a nail from a crucifixion (m. Sabb. 6:6, 9–10)." It is very interesting that archaeologists discovered crucifixion nails in the family tomb of Joseph Caiaphas. Certainly these were used as protective amulets, perhaps as ongoing protection from a crucified enemy, considered an "evildoer," such as Jesus of Nazareth.

50. Mark 15:43–46.

51. John 19:38.

52. To mitigate the historical risk associated with such a request, the gospel and early church make Pilate sympathetic to Jesus, and that Pilate tried to release Jesus as innocent. As *To Be Near the Fire* demonstrates (see 20–26), Pilate was brutal, cruel and only used the ruse of releasing Jesus so that at a public hearing his spies and assassins could identify, capture and kill any of Jesus' followers who spoke for him. This was a standard practice used by Pilate according to reports.

53. Matt 27:19 is coherent with the contemporary fear of magicians and evildoers like Jesus, where dreams acted as a warning of their malevolent power and pending danger; see Ogden, *Magic*, on dreams. Again, the gospel tradition is softened so that Pilate's wife, like Pilate, became sympathetic to Jesus, but nothing could be further from the truth.

54. Mark 15:43.

perilous risk context explains these actions (and also meets the criteria of dissimilarity and embarrassment).

Summary

As noted, the Galileans knew nothing of Jesus' claim to rise from the dead, only his warning of what would happen if murdered (although they had ironically witnessed his necromancy and expulsion of death on at least three occasions).[55] As the foregoing risk analysis has shown, Jesus had been destroyed, clearly dying under a divine curse.[56] The finality of Jesus' death supports the qualitative risk conclusions as to: (1) Jesus' warning to his enemies that if killed he would return to seek retribution; (2) his death on a cross as intentional, intended to annihilate him body and soul; (3) the elite's claim on the body and placement in a tomb to be sealed and watched to ensure annihilations; (4) the confusion of the Galileans as to reports of an empty tomb; and (5) their vehement refusal to accept that he was active post-crucifixion.

Given these conclusions, which are coherent with an analysis of perilous risks and countermeasures, we are left with another conundrum. Why would the elite then charge that Jesus' followers had stolen his body when the tomb was ultimately found empty to their horror? What was the significance of such a charge in its historical context, what was the perilous risk, and why this countermeasure? That the elite were taken by surprise is certainly accurate.[57] But something more ominous was at play here. Since qualitative risk analysis (and the criterion of embarrassment) demonstrate that the elite employed the tomb as a countermeasure to Jesus' warnings of retaliation, and that it was unsuccessful, why would their next countermeasure be to accuse Jesus' followers of the theft of his body? It is to these questions we now turn.

---

55. Matt 9:18, 19, 23–25; par. Mark 5:22–24; Luke 7:11–15; John 11:1–44.

56. Gal 3:13.

57. What is clear is that very early the rumor spread (and remained prevalent) that Jesus' followers had stolen his body to make a claim that he was raised (Matt 28:11–15). This tradition not only confirms, via the criterion of embarrassment (i.e., for the Jewish elite), that the tomb was empty, but more, that in order to counter that fact of the empty tomb, they provided an elaborate explanation that Roman guards had fallen asleep, missing the theft. This countermeasure to discredit the empty tomb, and the embarrassment for the elite it engendered (they could not even watch a tomb for a night with Roman guards at the ready!), simply establishes the historical fact that the tomb was found empty by their guards, and later, by women who were followers of Jesus.

5

Hunting Jesus' Followers
The Urgency to Neutralize Jesus' Exorcists

Why Were Jesus' Exorcists Charged with Grave Robbing and Necromancy?

To analyze the charge of grave robbing, or worse, necromancy (usually dark magic to summon back into a body the soul of the dead, as well as control the dead for evil purposes),[1] we must first take the view of the elite in order to understand the charge as a countermeasure to perilous risk. It is this context that will establish the risk conflict for the elite, which is not necessarily the same for the Galilean exorcists. In fact, the risk perception of the elite, and thus the countermeasures employed, may not even have been comprehensible to the Galileans.

Jesus' Followers Were more Dangerous than Other Galilean Rebels

For the elite, Jesus was a dangerous illegal magician and exorcist,[2] an agent of Satan,[3] and therefore, feared because of the threat he posed,[4] both from the rabble who supported him in rebellious Galilee and the dark powers he possessed that could be brought against them.[5] He was known to be able to

---

1. Odgen, *Magic*, in his section on necromancy, 179–209; Smith, *Jesus the Magician*, 118.
2. John 18:30.
3. Luke 11:15.
4. Luke 9:7, Mark 6:14.
5. See Bolt, "Life, Death and Afterlife," 55–59.

control all classes of malevolent demons and spirits—those that caused death, disease, disability, deafness, loss of speech, and insanity. More, he could even call the souls of those infected with death back to their bodies.[6] The elite and their supporters understood Jesus was the epitome of a Hellenistic magician, perhaps even an Egyptian *goetes* (and there were contemporaneous accounts of him spending time in Egypt).[7] Only an agent of evil, indeed of Satan, could control such demons and the spirits of the dead. While Jesus made claim to this power by the "finger of God," for his opponents this was a ruse, as Satan's chief demon possessed him and gave him unbridled malevolent powers. He was a deceiver and must be destroyed. It became publicly known that Jesus admitted to having conversed with Satan in the Judean desert, the desolate and forbidden place where demons, including the queen of demons Agrath bat Mahalath (except Wednesday and Sabbath nights),[8] were expelled and roamed[9]—a terrifying admission.[10] Even after his death, later Christians, as well as pagan and Jewish magicians and sorcerers,[11] used the invocation of his name to control and expel malevolent spirits for centuries.[12] His name was feared. Employing Jesus' name was the ultimate countermeasure to control evil and dark forces, a practice that terrorized the Palestinians Jews, unless it was used to aid them, whether the elite or the peasant.

This invocation of Jesus' name confirms that his authority over demons was still believed to be potent even after his death.[13] This reflected the worst fears of the elite who were terrorized that he may escape the tomb and be active or be available to his exorcists. Consequently, the most influential tradition supporting the use of Jesus' name to control or combat demons and evil spirits was the empty tomb, i.e., that he had not been annihilated, had overcome death and was available and active—and so, just as Paul later states, Jesus' "name" was "above" (greater than) all spirits;[14] he was "raised," with the undisputed "empty tomb" as proof—a fact accepted even by his

6. Smith, *Jesus the Magician*, 126–27.

7. Luke 2:14.

8. Costa, "Exorcisms and Healings," 133; http://www.jewishvirtuallibrary.org/jsource/Judaism/demons.html.

9. Matt 12:43.

10. Smith, *Jesus the Magician*, 104–6.

11. There are numerous examples in the Talmud, e.g., *Tosefta Hullin* 2:22f.

12. Ibid., 62–64, 114–15; also see *Sanhedrin*, 43a.

13. See Origen, *Contra Celsus*, 6:40.

14. Eph 1:21. While not Pauline, this passage reflects the continuation of earlier practices where Jesus' name could take command of any evil spirit or demon, as more powerful that all others available. Koester dates Ephesians to the end of the 1st century (*Introduction to the New Testament*, 273).

ardent enemies.[15] The elite faced perilous risk, and must respond to extinguish the new threat of an active Jesus, available to the exorcists. It is this risk response that informs the contextual response of the elite to the empty tomb and charges against the Galilean exorcists.

The Galileans and Dark Magic— the Deadly Charge of Necromancy

Grave robbing and necromancy was clearly the furthest thing from the minds of the Galileans. They were desperately trying to hide and escape Jerusalem after the capture and execution of Jesus. The infiltrator, informant and assassin Judas had compromised their secret nighttime retreat, a large cave in the olive grove of Gethsemane. Ultimately, they were forced to escape Jerusalem, perhaps only briefly hiding in the "upper room," where they had only hours before shared their last communal meal with Jesus. They had entered into a protective union with their master's divine spirit by mystically participating in a ritual, where they ingested bread and wine, his body and blood, a practice similar to magical rites of the Greco-Roman world also used for union and protection.[16] But the mystical security afforded them was made impotent, dissolved, by Jesus' capture and then death under a divine curse by men they perceived as possessed. They were terrified of being captured and killed, no longer protected by Jesus and "the finger of God."[17] In fact, at least three of his band of exorcists had abandoned or betrayed Jesus—Kayfa, Jesus' leading exorcist,[18] Thomas,[19] and of course Judas, Jesus' treasurer, who was the elite's embedded assassin, infiltrator and informant.[20] It is clear that after Jesus' death these men did not completely trust each other.[21] Indeed, everyone in Jesus' band fled when he was taken by his opponents in Gethsemane—no one stayed with him;[22] and despite the tradition that a young disciple was present with Jesus' mother Mary at the cross,[23] it is uncertain if this was even one of the exorcists, but more, in the context of dire risks facing Jesus' band, the historicity of this tradition seems quite improbable that is was.

15. Koester, *History*, 67.
16. Smith, *Clement of Alexandria*, 217–19.
17. John 20:19.
18. Mark 14:66–72.
19. John 20:25–27.
20. Busse, *To Be Near the Fire*, 27–30.
21. Some apparently decided independently to escape to Galilee.
22. Mark 14:50.
23. John 19:26–27.

The risk response of the Galileans in the context of their dire situation *absolutely confirms that grave robbing was not a possible or even conceivable countermeasure*. Everything they believed about Jesus, his mission and authority, as well as the powers he had given them to control demons in his name, were made moot. Perilous risks now surrounded them, and they were want for any countermeasure but to escape, get to kin, and hide. They could not even retreat to the cave at Gethsemane.

The Charge of Grave Robbing—Neutralizing Retribution

Jesus' threat to return after three days could also be understood by his opponents as a threat to make himself available to his followers after death, i.e., that his spirit could be conjured by them for malevolent purposes. Exorcists and magicians would be expected to conjure spirits from the dead, take control of demons using the spirit and name of Jesus, and continue to attack and expel pagan domination from the land—to make "Satan fall like lightening from heaven."[24] As such, the Galilean exorcists would be perceived as capable of bringing the retribution of the murdered Jesus, a *biaeothanati*; able to curse, punish and harm, even kill his murderers, under the authority that empowered him[25]—physically, politically and spiritually. Consequently, the elite would seek and employ a countermeasure to ensure the remaining exorcists still at large would be neutralized.

In order to neutralize such a perilous risk (other than with magical incantations and amulets—see above), the elite would need to annihilate the exorcists. The most effective risk mitigant would be to make them *targets meriting immediate execution*—stoning by a mob, or capture, handing them off to the elite for execution. Qualitative risk analysis would suggest that the Gospel of Matthew provides a version of the elite's actual countermeasure to accomplish just this, but it has been tempered from its original contemporary risk setting. Matthew 28:11–20 reports that the elite charged Jesus' disciples with stealing the body from of the sealed tomb while Roman soldiers slept. We have already established that Jesus' body need not be "freed" from the tomb. The expectation in the first century was that bodies of the dead could be reanimated, pass through solid enclosures and vacate even sealed tombs, then commence their activity and execute purposes, good or malevolent. The very idea of the stone having to be removed to free Jesus was never the concern of the elite. Even more, the idea of Jesus' terrified disciples rolling back the stone is completely improbable. With regard to

24. Luke 10:18.
25. Ogden, *Magic*, 152–53; 158; and as disputed by Tertullian in 200 CE, 149–50.

the story, no one would believe it. At least two men were required to lever the rolling stone away from the entrance to the tomb (i.e., the stone was very large, Mark 16:4). Doing so in the middle of a still night would cause a considerable stir that hardened Roman soldiers could hardly ignore.

As we have suggested, based on qualitative risk analysis, the actual "guards" placed at the tomb were white-robed ritual priests, wearing amulets and other protective items to ward off malevolent spirits and ghosts (perhaps even carrying brass or iron swords).[26] They were responsible for checking the tomb each day at dawn to ensure the body of Jesus was still present or report its absence to the elite and warn of the perilous risks faced. As such, it is clear that the Matthean tradition has been detached from its original setting. But a remnant of the elite's countermeasure is present. The core tradition, the countermeasure, is centered in the charge that the disciples stole the body of Jesus. Appropriate risk questions begin to emerge: First, why would the elite charge the disciples of Jesus with stealing his body? Second, what would taking a dead body of a presumed dark magician and agent of Satan actually imply about them? Clearly, the elite would never be concerned if a benign group of eleven disciples simply stole a body to make puzzling claims (who would care?)—that is, unless it was because such an act was feared and was originally associated with powerful, illegal dark magic.[27]

Recovering the original risk setting, it is clear that the elite charged the Galileans with the most heinous and repugnant of all crimes immediately punishable by death, namely, taking the body of Jesus for dark magical purposes—necromancy.[28] Their legitimate fear would be centered in the belief the body of Jesus, if truly stolen, would be used for malevolent purposes, using forbidden dark practices. But they knew better—the Galileans were hiding, several of them having denied or betrayed their master. But the fact remained that Jesus' body was still missing and he and the Galileans were dangerous. If they were to conjure their master and use his name to take control of demons and retaliate, their lives and souls were in danger—to conjure Jesus' soul and assuredly use it to attack and harm his enemies! Thus, this accusation against the Galileans of stealing Jesus' body is a legitimate countermeasure to the perilous risk they faced, and therefore is

---

26. See Ogden, *Magic*, 179, 181.

27. It must be remembered that the elite accomplished the desired outcome with the crucifixion of Jesus. The evildoer was dead under a curse and the disciples scattered, until the empty tomb was found, and more probably, rumors arrived from Galilee that Jesus had been seen. The elite never considered it just a matter of theft—it was a matter of perilous risk and danger that Jesus had vacated entombment. The accusation was designed to crush the Galileans, labeling them as dangerous necromancers and dark magicians that must be arrested and killed immediately if found.

28. Burton and Grandy, *Magic, Mystery and Science*, 150–51.

certainly accurate in its contemporary setting. It represented to the elite the most potent response to perilous risk that they believed the exorcists could employ against them once back in Galilee.[29] The charge empowered anyone to immediately inform (for money), or even attack, stone and kill a follower if discovered—exactly what happened later to one of Jesus' band.[30] Interestingly, this is the earliest charge brought against Jesus' followers, that is, that they practiced necromancy and dark magic, and so were to be associated with Satan—a charge that followed them for decades.[31]

As such, the tradition of the empty tomb, and particularly the charges that Jesus' disciples would steal his body to claim he "had risen from the dead," are often today treated as ridiculous, abhorrent, or puzzling—a shocking concept. However, in the context of the first-century Roman world, traditions ascribed to dark magicians of stealing bodies and, using magical practices, reanimating them to effect some spell or action, or even to learn the secret of life, were prevalent.[32] The rites surrounding this dark magic were strictly forbidden under Roman law under penalty of death, and the penalties were thoroughly described in early literature.[33] The body was stolen and manipulated, ultimately set up standing, filled with magical ingredients and potions and commanded to speak to reveal secrets, or perform acts to the benefit of the magician or sorcerer. Examples included consultation and oracles, understanding dark secrets and mysteries, correcting drought, or revisiting one's dead relatives and speaking again with them, or harming others in the most vicious of ways.[34]

Summary

The charge of grave robbing and necromancy, arising from the fear of the evocation of Jesus' spirit and power by the disciples, was thus perceived by the elite as a countermeasure to the empty tomb and a way to quickly find and capture them. While it was a fear, the intent of the charge was to find and kill them before they could harm those who executed Jesus and evoked his powerful and retributive spirit.

29. Remarkably, however, this possibility is completely absent from all traditions, including antagonistic writings against Christians, other than general comments such as a "disgusting," or evil superstition" (see Tacitus, *Annals*, 15:44). Consequently, something else was ascribed to the empty tomb, completely absent any tradition of this sort, and the least concern for such a body theft.

30. Acts 7:54–60.
31. Roman historians such as Suetonius and Celsus.
32. See Ogden, *Magic*, 179–209.
33. Smith, *Magician*, 75–76.
34. Ogden, *Magic*, 152–53, 184, 199–201.

6

Post-Crucifixion Encounters with the Dead in the First Century

Traumatizing Post-Crucifixion Encounters as Evidence of Risk Event

Tradition is consistent in portraying the response of Jesus' exorcists as one of shock and surprise, discomfort and denial—even fear that the accounts might be real, as most fled and abandoned him to his deadly enemies. They ridiculed those who claimed to have had any form of encounter (even ghostlike).[1] Jesus is said to have had to "remind" them that he predicted his death and resurrection. These and other traditions all fit the criterion of embarrassment.[2] The early church would never have included such traditions, nor would it have admitted that they hid in fear behind locked doors, if there was an expectation of post-crucifixion encounters, or certainly of predictions of resurrection. Consequently, it is certain that there was no expectation of his appearance, *particularly* by the Galileans. The risk-based question is why is this?

In the canonical gospels, post-crucifixion encounters with Jesus were universally described as unexpected and often traumatizing. There are at least thirteen post-crucifixion encounters embedded in the four canonical gospels. Some of these have been recast as events occurring during the life of Jesus. These will be described in more detail below. At the outset, it must be stated that any attempt to harmonize these encounters is simply impossible, confirmed by critical analysis.[3] More, it is apparent that these

---

1. John 20:19; Luke 24:37.
2. Luke 24:44.
3. Marxsen, *Resurrection*, 72–74.

traditions were quite varied and circulated independently, as the editors/ evangelists themselves make no attempt to bring coherence to the tradition, even though Matthew and Luke, and certainly John, may have known the narrative framework and events recorded in others. As Willi Marxsen correctly states: "There was no longer a unified view in the primitive church about the mode of the Easter happening."[4]

Part of the reason for the varied accounts is that encounters with the dead could take a multiplicity of forms. Yet, evidence will show that these encounters were adapted for theological purposes and were often disassociated from their original perilous risk context. Consequently, the resurrection appearances should be understood to reflect the editors'/evangelists' theological intent in servicing the communities to whom their gospels were directed.[5] The evangelists have one objective—to confirm that their community is an extension of the activity of Jesus, who is still active and alive, and whose encounters with disciples engendered the legitimacy and ongoing activity of the *ecclesiae*.[6] While the dates of final composition are suggested below, it is recognized that these traditions circulated for decades before their inclusion into these gospels. But their final form fits the intent of the editors and reflects the dynamic independence of the resurrection tradition.

The post-crucifixion encounters embedded within the four canonical gospels are as follows:

Mark (69 to 72 CE)[7]

- The original ending of Mark, Mark 16:1–8, records no post-crucifixion encounters with Jesus, only discovery of an empty tomb.

    However, the appendix, Mark 16:9–20 does include the report of several encounters. Yet this section is most likely a conflation of

---

4. Ibid., 76.

5. Ibid., 77: "It can be shown, for example, that Luke works out his conception with the help of geographical information, among other things. The Church starts from Jerusalem. Galilee's greatness is a thing of the past. Hence Luke, in contrast to his Markan source (16.7) leaves out the sending of the disciples to Galilee. Instead, he reminds his readers of what Jesus *had earlier programmed* in Galilee (24.16). Consequently, the Easter events are localized in and round Jerusalem."

6. Koester, *Introduction*, 83–86; "The resurrection and the appearances of Jesus are best explained as a catalyst which prompted reactions that resulted in the missionary activity and founding of the churches, but also in the crystallization of the tradition about Jesus and his ministry" (84). This is echoed in Paul's statement: "And if Christ be not risen, then is our preaching vain, and your faith is also vain" (1 Cor 15:14).

7. These dates are assigned based on analysis of scholars and generally follow the composition dates provided by Koester.

later gospel narratives of events, and so most scholars considered it a later addition (105 to 125 CE).[8] The ending is not included in most other key manuscripts, although there are iterations that vary even this ending. Nonetheless, at the conclusion of this section is an interesting "signs" statement attributed to the risen Jesus and addressed to his exorcists, i.e., that they will be able "*in my name* to cast out demons, they will speak in new tongues, they will pick up serpents, and if they drink any deadly thing, it will not harm them; they will lay their hands on the sick and they will recover." This does not appear in any other New Testament document and therefore must be considered a separate encounter with Jesus absorbed into the appendix added to the Marcan tradition. These charismatic activities are coherent with the activities of Jesus during his ministry. As such, this encounter will be treated on its own merits and tested.

- Mark 9:2–8; the ecstatic experience of three exorcists, Simon (i.e., Kayfa), James and John, known as *the transfiguration*, was most likely a post-crucifixion encounter with Jesus reinserted into the narrative and his itinerant activity. The literary unit begins, "After six days," and is set in Galilee, which is consistent with the aforementioned risk context with the exorcists fleeing Jerusalem and meeting with Jesus there (a command given to the women, passed on to the Galileans).[9] The nature of this ecstatic experience in Galilee is markedly different than other post-crucifixion encounters reported in Jerusalem. As it is an ecstatic vision, its placement as a resurrection event was certainly problematic.

Matthew (75 to 85 CE)

- Matthew 28:1–10; Mary Magdalene goes to the tomb, then later with "the other Mary" meets the risen Jesus on the way back to Jerusalem who tells the women (who hold onto his feet) to instruct his fellow exorcists to "go to Galilee where they will see me."

- Matthew 28:16–20; Jesus meets the exorcists (or a larger crowd) in Galilee on a mountain. Some doubt even after seeing Jesus (indicating a larger circle perhaps than the exorcists). He gives them a commission to go out into the world and "make disciples of all nations, baptizing them. . . ." He promises to return at the end of the age (as messiah).

8. Funk and Jesus Seminar, *Acts of Jesus*, 449–95.
9. Mark 16:7.

Luke (80 to 85 CE)

- Luke 24:13–35; two followers of Jesus, one named Cleopas, walking to a village Emmaus meet a stranger who they ultimately recognize as Jesus, but he vanishes out of their sight at supper when he breaks bread. They return to Jerusalem to let other know they had "seen Jesus."
- Luke 24:34; when the two Emmaus travelers return to Jerusalem they are told that the "Lord has risen indeed, and has appeared to Simon [presumably Kayfa]." There is no expansion of this provided in the canonical gospels, however, Paul later confirms the primacy of this encounter in his listing, 1 Cor 15:1–5.[10]
- Luke 24:36–39; hiding in Jerusalem, Jesus suddenly appears in a locked room. Those present think they see a *phantasm*, but Jesus shows his wounds and invites them to handle him to see he has flesh and bones. There is no indication they do. They disbelieve "for joy." Jesus eats in front of them. The disciples are instructed to remain in Jerusalem until they receive power "from on high."
- Luke 24:50–53; Jesus takes the followers to Bethany, blessed and then "parted [*dieste ap auton*, withdrew] from them." The implication is he dematerialized or ascended to heaven.

John (95 to 110 CE)

- John 6:16–24 (also Mark 6:45–56; Matt 14:22–36); Jesus is seen walking on the Sea of Galilee at night. The exorcists leave shore without Jesus, for "he had not yet joined them." They row against heavy winds toward Capernaum, about three or four miles out. Jesus later approaches the boat walking on water. The exorcists are terrified when they see him, but when he is helped into the boat they suddenly appear at the shore of Capernaum.[11] This tradition has led to debate as to its

---

10. Conzelmann, *1 Corinthians*, 248–57. Conzelmann agrees that the primacy of Kayfa's encounter with the risen Jesus as recorded in Paul's listing (taken itself from a very early formulae) is a variant tradition of a primitive event recognized by the earliest church as primary to the confirmation of Jesus' resurrection, and, therefore, is not reliant on Luke 24:34.

11. This event is also found in Mark 6:45–56 and Matt 14:22–36. In Mark, Jesus is trying to pass by the disciples without notice about 3–6 a.m. as they fight the strong winds, but the exorcists see Jesus and think he is a *phantasm*. He joins them in the boat and the wind ceases. In Matthew, Jesus sees them in trouble and comes directly to

original setting. Recent analysis has shown that this event was most likely a resurrection account, later transposed into Jesus' Galilean ministry.[12] The tradition was problematic as a resurrection event, as Jesus was identified as a *phantasm*, a ghost, reducing the experience as ethereal, subjective—a common ghost story. By placing the tradition back into the ministry of Jesus, concern that the resurrected Jesus was nothing more than a ghostly experience is eliminated.[13]

- John 20:11–18; Jesus appears to Mary of Magdala outside the empty tomb, she assumes he is the gardener, until she hears his voice calling her name. She attempts to hold him, but he stops her, saying he has not yet "ascended."

- John 20:19–23; Jesus appears to the exorcists despite the doors being locked (for fear of the "Jews"). He shows his hands and side and is recognized and gladly received. While the appearance feigns materiality, there is no indication it is material. Jesus breathes the Holy Spirit, authorizing them to forgive sins or "retain" them, and they are sent out to do so. Not all the exorcists are present.

- John 20:26–29; Eight days after the foregoing appearance, Thomas, who has reluctantly returned and found refuge from the elite with some of the other exorcists, refuses to accept that Jesus is active and risen. He takes their experience as a ghostly experience. Jesus materializes behind closed doors and asks Thomas to feel his wounds, although it is unclear if he does. Thomas falls to his knees and believes. Jesus blesses those who believe without seeing him.

- John 21:1–23; The longest of the resurrection encounters of the four gospels, Jesus appears at dawn, cooks breakfast and eats with Kayfa, Thomas, Nathanael, James and John, and two others—seven exorcists. Kayfa is fishing with these men off the shore, curiously at night, and they catch nothing. At dawn, Kayfa sees a figure standing on the shore,

---

assist. Again, they believe they also see a ghost. Kayfa tries to join Jesus on the water but begins to sink, only to be taken by Jesus' hand and rescued. The winds cease.

12. Patterson, *Beyond the Passion*, 113–14; Madden, "Jesus Walking on the Sea," 79–86.

13. The development of the tradition is also apparent. While Mark and Matthew use the word *phantasm*, Matthew expands the tradition with the inclusion of Kayfa, showing that Jesus was more than ghostly, he was material and extraordinarily powerful. John, eliminates *phantasm* altogether and has the boat arrive at its destination when Jesus boards. Mark's version is the earliest form. The event happens in Galilee, where the exorcists are to meet Jesus after the crucifixion. They row onto the sea, where ghosts roam at night, and they encounter Jesus. Jesus has no plan to assist them, but tries to pass by. The risen Jesus, as a *phantasm*, is encountered. This is a resurrection account.

and answers that they have caught nothing. Jesus, famous for controlling the spirits of animals, orders them to cast their net to another spot. The quantity of the catch is overwhelming. "The disciple whom Jesus loved" identifies the figure as Jesus. Kayfa dives into the water. They meet the figure. Curiously, Jesus is not necessarily recognized, just the actions that have taken place identify the man, but "they dare not ask him, 'who are you.'" Interestingly, the section ends with this event being the "third" time Jesus was revealed. Obviously, the appearance to Mary was not counted, some contend because the witness of a woman was unacceptable in Jewish courts and in tradition.[14] Rather, there was only a single witness, which was unacceptable as "proof."[15]

Selected Noncanonical Gospel Accounts

- *Gospel of Peter* 37–41 (150 to 190 CE): The "elders," a centurion Petronius and soldiers guarding the tomb witness two figures from heaven enter and walk out of tomb with a third figure, a cross following behind. There is no speaking or identification of the figure, but it is presumed to be Jesus. There are three witnesses, despite a combination of groups and individuals, which was required for confirmation of an event. It is also important that all of the witnesses are independent of disciples of Jesus.

- *Gospel of Nicodemus* (Acts of Pilate) 10:20–21, ch. 13 (350 to 375 CE): A priest named Phinees, a schoolmaster named Ada, and a Levite named Ageus (three witnesses, so reliable) report that they saw Jesus with his eleven disciples on the Mount of Olives. Jesus is then seen ascending. Pilate reports that the guards also saw the risen Jesus. None of these witnesses are disciples of Jesus. There are three witnesses, once again, indicating corroboration of an event.

Pagan sources are void of post-crucifixion encounters with Jesus. They are primarily polemics against Christianity as a "vile superstition." These

---

14. E.g., see Josephus, *Antiquities*, 4:219.

15. The discussion between Jesus and Kayfa, commanding him to feed his sheep (John 21:15–24) is clearly a later Christian tradition. It's purpose is to explain the reinstatement of Kayfa as the primary leader of the church (apparently James, Jesus' brother and leader of the Jerusalem *ekklesia*, was forgotten) and provide the prediction of his death, and the tale of the "the disciple whom Jesus loved," the source of many of the accounts in the gospel, who lived to an old age, but who did not live to see the return of Jesus as expected (creating dissonance in his community).

include Roman writings of Tacitus[16] and Pliny.[17] Flavius Josephus, a Romanized Jew, in the infamous *Testimonium Flavianum* (a Christianized passage that has corrupted Josephus' original report)[18] alludes to Jesus being seen alive again, but nothing more.[19] References in the Talmud refer to Jesus as a magician, sorcerer and deceiver, that he was punished in hell, thereby denying the resurrection (for him or his followers), and so provide no additional information.[20]

Risk Analysis of the Post-Crucifixion Encounters in Their Contemporary Setting

It is possible to analyze the various traditions that relate these encounters using risk analysis, seeking those that are contextually coherent with risk and criteria employed in this study. The results of this analysis should isolate the most reliable encounters and forms within the original setting, rendering conclusions as to the "contextual historicity" of the resurrection encounter. Risk analysis can thus suggest which encounters, in their original form, are coherent with that setting.

Based on our foregoing analysis, the risk criteria to be employed are as follows:

1. Qualitative Risk Analysis: The encounter cannot be a countermeasure to the elite (this is a later development of the church), but must heighten the perilous risk of the Galileans.

2. The Criterion of Dissimilarity: Encounters must differ from the needs of the early church on the one hand and the context of first-century Judaism in Palestine on the other.

3. The Criterion of Embarrassment: Encounters should create embarrassment for the early church, or create additional perilous risk.

Once these risk criteria are employed, the remaining encounters must pass contextual coherence tests using the contemporary setting recovered in

---

16. Tacitus, *Annals*, 15:44.
17. Pliny, *Epistles*, 10:96.
18. Busse, *To Be Near the Fire*, 18–19.
19. Josephus, *Antiquities*, 18:63–64.
20. The references to Jesus in the Talmud may not predate the fourth century, and they presume a comprehensive knowledge of the canonical gospels, but they also likely capture earlier traditions ascribed to sages who lived in or around the time of the early Christian movement. By assigning Jesus to punishment in hell, these traditions deny the resurrection for Jesus, or for his followers.

this study, with emphasis on Galilee, including Jesus' activity there among his exorcists. It is into this unfamiliar and radically different world we must enter, a world seemingly controlled by Satan, whose demonic influence had previously engendered the Galilean exorcists to risk everything, abandon subsistence existence, and follow Jesus into perilous danger. The encounter must therefore be coherent with the sociological risk setting, including the subsistence struggle of the Galileans, the background from which they came to join Jesus' band of exorcists.

The contextual risk tests are as follows:

4. Encounters with original members of Jesus' band of Galilean exorcists, those who faced capture, death and social isolation and starvation, are given priority.[21]

5. Encounters should be consistent with the ecstatic practices of Jesus that engendered the original perilous risk with his opponents.[22] Specifically, encounters that encouraged the remaining exorcists to continue the ecstatic activity of Jesus and his war on Satan are preferred.[23]

6. Encounters near or on the lake of Galilee, particularly related to subsistence fishing, and similar to the animistic control exhibited by Jesus, are preferential (i.e., the remaining exorcists escaped there).[24]

---

21. However, because of their problematic nature (see the criterion of embarrassment), encounters with the Galilean women (also original members of Jesus' band) should take preference over those reported with men.

22. Koester, *From Jesus to the Gospels*, 231: "Historians are on very thin ice if they try to recover the historical person of Jesus through a critical analysis of the sayings tradition. A person of past history can only be understood if the extant sources reveal the traditions to which such a person belongs as well as the subsequent structures, practices and institutions of a community in which the memory of this person is preserved." This risk test does not violate the criterion of dissimilarity in that we are not finding coherence with the early church, but what may have existed that was continued, not being a help to the church, but remained problematic to it, but originated with Jesus. This is a further confirmation that the criterion of dissimilarity has been met.

23. Koester, *Introduction*, 84: "There is at least no doubt that whatever was experienced was not without relationship to a previous direct or indirect knowledge of or about Jesus."

24. Because of the nature of Jesus' activity there, combined with the tradition that the men returned to Galilee to take up their subsistence existence, any activity on or around Galilee relative to how they became followers of Jesus, i.e., as exorcists having witnessed Jesus' ability to employ animistic control (see the previous discussion on how Jesus' charismatic activity assisted with survival in a subsistence existence), such activities should be given preference.

7. Finally, encounters that may have led the Galileans to again abandon subsistence existence (i.e., to which they returned for survival post-crucifixion)[25] are also preferred.[26]

The original form of these post-resurrection encounters can also be recovered. These circulated orally for decades, and were retained for the benefit of the early church, but the use of these criteria will enable us to render the most original form of the tradition within its original context.[27] From this effort, conclusions as to contextual historicity of the encounter can be suggested, and perhaps affirmed, using these criteria of risk analysis.

---

25. There is ample evidence that the exorcists returned to subsistence fishing after the crucifixion of Jesus and their having fled to Galilee. Both John and the *Gospel of Peter* reference Kayfa's decision to return to Galilee and fishing. As Brown notes: "The verb 'to fish' has the form of an infinitive of purpose which is rare in John (iv. 7, xiv 2) and more frequent in Matthew and Luke; MTGS, 134–35, reports that this construction was becoming increasingly popular in Greek from ca. 150 B.C. on. McDowell, 430ff., argues that the present tense of the verb 'to go' expresses more than momentary intention: Peter is going back to his earlier way of life and will stay with it. The point of the story, then, is that Jesus caused Peter to change his mind, especially in vs. 15: 'Do you love me more than these [nets, boats, etc.]?'" Brown, *John*, 1068–69. Brown believes that this may be dubious, but it is compelling in a perilous risk context, so we must accept the premise.

26. Slovic, "Perception of Risk," 280–85. A discussion with Professor Slovic confirms that the human response to perilous risk has not changed in millennia, only the context of that risk. For the Galileans to perceive risk as perilous, but accept it as necessary, is a clear test of historicity, when the historical context can be adequately recovered.

27. An empty tomb is discovered by the guards placed by the elite to ensure the body and spirit of Jesus is still, that is, dead. The elite's worst fear is realized, the spirit of Jesus, whom they believed had been annihilated, is roaming, likely seeking revenge. In fear of the exorcists of Jesus who may conjure Jesus' spirit for malevolent purposes and retaliation the elite charge them with necromancy. The Galilean exorcists are baffled by the empty tomb, quickly deny it, and go into hiding. Some flee Jerusalem for Galilee, while others stay in hiding. Those who go to Galilee return to subsistence fishing.

7

Recovering the Risk Context of Post-Crucifixion Events in Mark

How to Identify Real Exorcists, Reinstating Kayfa and a Metamorphosis

What is really interesting about the Marcan tradition is it ended with an empty tomb, then provided a list of things that happened as if they were an afterthought. This list may have been either an appendix added much later, or perhaps was original. If original, it is a very puzzling aggregation of events, but more important, it incorporates a very primitive exorcist tradition that is rather startling in its placement. Even more mysterious, the editor of Mark appears to have hidden resurrection encounters by placing them within the lifetime of Jesus. Why? We will evaluate by order of primary source as represented in the New Testament, beginning with the Gospel of Mark.

Mark 16:9–20—Why Provide a List of Exorcist's Practices After the Empty Tomb?

Most scholars consider Mark 16:9–20 to be a conflation of all post-crucifixion encounters with Jesus found in the other canonical gospels, and so, consider it non-Marcan and a later addition (105 to 125 CE).[1] The different vocabulary and style of the unit is cited, and the text includes a classical Greek term that is unique to the New Testament. More important, the ending is absent from early key ancient manuscripts,[2] although there is signifi-

---

1. Lunn, *Original Ending*, 673–76. Funk and Jesus Seminar, *Acts of Jesus*, 449–95.
2. Examples include ℵ, B, 304, syr and several others.

cant manuscript testimony from post-apostolic fathers and other ancient sources. This has led to debate as to its date and origin.[3] More recently, scholars, such as Koester, have defended the section as Marcan.[4] Whether Marcan or not, embedded in this unit is a striking post-crucifixion "signs" saying of Jesus that is addressed to his exorcists and charismatics. It is a separate encounter from those recorded in either the gospels or Mark, and so stands alone. It raises important qualitative risk issues, as the saying not only echoes but it demands the continuation of the same charismatic activities that brought Jesus into deadly confrontation with his opponents, thereby creating continued perilous risk for Jesus' followers. According to Mark 16:17–18, Jesus commands the following:

> *In my name* to cast out demons, they will speak in new tongues [or in heavenly language, *glossais*, in ecstasy], the will pick up serpents [*opheis*], and if they drink any deadly thing, it will not harm them; they will lay their hands on the sick and they will recover.[5]

Consistent with their views of Mark 6:9–20, some scholars conclude that this saying is also a conflation of various charismatic events found in the Synoptic Gospels and Acts of the Apostles,[6] and is a reflection of the "signs" source of charismatic events that were embedded into the Gospel of John by its editor.[7] But, if so, questions immediately arise that challenge this view. Why would charismatic acts, indeed those of Jesus and the men he trained to be exorcists, need to be legitimized by Jesus *after* the crucifixion by repeating all the events found in the canonical gospels and John? Mark is filled with these events, and Jesus chose his disciples because they could be trained to be exorcists and drive demons from the land.[8] Indeed, charismatic practices and authority are clearly and authoritatively placed throughout the context of Jesus' ministry in Mark—no more needed be said.[9] The very formation of

---

3. Snapp, *Authentic*, one of the most exhaustive analyses by a textual scholar.

4. Koester states that the language is compatible with the Gospel of Mark (see *Ancient Christian Gospels*, 295).

5. Mark 16:17–18.

6. Acts 2:4; 5:15; 28:3.

7. First proposed by Rudolph Bultmann in his commentary on John. See Brown, *Community of the Beloved Disciple*, 31; and the Jesus Seminar, i.e., the Signs Gospel. See the reconstruction of the Signs Gospel by Andrew Bernhard for the Jesus Seminar, *Early Christian Writings*, http://www.earlychristianwritings.com/text/signs.html, which is based on the analysis of Fortuna, *Fourth Gospel*, 48–139.

8. Mark 3:14, Busse, *To Be Near the Fire*, 66–69.

9. Matt 17:19; Mark 9:38; Luke 9:1–6; and so on.

Mark recognizes the empty tomb, Jesus as risen Lord, and, as such, sayings of Jesus in the context of his ministry carry the same weight for the community.[10] Having Jesus reconfirm these specific charismatic "signs" during a post-crucifixion encounter in Mark is puzzling, even question begging, and deserves special attention, particularly as to its risk function in the context of not just a possible second-century setting, but in first-century Galilee and among Jesus' exorcists immediately after the crucifixion. Consequently, we will evaluate this saying as a separate post-crucifixion encounter with Jesus that has been absorbed into the Marcan appendix.

We begin with an application of qualitative risk analysis. Jesus appears (*ephanerothe*, i.e., "he was manifested") during a communal meal of the eleven remaining exorcists, chastising them for the stubborn unbelief (*skaerokardian*, i.e., "hardness of heart").[11] The location of the encounter is not specified. Jesus commands the exorcists go into the world and baptize. Those that refuse the charismatic message to be baptized are immediately *cursed* (they are of Satan), meaning separated from God and condemned, i.e., they are damned (*katakrithesetai*). A similar commission is found in Matthew, but the location is on a mountain in Galilee and there is no curse. The command to baptize is linked with liturgical rites, i.e., baptizing in the names of the God, Jesus and the Holy Spirit.[12] Mark's version is clearly earlier; it is charismatic (i.e., the curse); it shows no reliance on Matthew. The commission is therefore linked with continuation of charismatic activity and, therefore, heightened risk for the exorcists, compared to that of Matthew. Luke has no such commission. John does but there is no charismatic command, and the commission is tied solely to Kayfa who is warned that he will be captured and murdered.[13]

Mark 16:17–18 then radicalizes the post-resurrection community, narrowing the legitimate followers of Jesus to those who successfully continue dangerous, and illegal, public charismatic practices that could be considered magic. They must evoke "signs." Clearly, to embrace these practices is to dramatically heighten the perilous risk of post-crucifixion followers. The same charismatic activities that created the perilous risk and conflict between Jesus and his opponents *are commanded to continue*—Jesus demands exorcists expand their battle against demonic pollution of the land in specific acts. When *his name is conjured*, demons will flee—a reflection of

---

10. Mark 3:14; 6:7–13; 9:28.
11. Mark 6:14.
12. Matt 28:16–20.
13. John 21:18.

the very experience of Jesus' exorcists.[14] Consequently, to continue exorcism and release of demons is to continue Jesus' war on the pollution of the land, and by implication, demonic imperialism.[15] But for the exorcists, to employ Jesus' name in exorcisms was to conjure the name of an executed magician, condemned by the elite under Roman law;[16] an "evildoer" and "deceiver" who accused the elite of being under satanic control; a possessed Galilean agent of Beelzebul, who not just condemned the temple as polluted, but stated it should be destroyed.[17] Even though the lower castes, the oppressed and subsistence workers would have embraced the protection of the exorcists, the perilous risks for these exorcists was just as extraordinary as it was for Jesus in conflict with his opponents.[18]

The expectation of "speaking in new tongues (*glossais*)" has been often cited as the principal evidence that this section is a conflation of later practices.[19] Indeed, this charismatic practice has become quite problematic in 1 Corinthians (54 CE), and Paul has to devalue it as a "gift."[20] However, it has an origin among the itinerant exorcists, including those that visited Corinth like Paul, perhaps also Kayfa, who practiced and condoned it,[21] and who may have introduced it there along with the "super apostles" that followed.[22] The laying on of hands resulting in one's possession by the Spirit between believers often resulted in ecstatic speech.[23] Paul boasts that he is able to speak in tongues more than any of the other itinerants, but finds it unnecessary to do so, implying it was a practice associated with the early exorcists and legitimate followers of Jesus, including the Galileans with whom Paul counts himself.[24] But interestingly, Paul speaks of it in terms of the language of angels (which he can understand and speak). By implication, Paul affirms

---

14. Luke 10:17; Mark 9:38–39.

15. Busse, *To Be Near the Fire*, 70–88.

16. Roman Law, *Twelve Tables, Crimes*, table VII.3 and 15, also table VIII.9 See Plessis, *Borkowski's Textbook*, 5–6, 29–30.

17. Mark 14:58.

18. Lewis, *Ecstatic Religion*, 88–89. Lewis describes the vulnerability of the lower castes, caught between the oppression of the elite and fear of demonic attack. Their reliance on exorcists (as "masters of the spirit") to mitigate the risk of demonic attack is found to be a cultural phenomenon that crosses all cultural barriers.

19. Hull, *Mark*, 673–74.

20. 1 Cor 13:8.

21. Acts 10:45; 2:4; and others.

22. 2 Cor 11:5–6.

23. From the earliest times, including Acts 2:1–13.

24. 1 Cor 14:8; 1 Cor 15:1–9.

that there was also a language of demons.[25] If one speaks in heavenly language an interpreter must be present, or the speaker is to remain silent.[26] Paul's charismatic and ecstatic speaking in tongues is also associated with either a trance or ecstatic experience.[27] Jesus is never explicitly tied to speaking in tongues in the synoptic or Johannine traditions, however, the multiple interactions with demons, identifying and silencing them, his groaning in spirit and prayer,[28] must be assumed to have included understanding and speaking in angelic and demonic language.[29] Indeed, when Jesus' exorcists fail to expel the demon of a young boy, they ask why, to which Jesus replies that only prayer (implying a special type of prayer) and fasting could succeed.[30] That this expectation immediately follows the command to exorcise is additional evidence that this charismatic power is associated with communication with demons, spirits, as well as special words or commands that are used to exorcise demons. Muting curses, some of which invoked demonic activity, were often written in secret languages, or on hidden tablets covertly placed in homes.[31] Jesus and his exorcists were able to release victims from such demonic curses,[32] understanding and affecting exorcisms that neutralized them using special words. Consequently, this practice is contextually coherent with the others in Mark 16:17–18, and is to be associated with the continued itinerant activity of the exorcists as they encounter and communicate with demons and neutralize curses and evil spirits that they must control and expel to continue the war on Satan.

Jesus also commands the charismatics/exorcists to raise up (*arousan*) serpents (*opheis*). The significance of this charismatic power is lost on many

25. 1 Cor 13:1.

26. 1 Cor 14:27.

27. 2 Cor 12:2; also Mark 9:2–13.

28. John 11:33, or Mark 7:34, and the use of specific words that are interpreted by the gospel editors, but whose original use may have parallels with unintelligible words (Morton), such as his words in Mark 5:41, "talitha, koum."

29. For further discussion on the use of special language in Jesus' exorcisms, see Smith, *Jesus the Magician*, 95. "Talitha, koum" was also circulated without translation as a magical formula.

30. Smith believes this was "secret" prayer, but the implication are for prayers that may be said ecstatically and under the influence of the Spirit, and so, in heavenly language. That fasting is associated with this prayer implies that a special state of ecstatic experience and language is possible.

31. Ogden, *Magic*, 211: "A legal, tongue-binding, lead curse tablet from Selinus"; also see 215.

32. See discussion above on the deaf and mute man of Bethsaida, whom Jesus commands not to reenter his village, as he likely had been cursed by someone there, i.e., a person who would repeat the process.

translators, as if this were simply snake-handlers holding up snakes, or a recast of the events in Acts 28:3 where Paul, while picking up brushwood for a fire is accidentally bitten by a poisonous serpent, but remains unharmed. Indeed, such stories did exist and were known, as Pythagoras is said to have handled a snake without harm, as did Hanina be Dosa.[33] But Jesus is not talking about accidental events. Jesus is saying, if not commanding, that his exorcists are to raise up, or perhaps better in Greek, "take away," poisonous serpents.[34] In the ancient world, particularly in Judaism, snakes were often the personification of Satan, evil, and capable of possession or engendering dangerous, and sometimes fatal deception.[35] Consequently, this is a charismatic directive of Jesus and appears to imply that the exorcists held animistic powers over snakes as creatures of Satan, i.e., they could take control, just as they controlled demons, and render them harmless, or even destroy them.[36] If to destroy them, this raises interesting and contemporary parallels where serpents are killed by "blasting." Blasting was a well-recognized charismatic power, albeit considered sometimes a dark power (conducted by incantation, or often by those who practiced manipulation of the dead, i.e., necromancy). In the Hellenistic world, this authority was associated with powerful sorcerers or magicians, often foreigners, such as Chaldeans, Babylonians, Assyrians or Egyptians.[37] The charismatic, using animistic powers, would communicate with the snake(s), collect or call them together by command, then destroy them, in many cases by breathing on them with fire—i.e., blasting[38]—or would trap them in tombs. Jesus gave his charismatics a similar authority to destroy creatures that were thought to be controlled by Satan, or by his demons, *particularly snakes and scorpions* in Luke 10:19: "I have given you authority to *trample (pantein)* on snakes and scorpions and to overcome all the power of the enemy; nothing will harm you." This power is the equivalent of crushing serpents and scorpions,

---

33. See Vermes, *Jesus the Jew*, 74. Sources from Bar-Ilan, "Exorcism of Demons," include: Hyman, *Sefer Toledot Tannaim we-Amoraim*, 481–84 (Hebrew); Vermes, "Hanina ben Dosa," 178–214; Freyne, "Charismatic," 223–58; Boxer, "Wonder-Working," 42–92. Also see Kee, *Origins of Christianity*, 225–28.

34. For the various translations, see, e.g., John 11:48, i.e., "take away."

35. See Rev 12:9 and Gen 3:14; also see 2 Cor 11:3 for a comparison of Eve and the serpent and the deception of the Corinthian believers. Jesus equates the Jerusalem religious elite with vipers and serpents in Matt 23:33, again because these creatures were controlled and possessed by Satan and demons and used to hamper or kill enemies.

36. Jesus was known to have animistic powers; the directives on catch of fishes, the coin in the fish's mouth and others previously described. See Mark 1:16–20; Matt 4:18–22; Luke 5:2–11; John 21:6; Matt 17:27.

37. Odgen, *Magic*, 49–50.

38. Ibid., 50.

and so, the original intent of this saying was to "take away" or blast the serpent, and hold it up, showing it destroyed, exorcised.[39] Satan would then be shown powerless, as even the creatures of evil that attacked could be annihilated when encountered by Jesus' command and authority. Ultimately, the use of Jesus' name alone was able to neutralize serpents, including their venom, among Jews.[40] Consequently, this reference is clearly not a conflation of gospel texts, nor is it a reflection of Paul's experience in Acts. Instead, the risk setting is in the itinerant charismatic activity of Jesus and his fellow exorcists, including a post-resurrection setting and encounter. It is unique and original. Jesus commands a continuation of the perilous conflict with Satan and his demons in the context of first-century Palestine.

The next command, drinking poison unharmed, is without parallel in the New Testament, with only a single reference found in Eusebius.[41] Barsabas Justus, the exorcist not selected to replace Judas, is said to have survived drinking poison. The reference to "poisons" again should not be thought of as toxic chemicals that immediately kill, but instead, are the result of witchcraft and evil potions and concoctions intended to harm the recipient in multiple ways, even driving one insane.[42] Poisons were slipped into water, wine or other drinks, or added to foods, and depending on their intent, could be deadly to soul or body, or were sometimes even intended to engender love or eroticism.[43] Such poisons were also combined with spells and curse tablets often hidden in the walls or floors of homes by enemies, which caused illness to accelerate, or bring on death. One famous case of this type was told about Germanicus, a powerful general and leader, rival of Piso, who died by magical assassination in Antioch in 19 CE.[44] Poisons had wide application and were placed in contact with the victim for malevolent intent, many times secretly. For the Galilean charismatics, opponents would seize every opportunity, including the use of magic and witchcraft (even hiring famous witches if needed), to kill them, a common practice in the Roman world.[45] Conse-

---

39. Ibid., referencing Lucian in *Pharsalia* (6.413–587), *Philopseudes* (11–3), and Ovid, *Amores* (2.1.23–8); *Magic*, 49–50, 121–24, 238.

40. This was said by Jews about 120 CE, see Hull, *Hellenistic Magic*, 71.

41. Eusebius, *Ecclesiastical History*, 3:39.9.

42. Ogden, *Magic*, 115: "Canidia and Sagana perform necromancy and erotic magic," as reported about 30 BCE (Horace, *Satirea* 1.8); "so much as the women who try to twist about human minds with spells and poisons (*venena*)."

43. Ogden, *Magic*, 117–18, a love potion considered a type of "poison."

44. Ibid., 217; Germanicus was the nephew of Tiberius, so the account was widely known. Piso filled Germanicus' residence with poisons, spells and binding curses.

45. So with Germanicus. To counter the poisons and spells, Germanicus' wife hired a woman "renowned for poisoning/witchcraft (*veneficia*) in that province (Syria)" to

quently, this charismatic expectation comes with reassurance and protection from magic, curses and dark spells, and so, Jesus' exorcists are to not fear any poison, as they will remain unharmed if ingested. This risk context of this saying is clearly to be set in the post-crucifixion itinerant ministry of the exorcists and the mission to drive Satan from the land.

In this final expectation, Jesus commits his exorcists to the *laying on of hands* (*keiris epithesousin*), as required to drive out demons of illness,[46] i.e., another very specific form of exorcism, since illness was associated with demonic possession or evil, whether undeserved, or more commonly, resulting from a curse or contamination arising from evil actions or wrongs against a deity (e.g., the presumption of "sins," willful acts of defiance, committed by the victim or members of the victim's family).[47] Jesus used this practice of exorcism only after all other methods had failed in Nazareth.[48] Touching with hands was not just a soothing element, but a powerful charismatic act to drive off evil that required special technique and knowledge.[49] There are multiple examples to be found in ancient sources, both Hellenistic and Jewish.[50] Jesus affected several cures with the use of his hands, either in terms of touching the affected victim or in creating substances for application to the areas infected with evil. For example, in Mark 7:32–35, Jesus is asked to lay his hands on a man possessed with a demon causing deafness and confused language. Jesus takes the man aside, privately, most likely because the exorcism may not succeed. We are then provided one of the most thorough descriptions of a charismatic exorcism in ancient literature. Jesus first places his fingers in the man's ears. He then uses spittle, a substance previously described as a powerful healing substance of magicians and charismatics. Jesus spits on his fingers and touches the man's tongue. Then he goes into a trance, blows out his mouth in a "deep sigh," likely to release power and blast

---

counter the poisons, curses and spells found.

46. Mark 6:5, 7:32; Luke 4:40. It is important to note that Jesus' charismatic activity in Nazareth, the Galilean town where he was raised, was limited to laying on of hands to drive out illness, i.e., direct contact to convey power to drive out demons. As such, Jesus' use of touch, or the laying on of hands, to drive out demons of illness was passed to his exorcists, and so references to this practice have the highest claim to authenticity.

47. See John 9:3.

48. Mark 6:5, dealing with only a few and likely in private.

49. Also to pass along charismatic power and authority: see Acts 9:17; also Acts 8:17–18, the baptized received the gift of the Holy Spirit, the dominant of all Spirits and so the most powerful available to charismatics and others who take on the risk of following the crucified man, the accused "evildoer" of Galilee. Other references include Heb 6:2.

50. E.g., Apollonius who is said to have learned this from the priests of Asclepius in Aegae; see Eshel, "Jesus the Exorcist," 183–85.

the demon, followed by pronouncement of command, "*ephphatha*," or "be opened." The man is freed.

This remarkable account of "laying on of hands" provides descriptive evidence that specific practices taught by Jesus to the exorcists stood behind this command, most of which are now lost. There must have been multiple techniques employed by Jesus, evidenced by Luke 4:40. John 9:6 mentions Jesus making an application of mud and saliva. Another example is the encounter with a blind man, Mark 8:22–26. Here Jesus is specifically asked to lay his hands on the man who appears to have been cursed and attacked by a demon. Taking him out of the village of Bethsaida, perhaps to avoid those affecting the curse on the man, Jesus spits on his eyes. The cure is incomplete. Jesus then rubs his eyes with his hands and the man is able to see. He then orders the man to go to his home and avoid the village, indicating that Jesus was concerned that the cure would either be temporary, or that there was a risk of return of the demon if the man was cursed again by his attacker in the village. Jesus would have trained his exorcists with these methods.[51]

The "laying on of hands" was common to Jesus' practice of exorcism-healings, driving out demons and releasing the afflicted from curse or possession. As such, this final command to the exorcists, i.e., the expectation of laying on of hands and the special techniques employed, is coherent with the foregoing list of charismatic practices to be embraced by Jesus' exorcists. It is clear that this activity was also fraught with risk and danger. For example, Jesus was undoubtedly using techniques such as in Mark 7:32–35 when he was accused of being possessed by Beelzebul, the accusation that brought Jesus into deadly and perilous conflict with his opponents. Jesus, and now the exorcists, would be accused of being "evildoers," dark magicians possessed by Beelzebul. Deceiving the people, announcing the end of demonic rule, and by implication the end of elitist rule that supported demonic imperialism, they would be sought out and destroyed like Jesus. Consequently, with this segment properly assessed in its contemporary setting, and perilous risk found to be inherent in its practice, we can now summarize our analysis of the qualitative risks present in Mark 16:17–18.

Recalling Helmut Koester's criterion, where one can only discover the historical practices of a leader (a leader like Jesus whose teachings and practices have become obscured by layers of theological interpretation) by looking to the practices of those who followed him or her, we find Mark 16:17–18 to be an accurate reflection of Jesus' actual activity. More, these

---

51. As implied by Luke 10:9, i.e., Jesus' sending of the exorcists into the towns and villages to drive Satan and demonic pollution out. They are to "heal" the sick, or employ the laying on of hands and the techniques taught by Jesus to drive demons out and away. They also were effective by employing Jesus' name in exorcising demons.

charismatic activities clearly continued the most dangerous and perilous practices of Jesus' war on satanic pollution of the land, including his war on demonic imperialism, which ultimately led to deadly conflict with his opponents and his execution. Clearly these sayings, embedded within the Marcan appendix, are very early, and must come from a period in time when those who were Jesus' most intimate followers—the exorcists of Galilee—decided to continue the perilous mission of Jesus. From the standpoint of qualitative risk analysis, the only event that would have engendered such a radical decision would have been a post-crucifixion encounter with Jesus.

In a post-crucifixion environment, Jesus' exorcists would only have perceived more perilous risk by not engaging in dangerous behavior (i.e., continuing the very activity that led to Jesus brutal death and execution), unless they had an encounter post-crucifixion. In other words, they believed they were at greater risk by remaining silent or in hiding in Galilee as subsistence fishermen. Paul's own expression of dread and fear if he did not do the same is evidence that his post-crucifixion encounter was decisive.[52] Such encounters demanded one embrace perilous risk, and it is the acceptance of heightened perilous risk that seems to authenticate this post-crucifixion encounter with Jesus in the form of a command to his exorcists. Consequently, what is unique in this instance is that it is not his spirit that possesses them, but the encounter itself experienced by a command. We now move to our next risk tests, employing the criteria of dissimilarity and embarrassment, in our assessment of Mark 16:17–18.

Applying the Criteria of Dissimilarity and Embarrassment to Mark 16:17–18

We begin with the *criterion of dissimilarity*. In this study, we will expand the criterion to address what is distinctive and different from both the needs of the early church and first-century Palestinian Judaism with regard to Jesus' charismatic demands placed on his exorcists in Mark 16:17–18? This is a challenging question in that it would appear the appendix in Mark may have been a conflation of synoptic and Johannine materials, which would imply it is late and intended to serve the needs of the early church. However, our analysis, using both contextual and qualitative risk analysis, has demonstrated that these specific sayings were not a later conflation. Instead, they are best placed in the period immediately after the crucifixion. They contain rigorous and dangerous demands (one of which is found nowhere else in the New Testament) directed at individual exorcists, and may have

---

52. 1 Cor 9:16.

identified those who should be considered legitimate followers of Jesus. A test of legitimacy seems to imply that these exorcists were part of a Marcan community. Yet, it must be emphasized that all these practices created heightened perilous risk, and so would have put any community in dire jeopardy. As such, these demands would *not* have met the needs of the early church at all, and indeed, were not intended for any nascent community, only for exorcists who were trained in the practices taught by Jesus. If we presume that Koester and others are correct, that this section is Marcan, it is also noteworthy that such demands are absent in Luke and Matthew, both of which utilized Mark as one of their sources. These later communities (80 to 110 CE) either chose to exclude these sayings or did not know them. If known, their absence in Matthew, Luke and John suggests their demise or devaluation. They were illegal and dangerous in the Roman world.

Given this, it seems abundantly clear that these demands could only have been directed at Jesus' own exorcists; and in particular, those who had been trained in the laying on of hands. As noted, aside from a few examples noted in Mark and John, most of the specific practices and techniques have been lost to history. Consequently, Mark 16:17–18 is a remarkable passage. It allows us direct access the perilous risk world of Jesus and his exorcists and what they did in that world. Only Jesus could have explained these techniques to the Galilean exorcists, as they were the source for the oral traditions as to what happened at these private events, if not the direct witnesses; whether using spittle, blasting or breathing, special words of authority over demons, or fingers in the ears. Jesus must have explained these techniques privately (certainly not just the meaning of his parables).[53] Finally, none of the sayings would have benefited those who employed only Jesus' name for magic or exorcism only, whether in or outside a nascent community, as the sayings are intended for trained practitioners.[54] Consequently, Mark 16:17–18 stands apart from the needs of the early church.

As to the Jewish context of these sayings, we can evaluate the contemporaneous charismatics of Jesus' time, including Choni, Hanina ben Dosa, Eleazar and various rabbis.[55] Even though there is evidence that some of the traditions associated with these charismatics have been altered to remove controversial and troubling activity, Jesus' radical charismatic activity as an exorcist in his battle with demonic imperialism and Satan has no parallel and is distinct from his contemporaries. Choni and Hanina are hailed not only

---

53. Mark 4:34.

54. Luke 9:49.

55. See Busse, "Palestinian Judaism and Ecstatic Activity: Demonic Activity and Possession," in *To Be Near the Fire*, 31–53; for examples, Vermes, *Jesus the Jew*, and also Kee, *Origins*, 226–28.

as Jewish sages, but as having an intimate relationship with God. They have these powers as a gift, and as such, there is little if any risk to them or their position within the community, i.e., it is coherent with charismatics who are favored by God and benefit the community. Jesus' activity is controversial, divisive and fraught with peril and risk. As such, the passages in Mark are also distinct from their Jewish context. Consequently, Jesus' sayings as recorded in Mark 16:17–18 pass the test of the criterion of dissimilarity as to its probable historicity. Next, we move to the criterion of embarrassment.

The *criterion of embarrassment* identifies those sayings or events in the New Testament that created difficulties for the early church, implying that they were undeniable or else these traditions would never have been included, let alone created. They are problematic to the early church. The betrayal by Judas (one of Jesus' chosen exorcists), Jesus' baptism by John (why would Jesus need baptism?), and the crucifixion (Jesus was brutalized on a cross like a common criminal) are all example of problematic events that would have never been included by gospel editors were they not well known, and so undeniable. They were embarrassing and yet included.

When we turn to Mark 16:17–18, the test is whether these sayings and the practices they encourage were, in whole or part, problematic, and therefore an embarrassment to the early church, but were undeniably part of the activity of Jesus and his followers. Yet, that Matthew and Luke-Acts omit the sayings on raising up (or blasting) snakes, as well as drinking cursed or poisoned potions, stands as evidence that they were problematic in the later church.[56] If Mark 16:9–20 could be conclusively shown to have been part of the original Marcan composition then omission of the sayings would provide conclusive evidence, as Matthew and Luke used Mark as a source.[57] Nonetheless, since they reference very specific radical charismatic practices that were abandoned or were obscured by the early church, evidence is strong that they were problematic. For example, the charismatic techniques employed by Jesus in the laying on of hands (some of which were very simi-

---

56. The fact that these charismatic sayings and practices, i.e., on raising up snakes and particularly laying on of hands, are omitted in Luke and Matthew provides strong evidence that the entire section, Mark 16:19–20, was very early, and was likely the original ending to Mark. The practices are problematic to the later church communities, and so were very early, then later recast or dropped. This would explain the ending's omission is some ancient manuscripts of Mark. The development of these practices, such as the laying on of hands, dramatically changes in these later gospels and Acts. For example, the laying on of hands for Luke becomes the ordination of apostles or leaders, e.g., Acts 18:17–18. The raising up of snakes becomes the tradition that Paul was bitten by a viper while collecting wood but remained unharmed.

57. As noted, Mark was used as a primary source by the author/editors of Matthew and Luke.

lar to contemporaneous magical practices noted) are omitted or radically emended in other later gospels. The tradition of the blind man of Bethsaida (Mark 8:22–26) is dropped completely by the author/editors Matthew and Luke, both of whom used Mark as a source. Matthew drops the reference to Jesus' common practice of laying on of hands found in Mark 6:5, while Luke omits the section entirely. In Mark 1:29–31, Jesus is said to have laid his hands on Kayfa's mother-in-law when driving out a demonic fever;[58] but in Luke, Jesus stands over her and commands the fever depart. Matthew omits the tradition entirely. Indeed, analysis has convincingly shown that Matthew goes to great lengths to purify the tradition, particularly of any references or instances that might infer Jesus was a magician.[59]

Even the saying on exorcism, Mark 16:17, became problematic to the early church. It is clear that Jesus' sayings related to exorcism have the highest claim to authenticity.[60] But, exorcism was considered illegal in the Roman world, and continuation of the very practices that led Jesus into deadly conflict with the elite and Roman authorities was *most problematic*. Certainly Paul knew of Jesus' exorcisms, and his itinerant activity continued from approximately 34 CE in Palestine to 63 or 64 CE in Rome. Yet, in his authentic letters, where any reference to exorcisms might be detected, Paul is very careful in his descriptions of "working powers" (Gal 3:1–4), and "miraculous powers" (1 Cor 12:10), avoiding reference to exorcisms or to Jesus' exorcisms, particularly the laying on of hands (considered magical).[61] Paul's healing "miracles" in Acts were associated with the passing on of handkerchiefs, or work-cloths, that came into contact with him.[62] It is these that touched and healed others, never touching of his hands.[63] Other charismatic events included Paul's resuscitation of a young man who had apparently died (i.e., the young man Eutychus, fell asleep, because Paul spoke "on and on," out of a third-floor loft[64]

---

58. That fevers were demonic possession, see Smith, *Magic*, 107.

59. Hull, *Hellenistic Magic*, 116–41. Hull makes a broad comparison, for example, with regard to the "signs," where Mark and Luke identify signs as exorcisms and the call to return to God as king, where Matthew only emphasizes one sign, the resurrection (118). "Unlike Luke, he (Matthew) refrains from drawing attention to the sign aspect of exorcism; he does not attach the demand for a sign to the actual Beelzebul controversy itself, but instead defers it" (119).

60. Koester, *History*, 78–79.

61. See also 2 Cor 12:12.

62. For additional reference on the use of handkerchiefs in the ancient world and magic, see Eshel, "Jesus the Exorcist," 184. The handkerchiefs mentioned in *Greek Magical Papyri* (7:826) had incantations written on them.

63. Acts 19:12.

64. This was in Alexandrian Troas, a very large Hellenistic-Roman seaport on the Adriatic. The site covered almost a thousand acres, including the typical public

and seemed as dead);[65] the blinding of Bar-Jesus, the sorcerer on Cyprus, for trying to convert Sergius Paulus;[66] the various miracles at Iconium;[67] and his surviving a stoning.[68] But the "laying on of hands" or any other form of charismatic practices in Mark are avoided or are intentionally diminished. Consequently, as a group, any expectation that the charismatic practices of Mark 16:17–18 were to continue post-crucifixion are problematic. Conducting any of them after Jesus' death would create perilous risk under law and from the elitist opponents.[69]

In sum, as a whole, Mark 16:17–18 reflects the most controversial activities of Jesus. The author of Mark, or the Marcan appendix, would never have created these expectations were they not understood to be unconditional expectations and to have come from Jesus—and specifically, a post-crucifixion Jesus. More, the author would never have invented a tradition that implied that the failure to perform these practices would imply condemnation of the exorcist, or that these practices must be continued in their most radical form! Consequently, Mark 16:17–18 passes the test of the criterion of embarrassment.

Mark 16:17–18 and the Contextual Tests

We now turn to contextual analysis. If an encounter has successfully passed the foregoing risks tests, it must also pass four contextual coherency tests. The event must be coherent with the sociological risk setting, including the subsistence struggle of the Galileans, the background from which they came to join Jesus' band of exorcists. The contextual risk tests previously established are as follows:

---

buildings, only a handful of which remain. If like other Roman cities, there were certainly three-story buildings, likely apartments like those near the forum in Rome.

65. Due to Paul's long sermon, still referenced today in many sermons as an anecdote for a preacher's long and laborious sermon; Acts 20:9.

66. Acts 13:6–11.

67. Acts 14:3.

68. Acts 14:9–20.

69. 2 Cor 12:12 includes Paul's description of his being a true apostle, which is linked to his ability to perform signs, wonders and miracles much like Jesus' exorcists (including the "super apostles," 2 Cor 12:11–12). In fact, this section is Paul's defense of his apostleship, and by his referencing these specific activities as defining a true apostle, Paul confirms that they were linked to the very activity of Jesus' exorcists. This confirms that this passage in Mark is an authentic reflection of the earliest activity of Jesus' exorcists post-crucifixion, and that Paul uses it to assert he was a legitimate apostle like they.

1. Encounters with original members of Jesus' band of Galilean exorcists, those who faced capture, death and social isolation and starvation, are given priority.
2. Encounters should be consistent with the ecstatic practices of Jesus that engendered the original perilous risk with his opponents. Specifically, encounters that encouraged the remaining exorcists to continue the ecstatic activity of Jesus and his war on Satan are preferred.
3. Encounters near or on the lake of Galilee, particularly related to subsistence fishing, and similar to the animistic control exhibited by Jesus, are preferential (i.e., the remaining exorcists escaped there).
4. Finally, encounters that may have led the Galileans to again abandon subsistence existence (i.e., to which they returned for survival post-crucifixion) are also preferred.

We can now turn to assess these sayings in Mark employing the contextual tests, each in turn:

Mark 16:17–18 passes the first contextual test based on our foregoing analysis. The charismatic expectations delineated in this section could only have been directed at Jesus' Galilean exorcists, i.e., those that witnessed for example the specific techniques and practices associated with the laying on of hands. Since laying on of hands as practiced by Jesus passed into obscurity very early, evidenced by its omission in other gospels and in the authentic letters of Paul, only the eleven and the Galilean women/exorcists, or those trained by them, could have been addressed. These were Jesus' most controversial and problematic practices, but were familiar only to these exorcists. When combined with raising up snakes, or blasting, and harmlessly drinking cursed potions and other concocted poisons, there is little doubt that these practices were directed at this intimate band of followers. The danger of continuing these practices was perilous. Yet, no other group would have been able to physically embrace them. However, it is unlikely that any of them, having escaped to Galilee and resumed subsistence fishing, would have embraced the risk if it were not for a post-resurrection encounter with Jesus that demanded their continuation.

This is also true for the second test, as the continuation of these radical charismatic practices by the Galileans is not simply encouraged but is expected, and become the true and only valid test of charismatic legitimacy, which in turn is what defines Jesus' true and only followers. Consequently, there is little doubt that what is required is the continuation of Jesus' ecstatic practices that engendered the original perilous risk with his opponents.[70] These extend

70. An interesting correlation with our tests of historicity related to risk is found

the ecstatic activity of Jesus and his war on Satan, and ensured that demonic possession and pollution of the land continued to be attacked and destroyed. Satan would continue to fall from power through these exorcisms.[71]

With regard to the third test, we are unable to confirm if the encounter was near the lake of Galilee. However, some of the events listed in Mark 16:9–20 have Galilean connections. Indeed, Jesus' final encounter with his eleven was on a Galilean mountain.[72] It is clear that Luke's theological agenda was to recast the final encounter with Jesus in Jerusalem to demonstrate the spread of the gospel from Jerusalem to Rome, i.e., the focus of the Luke-Acts composition.[73] We have discussed the ample evidence that Jesus' exorcists fled to Galilee after the crucifixion and the report of the empty tomb. Consequently, the shift in location in Luke for theological purposes would confirm that the original encounters with Jesus were near Galilee. Further, the charismatic expectations listed in this event include animistic powers, which is a power also exhibited by Jesus in Galilee. Yet, the animistic control over scorpions and snakes represents a more radical and authoritative power than that reported of Jesus, e.g., in the repeated catch of fishes for the subsistence Galilean fishermen. Jesus' exorcists are given unparalleled animistic authority, as they will be able to control the very creatures of Satan and render them impotent to possess, deceive or harm others. In sum, while there is evidence to support satisfying the third test, it is not conclusive.

Lastly, the final test evaluates whether the encounter led the Galilean exorcists to again abandon subsistence existence as fishers of Galilee (i.e., to which they returned for survival post-crucifixion). In Mark 16:7, the women report to the remaining exorcists that Jesus had told them to immediately go to Galilee where they will see him (*opsesthe*, i.e., will be seeing him). The inference is clear—they will not encounter Jesus until they return to Galilee. As noted, some scholars hold that some of the exorcists fled to Galilee for safety after the crucifixion, based on this passage, and that Galilee was the only cultural context in which a sighting of Jesus would occur due to his (and their) extensive charismatic activity near and around the lake.[74] It made no sense to remain in Jerusalem. The exorcists, particularly Kayfa, were easy to identify, having been sighted with Jesus in the city, or by the special clothing

---

in Morton Smith's *Magic*, 95. Smith states: "Details can never be guaranteed, but those general characteristics of a tradition that accord with and explain both the opinions of a man's adherents, and those of his opponents, have a claim to authenticity far stronger than that which can be advanced for supposedly idiosyncratic sayings."

71. Luke 10:18.
72. Matt 28:16–20.
73. Koester, *History*, 51.
74. See, e.g., Frye, *Galilee*, 51–68.

Jesus required they wear, and their heavy Galilean accents.[75] A risk response such as a flight to Galilee to counter peril is, as we have noted, consistent with qualitative risk analysis as an effective countermeasure. Indeed, why would they stay in Jerusalem for ten or more days and in danger? There was no protection.[76] Our previous analysis has shown that none of the exorcists expected to ever encounter Jesus again, his having been annihilated by crucifixion body and soul. A report of an empty tomb was just as frightening and puzzling for them (those who had denied and abandoned him) as it was for the elite (who now feared the ghost of Jesus would seek vengeance, like in the murder and wanderings of the untimely dead, particularly in light of their belief he was a minion of Beelzebul, prince of demons). Risk evidence would strongly support their flight to Galilee and a return to subsistence fishing, hidden by their extended families[77] and sent out at night[78] (a great risk they were willing to take, given the danger, as the lake was haunted).[79]

Conservative scholars cite the command of Jesus to stay in Jerusalem until they receive "power from on high," i.e., the Spirit.[80] However, as we have noted, this is Luke-Acts' theological agenda to track the gospel from Jerusalem to Rome. Consequently, the command of Jesus to tell his disciples to meet him in Galilee, supposedly passed on by the women, would help explain an embarrassing situation, where all of the exorcists, including Kayfa, fled to the safety of Galilee to hide. John 21:1–3 places at least five of the exorcists back in Galilee struggling to make their catch as nighttime subsistence fishermen. Of course, this passage contradicts all other passages concerning encounters with Jesus in Jerusalem (other than with the Galilean women), or to remain in Jerusalem, and so, its controversial nature makes it more reliable based on the criterion of embarrassment. In fact, none of the events in the Marcan appendix 16:9–20, other than an appearance to Mary Magdalene, are necessarily in Jerusalem. These encounters could have been expanded in Luke and Matthew. Based on the foregoing analysis, the last test is satisfactorily met.

---

75. Mark 14:70.

76. Our analysis has suggested that none of the Sanhedrin were acting on their own with respect to claiming and entombing the body of Jesus. They were concerned about attack, and to make sure the body of Jesus had not vanished indicating his vindictive ghost would seek them and the other Jerusalem elite out.

77. See Freyne, "Herodian Economics," 43–44, on *homophylia* and subsistence activity in Galilee.

78. As reported in John 21:1–3.

79. Keeping also in mind the events they had witnessed in Jerusalem, where the very evil forces they had attempted to cast out had overwhelmed Jesus, beginning in the olive grove of Gethsemane where they believed protection from demonic forces was certain.

80. Luke 24:49.

Conclusions on the Veracity of Mark 16:17–18

Based on the risk and the analytical criteria employed, combined with contextual analysis, Mark 16:17–18 should be considered a contextually reliable post-crucifixion encounter with Jesus. In the context of human risk experience, this encounter is reliable in its original context and setting. The setting of the encounter was in Galilee at a communal meal, where there was an ecstatic experience. Jesus' spirit was present, likely possessing and speaking through one of the exorcists his commands to continue the war on Satan in preparation for the arriving kingdom of God. Such events are familiar to Paul who receives words of the Lord in dreams, trances and ecstatic experiences as commands or instructions,[81] or hears words that cannot be uttered after ecstatic transportation to the third heaven,[82] or describes how those who receive revelations who are among others should test the words received by consideration and the help of the Spirit.[83]

Corollary Observations, Mark 16:15–16

There is a demonstrable link between the perilous risks of extending these charismatic practices in Mark 16:17–18 (i.e., those that Jesus expects his itinerant exorcists take) with instructions that precede them. The command to baptize in Mark 16:16 includes a startling condemnation, if not a powerful curse, on those that refuse baptism (more than "condemned" is intended in *katakrino*). Here Jesus' curse is similar to one he placed on the Galilean villages that refused to accept and institute the changes he demanded,[84] including democratized *agape*, the inclusion of all outcasts, as well as acceptance of the men and women he released from satanic possession by the "finger of God." By refusing, these villages rejected not just him and his exorcists' legitimacy, but deny that their command over demons is of God. This suggests these villages hold Jesus to be possessed by Beelzebul, which as we have seen is the charge of his enemies. For Jesus, village leaders not only remain subject to Satan and demonic imperialism, but they will suffer

---

81. 1 Cor 7:12; 11:23–26; 15:3; Gal 1:12.
82. 2 Cor 12:2–4.
83. 1 Cor 14:26–33.
84. These include the principal villages he had visited and also failed in this attempt to cleanse them and win over the village: Chorazin, Bethsaida (the village of at least two of Jesus' exorcists), and Capernaum (the village of several other followers, and where Jesus lived with Kayfa, Kayfa's wife, mother and his brother's family—the typical extended family in first-century Palestine)

devastation—they accept a divinely cursed fate. God alone is king, a king who is coming with judgment against his enemies.[85]

More important, Jesus had once suspended baptism due to the risk of capture after the execution of John the Baptist. To command that the exorcists recommence baptism (i.e., to publicly administer the now lost practices allowing for the absorption of evil and the containment of demonic pollution into sacred waters) was still fraught with perilous risk; it was an echo of the murdered John's call for condemnation of Jerusalem, the temple, and the Roman sympathizers and elite in Jerusalem. As such, the command to reengage in baptism is startling, and is coherent with perilous risks associated with Jesus' foregoing commands to return to illegal practices in vv. 17–18.

But why baptize if it could be perilous? Baptism was linked with the demand to continue itinerancy and expand the "gospel," the *euangelion*. While the command to "go into the world" (*kosmos*, Mark 16:15) is later seen in light of Luke's theological program (Christianity's expansion from Jerusalem to Rome in Luke-Acts), in Mark, there is a different sense evident, one of uncertainty and unlimited danger in carrying out such a demand, particularly by Galilean exorcists who did so in the name of a crucified Jewish criminal! As noted, *euangelion* should be thought of as a verb, it was a charismatic power, imbued with authority for immediate transformation, and baptism, post-crucifixion, was the charismatic response to unite one for protection with the Spirit of God (i.e., what Jesus had termed the "finger of God"), active in protection from the terror of Satan and demonic possession and doom at judgment, which was so near. Indeed, the exorcists could proclaim that it was this spirit that had denied the annihilation of Jesus, the man "approved by God" by miracles, signs and wonders (i.e., Mark 16:17–18). They had encountered him in post-crucifixion events in various forms, and therefore, continued under his authority to practice exorcism.[86] Consequently, the command for itinerancy and baptism are coherent with the risk practices of Jesus and his exorcists at war with Satan. Indeed, the *criterion of coherence* can be appropriately applied to support these conclusions since the *criterion of dissimilarity* has been employed in our analysis. As Norman Perrin states: "Material from the earliest strata of the tradition may be accepted as authentic if it can be shown to cohere with material established as authentic by means of the criterion of dissimilarity."[87]

---

85. Luke 10:13; Matt 11:20.

86. Acts 2:22, "a man approved by God by miracles, signs and wonders," the same words used by Paul to describe the authority of authentic apostles, 2 Cor 12:12.

87. Perrin, *Rediscovering*, 20–22, and 43; also Jeremias, *Parables*, 11.

Given these findings, the most original and primitive stratum of tradition supports the authenticity of this encounter with Jesus, where these instructions were communicated to Jesus' original exorcists in Galilee. It is possible that this was the first encounter with Jesus due to the intensity of perilous risks created and contextual tests met in association with exorcism, and was the encounter with Jesus' chief exorcist Kayfa that is acknowledged in all strata of tradition,[88] the contents of which are now lost, but the event was known to the original community. It is likely that this encounter was thus to Kayfa and that these instructions were given to him and then passed on to the other exorcists who had fled to Galilee.

Mark 9:2–8: Was the Metamorphosis of Jesus a Post-Crucifixion Encounter?

Mark 9:2–8 recounts the ecstatic experience of three of Jesus' exorcists, Simon (i.e., Kayfa), Yecob and Yohannes. They are separated from the other exorcists by Jesus and taken up to a high mountain (*oros hupselon*). There they witness his metamorphosis *(metemorphothe)*, also known as *the transfiguration*. The common translation of *anapherei* implies that Jesus physically leads these men up the mountain, but this word can also be translated as "carries up," as in a spiritual journey. As such, we must be cautious not to assume this event is a physical hike guided by Jesus any more than it is a spiritual journey, séance or vision, where Jesus reveals his true self—his glory.[89] There is evidence this is indeed a shared séance or spiritual journey among Jesus' exorcists that is guided by an encounter with Jesus because the event ends when Kayfa interrupts it with a question, a common feature of séances.[90] Shamans are able to produce group visions, but usually through rhythmic music and dancing, however, there is no evidence this is a shamanic experience.[91] To recover the original form and setting of this event, the tradition should be tested using comprehensive risk analysis and rigorous contextual evaluation. This may reveal the most likely setting and use of the tradition, and more, if this event was a post-crucifixion encounter.

The unit begins, "After six days," and is set on a mountain in Galilee. The count of days stands out,[92] as "six days" is the most specific description

---

88. Paul, 1 Cor 15:5; Luke 24:34.
89. See Smith, *Magician*, 120–22.
90. Ibid., 122.
91. Lewis, *Ecstatic Religion*, 53.
92. Lunn, *Original Ending*, 359; Lunn also mentions the six days that Moses was on the mountain before the voice of God called him from the cloud. While this may be

of passing time found in the Gospel of Mark aside from the predictions of the passion, a perilous risk event. As such, this unit must also have been originally tied to a similar perilous risk event, one absent from the current context. This indicates that the unit has been awkwardly placed in a new setting. Consequently, the original risk context has been neutralized. Form critical analysis long ago identified the event as resurrection appearance,[93] while other scholars argue it as an epiphany or representation of Mark's redactional program to reveal Jesus as the glorified Son of Man at the *Parousia*.[94] However, from a risk analysis perspective, the designation of days demands a relationship with a perilous risk event, namely the crucifixion, consistent with the Marcan editor's use of days elsewhere, which reference that event.[95] Consequently, Mark 9:2-8 is a post-crucifixion encounter with Jesus that has been reset back into the days of Jesus' itinerant mission.[96]

The location is consistent with the aforementioned risk context of the exorcists fleeing Jerusalem for the safety of Galilee. According to Matthew and Mark,[97] the women share the command of Jesus to meet him in Galilee.[98] While this tradition may have been used to explain why the exorcists were in Galilee, there is little doubt that within a week they were there.[99] The mountain in Galilee was familiar to the exorcists[100] and to Jesus,[101] and so must have been a specific location where he sought ecstatic prayer,[102] soli-

---

an important parallel, the location and temporal reference when combined are more significant. Six days would allow the exorcists to return to Galilee after the crucifixion and be hidden by kin among night fishermen.

93. Bultmann, *History*, 259-60. Bultmann is followed by Robinson, "On the Gattung of Mark," 116-18. Robinson finds support for his conclusions based on a review of Gnostic writings, including *Pistis Sophia* 2-3 and the *Apocryphon of James*, 14:25-26. Contrasting this view very early was Boobyer, *St. Mark*. For a current analysis of the debate, see Litwa, *Iesus Deus*, 114n4.

94. E.g., Perrin, "Towards an Interpretation," 8-9, 27-28; also the transfiguration as a proleptic of the Parousia, Kee, "Transfiguration in Mark," 137-52.

95. Not a reference back to a theological point! Perrin, *Christology*, 8-9, 27-28.

96. Stein, "Is the Transfiguration," 79-96; also for a thorough analysis of the account from a christological perspective and brief review of scholarly view of the original form of the unit, see Rothschild, *Baptist Traditions*, 134-40.

97. Matt 28:7; Mark 16:7.

98. Mark 16:7.

99. As we have already confirmed, Luke's theological agenda is to have the gospel preached from Jerusalem to Rome, but Mark, followed by Matthew, confirms that Jesus' followers met with him in Galilee.

100. Mark 3:13-19.

101. Matt 8:1; 14:23; Luke 5:16; 6:12; also see Mark 1:35.

102. Mark 6:46.

tude and encounters with the divine. Jesus' history with ecstatic mountain experiences began with his confrontation with Satan (Matt 4:8). It ends with his metamorphosis in Galilee at the "appointed" mountain.

The nature of this ecstatic experience in Galilee is markedly different than other post-crucifixion encounters reported in any of the canonical gospels. As it clearly could be construed as simply an *ecstatic vision or trance*, its placement as a resurrection event was considered problematic.[103] More, the three exorcists suddenly seem to awake and find they are alone with Jesus, i.e., they "looked around" (v. 8) and saw no one else.[104] The trance, or revelation, abruptly ends. The experience was ethereal and otherworldly, reliant on the report of itinerant Jewish exorcists—men who were reputed by their opponents to follow a divinely cursed dark magician possessed by Beelzebul. As a result, the metamorphosis of Jesus witnessed in a trance or séance by three peasant exorcists was too problematic to the Marcan community in that it was unremarkable, too common an event in the Hellenistic world to be advantageous in early Christian missionary propaganda.

Relative to this experience, we find a similar event reported by an undisputed historical figure, Paul of Tarsus, sometime between 35 to 42 CE. We learn of this experience from Paul's own hand as recorded in two of his undisputed letters, principally to the Corinthians (52 to 54 CE) and Galatians (49 to 56 CE).[105] In 2 Cor 12:2–4, Paul reports of an ecstatic experience where he is transformed and taken to *tritou ouranou*, "the third heaven," by God (*theos oiden*, is repeated, which implies that God was fully involved in this transportation and experience). This transport is to the highest heaven, paradise, the place God and the angels reside, a description common in Judaism before the second century and in rabbinic literature.[106] It is where God takes the heroes of the Hebrews, such as Moses and Elijah. Paul is insistent that God was involved not only in this ecstatic experience, but that it was God who chose him from his mother's womb,[107] and who "revealed (*apocalupsai*) his son to me."[108]

---

103. The disappearance of Apollonius of Tyana from a temple led to presumptions he was taken to paradise. The subsequent appearance of Apollonius in a dream to a follower, attempting to convince him of eternal life, is a good example of the contemporary appearance of the dead in a dream. See Philostratus, *Life of Apollonius*, 3i.

104. The experience is characterized as puzzling and ethereal, and so is less tangible than seeing Jesus with the marks of the crucifixion evident on his body.

105. Koester holds that Galatians was written after the council of Jerusalem, about 56 CE. See Koester, *Introduction*, 114. The other theory is of course that Paul's discussion should be thought of as pre-council, or about 47 CE. Since Paul cites multiple revelations and visions in 2 Cor 12, the dating of these events is irrelevant for our purposes.

106. Schweitzer, *Mysticism of Paul*, 153–54.

107. Gal 1:15.

108. Gal 1:16.

The risk context of this event is defined by Paul as *optasias* and *apokalypseis*, "visions" and "revelations," that is, one of *multiple ecstatic experiences* (more than any of the super-apostles), where he is taken in or out of body to be with the divine, which includes the post-crucifixion Jesus. For Paul, these experiences redefine perilous risk (he was now subject to attack by *messengers* of Satan),[109] and to disavow these was to bring on a divine curse.[110] Paul reports that he heard *arreta remata*, "unutterable words" that are forbidden to repeat by humans, a term used in mystery religions and rites, where the secret of the cult or divine revelations are to be kept to the initiate.[111] Paul's transportation was immediate, and he is uncertain if he was transformed from his body or not, which is evidence a metamorphosis occurred that was beyond his comprehension to discern.

Paul's metamorphosis and charismatic experiences at first do not appear to have a direct correlation to Mark 9:2-8, however, they confirm that Jesus' exorcists and chosen charismatics (and note that in 2 Cor 12, Paul considers himself one of them; that he is equal to Kayfa because of his charismatic powers of *signs, wonders and miracles*) received divine visions (in dreams or by trance) and revelations (transportation with or to divine beings to receive mysteries, wisdom or special insight) by God, where they heard divine voices directed to them. Consequently, Paul confirms that this type of ecstatic experience was *common* and *expected* among Jesus' authentic exorcists, post-crucifixion, just as Mark 16:17-18 implies. More, it was a sign of those who claimed to be true and authoritative representatives of Jesus, before and after the crucifixion, whether "fourteen years ago," or "after six days." From a risk context, it also meant that these men and women were at great risk, and if they refused to embrace these experiences as itinerant messengers whose lives were no longer their own[112] and the danger,[113] the consequences were dire. Indeed, Paul is terrified of his fate.[114] Their heightened perilous risk was centered in a refusal to embrace the encounter as transformative, and to deny was to thumb one's nose at God. Their greatest risk was no longer in danger from enemies, but being turned over to Satan for destruction.[115] In fact, Paul understood his precarious situation: To prevent his believing himself superior to all men

---

109. 2 Cor 12:7, *aggelos*, used as angels, messengers, which in this case can also infer the demons of Satan.

110. Gal 1:8.

111. Furnish, *2 Corinthians*, 527.

112. Gal 2:20; and the tradition as to Kayfa's fate remembered, John 21:18.

113. 2 Cor 11:24-26; Gal 1:13, 23; Acts 8:3; 7:54-60.

114. 1 Cor 9:16.

115. Such as the tradition represented in Matt 12:45.

due to his multiple visions and revelations, demons of Satan were allowed to attack him.[116] This was a deliberate perilous risk warning to caution Paul that to turn his back on his commission and selection as an itinerant *apostolos* of the "gospel" meant that he would be turned over to Satan for destruction, something akin to Paul's curse on an adulterer in 1 Cor 5:5, *olethron tes sarkos*, the destruction of the flesh.[117] This is also an echo of Jesus' dire warning to this exorcists in Luke 9:62, "No one who puts his hand to the plow and looks back is fit for the kingdom of God." Consequently, the tenor the danger for refusal to embrace the risks of being an *apostolos*, a charismatic messenger, meant only doom.

Mark 9:2–8 and Qualitative Risk Analysis

With this context set, we can begin our risks analysis of the unit, employing first, qualitative risk. In this analysis, the encounter cannot be a countermeasure to the elite, but must heighten the perilous risk of the Galilean exorcists and the conflict with opponents.

To begin, unless we hold the unit to be a post-resurrection event on the sacred mountain in Galilee[118] (near the lake to which some of the exorcists fled in terror after the crucifixion), the metamorphosis of Jesus becomes a neutral risk event slipped into his itinerant mission and war on Satan. As noted, this is an awkward and unlikely setting for such an event. Placement into the ministry of Jesus serves to extend the theological motif of a Marcan redactor.[119] Scholars have shown that if this were the purpose of the unit, the redactor sought to confirm Jesus' christological standing as *bar nasha*, the Son of Man, and Son of God, i.e., the transfiguration confirmed his glorified state to be realized at the *parousia*.[120] An alternate theological motif is also possible. The event becomes the pivotal moment in Mark when the benefits of being a disciple are made apparent, i.e., despite the disciples' struggles and hardships, the reward promised is to be with Jesus at the *parousia*, which is near.[121]

---

116. 2 Cor 12:7.

117. Smith, *Hand This Man Over*, 7–37.

118. This mountain was the location of several ecstatic experiences during Jesus' lifetime, see references later in this section.

119. This argument dates back to Perrin's "Composition of Mark IX, 1," 67–70, and has continued.

120. Perrin, *Modern Pilgrimage*, 93.

121. Morrison, *Turning Point*, 140–43.

Perhaps such theological motifs met the needs of the Marcan community at the time of the gospel's assimilation in late '60s CE, facing the crisis of the destruction of Jerusalem (a sign of the *parousia*),[122] albeit any reconstruction is completely theoretical.[123] And when such theories ignore the possibility of an original risk context in the post-crucifixion period in which the oral tradition was being formed, such as this unit, they forgo the risk context and a more prudent effort to recover its more original form and function. Since this study has shown that the unit in some form had a well-defined risk context, and that it was originally linked with a perilous risk event that preceded it by "six-days" (the specific passing of time and the most specific in Mark),[124] it is clear it had an earlier oral form and was dislodged from its original setting.[125] Since the unit was dislodged, we must ask what editorial work (theological redaction) was done to reset it within Jesus' itinerant mission, and so, attempt to recover its original form as a post-crucifixion event. If it can be recovered, perilous risk analysis can more accurately commence.

Scholars have identified the remnants of a core tradition within Mark 9:2–8 that has been expanded. As it stands today, there is unanimity that the unit is the result of editorial work of a redactor, one whose theological intent can be recovered by examining Mark 8:27—10:52.[126] In these studies, the metamorphosis of Jesus is linked to Mark 8:38, Jesus' prediction of the coming Son of Man, which for Mark was understood to be the arrival of the all-powerful divine messianic and eschatological figure. In Mark, this is a combination of the divine attributes in *1 Enoch* and *IV Ezra*.[127] The Son

---

122. Mark 13:14–27.

123. We must recall the early traditions related to the composition of Mark written by Eusebius, church historian, citing Papias, bishop of Hierapolis, 60–130 CE: "This also the presbyter said: 'Mark, having become the interpreter of Peter, wrote down accurately, though not indeed in order, whatsoever he remembered of the things done or said by Christ. For he neither heard the Lord nor followed him, but afterward, as I said, he followed Peter, who adapted his teaching to the needs of his hearers, but with no intention of giving a connected account of the Lord's discourses, so that Mark committed no error while he thus wrote some things as he remembered them. For he was careful of one thing, not to omit any of the things which he had heard, and not to state any of them falsely'" (*Ecclesiastical History*, 3.39:14–17). Mark's composition was not in chronological order, was related to the needs of Mark's community, and adapted (redacted) the traditions, and was second hand. Since Matthew and Luke retain Mark almost completely and in the same sequence, it is arguable as to the apostolic composition of any of the Synoptic Gospels.

124. See Lunn, *Original Ending*, 673–76.

125. Mark 8:31–32; 9:30–32; 10:32–34.

126. Perrin, *Pilgrimage*, 100–101; Todt, *Son of Man*, 145–47.

127. These eschatological and apocalyptic tests provide different portrayals of the Son of Man as a messianic, redemptive or judgmental and retributive figure. See Todt,

of Man would powerfully subdue Satan and all God's enemies in the last days. The subsequent placement of Jesus' metamorphosis following this section confirmed for a community in crisis (i.e., the pending destruction of Jerusalem by the Romans) that Jesus was this powerful being and that their protection and hope for justification was assured.[128]

The presence of Moses and Elijah appear to be later additions to the unit, as they serve as confirmation of Jesus' authority as the divine Son, i.e., the Son of God who now stands ready to fulfill and expound the Law and prophets. Bultmann argues that the presence of Moses and Elijah were not original to the unit, but instead were angelic figures present, similar to those who appeared at the tomb.[129] Other scholars omit these verses altogether as part of the earliest version. However, there is general agreement that the original unit included the following: A miraculous transportation to a mountain (possibly to a sacred mountain) or to paradise (like Paul's transportation in 2 Cor 12); the metamorphosis of Jesus (including the change in appearance, dazzling robe, which likely included his face shining in glory); the appearance of an angelic figure (to confirm presence in the third heaven); Kayfa's question, which shatters the trance; the covering of a cloud (the sign of divine presence); a divine pronouncement; and an awakening alone with Jesus, i.e., an ecstatic trance or vision. It is this form of the unit that more accurately represents the original post-resurrection event and oral unit.

While the vision is reported to have been witnessed by three of Jesus' exorcists, Kayfa's presence is significant. He was the acknowledged leader of Jesus' exorcists in all strata of tradition. The Synoptic Gospels confirm that Kayfa's encounter was the lightning rod event that assured other exorcists that Jesus was active, and, ultimately, his report led to the formation of the nascent assembly of exorcists, the first primitive community.[130] Paul describes Kayfa as one of "the pillars," an indication surely associated with his priority among the other exorcists resulting from their revelations and visions of Jesus, and being the principal witnesses to the event.[131] While this may have been a shared vision, Kayfa's presence was decisive.

Son of Man; also Cullmann, *Christology of the New Testament*, 137–88; Bultmann, *Theology*, 30–31; Bornkamm, *Jesus of Nazareth*, 228. For a thorough discussion of sources and the Son of Man in eschatology and apocalyptic tradition, see Reynolds, *Apocalyptic Son of Man*.

128. Lunn, *Original Ending*, 361.

129. Bultmann, *History*, 259–61, 309, 432–33.

130. Luke 24:34: "It is true, the Lord is risen and has appeared to Simon" (NIV), also translated, "The Lord has risen indeed and has appeared to Simon" (ESV).

131. Paul's description, Gal 2:9.

As a post-resurrection encounter, perilous risk would have been significantly heightened, particularly for Kayfa. From a risk standpoint, this event (along with Mark 16:17–18) clearly acted as the catalyst for his abandoning a kinship assisted escape into hiding with other workers as a night subsistence laborer on Galilee. It was this escape that served as the mitigation to the perilous risk of the Jerusalem crisis, the crucifixion and the hunt for Jesus' remaining followers. Kayfa clearly communicated his ecstatic experience to others that had fled to Galilee post-crucifixion, principally three to five of the exorcists who, like he, had returned to subsistence fishing at night, hidden and protected by kin.[132] By convincing others to join him and abandon subsistence labor and embrace illegal practices as exorcists (as known followers of the crucified criminal Jesus), they made themselves completely vulnerable. Informants and assassins of the Jerusalem elite ultimately succeeded. At least three of Jesus' followers were murdered, whether by the action of an informant or minions of the Jerusalem elite, including Paul. Consequently, based on risk and contextual analysis, this event passes the test of qualitative risk analysis.

Mark 9:2–8 and the Criteria of Dissimilarity and Embarrassment

In this test, encounters must differ from the needs of the early church on the one hand and the context of first-century Judaism in Palestine on the other. To accurately test the tradition, the most original form of the unit should be employed, as best as can be recovered. Analysis has confirmed that the unit differed significantly from the current structure, and occurs only a few days after a perilous risk event, most certainly the crucifixion. The core tradition recovered is as follows:

> Late at night, or in heavy sleep,[133] there is ecstatic transportation by a trance or vision[134] to a sacred mountain in Galilee, a place familiar to the exorcists,[135] or to paradise itself (e.g., 2 Cor 12); the metamorphosis of Jesus occurs revealing his glorified state (the change in appearance, dazzling clothing, and

---

132. John 21:13–15.

133. Luke 9:32.

134. Esler, *Modelling Early Christianity*, 57–64; Scharlemann, "Transfiguration," 886–88.

135. Shillington, *Jesus and Paul*, 42. As noted, the mountain in Galilee (likely modern day Mt. Tabor), was sacred to Jesus; it is where he escaped to have ecstatic encounters and pray (Mark 6:46), sometimes for days; where he selected and trained his exorcists (Mark 3:13–19; Busse, *To Be Near the Fire*, 76), and contested with Satan (not necessarily a mountain in the Judean desert).

shining face[136]); angelic figures appear (to confirm presence in paradise); Kayfa, in a trance[137] and likely the only one present, is terrified (*ekphoboi*) and inappropriately speaks, bringing the vision to a close; there is covering by a sacred cloud (the sign of divine presence); Jesus now resides in the third heaven with God and the angels; there is a pronouncement, God speaks and identifies Jesus as "my son"; Kayfa awakes on the mountaintop; he goes down the mountain to tell others.

In this form, there are no other contemporary Jewish traditions that report an encounter with a deceased crucified criminal and exorcist who was considered a dark magician, or one who then communicates with exorcists he trained, ordering them (after they have abandoned him) to continue the very practices that brought about his brutal death under a divine curse. There is no question that the unit differs from the context of first-century Judaism in Palestine. Should we consider this form representative of a unique segment within Judaism contemporary with the activity of Jesus and his exorcists? That these ecstatic practices were evident within first-century Judaism, the unique practices find no parallel on an equivalent level and by way of contemporary example.

The unit also differs from the needs of the early church. Indeed, by recasting the unit as an event occurring during the itinerant activity of Jesus in Galilee, it is confirmed as problematic to the early church as a post-crucifixion encounter, which this analysis has shown it was. Indeed, there is evidence that 2 Pet 1:15–18 demonstrates that there was an independent tradition of a post-crucifixion of Jesus having appeared to Kayfa,[138] one that the author took up. The sacred mountain is mentioned, the voice, and all coming with the "majestic glory" to which the author was a witness—that is, the post-resurrection encounter of Kayfa with Jesus on the mountain in Galilee, or through a trance where Kayfa transported to paradise, or the third heaven. With the vision-trance content of this encounter emphasized as the risk-context in the unit, it became difficult to sustain confidence that the resurrection of Jesus was more than a dream of a poor, displaced Galilean fisherman-turned-exorcist—one who had abandoned Jesus and fled. Such an encounter was insufficient to inspire new charismatics to embrace perilous risk, indeed the risk of death and annihilation under a divine curse.

---

136. Luke 9:29, while praying, Jesus face begins to change. This tradition portrays the metamorphosis more accurately.

137. Just as he did in Acts 10:10 while praying, i.e., deep spiritual breathing and meditation.

138. E.g., see Wells, *Historical Evidence*, 113n3, for a detailed and exhaustive analysis of the sources and scholars debating the original use and for of the tradition.

The event was isolated, personal and, while certainly considered to be a significant event for Kayfa, it was nonetheless ethereal.

In sum, the original and recovered form of the unit differs from the needs of the early church on the one hand and the context of first-century Judaism in Palestine on the other, and as such, passes the test of the criterion of dissimilarity.

The *criterion of embarrassment*[139] identifies those sayings or events in the New Testament that created difficulties for the early church, implying that they were undeniable or else these traditions would never have been included, let alone created. In evaluating the unit in its original form, Mark 9:1–8 meets the criteria. It was embarrassing as a post-resurrection encounter, evidenced by its displacement and recasting as an event that occurred during Jesus' itinerant war on Satan. More, placed in its new context, the metamorphosis served the needs of the early church, as the redactor of Mark linked the event to Jesus' prediction of the coming Son of Man, the messianic apocalyptic figure that would render justice to the righteous of God and crush all enemies. Set in the context of Mark 8:24—10:47, the metamorphosis of Jesus confirms he is both the Son of Man *and* the Son of God, revealing to his disciples his glorified self as he will appear at the *parousia*, the judgment. Therefore, a community in crisis, one that was facing the catastrophic destruction of Jerusalem, becomes comforted by the assurance that Jesus will act as the divine Son of Man on their behalf, mitigating all perilous risk and rescuing them from destruction. Consequently, the change in setting helps to confirm its original function in the oral tradition—that is, it was a resurrection event, experienced by Kayfa as a vision or trance, confirming for him that Jesus was not only active, but taken to paradise. As such, this unit also passes the criterion of embarrassment.

Summary of Risk Analysis

An analysis of Mark 9:2–8 has isolated the original form of the unit by employing the criteria of risk analysis. Based on this analysis, the event may be considered reliable, subject to passing the remaining contextual tests.

Mark 9:2–8 and the Contextual Tests

We now turn to contextual analyses. Here an event must be coherent with the sociological risk setting, including the subsistence struggle of the Galileans,

---

139. See Meier, *Marginal Jew*.

the background from which they came to join Jesus' band of exorcists. Once again, the contextual risk tests previously established are as follows:

1. Encounters with original members of Jesus' band of Galilean exorcists, those who faced capture, death and social isolation and starvation, are given priority.

2. Encounters should be consistent with the ecstatic practices of Jesus that engendered the original perilous risk with his opponents. Specifically, encounters that encouraged the remaining exorcists to continue the ecstatic activity of Jesus and his war on Satan are preferred.

3. Encounters near or on the lake of Galilee, particularly related to subsistence fishing, and similar to the animistic control exhibited by Jesus, are preferential (i.e., the remaining exorcists escaped there).

4. Finally, encounters that may have led the Galileans to again abandon subsistence existence (i.e., to which they returned for survival post-crucifixion) are also preferred.

In each of the foregoing tests, the original form of the unit recovered through risk analysis is evaluated.

To begin, it is readily apparent that the unit passes the first, third and fourth contextual tests, as Kayfa was not only one of Jesus' trained exorcists, he was considered their leader even two decades later[140] and continued to practice as an exorcist.[141] More, risk analysis has suggested that Kayfa fled to Galilee immediately after the crucifixion, returning to agrarian subsistence existence in desperation and to support his family (e.g., his wife and mother-in-law). Hiding under the protection of kin (and other fishermen), they arranged night work, where trammel-net fishing would allow him to avoid detection and capture by spies or informants.[142] Kayfa's subsequent trance and vision on the sacred mountain in Galilee of the glorified Jesus (a secret or special place familiar to Jesus[143] and his exorcists; indeed the place where they were selected and trained[144]) was certainly the pivotal ecstatic experience that drove him to abandon that life and, once again, embrace perilous risk; it led him to gather up Jesus' remaining (and willing) exorcists[145]—

---

140. Gal 2:9, written between 48–52 CE; Koester, *History*, 104 (52–55 CE)

141. Acts 5:12–16, 8:14–17, 9:33, 34, 36–41.

142. For the design of the net and the methods employed by Galilean fishermen, see archaeologist Nun, "Let Down Your Nets," 11–13.

143. Luke 5:16 and 6:12.

144. Mark 3:13–19.

145. The "twelve" were eventually gathered and selected by Kayfa, and included perhaps all of those chosen by Jesus on the mountain, assuming they returned to Galilee

thereby passing the second test—and report that Jesus was not only active, but in paradise and available. Kayfa's trance was also consistent with the ecstatic activity of the exorcists trained by Jesus. Jesus himself experienced trances and visions, as did his exorcists, particularly Kayfa, as confirmed in Acts 10:10. Later, Paul verifies that ecstatic visionary and trance experiences were confirmation of one's authenticity as an *apostolos*, such as Kayfa and the other "super-apostles." Given this, the unit passes all contextual tests.

Conclusions on the Veracity of Mark 9:2–8

Based on the risk and analytical criteria employed, combined with contextual analysis, the recovered form of Mark 9:2–8 should be considered a reliable post-crucifixion encounter with Jesus. In the context of human risk experience, this encounter is coherent with its historical context and setting. Jesus was understood to have survived annihilation, and was now enthroned with God in the third heaven.[146]

---

and remained, as some still were not convinced (Matt 28:17). The variation in the names of the twelve in the gospel lists, as well as the question of who followed Kayfa to Galilee, suggests that there may have been changes over time. Clearly, an early tradition confirmed that vacancy among the twelve was filled by casting lots, a practice used by even the high priest to decide religious issues.

146. Analysis will show below that this encounter then extends Mary's, where Jesus was clearly active and available but "not yet ascended," to his acceptance to the place with God. This difference set Kayfa's encounter as significant and different from Mary's, and ultimately took precedence over Mary's in the primitive Christian tradition, and as reflected by Paul in 1 Cor 15:1–5.

8

The Risk Context of Post-Crucifixion Encounters in Matthew

The Exorcist Magdalene, Magdalene and Kayfa, and the Sacred Mountain

The next section applies the risk and contextual methodology to Matthean post-crucifixion encounters. As with the former section on the Marcan tradition, the outcome of each risk analysis is to ascertain the original form and risk context and render whether that form recovers a reliable post-crucifixion encounter with Jesus, thereby suggesting veracity. There are key personalities in these traditions that faced daunting risks. The *Gospel of Mary* is included in the analysis of Matt 28:1–10 due to the thorough evaluation of Magdalene in recovering the original risk form and context of this post-crucifixion event.

Matthew 28:1–10: Why Would Magdalene Go to the Tomb at Perilous Risk?

In Matt 28:1–10, Mary *the Magdalene* (and "the other Mary") has the first ecstatic encounter with Jesus, post-crucifixion.[1] According to the Matthean report, they had gone to see the tomb the evening after the Sabbath "toward the dawn," which, from a risk perspective makes their effort striking—not because it was dark, but it was exactly when malevolent ghosts, evil spirits and demons were believed to roam seeking victims, particularly near tombs

---

1. The problematic nature of a report coming from the witness of a Jewish woman in first-century Palestine will be addressed below when applying the various risk criteria, including the criterion of dissimilarity.

and graveyards![2] Why would the women have taken such a perilous risk, particularly when these very demonic forces[3] had just succeeded in overwhelming and killing Jesus, the man they thought to be a powerful exorcist possessed by the "finger of God?" If it were only to be near the tomb, then their courage should be considered remarkable, but also quite puzzling and even incoherent. Indeed, our previous qualitative risk and contextual analyses would suggest their visit to the tomb had a specific risk motivation and one that can be recovered.

To begin, both Marys, particularly Mary the Magdalene, were most certainly itinerant ecstatics and exorcists,[4] just as were the men who followed Jesus—a tradition that was undoubtedly later suppressed.[5] The Matthean tradition confirms that, unlike the male exorcists who fled, they made a conscious, perilous risk decision—they *chose* to remain and risk being captured, *secretly* following (at a distance)[6] to see not only who took the brutalized body of Jesus (noticeably, a member of the Sanhedrin, Joseph of Arimathea, whose membership in this group included Roman sympathizers, the deadly enemies of Jesus—he was likely *not* a secret follower of

---

2. Ogden, *Magic*, please see previous citations in ch. 1.

3. The satanic forces included Satan's control over the Jerusalem elite and Roman imperialism under Pontius Pilate, see Busse, *To Be Near the Fire*, 23–34.

4. See Janowitz, *Magic in the Roman World*, ch. 6, and footnote on p. 100. While not explicitly tied to women "exorcists," women were directly linked to healings (i.e., driving out demons), with more than fifty-one of those associated with women married to or associated with rabbinic families. Paul does make this association; for Junia in Rom 16:7, whom he names as an apostle (and as defined by Paul in 2 Cor 12:2, as one who could exorcise demons and heal and would be itinerant; one who was so named before Paul's post-resurrection encounter with Jesus and held by all the apostles to be superior). Consequently, Paul clearly supports that women were exorcists in the Jesus movement from its inception. Why then in Paul's list of appearances in 1 Cor 15 does he not cite Mary the Magdalene? This question has puzzled scholars for decades without definitive resolution. The most compelling argument thus far is that Paul does include women in his lists of apostles, including a Mary he lists with other prominent apostles (Rom 16:6). Further, as his argument with the Corinthians demands unquestioned witnesses (and a woman's testimony did not carry the weight of men in the Graeco-Roman and Jewish worlds of the first century), he emphasizes particularly the report of Kayfa, who likely visited Corinth in 54–55 CE (1 Cor 9:5; Acts 9:32).

5. See the discussion below on the suppression of women in subsequent gospel traditions, particularly Kraemer, "Autonomy, Prophecy and Gender," 130–31. We know that Junia and Phoebe were likely itinerant ecstatics, as Junia is identified by Paul as an apostle of note among the others, and was known to be one long before he had his own encounter with Jesus, Rom 16:7. Paul is very clear about the qualities of true apostles like himself in 2 Cor 12.

6. Matt 27:55.

Jesus who went to Pilate), but more important, to see *where* it was taken.[7] For these two exorcists, the perilous risk of doing so is outweighed by the even greater risk of failing to do so. They watched as it was sealed in a rock tomb, the entrance blocked by a heavy rolling stone. Finally, when alone and before guards arrive, they face or sit over against the tomb. The tomb is then guarded (as noted, by special priests, not soldiers).[8]

Why these women would take such a risk is critical to ascertain. Indeed, to assert there was no risk because, as women, they would be immune from attack is completely inaccurate and neutralizes perilous, dangerous actions. There are numerous contemporary accounts of brutal attacks on men and women, even innocent bystanders, by Pilate, the elite and their spies, recorded by Josephus and others.[9] Saul, an agent and spy of the Jerusalem elite, brutalized both men and women of the early followers of Jesus movement. Indeed, as will be seen, the actions to secure the body by Jesus' enemies do not just fit the risk context (and so are most assuredly reliable), but underscore the risk of being seen or even thought to be his supporter.[10] These exorcists must have had a different risk motivation.

After the Sabbath ended, and at the most dangerous time of night, the two Marys return. Mark and Luke include that it was to "anoint the body" (Mark 16:1–2 or Luke 24:1), adding also the names of other women present with them.[11] However, the editor/redactor of Matthew knew Palestine and that anointing a decaying body would have been inconceivable and repugnant after three days;[12] and with the brutalized condition of Jesus' body, simply too horrible. For the editor/redactor of Matthew, such a tradition was an embarrassment, and so it was dropped. Further, carrying heavy spices at night (let alone purchasing them while in hiding) would have been very difficult, if not impossible, and since the tomb was guarded and ritually sealed,[13] any approach would have led to their being attacked

---

7. If these men were sympathizers of Jesus, the women would not have had to follow at a distance, or wait until their departure, and only then approach the tomb.

8. Matt 27:61: Guarding the tomb was indicative of fear of retribution, i.e., to monitor it to ensure it remains still and inactive.

9. See Horsley and Hanson, *Bandits, Prophets and Messiahs*, 29–32, 41–42; Josephus, *Antiquities*, 8:60–62, 18:3.3, 18:85–89; Philo, *Embassy*, 302; see also Busse, *To Be Near the Fire*, 20–27.

10. Mark 14:70; Luke 22:58; Matt 26:73; John 18:17.

11. Other women are mentioned in Mark 16:1–2: Mary Magdalene, Mary the Mother of James and Salome; other gospels have different groups and interactions, but are unanimous that women found the empty tomb and tried to report it to Kayfa, only be told it was an "idle tale."

12. The very point of John 11:39 within the canonical gospel tradition.

13. To keep the body of Jesus and his spirit trapped, preventing retributive attack on

(i.e., not knowing if they were spirits, ghosts or exorcists of Jesus). Those monitoring and guarding the sealed tomb would have used special protective weapons, including bronze swords, magical amulets or special tokens for driving away evil or casting (throwing) deadly protective curses.[14] More, no anointing was needed, as according to John 19:38–42, the body already had been anointed, covered with unusually large amounts of burial spices (over one hundred pounds of myrrh and aloes, while only forty pounds were used for the highly respected and revered Rabbi Gamaliel).[15] That Jesus' body had been dressed is certainly correct. However, based on the risk and contextual setting previously analyzed, Jesus' body was more likely covered with a concoction of magical herbs, amulets and written spells.[16] Large quantities of this mixture were placed on the body to ensure the dark magician's spirit, if not annihilated by crucifixion, was trapped. His enemies feared that, as a minion of Satan's demonic prince, Beelzebul, he would seek deadly retribution.[17]

Consequently, going to the tomb had nothing to do with anointing a decaying and mutilated body. Employing a contextual risk perspective within the contemporary setting, we must postulate that, as ecstatics and exorcists who had been abandoned (the male exorcists had fled) and who were desperate for escape (fearing discovery and attack), these exorcists went to raise up, claim or communicate with Jesus' spirit, intending to seek his protection, or that of "the finger of God," the spirit that possessed him. It is more likely that they brought esoteric herbs and spices used by exorcists[18] to carry out ecstatic prayer near the tomb with the intent of having an ecstatic vision, that is, to determine if Jesus' spirit had been annihilated,

---

enemies as was expected by the "untimely dead."

14. Jesus' body was taken by his enemies to ensure he had been annihilated, both body (they brutalized and mutilated it as a first precaution) and spirit (killing him under a divine curse, being "hung on a tree"). It was then sealed in the tomb and guarded by special priests ordered to monitor the body, rolling back the stone at dawn each day to verify it remained still, i.e., to ensure his spirit was not "restless" to seek retribution as one of the untimely dead. See Ogden, *Magic*, 179, 181.

15. Josephus, *Antiquities*, 17:8.3.

16. For the use of amulets by Jewish rabbi's and others, see ch. 1.

17. See Busse, *To Be Near the Fire*, 55–56.

18. The tradition about Rabbi Zakkai is referenced in Kohler and Blau, "Exorcism," in the *Jewish Encyclopedia*, http://www.jewishencyclopedia.com/articles/5942-exorcism. A root was used by the exorcist Eleazar according to Josephus (*Antiquities* 8.2.5). While the practice has been lost, the women coming to the tomb during the peak hours of demonic activity, using similar herbs and roots to drive demons away, could have augmented a state of prayerful trance free from attack while hoping for contact with Jesus.

or if he could be contacted. To accomplish this, ancient ecstatics, exorcists and *goetes* went to the tomb of the victim, particularly during predawn hours. Spices and herbs could be burned or inhaled to activate ecstatic experiences, or digested. This presents the possibility that these exorcists were responsible for the first critical encounters with Jesus post-crucifixion as a result of these practices—the origin of primitive Christianity. Only these circumstances adequately address the contemporary risk context of the two Marys visitation to the tomb.[19]

Accordingly, the women then do have an ecstatic experience, when in a trance or vision, not unlike that of Kayfa,[20] near the site of the tomb. They witnessed the descent of an angel, felt a tremendous earthquake, and then the rolling back (*kulio*) of the large stone that sealed the tomb. An angel of God instructs the women to tell the remaining exorcists that the tomb had been vacated. Jesus' body did not appear; the tomb was already empty, just as in the tradition of Phlegon previously noted in the account of a deceased girl, Philinnion.[21] The vision may end at this point, but the exorcists have confirmed Jesus is available and active to them.

The extant tradition then has the women rush to the exorcists, who were either in hiding or already in the process of fleeing to Galilee. While on the road they encounter Jesus. Whether this occurs in the vision or on a road as they seek to find the exorcists is uncertain,[22] but Jesus appears suddenly and is in a visible and substantive form. They fall to their feet, wrap their arms around and worship him. Jesus commands the women to tell the male exorcists, "Go to Galilee where they will see me." These instructions are contrary to those reported in Luke (i.e., they are to remain in Jerusalem, see Luke 24:49), and so certainly reflect the earlier form of the tradition of Jesus' first encounters, i.e., since it retains the more controversial event, the exorcists "fleeing to Galilee," versus remaining in Jerusalem.

The tradition of women conversing with Jesus, as well as Mary the Magdalene having equal standing with Kayfa, are deeply rooted in early Christian literature. More, these traditions are multiply attested.[23] Conse-

---

19. See examples in Ogden, *Magic*, 64–65, 146–47, 149–52, 161–62, 164–65, on tombs and encounters with ghosts and spirits there.

20. As determined in our previous analysis of the metamorphosis of Jesus, or as in Act 10:10.

21. Phlegon of Tralles, *Mirabilia I*, in Ogden, *Magic*, 159–60.

22. If on a road, the tradition may have been created as an echo to Paul's Damascus experience. Were this the case, the encounter was during the trance.

23. See the excellent analysis of sources and the *Gospel of Mary* by King, *Gospel of Mary*, 175–76; Mary is known as an apostle in various early Christian writings, from the *Dialogue of the Savior*, *Apocalypse of James*, and the confrontation with Kayfa is

quently, the tradition that "the Lord is risen indeed and has appeared to Peter (Kayfa)"[24] should not be understood as proof the women exorcists were ignored, perhaps for days or weeks. It is not a reflection that they were simply women and their report could not stand as an "idle tale," which devalues their report in a ridiculous way given the contemporary contexts noted! Instead, until Kayfa had a post-resurrection encounter, *the male exorcists remained outsiders*, vacated of all authority, and were hunted by spies of the elite on orders of the Jerusalem elite. These men believed that Jesus had been annihilated, that they had failed. They publicly rejected and abandoned him. Any report of a post-crucifixion encounter by a male or female (so Thomas, John 20:25 by males) was *leros*, i.e., nonsense—that is until the encounter with Kayfa. Paul, like the other male exorcists listed in 1 Cor 15:1–8, traced their charismatic and divine authority to Kayfa's encounter as confirmation of inclusiveness as male *apostolos*. Consequently, until the encounter with Kayfa, primitive Christianity was strictly associated with female *apostoloi*, thus explaining the primacy of the women in the earliest traditions, and Phoebe and Junia in Paul's greetings and ascription to them as an *apostlos* and leaders in Rom 16.

So, who is this apostle, Mary the Magdalene, and what of the first post-crucifixion encounter with Jesus?

Mary Magdalene is mentioned in only one other canonical tradition prior to her ecstatic encounter with the risen Jesus, i.e., Luke 8:1–3:

> After this, Jesus traveled about from one town and village to another, proclaiming the good news of the kingdom of God. The Twelve were with him, and also some women who had been cured of evil spirits and diseases: Mary (called Magdalene) from whom seven demons had come out; Joanna the wife of Chuza, the manager of Herod's household; Susanna; and many others. These women were helping to support them out of their own means.

There are many curious elements in this tradition. First, Mary is portrayed as an itinerant follower of Jesus, traveling with the male exorcists, taking the same perilous risk as they, after having been freed of "seven demons"—that is, she had been overwhelmed by Satan.[25] Scholars have rightly challenged this tradition on the basis of careful research, detecting an attempt to devalue Mary and her role in the early church by claiming

---

recorded also in the *Gospel of Thomas*, 114. The multiple attestation of Mary's role as an apostle and women as apostles is indisputable.

24. Luke 24:34.
25. Ehrman, *Peter, Paul and Mary Magdalene*, 206–7.

she was a demonic survivor of possession.[26] However, there is much to be said for her role as an exorcist and leader of the women who were ecstatics in support of Jesus' war on Satan as it moved from village to village. There is much also to be said of the tradition in the *Gospel of Thomas*, saying 114, of her "becoming male," i.e., cutting her hair and wearing the clothing of a male exorcist, as there is evidence ascetic females neutralized their sexuality in a spiritual transition and to be equal with men.[27] Even more, instead of being possessed, she most likely instead *exorcised* seven demons, which she took into her—a common practice of exorcists and shamans, as previously described.[28] Mary was undoubtedly an exorcist *par excellence*.

Second, she is called *the Magdalene* (*Maria he kaloumene Magdalene*), which is commonly associated by many scholars with her having resided in the village of Magdala on the western shore of Galilee. The village name[29] derives from a tower there and the fish brought for market, i.e., "fish tower." This is where the various fish caught on Galilee were taken and processed, whether salted or pickled. This is also where fish oil was extracted to create popular sauces, all for export throughout the Roman Empire, generating high taxes and income for the Romans, as well as the Herodians and Jerusalem elite. Magdala was the largest settlement on the western shore prior to Herod Antipas' construction of Tiberius (about 20 CE). The location of the village and its first-century synagogue (with the oldest Menorah ever found, carved on a stone table laying within the synagogue) have been excavated, along with ritual Jewish baths still fed by springs, other buildings and a main road.[30] In this traditional view, she is to be identified as Mary *of* Magdala. Certainly, Jesus did visit this village, as it was on the main road from Nazareth to Capernaum and Bethsaida, and Mary could very well have come from this village, having obtained enough wealth to be a patron of Jesus' activity, a position now confirmed as wholly probable for first-century Jewish women.[31]

However, another and more probable translation is Mary, *the Magdalene*, which in Hebrew and Aramaic is translated "tower," the "fortress," or the "high one."[32] It is this identification that renders the proper under-

26. Kraemer, *Her Share of the Blessings*, 129–33.
27. Castelli, "Virginity and Its Meaning," 75–77.
28. See Lewis, *Ecstatic Religion*, 51–53.
29. Josephus, *War* 1, chs. 8 and 9.
30. Avshalom-Govi and Najar, "Migdal," 121–25.
31. Kraemer, *Her Share*, 174;
32. This is a very old tradition that was retained in early Christianity, even repeated by Jerome in 412 CE in his letter to Principia, recounting the life of Marcella: "and how specially Mary Magdalene—called *the Tower* the earnestness and *glow* of her faith [glow

standing of Mary's position within the original risk context, i.e., Mary's new name awarded by Jesus,[33] following successful training as an exorcist in his war on Satan. She joined in his attack on demonic pollution of the land, likely providing monetary support to Jesus' band donated by victims freed from demonic malady and possession. The name is significant and must be considered to have been equal in importance to the leader of Jesus' male exorcists, Simeon. As noted, Simeon was given the name Kayfa, "the rock," a leader of Jesus' band of exorcists. He was the rock on which Satan's power would be broken. It was he who was given the "keys," that is, the methods to access the authority and power of Jesus' Spirit, the "finger of God," to "bind and loose"[34] victims from demonic possession, whether it arose from arbitrary attack, the retribution of enemies, or divine retribution for offense (or potential for offenses)[35] against God. Mary is similarly given the name of authority over Satan, "the fortress," perhaps the original leader of the exorcists who joined Jesus' band. This name would confirm that Mary was considered a powerful exorcist, apparently having taken control of at least seven demons. Jesus may have later freed her from taking these, by his absorbing them or loosing them into Galilee or the desert wilderness.[36] Her role as a powerful exorcist, one who would have embraced perilous risk in hopes of encountering Jesus at the proper hour out of mourning, would more adequately explain why she went near the tomb with the intent of having an ecstatic experience and encounter with Jesus.

Mary is said to have "ministered (*diekonoun*)" to Jesus and his exorcists, implying she provided monetary and subsistence support. This has been interpreted not as her contributing to the common purse from donations related to her exorcisms (the most likely explanation), but being wealthy, speculating that she was a widow or matron, perhaps associated with a family business associated with the fish trade in Magdala. This was possible, as one of the women mentioned in Mary's company was Joanna,

---

here can also infer ecstatic behavior]—was privileged to see the risen Christ first of all before the very apostles" (Kraemer, *Maenads, Martyrs, Matrons*, 181).

33. See previous discussions in ch. 3, "Galilean Subsistence Fishing and Haunted Waters—From Fishers to Exorcists," and ch. 8, which describe how Jesus renamed his exorcists to give them power and authority over demons of Satan.

34. Matt 16:19.

35. Paul's thorn in the flesh, i.e., a messenger of Satan, to bring Paul to humility after his receiving multiple revelations, 2 Cor 12:7.

36. While the tradition in Mark 16:9 was late and recasts Mary as the possessed (a devaluation of her role as noted), it still may reflect an authentic tradition where Jesus would have taken these demons within himself from Mary, or set her free from them without any intent to devalue her role—it was an act that Jesus, as possessed by the Spirit, would have been able to execute for other exorcists.

the wife of Chuza, Herod Anatipas' householder (the head of financial and business affairs of the emperor or his designee), an *epitropos*, who would have had the means to support Jesus.[37] Joanna was also associated with women whom Jesus is said to have expelled demons, something Jesus would have expected given her association with Herod and demonic imperialism. Joanna could have become an acquaintance of a wealthy Mary, and met her while with her husband at Herod's royal retreat in nearby Tiberius, during or after construction and development of this elaborate pagan town.[38] Mary's income would have been heavily taxed if trading in exporting salted fish or oils. An invitation to Mary of a supportive and important patron of the Herodians and Rome would be expected. Perhaps both sought Jesus to be freed of demon-associated afflictions, and then continued to support him monetarily to remedy women of afflictions. However, there is a very dark and dangerous association that overshadows all of this speculation. If Joanna were to have been a supporter of Jesus, this would mean that Herod's fear of infiltration into his inner circle was not a paranoid illusion,[39] but a reality, making Jesus all the more dangerous a threat. Mary may have very well been a "patron to Judaism," supporting synagogue worship as a benefactor, receiving an active and important title of leadership with the local synagogue. That such roles and titles for Palestinian Jewish women were prevalent has been shown to have substantial support based on archaeology and inscriptions.[40] However, risk analysis demands further explanation related to Luke 8:1–3.

The tradition in Luke clearly suggests that Mary was not a wealthy patron, but an itinerant exorcist who traveled with Jesus from village to village in Jesus' war on Satan.[41] The living conditions of an itinerant ecstatic were subsistence level, and for women even more difficult. In the Greco-Roman world such women were considered wandering magicians and sorceresses who were to be avoided and were considered dangerous.[42] By joining with

37. *Epitropos*, was an important position, evidenced by Josephus' use of the term to describe the role of the procurators (see also Josephus, *Antiquities*, 14.143). The name Chuza has been found in Nabataean inscriptions, and so would be someone from the area from which Herod came, i.e., he was trusted and a countryman of Antipas.

38. Josephus, *Antiquities*, 18:3.2.

39. Busse, *To Be Near the Fire*, "Herod Antipas" and his fear of John and Jesus.

40. Brooten, *Women Leaders*, 15–64, 141–44; also see Kraemer, *Maenads, Martyrs, Matrons*, 27–32, 90–99.

41. It is possible to see the tradition of her support as the example of what women patrons were expected to provide "out of their means." However, Mary, as an exorcist, would have received donations, which would have contributed to the common purse. Klutz, *Exorcism Stories in Luke-Acts*, 119–21.

42. See, e.g., some traditional analyses by Gager, "Social Practice of Magic," vol. 14,

Jesus, she was counted with him and considered possessed by Satan and an evildoer. She was publicly charged with illegal black magic by very powerful enemies, and was hunted for betrayal by spies of the elite, one of whom was successful—Judas. Like Jesus, she was considered a demonic servant of Beelzebul, a deceiver and blasphemer. While wealth could explain Mary's ability to find shelter for her and the other exorcists, this is inconsistent with the risks that surrounded her itinerant travel with Jesus, as wealth was no protection from such charges, particularly that of sedition. Consequently, to conclude she was a wealthy patron fails to fit the risk context.

This allows a contextual reconstruction of *the Magdalene*, the "fortress," a leader Jesus' exorcists. Mary had embraced the perilous risk of joining in Jesus' war on Satan. She clearly knew that Jesus was hunted because he was considered possessed and a dark magician, an "evil-doer." She also knew that Jesus had made powerful enemies, which included Herod Antipas[43] and the Jerusalem elite,[44] and that Herod himself considered Jesus a conjurer of the dead and a dangerous threat. Herod believed that Jesus had raised and invoked the spirit of the beheaded John the Baptist (the Jew he had brutalized and beheaded to prevent retribution) in order to seek revenge.[45] Consequently, Mary's deliberate association with Jesus was fraught with perilous risk, which included being charged with illegal magic, capture, and execution. For Mary to travel with men, particularly those who had been demonized, was to embrace scandal and certain controversy, including charges of being a prostitute. For this reason and others noted earlier in this study, Mary could not have been a wealthy patron. Her property would have been confiscated and sold. She may have been a dispossessed subsistence worker who knew the other exorcists and embraced the opportunity to abandon that life under the harsh conditions in Galilee. More likely, Mary was a Therapeutrides, a healer who joined Jesus.

Contemporary examples confirm there were charismatic women who traveled and lived with male aesthetics and charismatics. Most interesting, these examples point to communities along lakes being healers, both men and women.[46] The Therapeutrides (20 BCE to 40 CE) included Jewish women who were aesthetics. They cut their hair, wore men's clothes (including special robes) and lived in various cities of the Graeco-Roman

---

set 1; and Dickie, *Magic and Magicians*, especially ch. 8.

43. Luke 13:32, Herod as "the fox," and Jesus, being hunted, has no where to lay his head, Luke 9:58.

44. Mark 3:6, 12:13.

45. Mark 6:14.

46. The Therapeutrides, 20 BCE–40 CE; see also Brooten, *Women Leaders*, 87–88.

world. In Alexandria, they lived along a lake, Mareotis. The name derives from the Greek word, *therapeuo*, which infers that these were women that cured maladies, i.e., in the ancient world this meant that were able to control spirits and exorcise demons and do so near lake waters. Philo (*Da Vita Contemplativa*) indicates that the Therapeutae were living in many cities and locations, perhaps including Palestine. Philo states that the name may have indicated that they were "physicians of souls as servants of God," or the gods (e.g., in pagan religion, as in association with the Therapeutae of Asclepius). Magdala was a village along the Sea of Galilee. This would explain why Mary would be living among non-kin Jewish males. In a new association of men and women in Jesus' war on Satan, it is possible that Jesus proclaimed those with him as his kin and under his protection, i.e., his true mother and brothers and sisters,[47] or that these women had become men. Saying 114 in the *Gospel of Thomas* has Jesus saying to Kayfa: "See, I will draw her so as to make her male so that she also may become a living spirit like you males. For every woman who has become male will enter the Kingdom of heaven." This saying accurately reflects why Mary, a healer and exorcist, was accepted and lived with the other males, and was on equal footing with them. And it is coherent with the Therapeutae who physically became like men. Consequently, it is evident that Mary Magdalene was a member of Jesus' exorcists, undoubtedly trained and empowered by Jesus, but who came with prior practices and powers to control demons and spirits. More, she was the exorcist that facilitated the first post-crucifixion encounters and ecstatic experiences near the tomb. But, even more, evidence demonstrates that Mary the Magdalene was one of Jesus' leaders among the exorcists.

Indeed, the leading role of *the Magdalene* is multiply attested in all layers of tradition, i.e., in the four canonical gospels,[48] noncanonical gospels,[49] esoteric writings and in Thomas.[50] She is reported as having multiple direct conversations with Jesus, both pre- and post-crucifixion. She was said to be in conflict with Kayfa, and yet considered an equal, and Jesus demands her acceptance and authority. We must conclude that Mary the Magdalene was not just considered a powerful exorcist, but was as well known as Kayfa in the primitive community for her courage, authority and close relationship with Jesus. Magdalene had not abandoned Jesus like the male exorcists (led by Kayfa, fleeing to Galilee to return to fishing). Indeed, Magdalene went to

47. Mark 3:35; Matt 12:50.
48. Mark 16:9–10; Matt 28:1–8; Luke 8:2, 24:10; John 20:18.
49. *Gospel of Mary, Codex Berolinensis* 8502; *Gospel of Phillip*; *Pistis Sophia*.
50. *Gospel of Thomas*, 114; see Gnostic Society Library, Nag Hammadi Library, *Gospel of Thomas*, translated by Stephen J. Patterson and James M. Robinson, http://gnosis.org/naghamm/gth_pat_rob.htm.

the tomb and successfully encountered Jesus. Consequently, gospel traditions of her being possessed, ordered to run and tell the men he was risen (i.e., her role being only a messenger to the men), are evidence of collusion in devaluing the role of Mary by a male-dominated hierarchical church in the late first century, that continued into the second century and beyond; just as it was for Junia, as later scribes changed her name to *Junias*, i.e., a male name. As Helmut Koester notes about Paul's list of women:

> Most of the persons named in this list are not simply personal friends of Paul in the church of Ephesus, but associates and co-workers. This is shown by the repeated references to their functions. The fact that such a large number of women appear in this list is clear and undeniable evidence for the unrestricted participation of women in the offices of the church in the Pauline congregations.[51]

In 1 Cor 14:34, Paul is said to require that women remain silent, but this passage has convincingly been shown to be a later emendation and not Pauline.[52] In 1 Cor 11:5, Paul states that women prophesied (including speaking words inspired by the risen Lord) as well as participated in ecstatic prayer, and so, had an indispensible role in the primitive community, which must have originated in Galilee and Palestine. Women leaders, such as Magdalene, Junia and Phoebe (a full letter of recommendation was written by Paul for her and her authority), held preeminent roles among the exorcists and apostles in the early Jesus movement, and one is indisputably named an apostle equal with Paul. As Luke 8:1–3 shows, Magdalene's authority over demons was feared and respected, and her relationship with Jesus was revered as equal with that of Kayfa.[53]

Matthew 28:1–10 and Qualitative Risk Analysis

With this context set, we can begin our risks analysis of the unit, employing first, qualitative risk. In this analysis, the encounter cannot be a countermeasure to the elite, but must heighten the perilous risk of the Galilean exorcists and the conflict with opponents.

Magdalene's post-crucifixion actions and the subsequent ecstatic encounter with Jesus heighten perilous risk on several levels. Risking discovery,

---

51. Bruce Robinson, "Women as Clergy," http://www.religioustolerance.org/ord_bibl.htm.

52. Koester, *Introduction*, 215.

53. *Gospel of Thomas*, 114.

capture or attack, Magdalene goes to the sealed and guarded tomb that holds the brutalized body of Jesus. She does so at the hour that spirits, demons and ghosts roam, looking for victims and souls to seize. She knows and understands this danger; that being near tombs brings contact, particularly with the untimely dead or the dead by violence seeking revenge while they wander at night. Magdalene is in perilous danger. But as an exorcist trained by Jesus, she comes to the tomb accepting the deadly risk of either conjuring or communicating with him to discover if he had been annihilated. The practices she employs were related to necromancy, the darkest of magic, and if discovered would have led to her immediate execution.[54]

For her to remain in Jerusalem was also to risk all. There was perilous danger from enemies, whether demons or the enemies that had killed Jesus, all of whom were under satanic control. Magdalene could not hide easily. She was identifiable—a Galilean with that telltale accent, wearing clothing that Jesus prescribed of his exorcists (another reason for nighttime travel and moving from place to place). She had been seen with Jesus and the exorcists.[55] Magdalene's incursion and perilous practices near the guarded tomb cannot be understood as benign.

Magdalene's ecstatic experience also heightened her perilous risk. In Matthew, the event follows a vision or more likely a "possession trance."[56] The angelic appearance signifies the tomb has been vacated, and she immediately becomes the first witness, bearing the risk of the message and recommitment to the war on Satan—but she stands alone at this point and is completely vulnerable. The Matthean redactor attempts to neutralize her perilous risk and standing. Her role is simply to be a messenger, traveling a short distance to the male exorcists in Jerusalem, which significantly devalues both Magdalene's importance and the significance of her encounter.[57]

54. Jesus' "laying on of hands" described in detail above, including using mixtures of spittle and mud to exorcise demons; Mark 7:33, 8:23; John 9:6; Luke 8:55; this food was likely herbs or roots to sustain her spirit's return after Jesus cast out the demon of death, i.e., the translation can be the "he prescribed she be given something to eat."

55. Luke 9:3; Matt 10:10.

56. For characteristics of a possession trance, which includes introducing artificial means to produce the trance (such as spices, roots or herbs), see Aune, *Prophecy*, 20–22. These are typically associated with prophetic experience, but in this case, Mary became prophetic by spreading the news of her vision and the vision's meaning, then relating it to the encounter. Christian prophets, described by Paul in 1 Cor, also may have had similar experiences (Paul himself), in visions and revelations, which were then adopted as sayings of the risen Lord, paranesis and instruction, or clarification for the benefit of the community. Aune confirms that these traits were prevalent in the Graeco-Roman and Jewish worlds.

57. The same fate is found in the tradition of Jesus and the Samaritan woman, John 4:1–42. According to my discussion with Stephen Patterson in 2013, Jesus' discussion

Magdalene encounters Jesus and reports the experience first to the other women. Now her perilous risk is dramatically heightened. She becomes a witness that the "evil-doer" Jesus is active despite the efforts of the religious elite and Roman sympathizers to annihilate him. She thus becomes complicit as a participant in the return of Jesus, the dark magician and one of the untimely dead; the servant of Beelzebul who was most certainly going to seek revenge against his enemies. Mary's action therefore meets the test of qualitative risk analysis.

Matthew 28:1–10 and the Criteria of Dissimilarity and Embarrassment

In this test, encounters must differ from the needs of the early church on the one hand and the context of first-century Judaism in Palestine on the other. To accurately test the tradition, the most original form of the unit should be employed, as best as can be recovered. Analysis has confirmed that the unit in Matt 28:1–10 differed significantly from the current structure. The core tradition recovered by risk analysis (i.e., that Mary was herself an exorcist and not that she had demons exorcised, as held by most scholars)[58] is therefore markedly different from the needs of the early church in that her role as an exorcist (and that tradition as a whole) was devalued and made subservient to the traditions of the male exorcists. But can we say that the recovered tradition differs from the context of first-century Palestinian Judaism?

Based on contextual and risk analysis recovered, Mary is a trained exorcist of Jesus. Like Kayfa, she is given a new exorcist's name, *the Magdalene*, the fortress, having overcome and taken control of multiple (i.e., seven) demons. Magdalene becomes an itinerant exorcist and charismatic with Jesus, taking the risk of participating in his war on Satan and on demonic imperialism, traveling from village to village, driving out demonic possession. Other women are added as exorcists (at least four) to Jesus' band. They contribute to the common purse by sharing their donations for cures and exorcisms.

Magdalene was not wealthy, not a harlot, nor a Jewish patron. She lived a subsistence existence among the fishing villages of Galilee until she

---

with her, based on the Greek used, is harsh, but the tenor of the tradition is that she is like an *apostolos*.

58. See Adna, "Encounter of Jesus," 299–300. Adna cites the tradition of exorcism of demons from Mary, and that scholars, such as Meier, *Marginal Jew*, find that it has a reasonable claim as historical following detailed inquiry. However, risk analysis has recovered the original context and tradition, which has been subjugated by a male-dominated church hierarchy that owes its authority to traditions of Kayfa's encounter with Jesus.

encountered Jesus, or was a Therapeutae. Her fate has been lost to history, but traditions as to her importance in the early risk encounters with demons and demonic imperialism, as well as crucifixion and her incursion at the tomb, are found in some capacity in all layers of the tradition. This multiple attestation confirms that Magdalene's risk activities held a prominent place in the early Christian movement, and even in their original form (i.e., before subjugation by male leaders) were recited and orally circulated, i.e., they were thought to have been instrumental in the formation of the early movement through her first encounter and subsequent interaction with Jesus, post-crucifixion. As such, Magdalene's role is unlike any known in contemporary Judaism. While there are some similarities with Graeco-Roman women sorceresses and charismatics, the closest similarity within Judaism is with women of rabbinic families who are said to have had charismatic authority. However, there is no contemporary correlation. The conclusion must be that the tradition of Mary, the fortress and exorcist, is dissimilar to Palestinian Judaism. Consequently, this tradition *passes* the test of the criterion of dissimilarity.

With regard to the criterion of embarrassment, it is clear that the traditions of Magdalene became problematic, as they are devalued and made subservient to the traditions associated of the male exorcists, both in the canonical and extrabiblical literature. Later traditions include esoteric sayings and confrontation with Kayfa.[59] While the revised tradition in Matthew and the other canonical gospels make Magdalene the catalyst of communication with the male exorcists, this trend only confirms that these traditions were problematic. Paul excludes her encounter completely. As such, the traditions related to Magdalene's encounter meet the criterion of embarrassment.

Summary of Risk Analysis

An analysis of Matt 28:1–10 has isolated the original form of the unit by employing the criteria of risk analysis. Based on this analysis, the event may be considered reliable in this revised form, subject to passing the remaining contextual tests.

---

59. *Gospel of Thomas*, 114; see Patterson, *Gospel of Thomas*, 249–51. In a discussion with Steve Patterson, August 19, 2015, we discussed the charismatic nature of the *Gospel of Thomas*, and the ecstatic nature that stood behind sayings tradition, i.e., in visions and revelations, that must have accompanied them. These sayings were likely part of visionary experiences, and so an ecstatic background to the *Gospel of Thomas* and it sapiential material must be considered.

Matthew 28:1–10 and the Contextual Tests

We now turn to contextual analyses. Here an event must be coherent with the sociological risk setting, including the subsistence struggle of the Galileans, the background from which they came to join Jesus' band of exorcists. Once again, the contextual risk tests previously established are as follows:

1. Encounters with original members of Jesus' band of Galilean exorcists, those who faced capture, death and social isolation and starvation, are given priority.

2. Encounters should be consistent with the ecstatic practices of Jesus that engendered the original perilous risk with his opponents. Specifically, encounters that encouraged the remaining exorcists to continue the ecstatic activity of Jesus and his war on Satan are preferred.

3. Encounters near or on the lake of Galilee, particularly related to subsistence fishing, and similar to the animistic control exhibited by Jesus, are preferential (i.e., the remaining exorcists escaped there).

4. Finally, encounters that may have led the Galileans to again abandon subsistence existence (i.e., to which they returned for survival post-crucifixion) are also preferred.

In each of the foregoing tests, the original form of the unit recovered through risk analysis is evaluated.

Applying these contextual tests to the original tradition recovered from Matt 28:1–10, given the risk analysis of Magdalene as an exorcist of Jesus (Luke 8:1–3), and employing the criteria of dissimilarity and embarrassment, the tradition clearly passes the first two tests.

With regard to the third, there is no evidence in the canonical gospels that Magdalene returned to subsistence existence as an exorcist, or to activity related to subsistence fishing in Galilee.[60] However, the report of Magdalene's encounter with Jesus must have been impactful to the original band of exorcists, as the tradition is multiply attested (the Synoptics and John) and is also found in noncanonical sources. Magdalene must have contacted the male exorcists in Galilee, certainly their leader, Kayfa, for this is remembered in all traditions. The risk criteria employed also confirm its impact. Both the *Gospel of Thomas* and the *Gospel of Mary* report Magdalene's discussion with Kayfa and other exorcists as to her interaction with Jesus

---

60. That the tradition has Jesus ordering Mary to tell the exorcists to go to Galilee (not to a hiding place in Jerusalem—as noted, a Lucan creation that conflicts with Mark, Matthew and John 20:17) that is a later addition, this is where the exorcists escaped who fled.

post-crucifixion, and Jesus' defense of Magdalene as an equal to the male exorcists, i.e., her becoming male.[61] Her presence with them would indicate that Magdalene continued to be considered an exorcist post-crucifixion. Consequently, contextual evidence suggests that Magdalene was considered an exorcist. She likely never abandoned her role as such. Elements of the tradition, based on risk analysis, would indicated that she reported that Jesus was active; that she had a vision at the tomb and then encountered Jesus, not as a ghost, but in a substantive form, whether in a vision or trance.[62] This tradition therefore passes the third test.

The last test evaluates whether encounters with Jesus, post-crucifixion, led the Galileans to again abandon subsistence existence and return to their war on Satan. Here we must count Magdalene fully as one of the Galilean exorcists whose perilous risk was heightened following her encounter with Jesus. While there is no confirmation that Magdalene continued exorcism in the synoptic tradition or in John, extra-canonical traditions confirm that Magdalene was an active and influential member among the remaining exorcists in Galilee and provided instruction to them about her vision of Jesus and her continuing relationship with him. The communication is portrayed as prior to their reengagement in their itinerant activity—indeed that she was a catalyst for doing so. The tradition of this influence is best captured in the *Gospel of Mary*, which is a fragmented document of the second century,[63] but may have traditions that predate the canonical gospels.[64]

Gospel of Mary, Chapter 5:

1. But they were grieved. They wept greatly, saying: How shall we go to the Gentiles and preach the gospel of the Kingdom of the Son of Man? If they did not spare Him, how will they spare us?

2. Then Mary stood up, greeted them all, and said to her brethren, Do not weep and do not grieve nor be irresolute, for His grace will be entirely with you and will protect you.

---

61. If she becomes like a "male," i.e., what was perceived in the ancient world as the complete human being reflected in male form. See Meyer, "Making Mary Male," 554–70. For this she would have cut her hair and wore male clothing. See below on the discussion of the *Gospel of Mary* and the analysis by Karen King.

62. As noted, encounters with the active spirits of the dead included material activity and contact.

63. King, *Gospel of Mary*, 148, argues for composition between 30–130 CE.

64. King, *Gospel of Mary*.

3. But rather, let us praise His greatness, for He has prepared us and made us into Men.

4. When Mary said this, she turned their hearts to the Good, and they began to discuss the words of the Savior.

5. Peter said to Mary, Sister we know that the Savior loved you more than the rest of woman.

6. Tell us the words of the Savior, which you remember which you know, but we do not, nor have we heard them.

7. Mary answered and said: What is hidden from you I will proclaim to you.

8. And she began to speak to them these words: I, she said, I saw the Lord in a vision and I said to Him, Lord I saw you today in a vision. He answered and said to me,

9. Blessed are you that you did not waver at the sight of Me. For where the mind is there is the treasure.

10. I said to Him, Lord, how does he who sees the vision see it, through the soul or through the spirit?

11. The Savior answered and said, He does not see through the soul nor through the spirit, but the mind that is between the two that is what sees the vision and it is [. . .]

Chapter 9

1. When Mary had said this, she fell silent, since it was to this point that the Savior had spoken with her.

2. But Andrew answered and said to the brethren, Say what you wish to say about what she has said. I at least do not believe that the Savior said this. For certainly these teachings are strange ideas.

3. Peter answered and spoke concerning these same things.

4. He questioned them about the Savior: Did He really speak privately with a woman and not openly to us? Are we to turn about and all listen to her? Did He prefer her to us?

5. Then Mary wept and said to Peter, My brother Peter, what do you think? Do you think that I have thought this up myself in my heart, or that I am lying about the Savior?

6. Levi answered and said to Peter, Peter you have always been hot tempered.
7. Now I see you contending against the woman like the adversaries.
8. But if the Savior made her worthy, who are you indeed to reject her? Surely the Savior knows her very well.
9. That is why He loved her more than us. Rather let us be ashamed and put on the perfect Man, and separate as He commanded us and preach the gospel, not laying down any other rule or other law beyond what the Savior said.
10. And when they heard this they began to go forth to proclaim and to preach.

A review of this tradition alone confirms that Magdalene was believed to have influenced the return to subsistence existence as exorcists and *apostoloi* of Jesus, post-crucifixion. As such, the last contextual test is also passed.

Conclusions on the Veracity of Matthew 28:1–10

Based on the risk and analytical criteria employed, combined with contextual analysis, the tradition that stands behind Matt 28:1–10 should be considered an authentic post-crucifixion encounter with Jesus. In the context of human risk experience, this encounter with Magdalene is reliable in its recovered contemporary context and setting. The order of appearances then is emerging.

Magdalene, "the fortress," a powerful Galilean female exorcist of Jesus that had taken control of multiple demons, has been abandoned in Jerusalem post-crucifixion. All of the male exorcists fled to Galilee and are in hiding. Magdalene, desperate to determine the fate of her master, goes to the tomb, facing deadly perilous risks. She intentionally arrives at the very time spirits, demons and evil are active and seek victims. This is also the time to engage in special rites to rescue the spirit and soul of Jesus. She brings special herbs and roots of the exorcist and then enters into a trance. An angel confirms Jesus' spirit has vacated the tomb and that he is free and active—he has not been annihilated under a curse. Magdalene's rites and activity at the tomb facilitates the return of Jesus by the power of the spirit that possesses him, the *daktuo theou*. Magdalene encounters Jesus. While the tradition is that she is to immediately contact the male exorcists, this tradition is clearly a subjugation of the Magdalene's encounter. Magdalene's perilous risk is significantly heightened. She has contacted a condemned dark magician executed by the powerful elite and now publicly admits she has been in contact with him. Her life is in danger, and if captured, she would be immediately stoned or killed. She escapes to Galilee and locates the male exorcists, still in hiding, protected by kin, working as fishermen through the night to avoid discovery. Magdalene communicates her encounter. There is no doubt at her report, and she begins to encourage a return to Jesus' war on Satan and demonic imperialism. Magdalene confirms that Jesus would contact them in Galilee.

Kayfa, the leader of the male exorcists, has returned to subsistence life on Galilee, hiding and working through the night to help feed himself and his kin. His perilous risk is significantly heightened by his escape, and his abandonment of Jesus to his enemies. Kayfa is now subject to capture and death, or attack by demons he expelled since he is no longer under the protection of Jesus and the "finger of God." He had also abandoned Jesus to demonic enemies and to satanic forces. Kayfa faces retribution. While on Galilee, Kayfa encounters the spirit of Jesus who approaches and communicates with Kayfa. Soon afterward, Kayfa goes to the sacred mountain where he and other exorcists had been selected and then trained by Jesus to be ecstatics and exorcists. He may bring others with him and enters into a trance where he encounters Jesus. Kayfa and the remaining male exorcists decide to abandon subsistence existence on Galilee and reenter the war on Satan. The list of practices to be embraced by the exorcists is then delineated through an encounter with Jesus, defining the authentic witnesses to Jesus, post-crucifixion, i.e., they must demonstrate these charismatic practices to be counted among the valid *apostoloi*.

These traditions represent the nascent post-crucifixion events that led to encounters with Jesus.

Matthew 28:16–20: Mass Visions and Trances in the Ancient World

Jesus is "seen," or is "perceived (*idontes*)," by the "eleven" (i.e., purportedly, the remaining male Galilean exorcists that fled Jerusalem *sans* Judas) on a mountain in Galilee. Who led them there or why they went to that particular mountain location is not fully explained, only that Jesus had "told them." Yet, curiously, the women who encountered Jesus after the crucifixion and were given instructions in v. 10 were also not provided a specific location in Galilee to pass on to the "brothers (*adelphois*)." Although, not named, some of the eleven "doubt (*de edistasan*)," meaning they do not believe they encountered Jesus, or the same Jesus, whether materially, in a vision or trance—*a shocking admission*. This implies that there were those of repute (i.e., of the original exorcists of Jesus—not necessarily those in the final lists of apostles named in Mark 3:13–19, Matt 10:2, Luke 6:12–19)[65] who doubt that they encountered Jesus post-crucifixion in one of these forms, and so, refused to embrace the same mitigating practices of perilous risks as the other exorcists who had. From the tradition of Jesus' metamorphosis (Mark 9:2–8, as noted, a post-crucifixion encounter),[66] we do know the names of three who reputably are said to have encountered Jesus—Kayfa and *Boanerges*, i.e., Yohannes, or Yecob, the "sons of thunder."[67] Yet, why was such a troubling oral tradition of doubt retained some fifty-five years after the crucifixion (80 to 85 CE) when Matthew was compiled by its editor/redactor? What risks existed within the Matthean community that necessitated such dramatic mitigation by retaining a tradition of doubt among the eleven; even more, why then crystallize it in a community document that was read to its members and to proselytes in charismatic gatherings?[68] While the scope of this study cannot reconstruct the Matthean community or its practices, it can examine specific risks.

Clearly, this tradition served a risk function in the Matthean community for some time. To evaluate how it functioned as a countermeasure, the tradition must be analyzed contextually. The most obvious explanation for its retention is rather stunning; namely, that some of Jesus' chosen exorcists (i.e., the original Galileans trained by Jesus) did not have (or were later claimed to not have had) a post-crucifixion encounter where Jesus was present—whether a *phantasm* that was seen with the eyes or present in another form, such as a spiritual journey or trance.[69] Rather, they had an alternate ecstatic, transformational encounter; one that was considered dangerous to the Matthean community.

---

65. See the discussion of the identity of the "twelve" being the same as Jesus' exorcists or others that became known as "The Twelve" in Koester, "History," 8–10. In fact, the Twelve mentioned by Paul in 1 Cor 15:5 cannot be exactly identical to the eleven who went to the mountain here in Matthew. Paul recounts that the Twelve were with Kayfa, and all were witnesses to the resurrection, active in defending this witness (i.e., many still available to confirm their experience). Matthew allows that some of the original exorcists did not believe they had encountered Jesus, and so, those listed in Matt 10:2 likely reflect the list of those who witnessed and did not doubt, drawn from the "disciples" who followed Jesus and named by Kayfa as the Twelve. See Jenott, *Gospel of Judas*, 40–44.

66. See discussion above on Mark 9:2–8 recovered by risk and contextual analysis.

67. Two of these are confirmed by Paul in Gal 2:9.

68. Hengel, *Four Gospels*, 19–20.

69. Such as Paul's journey to the third heaven, i.e., "whether in the body or not, I don't know" (2 Cor 12:2–3).

Paul's letters, particularly in 1 and 2 Corinthians, confirm a tension between claims of authority linked to various post-resurrection encounters and the practices they engendered. For example, his chronological list of encounters in 1 Cor 15:1–9 attempts to mute his opponents' claims to legitimacy by linking an encounter with Jesus to the legitimacy of Paul's gospel and his rites as an *apostolos*. Yet, Paul's own post-crucifixion encounters with Jesus were different than those reported in Luke, Matthew and Mark, as well as John. Paul's multiple encounters appear to have been *both* visionary (trance-like experiences and spirit transportation)[70] as well as substantive (*opthe*, that is, Paul saw Jesus *with his own eyes*).[71] They also include revelations, including spiritual insight, paranesis, and the understanding of mysteries and hidden secrets given to him by Jesus.[72] The *Gospel of Thomas* would suggest that there were other ecstatic experiences considered just as legitimate, and ones that were not reliant on an apocalyptic *Parousia* and future judgment, or reliance on a Galilean encounter. Instead, a union with the divine was realized immediately through mystical encounter with Jesus' words as the "living" one, where charismatic sayings awakened one's spirit and were salvific—a mysterious (if not magical) transformation by encountering the heavenly wisdom in esoteric sayings of the divine one, reuniting one's soul with God.[73]

One of Jesus' exorcists, *Toma* (the "twin," a name given by Jesus,[74] in Greek, *didymas*), is said to have been the source and authority for such esoteric wisdom sayings and practices passed to him by Jesus. Salvific esoteric wisdom trajectories, such as that in the *Gospel of Thomas*, are found in the earliest strata of tradition, originating perhaps during Jesus' charismatic activity in Galilee.[75] In 51 to 54 CE, Paul encounters well-established and popular "super-apostles (*huper apostolon*)" carrying persuasive letters of recommendation on their behalf (2 Cor 3:1, possibly from James, brother

70. Even Acts continues this tradition five decades later, Acts 9:1–19.

71. Gal 1:15–16; 1 Cor 9:1; 15:1–9, 50–54 (not a body of flesh and blood, but a spiritual body); 1 Cor 12:2 (the visit to the third heaven)

72. 1 Cor 13:2; 14:2; 15:5; 2 Cor 12:1–7; also 1 Thess 4:17; Rom 16:25; also in the sense of gnosis, special knowledge, 1 Cor 12:8, but given by the Spirit. Paul's receiving instructions from Jesus, 1 Cor 7:1–12; 11:23.

73. See the discussion below on the *Gospel of Thomas* and Stephen Patterson's research and conclusions.

74. This may have also been an exorcist name awarded by Jesus, i.e., the "twin" being Jesus' twin, an exorcist who shares the same authority and power.

75. An example is in Davies, *Gospel of Thomas*, xxxiv and xxxv, sayings 14 and 53. Also see Kloppenborg et al., *Q-Thomas Reader*, 102, saying 65, the parable of the wicked tenants, a familiar situation in Galilee. Both Q and Thomas may have originated from a common salvific wisdom tradition of Jesus' sayings. See Patterson, "Wisdom in Q," 194.

of Jesus, or Kayfa),[76] who may have espoused the salvific *logoi* tradition ultimately captured in Thomas. Paul's vigorous confrontation with these *huper apostolon* in 1 and 2 Corinthians includes his mimicking of esoteric sayings similar to those in Thomas, or in a primitive version of Q that stood behind the final version of Q and Thomas.[77] As Koester notes, "The basis of the Gospel of Thomas is a sayings collection which is more primitive than the canonical gospels, even though its basic principal is not related to the creed of the passion and resurrection."[78] Thomas has no expectation of a general resurrection to come; access to the divine is already present in the charismatic *logoi* of Jesus. The Matthean community is one that rejected the legitimacy of any *apostoloi* who did not experience a substantive, if not physical, resurrection encounter with Jesus (as defined above) as well as initiate new followers with baptism, a mystery rite of unification with the divine. Only these *apostoloi* had been given the right, through these certain rituals and practices, to effect escape from perilous risk of death and annihilation of the soul. Consequently, Matt 28:17 confirms there were competing risk traditions about Jesus post-crucifixion among those who followed him. These risk traditions created conflict among vying communities and their ecstatic rites—rites that afforded safety and protection from evil, demonic pollution and death. The countermeasure was to reject what were considered errant communities and deny the legitimacy of their leaders—something Paul experienced from powerful opponents.[79] He was tersely rejected by the "super-apostles," and earlier by men (false brothers, *psuedadelphous*) sent by James,[80] both of whom (just like the Matthean community) practiced charismatic baptism. Consequently, it is important to further explore the command of Jesus to baptize embedded in the Matthean encounter.

For those exorcists that continue with the visionary encounter on the mountain, Jesus approaches (*proselthon*) and makes a demand: "Having gone [Go!], instruct and make adherents [*mathetuesate*][81] of all people, bap-

---

76. By implication, persuasive letters, like those of the super-apostles, must have come from those of substantive reputation, i.e., from Jesus' brother, James, or others of belonging to Jesus' original exorcists, including Kayfa or even Mary.

77. Patterson, *Gospel of Thomas*, 245–46, 257, and "Paul and the Jesus Tradition," 23–41. Koester believes that 1 Cor 2:9 was from an early version of Q. See *Trajectories*, 158–204, and *Ancient Christian Gospels*, 58–59. The saying of Jesus would indicate that competing views of its meaning are in play very early.

78. Koester, *Trajectories*, 186.

79. Thus the accusations against Paul in Galatians, 1 and 2 Corinthians.

80. Gal 2:4, 11–13.

81. Greek, imperative form—teach, inform, in this case give them understanding that, when accompanied by powerful rites, is risk transformative.

tizing them. . . ." This encounter and the accompanying demand is similar to contemporary examples in the Graeco-Roman world with the untimely dead and the dead by violence, where the restless spirit of the deceased makes demands on living relatives, or others, in order to find rest or to seek retribution on enemies.[82] Here, Jesus, makes a similar demand on his exorcists—but in this case they are commanded to remain itinerant exorcists whose primary role is now to perform an ecstatic, mystical rite that is founded on something unique to these other encounters—a charismatic act of love, not revenge; to rescue[83] those who are possessed and afflicted from the demon-possessed and Satan, in fact, even those who killed him, if they will. Instead of retribution, this post-crucifixion encounter with Jesus remarkably demands *agape*, which can only reflect a core teaching that echoes the message and practices of the historical Jesus, particularly when we employ Koester's criterion.[84] It is this unique response of love that differentiated the itinerancy of Jesus' exorcists from other magicians, exorcists, ecstatics and sorcerers who interacted with or were controlled by the spirits of the dead.[85] There are no other contemporaneous examples of instructions like these given to the living by those killed by violence. This command and its link to baptism must be considered reliable and a legitimate extension of Jesus' war on Satan by the itinerant exorcists who continued his conflict after this encounter. This became the bridge between the Jesus of history and the post-crucifixion experiences of Jesus by certain exorcists who practiced *agape*, love.

In Matthew, Jesus orders a mystical baptism of unification with powerful, divine names. Baptism, undoubtedly similar to the baptism of John,[86] is a substantive transformational rite, and may also have been accompanied by recitation of other sacred words. As such, baptism unites the disciple/learner with divine protection from perilous risks and death. They are to be immersed in water by legitimate *apostoloi*, those who are charismatics having had encounters with Jesus. For Matthew, legitimate charismatics and teachers of Jesus' words and wisdom, post-crucifixion, must baptize concurrent with these names being pronounced to enact a powerful union, a

---

82. Ogden, *Magic*, 146–48, 158, 322–23, and there are several other examples provided by Ogden.

83. And thus, mitigate perilous risk.

84. Koester, *From Jesus to the Gospels*, 231.

85. Herod assumed the spirit of the murdered John the Baptist had been taken by Jesus for retribution against him, Mark 6:16.

86. The baptism of John led Jesus to have an ecstatic experience and hear the voice of God, and then be driven to confront Satan in the demon-controlled hills of Judea, Mark 1:9–11.

new being, joined with and under the protection of the Father (the *Abba* of Jesus), *Abba's* spirit that empowered the exorcist Jesus (i.e., the "finger of God" who gives Jesus *pasa exousia*, unlimited authority, Matt 28:18), and the "Son" who is active and maintains this authority to abolish demons and cast out the curse that brings death. Such ritual acts "in the name of" were intentional,[87] that is, they extended the power of that entity to the individual receiving rites, thereby becoming united in the sense of imbuing, or saturating the initiate with divine protection, including the *immediate* award of authority that will be (or in some cases *is*) a countermeasure to death.[88] This form of baptism was a fully charismatic and ecstatic countermeasure, an act of unison and protection from evil and satanic forces, including as noted possession or the disease of death that led to the capture or annihilation of the spirit. Those receiving this baptism allow the adherent to achieve protection now, and if they die, to "sleep," only to be awakened when the general resurrection comes, which was immanent—an expectation held by Paul and Jesus.[89]

However, the post-crucifixion encounter and command of Jesus in Matt 28:16–20 to baptize points to the confrontation between various groups and trajectories that associated their safety with itinerant "apostles" or "fathers (*pateras*)"[90] who baptized them in primitive Christian *ecclesiae*; a confrontation that is evident in conflict between Paul and his opponents in 1 and 2 Corinthians. Paul is accused of being a false apostle, a charlatan—he does not require baptism and does not baptize.[91] Paul's saving "gospel" is in the mercy of the cross and its power—the death, burial and resurrection of Jesus (1 Cor 15:1–3)—and the *parousia* to come for those who suffer, hold fast to faith in the risen Son, and evidence the transformation to salvation by practicing love. The sacrifice of Jesus breaks the curse of death, brought on by sin that kills.[92] His sacrifice[93] holds out a promise of justification at

---

87. See Paul in 1 Cor 1:13 as an example.

88. These rites could also bring punishment and a curse of destruction, such as Paul's spirit transport to Corinth and condemnation in the name of Jesus in 1 Cor 5:4. There is no doubt that Paul practiced the use of Jesus' name in rites. This is exactly what is occurring mystically in this example.

89. 1 Thess 4:16; 1 Thessalonians was the earliest writing now found in the New Testament, written by Paul between 42–49 CE. A saying of Jesus: "Some of you standing here will not taste death until they see the kingdom of God coming with power" (Mark 9:1).

90. 1 Cor 4:15.

91. 1 Cor 1:14, 17.

92. For Paul, the curse is revealed and made active by the law, evoking death.

93. 1 Cor 5:17.

judgment for those who wait in faith for the return of Jesus as messiah, i.e., Jesus the *Christos*. When the *Parousia* occurs, a transformation into a spiritual body (*soma pneumatikon*), presumably like that of Jesus (seen by Paul), occurs for the faithful (1 Cor 15:44). Consequently, safety is justification by faith (like the faith of Jesus), the countermeasure to death, not in rites of baptism.

For Paul's opponents in Corinth, the "super-apostles" (2 Cor 11:5) and their followers who are already "kings" (i.e., in a state of union with the divine and freedom from death, 1 Cor 4:8), baptism is the essential, transformational mystical rite. Baptism must be conducted by special apostles; i.e., those who are the conduits of passage from death to life (where baptism is central in an initiation to safety). Baptism in these apostles' names unites the initiate with the divine immediately. Perilous risks, including death of the soul, are neutralized—one is no longer bonded to death.[94] Initiates find awakening in the *logoi* of Jesus. Paul goes so far as to recast an opponent's use of a saying of Jesus in 1 Cor 2:9, a saying similar to the *Gospel of Thomas* 17:

> I shall give you what no eye has seen and what no ear has heard and what no hand has touched and what has never occurred to the human mind. (*Thomas* 17)

The saying is about the awakening, revealing one's true state as united with the divine, the child, an androgynous being. For Paul, this saying is comprehensible only if understood in the context of his "gospel" of death, burial and resurrection, and thus, the future *Parousia*.[95] He executes a curse on anyone teaching otherwise![96] Paul's opponents share a similar trajectory to that reflected in Matthew, as Jesus further instructs, "teach[ing] [those baptized] to keep [or to act on] whatever I direct." The words of Jesus, indeed the divine wisdom and protection they provide (e.g., like the "living one" in Thomas), take the prominent position in Matt 28. Consequently, it is possible that the Matthean tradition reflects an ongoing confrontation with the Pauline *ecclesiae* (baptism was optional) and the legitimacy of Paul's "gospel." The Matthean community may have been more akin to the community of Thomas than thought, although a post-crucifixion encounter with Jesus was the link to legitimate baptism by its *apostoloi*. What may be evident is a primitive battle for orthodoxy.

---

94. Patterson, *Gospel of Thomas and Christian Origins*, 28, 31, 121, 137–38, 249–51.
95. Ibid., 251–58.
96. Gal 1:8. It is for this reason that Betz calls Galatians a "magical" book (see Betz, "Letter to the Galatians," 352-53.)

The location of the Mathean encounter is the sacred mountain in Galilee, the modern *Har Tavor*,[97] which, based on the number of events on this mountain,[98] must have been well known to the exorcists and the primitive community who later visited in the hopes of having a similar ecstatic experience.[99] The well-developed oral tradition repeated by Paul in 1 Cor 15:1–5 states that Kayfa and then the "twelve" saw Jesus. In Matthew we have eleven. So who then are these twelve?

The paid informant and assassin, Judas, had been killed,[100] and we know of one to three who did ultimately see Jesus based on traditional reminiscences of the metamorphosis (as noted, likely only Kayfa has this vision). The names of the twelve vary in the canonical lists. Acts 1:12–26 confirms that others were added to complete the twelve, using divination by lots,[101] a practice also used by the high priest to settle questions, as the lots were influenced by God. The redactor/editor of Matthew brings consistency to the events following the crucifixion by eliminating Judas, implying that eleven remained, that is until some doubted! As such, it is entirely likely that Jesus did select twelve, for as Koester notes, later practices of those who followed Jesus reflect the practices that the person established; so the sacred and mystical reconstitution of the kingdom of God and Israel's twelve tribes, being rescued from Satan's demons, is suggested and retained by Matthew. However, this does not confirm that twelve went to the sacred mountain.

---

97. Likely, Mt. Tabor (*Har Tavor*), held to be sacred by Jews (Ps 89:12) and pagans (Baal Tabor, Hos 5:1), like Mt. Hermon. See Freyne, *Jesus*, 57. Not as in Luke the Mount of Olives (as has been demonstrated, the editor/redactor of Luke wishes to show the Jesus movement having successfully spread from Jerusalem to Rome). Galilee is where the earliest tradition states the exorcists encountered Jesus. Risk analysis has demonstrated that this tradition coincides with the escape of the exorcists from Jerusalem, abandoning Mary, and perhaps other women exorcists behind. The Lucan theology attempts to smooth over the embarrassment of their abandonment of Jesus and flight to Galilee by having them remain in Jerusalem.

98. The selection and training of the exorcists; the location of Jesus ecstatic prayer and retreats to solitude for days; the metamorphosis of Jesus and trance of the Kayfa; the teaching to the exorcists and others to name the most prominent.

99. The location was attested in the early second century as 2 Pet 1:17–18 includes this tradition, which predates the letter likely by decades. In addition, pilgrims to Mt. Tabor for example, may have been visiting sites on this mountain as early as the second century, but is well attested by the fourth century, including visits by Melito Bisphop of Sardis, Origen, and Alexander from Cappadocia. See Charlesworth, *Jesus and Archaeology*, 167–68.

100. See Busse, *To Be Near the Fire*, "The Assassin"

101. Luijendijk, *Forbidden Oracles?*, 2–3. This is a fascinating analysis of a Coptic codex of oracles "retrieving them through a divinatory procedure ascribed by lot."

There is no evidence of a spiritual journey (versus a physical excursion) by vision or trance to the sacred mountain here. The trip is portrayed as physical. However, this is the place where visionary experiences did occur, including the visionary trance of Kayfa, and the visionary experience of John in the *Apocalypse of John the Theologian*. Origen (184 to 150 CE) quotes the *Gospel according to the Hebrews*, where Jesus says that the Holy Spirit had driven him (pulled by the hair) to *Har Tavor*.[102] These traditions continued well into the fourth century.[103] Thus, travel to the sacred mountain is emphasized, as it was most likely a well-known destination to the Matthean community that may have resided in Antioch, Syria.[104] When they arrived, a vision or trance experience is possible.

Since pagans and Jews considered *Har Tavor* a sacred mountain, for the exorcists to physically go to this place (some 17 miles from Capernaum for example) would constitute substantial risk, i.e., they accepted the risk of being seen, which, since they were hunted, would indicate that their perilous risk was heightened. It is possible that their travel was at night to reduce the chance of discovery (as they did when returning to subsistence fishing). Travel to this sacred mountain by several exorcists would have been suspicious and contrary to the Roman restriction of the gathering of any size group,[105] particularly Galileans.

The context of this tradition is complex. We now turn to risk analysis of Matt 28:16–20.

Matthew 28:16–20 and Qualitative Risk Analysis

With this context set, we can begin our risks analysis of the unit, employing first, qualitative risk. In this analysis, the encounter cannot be a countermeasure to the elite, but must heighten the perilous risk of the Galilean exorcists and the conflict with opponents.

Evidence of heightened risks for the Galilean exorcist is layered in the tradition. The travel to the sacred mountain and need to avoid detection and capture shortly after Jesus' crucifixion; the encounter with Jesus and his demand not only to continue itinerant travel and illegal activity as exorcists,

---

102. Charlesworth, *Archaeology*, 173.

103. Ibid., 173–75.

104. Kloppenberg, *Excavating Q*, 172: "The facts that Q was used by Matthew, whose provenance my be Syrian, and it bears some relationship to the Gospel of Thomas, which may have come from Syria (Koester 1971a: 127–8; Arnal 1995), might invite the conclusion that Q was composed in an area adjacent to Syria."

105. Livy, *Founding of the City*, 39.14.

but to conduct a very public mystical rite where abundant water was available, i.e., where people would gather, including spies and sympathizers of the Herodians in Palestine (but not out of Palestine). Initiates are to be baptized in the name of a crucified Jewish criminal now identified as the "Son of God," repeating this name and designation in association with a pseudonym of God, Father, as well as the Spirit, making Jesus the Son equal to God, a blasphemy. The danger involved in all of these activities is perilous and, therefore, passes the test of qualitative risk analysis.

Matthew 28:16–20 and the Criteria of Dissimilarity and Embarrassment

In this test, encounters must differ from the needs and influence of the early church on the one hand and first-century Judaism in Palestine on the other.

To begin, the tradition has been redacted to fit the needs of the early church. The presumption of the baptism and use of the names in association with such a public event would fit the contextual world of a Syrian, Matthean community some fifty years after the crucifixion of Jesus. Syrian Antioch became a center of Christian activity at this time, and as noted, was the area in which both a primitive version of an esoteric sayings tradition was composed, one that stood behind both Q and Thomas. The "doubt" of some of the eleven would fit the context of a tradition, such as the gospel ascribed to Toma, Didymas, where he, one of the eleven exorcists renamed by Jesus, was identified by a community as the source of these traditions and their authority—a competing tradition to that of Matthew—that's why he is typified as the "doubter" in later traditions. The redactor/editor of Matthew would only acknowledge doubt among the eleven if this troubling tradition were not used to mitigate a present risk to that community of significance. Perilous risk of this magnitude must be associated with spurious traditions ascribed to one of the twelve by the Matthean community, and one that was substantive and considered dangerous, meaning it was persuasive and divisive.

Further, the tradition legitimates the expansion of the practices and the Matthean gospel tradition into the Gentile world, such as Syrian Antioch,[106] based on a command of Jesus, post-crucifixion. In addition, the use of the words of rite and "Son" and association with Father and Spirit are well-developed christological titles and a formula, all reflecting a second- or third-generation usage in an equally developed liturgical rite of a Christian community.

---

106. Matt 17:24–27 correctly identifies two *didrachmae* as exactly equal to the *stater*, the official coin of Greece or Lydia used in the empire, which only occurred in Antioch or Damascus, i.e., the province of Syria. See also Streeter, *Four Gospels*, 500–523.

In this case, the liturgy is a reflection of the Matthean rites. Consequently, the tradition has been adapted to meet the needs of early Christianity.

Is the tradition unique to Palestinian Judaism, particularly with regard to Jesus' demand for charismatic baptism in Matt 28? This answer is made complex by the extant contemporary sources previously cited, from Qumran and among the Essenes[107] to John the Baptist at Aenon.[108] At first blush the command of Jesus to baptize and employ powerful names in a mystical union with the divine, which is very likely a reflection of the original practices of Jesus' band of exorcists, would appear to be distinct from the expectations of Judaism based on what can be recovered concerning these sources, including that of John the Baptist.[109] It is clear that even this tradition concerning John has been recast by Josephus to make the Baptist more acceptable to authorities and the literate of a Roman Hellenized society,[110] (as opposed to Herod and the Jerusalem elite, whom Josephus portrays as corrupted and evil). The use of the Jewish ritual bath, the mikveh to regain ritual purity by immersion (e.g., to enter the temple), and even the practices of John the Baptist (still in use at the time of Josephus' *Antiquities* throughout the Roman world) are carefully associated with words such as virtue, justice and piety toward God—not rebellion, secrecy or sedition. These are words good citizens of Rome would practice. Consequently, we cannot rely on these accounts fully without placing them in a risk context and evaluating their outcome.[111]

As such, it is certain that there were differing interpretations as to the Jewish and Hellenistic practice and meaning of baptism in the first century, and the use of immersion and water, particularly for conversion.[112]

---

107. Immersion was used in initiation into the cult, annual commitment and renewal, and then in daily purification—See *Community Rule, Manual of Discipline* (1QS 5:13–14) and the *Purity Texts* (4Q 274–76). See also Fitzmeyer, *Dead Sea Scrolls*, 19–21 The Qumran initiation and purification rites were full rituals with words and pronouncements.

108. See the introduction to this problem citing various scholars in Johnson, *Rites of Christian Initiation*, 2–17.

109. Josephus, *Antiquities*, 18.5.2: "Now some of the Jews thought that the destruction of Herod's army came from God, and that very justly, as a punishment of what he did against John, that was called the Baptist: for Herod slew him, who was a good man, and commanded the Jews to exercise virtue, both as to righteousness towards one another, and piety towards God, and so to come to baptism; for that the washing [with water] would be acceptable to him, if they made use of it, not in order to the putting away [or the remission] of some sins [only], but for the purification of the body; supposing still that the soul was thoroughly purified beforehand by righteousness."

110. The use of virtue, justice and piety toward God are all Roman traits and likely had nothing to do with the historical John and his charismatic practices, including his baptism.

111. See Busse, *To Be Near the Fire*, "John the Baptist."

112. Cohen, *From the Maccabees*, 43–44; Freyne, "Jewish Immersion," 221–46.

So the question is not necessarily if the Matthean practices were unique to Palestinian Judaism of the first century, as we don't know; but if the Matthean version is simply another expression of this diversity, and more, is a later "Christianized" version of the original understanding and practice of baptism among Jesus' earliest followers,[113] then it cannot be distinct from first-century Judaism. Thus, while the tradition in Matt 28 carries forward a similar charismatic and mystical baptism to that experienced by Jesus, and some of Jesus' exorcists were followers of John before joining Jesus band,[114] there is little correlation between the rites demanded in Matthew and the practices of the baptism of Jesus that can be recovered using risk analysis. Consequently, the baptism in Matt 28 is a fully Christian charismatic rite, even distinct from the experience of Jesus recorded in the same gospel. Indeed, there is no correlation between the charismatic and ecstatic experience of Jesus when baptized by John, which have been shown to have a claim to authenticity using the criterion of dissimilarity.

Lastly, with regard to the criterion of dissimilarity, the final element of the tradition to evaluate is the command of Jesus given to his exorcists attributed to this encounter: "Having gone [Go!], instruct and make adherents [*mathetuesate*][115] of all people, *baptizing* them. . . . " As noted, this encounter and the accompanying demand is similar to contemporary examples in the Graeco-Roman world with the untimely dead and the dead by violence, where the restless spirit of the deceased makes demands on living relatives or others in order to find rest or to seek retribution on enemies.[116] But, risk analysis has shown that Jesus' demand on his exorcists is in this case a commanded to remain itinerant exorcists whose primary role is now to perform an ecstatic, mystical rite that is founded on something unique to these other encounters—a charismatic act of love, not revenge. It is to rescue[117] those

---

113. Particularly given that the baptism of Jesus by John (that has itself been made more acceptable through the redaction of the Marcan editors/authors), is an undeniable fact given its difficulty and embarrassment (Jesus needing baptism by John—it had to be explained). Jesus was baptized by John in a ritually act, which Jesus' traced his calling by God, his possession by the Spirit, and being driven in the deserted hills of Judea when demons roamed and faced and conversed with Satan. Baptism was a charismatic event that brought about perilous risk and change, even the risk of demonic possession and death, based on Jesus' baptism. Recovery of this event can only point to the radical transformation that occurred for those baptized by John.

114. John 1:35.

115. Greek, imperative form—teach, inform, in this case give them understanding that, when accompanied by powerful rites, is risk transformative.

116. Ogden, *Magic*, 146–48, 158, 322–23, and there are several other examples provided by Ogden.

117. And thus, mitigate perilous risk.

who are possessed and afflicted from the demon-possessed and Satan, in fact, even those who plotted and murdered him, if they will. Instead of retribution, this post-crucifixion encounter with Jesus demands *agape*, which can only reflect a core teaching that echoes the message and practices of Jesus.[118] It is this unique response of love that differentiated the itinerancy of Jesus' exorcists from other magicians, exorcists, ecstatics and sorcerers who interacted with or were controlled by the spirits of the dead.[119] It is distinct in its original setting from both the later church's understanding of this tradition and Palestinian Judaism. Indeed, there are no other contemporaneous examples of instructions like these given to the living by those killed by violence. This command (and its link to baptism) must be considered a legitimate extension of Jesus' war on Satan by his itinerant exorcists, who continued his conflict after this encounter. Consequently, this recovered aspect of the tradition passes the test of the criterion of dissimilarity.

By employing the *criterion of dissimilarity*, the tradition in Matt 28:16–20 has been shown to reference later Christian baptismal liturgical rites. Only the command ascribed to their encounter with Jesus, who was one of the untimely dead killed by violence, that rejects revenge passes the test.

With regard to the *criterion of embarrassment*, one is confronted by the use of the "eleven," a confirmation that one of Jesus' original exorcists had abandoned and betrayed Jesus to enemies, leading to his brutal execution. Certainly, this tradition was an embarrassment to the community in its early years. But here the use of the "eleven" is linked to the "doubt" of some of the eleven; i.e., that they had not seen Jesus on the sacred mountain and that the encounter was not convincing. The embarrassment has been transformed into a polemic against some of the eleven who were outside the Matthean community. The implication is clear—any communities whose traditions are associated with one of these exorcists must be considered spurious.

Consequently, there is no longer embarrassment implied by the "eleven" or the betrayal by Judas, only a statement of fact that some of the eleven were not reliant witnesses and dangerous to the Matthean community. Our analysis of risk and mitigation has confirmed that this element of the tradition fails the test of the criterion of embarrassment. Indeed, even the aspect of the command of Jesus to not seek revenge has been so obscured by the tradition's development and application to a later generation of Christians that it no longer represents an embarrassment to the community. Thus, the tradition fails the criterion of embarrassment.

---

118. Koester, *From Jesus to the Gospels*, 231.

119. Herod assumed the spirit of the murdered John the Baptist had been taken by Jesus for retribution against him, Mark 6:16.

Summary of Risk Analysis

An analysis of Matt 28:16–20 has isolated the reliable elements of the unit by employing the various criteria of risk analysis. Based on this analysis, the event should not be considered contextually reliable, but reflective of a later Christian liturgical rite and a polemic against some of the original exorcists who did not make central the post-crucifixion encounter with Jesus where he was seen. However, the command of Jesus for *agape* versus retribution is distinct from its contextual setting, particularly with regard to encounters with the untimely dead. This piece of the tradition is a reflection of Jesus' ministry.

Matthew 28:16–20 and the Contextual Tests

We now turn to contextual analyses. Here an event must be coherent with the sociological risk setting, including the subsistence struggle of the Galileans, the background from which they came to join Jesus' band of exorcists. Once again, the contextual risk tests previously established are as follows:

1. Encounters with original members of Jesus' band of Galilean exorcists, those who faced capture, death and social isolation and starvation, are given priority.

2. Encounters should be consistent with the ecstatic practices of Jesus that engendered the original perilous risk with his opponents. Specifically, encounters that encouraged the remaining exorcists to continue the ecstatic activity of Jesus and his war on Satan are preferred.

3. Encounters near or on the lake of Galilee, particularly related to subsistence fishing, and similar to the animistic control exhibited by Jesus, are preferential (i.e., the remaining exorcists escaped there).

4. Finally, encounters that may have led the Galileans to again abandon subsistence existence (i.e., to which they returned for survival post-crucifixion) are also preferred.

In each of the foregoing tests, the original form of the unit recovered through risk analysis is evaluated.

To begin, the unit references the original and surviving exorcists—the "eleven." A twelve- to seventeen-mile traverse through Galilee to and up the sacred mountain would most certainly be fraught with risk. The risk of identification, capture, and execution (the men, were hunted and would be valuable bounty to spies) was real and perilous, particularly with the eleven known to have been fellow exorcists of the crucified Jesus. The trip having been made within days or weeks after his execution would heighten that risk of capture.

The post-crucifixion encounter on the mountain is doubted by some of the eleven. For those who accept the encounter as being a post-crucifixion revelation of Jesus, they see him approach and command them, not to embrace retribution, but to continue in perilous risk as itinerant charismatics, yet now specifically as *baptists*. Their role as ecstatic exorcists has been significantly altered, and is now focused on building community, the *ecclesiae*. Water immersion required abundant water, or the use of a private *mikveh*, both dangerous due to the possibility of discovery, or betrayal. Immersion was to be performed concurrently with esoteric words and in specific names, in this case, those that elevated Jesus to "Son," and with that, equivalency with God, which might suggest a continuation of Jesus' war on Satan. However, the focus on baptismal sacred rites and not exorcism points to a much different period than that immediately after the crucifixion. Indeed, it is possible to see this encounter as limiting, a recasting of exorcism and ecstatic activity, and thereby alters the specific activity of the exorcists. Finally, the unit presumes that the exorcists had already abandoned a return to subsistent existence as agrarian fishermen, something they had not yet done.

Consequently, while the unit includes contextual elements that are consistent with the majority of tests, the *sitz im leben* is centered in the expanding Gentile community, such as Syrian Antioch, among later generations of Christians.[120] As such, this unit fails the contextual tests, but allows that certain elements may warrant consideration as reliable fragments imbedded in it.

Conclusions on the Veracity of Matthew 28:16–20

Based on the risk and analytical criteria employed, combined with contextual analysis, the tradition that stands behind Matt 28:16–20 should not be considered a reliable post-crucifixion encounter with Jesus in its contemporary setting, but is a reflection on earlier encounters, which may include some actual events. In the context of human risk experience, this encounter with Jesus is therefore unreliable in the original post-crucifixion context and setting. The Matthean community is facing specific risk challenges. They respond to alternative and emerging communities that ignored the importance of a post-resurrection encounter with Jesus that was material and linked with Jesus' command to baptize—for example, the community of *Toma*.

120. See also Hartvigsen, "Different Ways of Relating Baptism," 657–709.

While the tradition does not pass the risk and contextual criteria as noted, one specific element does—an encounter that does not command retribution by one of the untimely dead killed by violence. Here instead the exorcists are to continue and charismatically baptize into powerful names *to rescue, provide safety and mitigate perilous risks to all people, including the enemy—i.e., to love.* There is nothing in contemporary literature relating similar encounters that reject retribution and command love from those killed by violence for their enemies. This element must be considered trustworthy and must also be associated with the call of Jesus. Risk analysis have confirmed that *agape* was the central charismatic power associated with the war on Satan, both before and after the crucifixion, and was the message of Jesus to his inner circle of exorcists, post-crucifixion.

9

Luke and the Refinement of the Post-Crucifixion Tradition

The Exorcist Cleopas, Ecstatic Meals as Encounter and Mass Encounters

The next section applies the risk and contextual methodology to the Lucan post-crucifixion encounters. As with the former sections on the Marcan and Matthean traditions, the outcome of each risk analysis is to ascertain the original form and risk context and render whether that form recovers a reliable post-crucifixion encounter with Jesus in its contextual setting, thereby suggesting veracity.

Luke 24:13–35: Why Were the Exorcist Cleopas and Village of Emmaus Named?

The material in Luke 24:13–35 (80 to 85 CE) is peculiar to Luke alone, other than a reference to a similar tradition from the oral tradition condensed in Mark 16:12 (see below). Here, two followers of Jesus, one named Cleopas,[1] are heading to a village called Emmaus when they meet a stranger, a "lonely

---

1. Attempts to identify Cleopas as Clopas (John 19:25, of Mary of Clopas, i.e., her husband), or later traditions of him being a relative of Joseph by Hegesippus (180 CE who is said to have received the tradition from the grandson of the apostle Jude; Eusebius, *Ecclesiastical History*, 3.11) is unconvincing. Who Cleopas may be is unknown. However, it is unusual that a name is cited, meaning that the tradition was once tied to a living person well known to the early community, said to have encountered Jesus post-crucifixion. Consequently, the name had meaning associated with the oral tradition by way of a strong connection, i.e., such as a nickname or a form of a name given by Jesus as in his normal practice with his exorcists, not necessarily related to the proper name of the person.

sojourner from Jerusalem," on the road. He joins them and reveals the secret, if not sacred, meaning of events[2] that occurred the same day in Jerusalem concerning Jesus of Nazareth (primarily the meaning of crucifixion and the empty tomb).[3] They ultimately recognize the stranger as Jesus when at an evening common meal he blesses and then breaks bread.[4] Upon recognition, he vanishes or disappears (*aphantos*)[5] out of their sight.[6] According to Luke, they return to Jerusalem that same night to let others know they had "seen Jesus."

2. This recounting of events has been thoroughly analyzed due to its striking similarity to the controversial account by Josephus of Jesus in the *Testimonium Flavianum*, such as by Goldberg, "Coincidences of the Emmaus Narrative," 59–77. A comparison of Greek language, structure and content suggests the tradition of Josephus may come from an independent oral tradition that ultimately was related to the Emmaus tradition in Luke. This analysis, however, as to the relationship between Josephus' account and Luke is outside the scope of our risk analysis study.

3. Mark 16:12 has a similar tradition: Jesus *en hetera morphe*, "he appeared in another form," to two. This tradition does not seem to be reliant on the Lucan tradition, but is distinct and primitive, which indicates this tradition was orally circulated with details known to the Marcan reader. Luke brings the tradition, which carried the original name of the village of Emmaus, and an exorcist, Cleopas, into his theological program (i.e., of the gospel spreading from Jerusalem to Rome) by artificially placing Emmaus near Jerusalem. This has been shown to be an artificial geographical placement, see Fitzmyer, *Luke*, 1562, note 2c. We must instead see a location in Galilee where the first appearances were said to have occurred (coming from the oral tradition).

4. This is an allusion to the passion narrative tradition, where Jesus "breaks" bread at the Last Supper; but why they would recognize this action as from Jesus is puzzling, particularly since neither of these men is named as one of the remaining eleven exorcists having shared that meal? It was too soon after the crucifixion for the oral tradition of the events at that last meal to have reached them. The answer is quite clear: Jesus' practice of sharing an eschatological meal with his fellow exorcists, i.e., where he prayed and broke bread, was a practice that continued after his death. It was so well known and recognized by early followers in Galilee that they continued this practice (Koester, "Memory of Jesus' Death," 335–50) Consequently, we cannon dismiss this recognition as strictly coming from a later tradition. A post-crucifixion encounter with Jesus by his exorcists (and others) at a common meal would not have been an unexpected setting.

5. *Aphantos egeneto*, which is connected with *ap auton*, making *aphantos* and adverb, a unique construction. "Nowhere else in biblical Greek does *aphantos* occur: in classical Greek it is poetical." In other words, the construction is unique to the New Testament and indicates a vanishing, or becoming invisible before their eyes. See Plummer, *Gospel according to St. Luke*, 557. According to Fitzmyer, *ap auton* is "a bit peculiar; but it imitates a phrase often used with the passive of the cognate verb *aphanizein*, ('to be made invisible, disappear'), in the LXX (Judges 21:16; Job 2:9). . . . In classical Greek the adjective is used of disappearing gods. See Euripides, Hel. 606." Fitzmyer, *Gospel according to Luke X–XXV*, 1568.

6. That physical manifestation after escape from a sealed tomb has parallels: As noted Phlegon, a Hellenistic writer and freedman of Hadrian, provides an account of a deceased girl, Philinnion, doing just this—leaving her tomb (after six months!) and physically interacting with a loved one, Machetes. In this account, Philinnion is able

This tradition has been thoroughly analyzed by scholars, and there is evidence that an earlier tradition stands behind the Emmaus encounter,[7] as there is a close parallel in Graeco-Roman literature.[8] Interestingly, Josephus identifies an Emmaus, "Ammathus," as a village *on the shore of Galilee*,[9] the very area of Jesus' ecstatic activity (i.e., where he freed villages and their synagogues from demonic possession)[10] and where his exorcists escaped immediately after the crucifixion (only 16km, or 10 miles from Capernaum).

> But Vespasian removed from Emmaus, where he had last pitched his camp before the city Tiberias (now Emmaus, if it be interpreted, may be rendered 'a warm bath,' for therein was a spring of warm water, useful for healing) and came to Gamala.[11]

There is also another Emmaus cited by Josephus twenty miles west of Jerusalem (referenced also in 1 Maccabees 3:40; 4:3; 9:50), and there are several others that have been studied by scholars and archaeologists.[12] The Lucan tradition suggests a location similar to a village near Jerusalem, but there are significant problems with this identification in the Lucan narrative itself—primarily time and distance and the implied return to Jerusalem and the archaeological evidence and uncertainties as to its placement and identification.

The most persuasive argument against identifying any potential village location of Emmaus as being near Jerusalem is that the traditions in Mark and Matthew suggest all post-crucifixion appearances (all encounters and revelations, other than to Mary the Magdalene) were in Galilee. Indeed, risk analysis

---

to vacate her tomb (still apparently sealed), appear at a location of choice, *physically manifest in bodily form, and even leave clothes and jewelry at sites visited*. Her ability to do so, according to Phlegon, was *allowed by "the gods,"* i.e., by divine caveat and out of love. When her parents, Charito and Demostratus, alerted by a servant (a nurse) about her presence in the house, find her in the room sitting with Machetes, they grasped her in joy. But when touched, she laments and says she is unable to remain any longer, all to their despair and disappears. The parallels are striking. See Phlegon of Tralles, *Mirabilia I*, in Ogden, *Magic*, 159–60.

7. Fitzmyer, *Gospel of Luke*, 1555–56; this is based on vocabulary and style, and the use of the name Cleopas found nowhere else in the New Testament.

8. Plutarch describes how Romulus met with a friend on a road after his death, then vanished after revealing he was now the god Quirinus: *The Parallel Lives of Plutarch*, vol. 1, 28:1–4, Loeb Classical Library, 1914.

9. Josephus, 18:36.3, near Tiberias with warm baths.

10. Busse, *To Be Near the Fire*, 79–80.

11. Josephus, *Jewish War*, 4:1.3.

12. Emmaus-Nicolas/Imwas, 18.6 miles west; al-Quebiba, 5 miles to the northwest of Jerusalem; Abu-Gosh, 9 miles from Jerusalem; and Motza (Latin Ammas, Greek Ammaous), 5 miles.

has confirmed that all of Jesus' exorcists fled to Galilee after the crucifixion, returning to subsistence existence, and that it was there the first encounters occurred. We cannot forget that the Lucan theological program in Luke-Acts is to demonstrate what Conzelmann (and also similarly in Bovon, Fitzmyer and others) correctly termed or refer to as "salvation history," and with it, that the gospel of salvation long promised for all nations began in Jerusalem and by divine inspiration spread to Rome.[13] It is for this redactional purpose that the author-editor of Luke must have the first appearances, as well as the first apostolic preaching and arrival of the Holy Spirit, all occur in Jerusalem.[14] Luke is developing sacred history, yet Mark and Matthew both support the more risk-centered contemporary events that can be reliably recovered—in Galilee. Consequently, Emmaus must be placed near Jerusalem in Luke-Acts, but the actual encounter is more appropriately placed in Galilee.

That Josephus mentions the village of Emmaus in Galilee; particular one near Tiberias is, therefore, significant. What was in the village of Emmaus that attracted Galilean followers of Jesus? Were they fellow exorcists? Why would they risk travel to a village so close to a town under Herodian/Roman control—a perilous danger?

While the location on the western shore of Galilee and proximity to other followers of Jesus would explain why their *phantasm* encounter was shared so quickly with other sympathizers (apparently those who knew Kayfa and had heard his reports of encounters, which as we have shown occurred in Galilee),[15] the more important implication, and one that is contextually coherent with the risks facing Jesus' followers (which are contrary to a leisurely stroll along a road debating the brutal execution of their leader by the bloodthirsty betrayal by one of their own suggested here!), is that Emmaus was a village where Jesus' followers may have both *lived and practiced* and was considered safe from satanic attack *and* demonic imperialism. If so, how and why was this possible? Was this a village that Jesus had liberated

---

13. Conzelmann, *Theology of St. Luke*, 13–14, 18–27, 96, 135, and 149–234. Bovon establishes two periods of salvation history, i.e., the present ecclesiastical situation of the church in the Roman world and the future and distant coming of the Son of Man and the resurrection. As he states: "Settled in the Roman Empire, which for some was peaceful and for others dangerous, Luke would have lived according to a gospel that had become a holy and ideal evangelical story as well as a hope in a distant resurrection from the dead. Associated with a certain, but as yet remote, return of the Son of Man, absent because of the ascension, this hope could no longer nurture, except in an ethical manner, an existence whose origin was more ecclesiastical than Christological." Bovon, *Luke*, 11. Kummel, *Introduction to the New Testament*, 316.

14. Acts 2:1–13.

15. The first encounter while subsistence fishing at night (being hidden by kin), and then his visit to the sacred mountain to communicate with Jesus.

from Satan and demonic imperialism? Did Jesus' exorcists flee to Emmaus to abandon Capernaum, Jesus' former "home," because it was known to be the fishing village and home of his exorcists by spies and enemies? We will attempt to address these risk questions.

In fact, if a Galilean Emmaus was the destination of these men, it is certain that the perilous risks that permeated an original Galilean-Emmaus-tradition is now lost, as its displacement by the Lucan editor/redactor as near Jerusalem acted to mute all perilous risk, changing a terrorizing escape from capture into a parabolic story of a believer's journey to reward (that is, a countermeasure to perilous risk, and why the tradition was likely retained by the community, and why after decades of oral transmission only residual elements of the original awkwardly remained, e.g., the name Cleopas and perhaps even the village of Emmaus). As we have consistently shown in this study, recasting traditions to eliminate embarrassment or to mute perilous risks often point to later redaction and embellishment, because the tradition was still useful to the early communities. Consequently, that an "Emmaus tradition" was even retained after decades of oral circulation is evidence that it had Galilean origins. Only a Galilean origin would adequately explain why recasting its location would mute increased perilous risks that are evident in such a tradition. Is there additional evidence for this?

Haunted and Sacred Waters

To begin, it cannot escape us that Josephus mentions the powers of the warm waters of Emmaus. As noted, springs and waters in Galilee were considered possessed by spirits and demons, i.e., that the waters were under their control and might even be cursed.[16] Waters in Emmaus were more than just warm springs that aided in health, they were considered powerful, able to pull out and absorb demons and spirits by the work of angels.[17] Exorcists and ecstatics such as Jesus would have frequented these sites, employing charismatic authority to call on these same angels to assist in freeing the possessed and trapping their demons in the waters.

---

16. Bar-Ilan, *Exorcism by Rabbis*: "Some springs have a complete family of spirits living in each; it is understood that hot springs, as in Tiberias (Galilee), are heated by spirits (acting on the basis of the commands of King Solomon). It can be generalized that there is hardly a source of water in the land of Israel without a spirit (one or more)." Bar-Ilan cites as additional support the *Pesachim* 112 p. 1, two baraitot: "The Rabbis learned: One should not drink water from rivers or lakes at night. And if he drinks, he risks his life because of the hazard. What hazard? The hazard of demons." Also cited by Bar-Ilan, "Haunted Springs," 153–70.

17. A similar tradition is reflected in John 5:4.

> Now there is in Jerusalem near the Sheep Gate[18] a pool, which in Aramaic is called *beth hesda* (or *beth Zatha*),[19] and which is surrounded by five covered colonnades (i.e., porticoes).[20] Here a great number of disabled people used to lie—the blind, the lame, the paralyzed—and they waited for the moving of the waters. For time to time an angel of the Lord would come down and stir up the waters. The first one into the pool after each such disturbance would be cured (*hugeis egineto*, became sound, or freed) of whatever disease they had (or, *depote kateicheto*, they had been bound).[21]

The exorcist Jesus is intentionally at that pool of *beth hesda*. This must have been a common practice of Jesus, where he and his exorcists went to drive demons out using various techniques with the aid of powerful angels, whose presence was made known by stirring waters, where the waters absorbed the demon.[22] As demonstrated from an examination of the Gospel of Mark alone,[23] Jesus employed many techniques to expel demons,[24] which included being near powerful waters, particularly where angels came to take or trap demons. Jesus was able to draw a legion of angels for assistance if requested.[25] Consequently, Jesus was capable of expelling and trapping demons into the

---

18. The sheep gate may have been near the temple, where the sheep to be sacrificed were cleaned before being submitted to the priests. There the waters may have been considered sacred or part of an act of sanctification. See Rousseau, *Jesus and His World*, 178–79.

19. A translation could be either the "house of shame" or the "house of grace," but more than likely the former.

20. In this case a five sided rectangular pool, which has been confirmed in recent archaeology.

21. John 5:1–4 (many manuscripts do not include v. 4 in whole or part, but the inclusion of this information was problematic and omitted for that reason).

22. Our study has demonstrated that the waters of Galilee and some of the springs and waters near it were considered the home of demons. This is the place the demons request Jesus send them, as noted, in the tradition of the Gerasene demons who possess swine and run into Galilee.

23. Mark 7:33; 8:23.

24. Jesus takes the possessed aside in private, a common practice for him. In the example of the man blinded by a demon in Bethsaida, Jesus uses his hands and physical contact, including contact with the location of demonic possession, the eyes, to help rid the man of his demon, Mark 8:22–26. In another, Jesus places his fingers in the ears of one possessed. The contact passes the authority of Jesus to the site of demonic attack and then the expulsion by command is given, i.e., Mark 7:31–37. See Busse, *To Be Near the Fire*, 83–84.

25. Matt 26:53.

LUKE AND THE REFINEMENT OF POST-CRUCIFIXION TRADITION   147

waters at locations like these. Indeed, in John 5, Jesus never disputes charismatic power of the angel(s) at the pool to expel and trap demons.

In another instance, Jesus expels a blinding demon using the powerful waters of the pool of Siloam (John 9:1–10). Common to the use of multiple practices in difficult exorcisms, Jesus here employs powerful substances, some considered magical in the Graeco-Roman world, and he does so in stages. First, mixes his saliva (his spittle and "water" transmitted power as an exorcist)[26] with mud to make an expulsion-clay (a substance that was used in many of his exorcisms).[27] Saliva, sometimes mixed with clay, was known in the ancient world,[28] and among the Essenes,[29] as an efficacious, magical substance, used to ward off or to control evil.[30] Jesus then rubs the mixture into the eyelids, transferring his authority and power to the area of demonic control. He then commands the demon to "go! (*hupage*, i.e., this is not a command to the man, but the demon to enter the clay), followed by the command to the man to "Wash!" at *Siloam*, the pool meaning "be sent." In this last stage, the demon cast into and captured by the clay, the substance of the exorcist and earth, is "washed" or expelled into the waters of Siloam (John 9:1–7), a sacred *mikveh*.[31] The tradition of John has retained the translation of Siloam known to locals for its power: "[Siloam] . . . which is interpreted, Sent (*apestalmenos*)," because it was where demons and evil spirits were expelled into it waters. Recovery of this risk practice is now made remarkably clear to us.

Consequently, the "healing waters" of Emmaus that absorbed demons would certainly have been a location where Jesus and his follow exorcists would have been active, and a village he would have liberated. It is likely that few in any Gentiles would have visited an area where the Jewish sick, diseased, possessed and lame waited by waters, and where many continued to be taken for years, long after Jesus' and his exorcists were active. As such,

26. Jesus' water was considered powerful, transformative and able to commute his authority to others. For example, even at the cross, the tradition of his side flowing with water was the release of his this authority and power, like that used in his saliva, i.e., John 19:34, and much later in 1 John 5:6.

27. That this tradition omits the use of spittle and mud (a magical clay) in Matthew and the tradition is missing altogether in Luke constitutes strong evidence that this controversial practice of Jesus (considered magic in the ancient world) was used frequently as one of his expulsion techniques. Just as he put his fingers in the ears of the deaf man to absorb the demon into himself through his hands (Mark 7:32–35).

28. Graves-Brown, *Dancing for Hathor*, 165. Isis tricks Re by using his spittle and clay to obtain his name and gain power.

29. Frayer-Griggs, "Spittle, Clay and Creation," 659–70.

30. E.g., Pliny, *Natural History*, 28:7; Petronius, *Satyricon*, 131.

31. Just as the waters of Bethseda were influenced by the angel in the mikveh.

148   JESUS, RESURRECTED

Galilean Emmaus would have been a village to which his followers would have fled post-crucifixion, and been in hiding, having vacated both Jerusalem and Capernaum for fear of spies and capture.[32] In this context, the name Cleopas, meaning "glory of the father," must have been an exorcist name given by Jesus, i.e., such as *Kayfa*, *Boanerges*, *Toma*, and *Magdalene*—each given to the exorcist he trained and accepted into his circle. Indeed, this would explain why this name continued to be attached to the tradition, i.e., if this were one of Jesus' recognized exorcists in the primitive community. This form of the recovered tradition of the Emmaus appearance is thus set within a context of perilous risk.

Ecstatic Meals and Prayers of the Exorcists

The action leading to the recognition of Jesus by the exorcist Cleopas is the blessing (*eulogesen*) and breaking (*klasas*) of bread by the traveler (*paroikeis*)[33] at the evening meal. Scholars have long identified this communal meal as having been established by Jesus. The meal is assumed to have anticipated the "messianic banquet" to be held in the kingdom of God.[34] As such, it was thought to be an *eschatological meal* celebrating the presence, but still future arrival of the kingdom. It was, therefore, an ecstatic experience of the kingdom emerging around them, yet in "their midst,"[35] and in which they participate as a community. As Koester states:

> Now, is it possible to infer that the Christian community meal has indeed its origin in meals that Jesus celebrated with his disciples? And my answer to this question is yes. There is indeed good evidence that Jesus celebrated common meals with his disciples and friends. What is told in the reports about Jesus' last meal, as well as in other information, indicates that these common meals must have been understood as *anticipation* of the banquet of God, the banquet in the kingdom of God.[36]

---

32. Mark 1:21–28. Jesus confronts the elite from Jerusalem in Capernaum, including their decision to try and capture and destroy him. It appears that Jesus is accused of being possessed by Satan there as well. From Capernaum his is followed and then hunted. See Iwe, *Jesus in the Synagogue of Capernaum*, 59–61.

33. The "different form" taken by Jesus according to Mark 16:12, i.e., the traveler who joins the escaping exorcists.

34. Koester, "Memory of Jesus' Death," 335–50.

35. Luke 17:21; *Gospel of Thomas* 113, it is "spread out over the earth and men do not see it."

36. "Story and Ritual in Greece, Rome, and Early Christianity," a lecture by Helmut Koester, May 30, 1998, Harvard University (italics mine).

But, does this go far enough? Does it adequately capture the risk context of Jesus' and his exorcists' activity in their daily war on Satan and his demons?

When placed in the context of Jesus' war on Satan, where Jesus' exorcisms and daily ecstatic activity were overcoming Satan village by village as he approached Jerusalem to reclaim the temple,[37] the evening communal meal was much more than just an innocuous "anticipation" of God's arrival. It was instead an ecstatic and powerful countermeasure to evil in the context of perilous risk and the daily threat of counterattack. Jesus certainly instituted it for this reason.[38] Indeed, by Jesus' own admission, Satan tried to possess victims multiple times,[39] and demons sought to return and attack bringing with them seven others.[40] Consuming special food, herbs, bread and wine, combined with apotropaic prayers (much like the Lord's Prayer) and rhythmic songs and incantations, provided protection from demonic attack, not dissimilar to multiple examples in the Dead Sea Scrolls and its community.[41] The ecstatic meal united Jesus and his authority with his exorcists. It was *Abba* and his Spirit who rescued and possessed him, and now protected his fellow exorcists, as it did Paul and his community.[42] But, they could still lose the war—Satan could still possess them, even that evening, like a thief at night when demons roamed[43] seeking victims.[44] Their prayer is to be preserved from "falling into the hands" of Satan;[45] from being possessed and tormented, just as those that they had rescued. Jesus warned that they could be overwhelmed by the demons that returned seeking retribution.[46] Consequently, the ecstatic meal

37. Luke 11:20.
38. Koester, *Introduction*, 96.
39. Luke 4:2 (as noted, this tradition could only have come from Jesus); Mark 8:33 (deception through one of Jesus own exorcists, Kayfa, through whom Satan spoke)
40. Matt 12:45.
41. See Lichtenberger, *Demonology*.
42. *Abba* was the unique and characteristic address of Jesus in his speech about and prayers to God, multiply attested as having originated with Jesus. See Jeremias, *Prayers of Jesus*, 54–55 (attested in all strata of the tradition—Q, Mark, Matthew and Luke, John and Paul; Paul's use the term Abba¢ in Gal 4:6 and Rom 8:15, i.e., an Aramaic word in the Greek speaking world of his itinerant activity is decisive proof that this was the way in which the historical Jesus' addresses God). Jesus authorized his exorcists to do the same in their ecstatic prayer, similar to the Lord's Prayer—a unique address in ancient Judaism to God most certainly.
43. Similar to 1 Peter 5:8, but found in the Dead Sea Scrolls, 1QH 5:9, 13–14; 4QpNah 1:5–7; 4QpHos 1. While alluding to individuals, the image still stands as how Satan seeks his victims, even through human manipulation.
44. Luke 12:39; Matt 13:19; or when Satan possesses, Luke 22:3.
45. Jeremias, *Prayers of Jesus*, 104–6.
46. Similar to Matt 12:45.

provided protection from perilous risk of the demonic dangers of the night, while also celebrating the day's victories and union with those who were rescued, the new children of the kingdom of God. Satan and his kingdom were collapsing, "falling as lightening."[47] However humble and lowly the meal may have been, it was anything but an anticipation of the coming messiah. Instead, it was a critical and daily ritual of Jesus and the exorcists who were steeped in battle with Satan to ward off evil.

The apotropaic prayer said at the meal is similar to the Lord's Prayer. It followed a solemn, liturgical pattern,[48] similar to contemporary Jewish prayers,[49] but was more urgent. Indeed, the reason the disciples had requested the prayer was because it afforded protection, just as it had for John the Baptist's followers.[50] The prayer cries out from the context of perilous risk.[51] Paul confirms that Jesus spoke it at the evening meal.[52] It was uttered, perhaps even sung[53] while holding the bread and breaking it, so as to imbue it with protective power. When it was ingested, the bread and food acted as the communal nourishment against Satan's forces that night, as well as for the next day's battle. The prayer would be said by Jesus or by the leading (i.e., most powerful) exorcist (such as Cleopas, the Magdalene or Kayfa) or by all present in unison.[54] But the prayer, bread (and wine if available) were a call to be possessed and protected by the "finger of God," the spirit given to Jesus by *Abba*.[55] It was mnemonic; it had rhythm and rhyme, and was simple.[56] The name of God as *father*, *Abba*, was invoked by the exorcist at its beginning, identifying their father, the provider of *daktulo theou*, as the one who is "hallowed," i.e., powerful and overwhelming, but intimately available to Jesus and his exorcists.

---

47. Luke 10:18.

48. Jeremias, *Lord's Prayer*, 15.

49. Such as the *Qaddish* and *Shema*; Jeremias, *Prayers*, 77–78; but transformed into a charismatic, urgent plea and invocation for protection and power in the face of perilous risk and danger.

50. Luke 11:1.

51. Jeremias, *Lord's Prayer*, 22.

52. 1 Cor 11.

53. See also Chase, "Lord's Prayer in the Early Church," 147–51, in the section, "Deliver Us from the Evil One," on "Note on the 'Songs' in St. Luke's Gospel in Relation to Ancient Jewish Prayers."

54. Luke 11:1–13; see also the *Didache*, 9:2–4.

55. Jeremias, *Lord's Prayer*, 20–21; Paul confirms: "When we cry out 'Abba' it is the Spirit bearing witness." Rom 8:16, also Gal 4:6, meaning the Spirit has entered the believer.

56. Jeremias, *Lord's Prayer*, 15–16.

The prayer included an appeal for victory and survival the next day, as it requested another divine meal, i.e., to "deliver the day" to them and bring about the next meal. Finally, there was a petition for continued protection from satanic possession and deception—words, once again, strikingly similar to what is now understood to be the Lord's Prayer that is multiply attested.[57] The final petition was abrupt, pressing, and an affirmation of their source of protection from the "evil one," Satan.[58]

Given the foregoing, the apotropaic prayer taught by Jesus is similar to the following:

> *Abba*,[59]
>
> I call on you and invoke your powerful name!
>
> Your kingdom comes by your power and will!
>
> Continue to give into our hands victory over your enemies
>
> and sustain us, your children, with the bread of life tomorrow.
>
> Protect us from Satan[60] and his demons![61]
>
> As you have saved us, let us rescue others to be your children!
>
> Yours alone is the kingdom, authority and glory.
>
> Let it be so tomorrow, Amen.

In fact, this form of the prayer is strikingly similar to the earliest version of the Lord's Prayer that has been recovered in Aramaic by scholars.[62] More,

---

57. Ibid. Lecture: Koester suggests that the prayers associated with the Eucharist in the *Didache* (last part of the 1st century CE) may be authentic sayings of Jesus. But these also may be better construed as a directly linked to his ecstatic activity and successful war against Satan, defeat of his demons, and the erosion of demonic imperialism (e.g., Jesus' conversion of imperially licensed tax collectors to his band of exorcists and supporters). These prayers reflect a later theology and eschatology overall in my view.

58. Jeremias, *Prayers*, 106; see also Chase, "Lord's Prayer," 85–101.

59. Jeremias, *Prayers*, 76, the unique call on the name of God using the most unique characteristic of Jesus' prayers, i.e., the address of God as "father," *Abba*, the intimate name of one's father here applied by Jesus to God; a term he allowed his exorcists to employ as well.

60. The original prayer referenced delivery from the "evil one," *apo tou panerou*, i.e., Satan, or *ho paneros*; see also the discussion on the "evil one" being Satan in Sim, *Apocalyptic Eschatology*, 77–78.

61. The context is perilous risk where one lived in the midst of the risk of satanic control, i.e., see Jeremias, *Lord's Prayer*, 30.

62. Ibid., 86–89. While Jeremias believes the earliest version of the Lord's Prayer is embedded in Luke, the petition to protect the exorcists from Satan, i.e., "but deliver us from the evil one," is absent. Jesus' conflict was with Satan and demonic attack. Therefore, the petition, "deliver us from the evil one," which is found in Matthew's version (Matt 6:13), is the more original.

there are parallels in the Dead Sea Scrolls to a sacred meal and blessing within the community—the bread, the cup and the ointment. These were communal elements, but were employed for ritual protection, reflecting similar practices within Jewish mysticism and among the Therapeutae (e.g., of Mary the Magdalene).[63] The "pure food" eaten was sacred, perhaps angelic food, affording mystical protection in the end of days as the Essenes prepared for battle against evil, the war against the sons of darkness and evil priest, expected any day, even the next day. These contemporaneous have strong parallels to the ecstatic meal instituted by Jesus in his active war on Satan.

The Emmaus event is remarkable, and, in its original form, a critical connection to the original ecstatic, powerful meal practiced by Jesus and his exorcists. In Emmaus, when the bread is broken and the ritual begins, the traveler is "recognized" as Jesus and then disappears. As such, the Emmaus event confirmed that Jesus was not only active, but was present and available at the ecstatic meals when the bread is broken. He can be made present, or is present at the meal, but like the traveler may be incognito, so beware. To abuse the meal (e.g., to be drunk) is to bring on peril, illness and death, that is, demons that curse and attack the participants.[64] They are made guilty for the murder of Jesus and receive retribution, much like the attack of the untimely dead on their executioners.

The Emmaus encounter was retained in the oral tradition because it redefined the original ecstatic meal and confirmed that at its practice Jesus was certainly present, perhaps as the stranger, but could materialize. The meal's focus retained its protective function, but also took an eschatological tenor, looking forward his return as Messiah. In the earliest stages of post-crucifixion practices in Galilee, Jesus was available,[65] his name carried power,[66] and he continued to direct the war on Satan—the kingdom was still inbreaking led by Jesus.[67] Ultimately, the story of the passion was linked to the meal, becoming the community sacrament of union with the risen Lord, the Eucharist, as found in Paul's letter to the Corinthians. But all this began with the Emmaus event.[68]

63. See, e.g., Chestnutt, "Dead Sea Scrolls," 397–401, 404, 405–8.
64. 1 Cor 11:27–30.
65. Matt 18:20.
66. 1 Cor 5:4.
67. Gal 4:6.
68. After Emmaus, the meal was transformed into complex christological and soteriological rituals to meet the needs of the early church. Indeed, Paul's reference is to a well-developed tradition that he had received points to its thorough development by 54 CE. Its history of development, fully formed in the gospels, 68–90 CE (i.e., where Jesus predicts his death, his broken body and shedding of blood for the new covenant with

Luke 24:13–35 and Qualitative Risk Analysis

With this context set, we can begin our risks analysis of the unit, employing first, qualitative risk. In this analysis, the encounter cannot be a countermeasure to the elite, but must heighten the perilous risk of the Galilean exorcists and the conflict with opponents.

In a recovered tradition that employs risk analysis, the follow reconstruction is suggested: Two men (Cleopas, an exorcists renamed by Jesus and another unnamed male, likely not an exorcist) flee to the village of Emmaus in Galilee in the evening, having abandoned Capernaum.[69] They fear capture or execution as exorcists of Jesus. They learn he has been executed as an "evildoer." There is perilous risk—spies and assassins, working for the Herodians and the elite, are hunting them (e.g., paid informants such as Judas). They expect to find safety in Emmaus of Galilee, a place freed of demons by Jesus in his itinerant village-by-village war on Satan. There he likely expelled numerous demons, driving them into the sacred waters of Emmaus (the "healing waters" cited by Josephus), as he had done at the waters of *Beth seda* and *Siloam*. In Emmaus they find fellow exorcists in hiding who share in the communal meal of protection instituted by Jesus. They know Kayfa, Jesus' chief exorcist, and have heard reports of his ecstatic encounters with Jesus, both on the lake at night and at the sacred mountain. A stranger joins the two men (a lonely stranger from Jerusalem)[70] on the road to Emmaus; Cleopas and his companion receive a revelation given by the stranger. Once in Emmaus, they have an ecstatic experience during a communal meal. Their "eyes" are opened and perceive the traveler as Jesus when he "breaks bread." Jesus then vanishes when recognized. The event is shared with the others.

The recovered tradition behind Luke 24:13–35 is coherent with the contemporary risk setting, and presents a compelling connection between the protective practices of Jesus during the evening meal in his war on Satan, and its continuation by his exorcists in Galilee. The danger from demonic attack prevented by the meal's ritual and aprotropaic prayers continued to be essential for the exorcists post-crucifixion. Jesus was thought to be present, even if in secret. To be drunk or irreverent brought the retribution of demons and cursed death. Given this heightened perilous risk, Luke 24:11–35 in its recovered form passes the test of qualitative risk analysis. However, the recovery in this case is circumstantial and based on the collection and recovery of multiple facts from varied traditions. Nonetheless, we will allow it based on the preponderance of this evidence.

God in the bread and wine), was recast into his last meal in Jerusalem.

69. Or escaping Jerusalem for Galilee after the crucifixion.
70. See Plummer, *St. Luke*, 553.

Luke 24:13–35 and the Criteria of Dissimilarity and Embarrassment

In this test, encounters must differ from the needs and influence of the early church on the one hand and first-century Judaism in Palestine on the other.

To begin, the recovered tradition meets the test of authenticity using the *criterion of dissimilarity*. The recovered tradition certainly differs from the needs of the Lucan community and is starkly dissimilar to the characterization of risk in the Lucan version of the event. The redactor/editor sought to insert a tradition near Jerusalem to meet its salvation-history theological program, i.e., the divine expansion of the gospel to all nations as promised from Jerusalem to Rome. More, the tradition confirms the presence of the risen Lord in the journey of faith among believers and in the communal meal.[71] However, the recovered tradition may no longer be considered unique to a charismatic Jewish setting in first-century Palestine. Our analysis has suggested that Jesus' activity, including his techniques and their use near waters, may have reflected the practices of contemporary exorcists and ecstatics. The differentiator is Jesus' public association of these events with his war on Satan and demonic imperialism and demand of acceptance of the demon possessed as children of God. This was the countermeasure to demonic control.

Given the distinct characteristics of the recast Lucan tradition from the needs of its community and first-century Palestinian Judaism (including charismatic Judaism), the tradition meets the criterion of dissimilarity, and therefore, should be considered reliable within its contemporary context.

With regard to the *criterion of embarrassment*, the redaction of the older oral tradition, which in Luke retained only the name of a forgotten exorcist and an obscure village, and includes a geographical displacement of that village to a near proximity to Jerusalem, provides no evidence that the tradition was an embarrassment to the community in its later form. It simply lost it original risk characteristics and was employed as a theological motif to meet the needs of the Lucan community. The question is whether the original tradition was an embarrassment to later communities, which necessitated its adaptation. The answer is unequivocally, "yes." The original tradition references a contemporary setting that was imbued with radical charismatic activity near waters that employed the techniques of exorcists that are subdued over time. The tradition in its original form leaves little doubt that it was emended gradually until only the rudimentary elements the remained, thereby providing a framework as a post-resurrection event allowing for its adaptation as a free oral tradition for use within the

---

71. E.g., see Esler, *Modeling Early Christianity*, 2–3.

community. Consequently, the recovered tradition does meet the *criterion of embarrassment*. It therefore passes this test.

Summary of Risk Analysis

The recovered tradition suggested in a qualitative risk analysis of Luke 24:13–35 provides a unique and powerful insight in the dangerous world in which Jesus and his fellow exorcists combated Satan, evil angels and his demons, particularly at sacred pools using the methods of an exorcist. Behind the encounter with Jesus at a common meal and vanishing stands a more primitive tradition of desperate escape from perilous risk, which is now lost; one between the exorcist Cleopas and Jesus, post-crucifixion. Based on the risk analysis, the preponderance of evidence behind the tradition establishes why the exorcists would have been fleeing to Emmaus, why this was an important village to the exorcists, and what happened there by way of an ecstatic encounter with Jesus during the practice of the ecstatic meal and its rituals. While not fully recovered, based on a risk analysis, reminisces of the original event should be considered contextually reliable.

Luke 24:13–35 and the Contextual Tests

We now turn to contextual analyses. Here an event must be coherent with the sociological risk setting, including the subsistence struggle of the Galileans, the background from which they came to join Jesus' band of exorcists. Once again, the contextual risk tests previously established are as follows:

1. Encounters with original members of Jesus' band of Galilean exorcists, those who faced capture, death and social isolation and starvation, are given priority.
2. Encounters should be consistent with the ecstatic practices of Jesus that engendered the original perilous risk with his opponents. Specifically, encounters that encouraged the remaining exorcists to continue the ecstatic activity of Jesus and his war on Satan are preferred.
3. Encounters near or on the lake of Galilee, particularly related to subsistence fishing, and similar to the animistic control exhibited by Jesus, are preferential (i.e., the remaining exorcists escaped there).
4. Finally, encounters that may have led the Galileans to again abandon subsistence existence (i.e., to which they returned for survival post-crucifixion) are also preferred.

In each of the foregoing tests, the original form of the unit recovered through risk analysis is evaluated.

The recovered tradition occurred in Galilee at the village of Emmaus. Jesus' remaining exorcists fled there from either Jerusalem or Capernaum to escape perilous danger, expecting to find others there post-crucifixion. Emmaus was a village known for Jewish ecstatic activity, and the waters there into which Jesus and his fellow exorcists expelled demons using various techniques described would not have been a location visited by Gentiles or the Herodians. As such, it was considered a safe haven, where Jesus and his fellow exorcists would be protected, if not hidden. Cleopas and his companion enter into the ecstatic meal, a practice begun by Jesus. During the breaking of bread they suddenly recognize the stranger, one who appears "in another form" while walking in the country, according to Mark 16:12, as Jesus. Whether an epiphany or a possession, their eyes are "opened (*de dienoichthesan*, a description implying ecstatic experience granted by God). Upon recognition, he vanishes (*opthalmoi*, disappears) from sight. This encounter is enough to convince them that Jesus is active and has transformed into another state of being, which is confirmed by a report that Kayfa has also encountered Jesus post-crucifixion. The implication of these events is that a return to ecstatic activity had begun, which would include the expelling of demons and other ecstatic activity.

Given the recovered tradition, all the contextual tests are met. If this form of the tradition reflects the risk and practices of the post-crucifixion exorcists, it is compelling.

Conclusions on the Veracity of Luke 24:13–35

Based on the risk and analytical criteria employed, combined with contextual analysis, the tradition that stands behind Luke 24:13–15 should be considered a reliable post-crucifixion encounter with Jesus; but one where the tradition is only partially recovered from an earlier encounter with actual events. The redactor/editor of the Lucan community has reset the events around Jerusalem and wishes to relate the original event to the *sitz im leben* of the current community, i.e., the perilous journey of the believer with the reward of one day begin with the resurrected Lord.

Luke 24:34: Why Did Kayfa's Report Stand Apart from Any Other of the Exorcists?

In Luke 24:34, when the two Emmaus travelers (including Cleopas) return to Jerusalem, they are told that the "Lord has risen indeed (*ontos*[72]), and was seen by Simeon [presumably Kayfa[73]]." There is no expansion of this tradition provided in the canonical gospels, however, Paul later confirms the primacy of this encounter in his listing of appearances in 1 Cor 15:1–5, and repeats a very early oral formula.[74]

Kayfa's encounter has been held as the primary catalyst validating the resurrection of Jesus from the very days after the crucifixion to today, the earliest witness to this tradition being Paul in about 54 CE. In 1 Cor 15:3–5, Paul cites a well-known formula[75] that orally circulated in the primitive community as early as 35 CE,[76] ascribing primacy to Kayfa's encounter. This was the watershed event, leading to multiple encounters, a "chain event"

---

72. The Greek word here, *ontos*, stresses the reality of the event, a fact, i.e., it is certain and critically important versus what is fictitious or conjectural. See 1 Cor 14:25. The emphasis is clear in a risk context: Jesus' chief exorcist has encountered him without doubt—Jesus has not been annihilated! All that this implied during these early days would not have been known or understood, only shocking and transformative in dealing with what was expected versus what this event meant to charismatics that fled Jerusalem (perhaps including their forgiveness for having abandoned him).

73. As noted, Simeon, son of Yona (bar Yona), was renamed "the rock" by Jesus after being trained as his leading exorcist. In Greek, "the rock" is Petros, but in Aramaic, Kayfa, the "s" being added to accommodate the Aramaic ending implying a feminine ending, thereby making it masculine. Consequently, Kephas, commonly used by scholars should be Kayfa, the original Aramaic, with the long "a." The other translation of Cephas improperly drops the hard "k" of Aramaic.

74. See Conzelmann, *1 Corinthians*, 248–57. Conzelmann agrees that the primacy of Kayfa's encounter with the risen Jesus as recorded in Paul's listing (taken itself from a very early formulae) is a variant tradition of a primitive event recognized by the earliest church as primary to the confirmation of Jesus' resurrection, and, therefore, is not reliant on Luke 24:34.

75. The formula Paul employs in 1 Cor 15:3–5 is much older and is set in orderly statements, each introduced by *hoti* (i.e., that), which is an introduction normally used to introduce scripture. For Paul, this tradition is on par with his Pharisaic training in scripture and law. A close look at each statement, or the formula as a whole, clearly shows that they do not reflect Paul's normal language or style found in 1 Corinthians, Thessalonians or Galatians. As such, this small section, which has appended to it the earliest order of resurrection appearances in the New Testament, originated from the earliest witnesses, likely Cephas and the apostles, or perhaps by revelation to Paul directly. In Galatians, Paul is emphatic—the revelation came directly from God, but the formula could have existed in parallel to Paul's own revelation of the "gospel," i.e., they are not mutually exclusive.

76. Luedemann, *Resurrection of Jesus*, 145.

of appearances.[77] Scholars, including critical scholars, concur that Jesus did appear to Kayfa in some form.[78] However, this appearance is never described, including by Paul (1 Cor 15:3–5). What is available, and has been recovered as a result of this study using risk analysis, is that Kayfa encountered Jesus on two occasions in Galilee: First, on the lake while in hiding,[79] that is, while night fishing under the protection of kin (Matt 14:22–36; Mark 6:45–56). Second, following the lake encounter, when Kayfa returns to the sacred mountain, i.e., to the place or cave where Jesus selected and trained him as an exorcist (Mark 9:2–13; Matt 17:1–13; Luke 9:28–36). One, or both of these encounters were reported to the other exorcists in Galilee.

The use of the Greek word *ontos*, stressing the reality of the event, is somewhat puzzling, particularly since the two men present, including the exorcist Cleopas, just reported having had an encounter at the common meal that evening! Why would their report not carry the same weight as that of Kayfa? Use of *ontos* is much more that an inference that they were right about their encounter. It is Kayfa's encounter, not theirs that is convincing to the others. The implication is clear: While they reported the event, they were still uncertain about its reality and the identification of the traveler as being Jesus. Indeed, their discussion about the traveler following the encounter demonstrates this—they *were* uncertain: "They asked each other: 'Did our hearts not burn'" (Luke 24:32), as if the event needed confirmation that they had experienced the same Jesus they knew. Was the traveler a *phantasm*, having walked with them, handled the bread, but then *dematerialized* in front of them? Could they believe the encounter as real? No matter, Kayfa is said to have seen[80] Jesus.

---

77. Ibid., 174–75.

78. Koester, *Introduction*, 84; Perrin, *Resurrection*, 80. See also Patterson, *God of Jesus*, 237–38, and the meaning of the appearances being the confirmation of Jesus' legitimacy as the resurrected martyr.

79. Kayfa fled Jerusalem to Galilee after the crucifixion, having denied he knew Jesus (Luke 22:60)

80. What is meant here by *opthe* is debated, but some hold the use here emphasizes to be seen with the bodily eye, not internally perceived (Plummer, *Luke*, 509–10, 558), particularly given its placement with the next section, Luke 24:36–39, where Jesus' offers those present to examine his wounds and see he has "flesh and blood." Paul's use of *opthe* seems to reflect both physical and internal, with more emphasis on seeing a nonematerial body and internal perception (see Gal 1:15–16; 1 Cor 9:1; 15:1–9, 50–54; not a body of flesh and blood, but a spiritual body); 1 Cor 12:2 (the visit to the third heaven).

Who Was This Kayfa?[81]

Kayfa was a struggling, subsistence fisherman living a back-breaking life in a small obscure village with his extended family (wife, mother-in-law and the family of his brother) along the western shore of Galilee called *Kfar Nahum*, "the village of Nahum" (or called in the gospels, Capernaum). As noted, excavations in the village of Capernaum have revealed some first-century Roman ruins, but a much larger peasant area, which dominated most of the original site.[82] These were simple structures, made with black basalt fieldstones and rubble/mud filled walls, and branch, grass and mud roofs, which provided only adequate subsistence living conditions.[83] Simple rooms surrounded a courtyard in which small clay ovens cooked meals for the families. More, these were not the house of any middle class folk, but the poor, heavily taxed, struggling families—the very villagers that embraced Jesus as an exorcist, a kind of village Shaman, or protector. No one stood up for the desperate poor, the subsistence peasants,[84] nor offered protection against demonic illness, injury, starvation, death, unending poverty and social persecution—other than fringe charismatic rebels, like John the Baptist, Jesus and his fellow exorcists. In fact, the real social, political and economic situation for poor peasants and their families during the time of Jesus' activity in Galilee was a daily struggle for survival under harsh tenant/landlord relationships and ever increasing taxation.[85] Production was funneled to

---

81. While we use Mark as a primary source to recover many of the traditions about Kayfa, it has been clearly demonstrated that Mark's tradition has suppressed and redacted older material that was much more favorable to Kayfa. Bultmann, *History*, 251. Bultmann has shown the influence of Hellenistic Christianity, what is thought influenced by Paul, actually resulted in a polemic against Kayfa and traditions about him. Consequently, the more ancient tradition can be recovered, particularly by employing risk analysis. The tradition of Papias (i.e., that the gospel is by Mark, one who followed Kayfa but had never seen or heard Jesus; one who faithfully wrote down what he heard to the best of his memory, but not in order) has been shown to be difficult, if not impossible to accept. For example, see Kummel, *Introduction to the New Testament*, 69–70, highlights the various difficulties. See also Koester, *Ancient Christian Gospels*, 32–34. Weeden has also shown that Kayfa holds Jesus to be an exorcist and wonder worker, but Mark presents him as the "spokesman of an erroneous Christology," where Jesus is shown to "correct them by insisting on a theology of suffering and the cross." Weeden, "Heresy That Necessitated Mark's Gospel," 145–58. This is an accurate assessment of the suppression of the Kayfa tradition and primacy of Kayfa in the earliest tradition. From a risk perspective, this absolutely confirms that Kayfa was an exorcist and that Jesus' historical activity centered on exorcism and his war on Satan with Kayfa at his side.

82. Horsley, *Galilee*, 115.

83. Ibid.

84. Patterson, *Lost Way*, 75.

85. Patterson: "Ancient cities were parasitic. Each was assigned a *chora*, a large

the cities, including Sepphoris, "leaving nothing for the peasant producers themselves to live on."[86] A village of only four to eight hundred, "it was small, poor, and uncultured."[87] Struggling daily for survival, and with confidence in Jesus' ability to control Satan's demons and evil spirits (having witnessed his exorcising demons from his mother-in-law)[88] even the spirit of animals (directing fish into their nets to meet their catch quotas),[89] they chose relief from the relentless risks and economic hardship of Herodian and Roman oversight and taxation,[90] and joined in his war on Satan to drive demonic forces out of the land—as exorcists for the villagers, who supported, housed and fed them. Their success led to "Satan fell like lightening,"[91] and as Satan fell so too would their pagan occupiers and their burden.

The speculation among some scholars that these fishers, including Kayfa, Yohannes and Yecob, were of "moderate means" is incorrect. It presumes that they owned their boats and were fairly well off "middle class" (there was no such thing) due to their cooperatives (*koinonoi*) with other family clans (the "Yonah-Zebedee" cooperative). This has been shown to be utterly false by K. C. Hanson.[92] Galilean fishermen were of the desperately poor, subsistence peasant class operating under duress. This included physical hardship and the onerous requirements of fulfilling tax lease obligations to the Roman licensed tax collectors on behalf of the elite. These were "game wardens" that monitored catch for collection (and to ensure "sacred fish" were not harvested). These cooperatives with other families were formed by necessity in order to survive and meet their contracted fishing quotas, having been provided the boats at fee as part of their lease: "Peasants did not voluntarily supply labor for the elites, nor did they work willingly for wages. Most traditional peasants are devoted to self-sufficient household economy as the elites are to the welfare of their estates."[93]

Antipas rebuilt Sepphoris, a Hellenized city near Nazareth, and constructed Tiberius on Galilee in honor of the emperor, exacerbating the

---

agricultural area surrounding it, upon which the city could draw for its basic food supply and income" (*Lost Way*, 69).

86. Horsley, *Galilee*, 45; Horsley references another excellent article, Reed, *Population of Capernaum*.

87. Erhman, *Peter, Paul and Mary Magdalene*, 25.

88. Mark 1:29–31, Kayfa's mother-in-law.

89. Luke 5:4 is one of several examples of Jesus charismatic direction and ability to control animals to assist his villagers.

90. Horsley, *Archaeology, History and Society*, 121–30.

91. Luke 10:18.

92. Hanson, "Galilean Fishing Economy," 99–111.

93. Ibid., 119.

taxation and quotas on villagers at this time of Jesus' activity.[94] Economically, the fishing cooperatives were by necessity organized, certainly due to being burdened with multiple taxes—Rome, Antipas, and the temple tax.[95] Taxation was so heavy[96] there was no surplus, as all production above subsistence was confiscated and sent to the urban centers and the elite for consumption and profit. Escape from this cycle of poverty, much like agrarian tenant sharecrop farming in first-century Palestine, was virtually impossible.[97] Fishing on Galilee was seasonal, susceptible to drought, poor inflow from the Jordan, and poor catch. Practices to appease spirits and gods were important, critical and prevalent.[98] The protection of an exorcist like Jesus, one who controlled the demonic waters; one who stood for the hopeless and economically helpless, denouncing the elite of Jerusalem as possessed and their displacement by the empire of God immanent, was ultimately persuasive to these fishermen, particularly when he began his mission to free the land of demonic control and retake Jerusalem.[99] Such tenant fishers and farmers were under the control of severe landowners who intended to bond them to dependence and economic destitution—slavery being a close analogy to their plight.

In the context of the Galilean fishing village harbors (i.e., stones built up to create docking areas along the lake), filled with poor and illiterate people struggling for survival, there were cultural practices employed to mitigate risks from death, demonic possession and attacks by spirits and ghosts (illness, insanity and deformation). These included not only prayer and supplication, but also sacrifice and divination, particularly among Hellenized Jews and Gentiles who looked for protection and safety on the waters and from forces below. Those who controlled such demons, provided protection, and could increase catch, were embraced, protected and fed.[100] Jesus' encounter with these soon to be exorcists, where he was able to increase catch (e.g., Luke 5:4–6, John 21.6, and Matt 17:27), confirmed that he held control over these dark forces and spirits and the fish that provided life.[101] Struggling for survival, falling short on fishing quotas and contracted requirements, it

94. Freyne, "Herodian Economics in Galilee," 23–46.
95. Matt 17:24–27.
96. Hanson, "Herodian Economics in Galilee," 115.
97. Freyne, *Galilee and the Gospels*, 161.
98. As noted, evidenced by the name Bethsaida, the "temple (or house) of the fish God."
99. The thesis of *To Be Near the Fire*.
100. Jesus is invited to remain with Kayfa and his family after driving a demon from his mother-in-law, Luke 4:38–40.
101. Craffert, *Life*, 302–3.

is no wonder that these men left fishing to learn control over demons and the lake, and agreed to be "fishers of men (*aleeis anthropon*)," i.e., trained *and paid* exorcists, able to pull humans, like fish, from the depths of evil, the waters that held demons and control of dangerous demons and deadly spirits that roamed.

Mark 16:9 presents a saying of Jesus, similar to what is equivalent to the bestowal of charismatic authority to exorcise demons and death on those he trained. Kayfa is given the "key of heaven" to bind and loose demons.[102] More, these men and women wanted to receive authority to increase fish catch, exercising release from subsistence survival and hunger—not just for themselves, but for other villages, any of whom they fed. Jesus, to them a remarkable charismatic and protector of these fishermen and their kin,[103] offered a way to escape poverty and control forces that threatened their and their family's survival and take back the empire from demons, returning it to God, for Satan was already falling like lightening.[104]

We cannot forget that this was exactly the outcome, as Kayfa (and others) continued to support not only himself, but also his wife (and kin) as an exorcist and charismatic[105] over twenty-four years after the crucifixion.[106] If they could be taught this charismatic talent, exorcise and control evil, especially the demons that controlled the waters, then they would be able to feed their extended families. For this, leaving nets behind to follow this Jesus was essential and urgent; particularly in the height of the fishing season when catch was not forthcoming and their quotas were not being met.[107] As noted, all was at risk! It was this event that drew them into the company of Jesus and, ultimately, his war on Satan as charismatics and exorcists.

Kayfa was widely known and considered centrally important and influential in the early church, primarily due to his receiving the first post-crucifixion encounter that was trusted (1 Cor 15:5). Paul went to Jerusalem to meet with Kayfa to validate his vision and understanding of "gospel" (Gal

---

102. Smith, *Jesus the Magician*, 186–87: "As to what Jesus' mystery [the mystery of the kingdom of God] could have been, the magical papyri give us a clue: A magician boasts that he is 'the keeper of the keys of the three-cornered paradise of the earth,' the kingdom (PGM III.54ff.). Jesus is said to have promised the keys to Peter."

103. Craffert provides a model and analysis of Jesus as Shamanic figures that has compelling features suggesting the villagers may have considered him such. See, *Life*, 353–82.

104. Luke 10:18.

105. Acts 8:9–24, his battle with Simon the Sorcerer; see also the *Acts of Peter*.

106. See Paul's objection, 1 Cor 9:5.

107. Luke 5:5, even risking life by staying out all night on the lake—they risked death to meet their quotas!

1:18), and is he called a "pillar" (2:9). Paul later confronts Kayfa and reports the outcome as his prevailing over the erring *apostole* (2:11–21) in front of the entire community. Kayfa was the head of what Paul terms as "the twelve" (1 Cor 15:5). He had a following, resulting from his ecstatic baptisms (1 Cor 1:12), his teachings and ecstatic activity (3:22), and carried on his itinerant activity. He was supported in this activity to a level that allowed him to travel with his wife and be fed and housed for free (9:5). All of these references demonstrate that Paul used Kayfa as a lightening rod on which to compare the legitimacy of his apostleship and activity, even his gospel. Since these ecstatic letters[108] are dated to the mid-fifties CE, and Paul calls himself a *presbytes*, an aged man (in his fifties), Kayfa too must have been the same, having survived, but still facing perilous risks and dangers, as well as starvation.

It was this Kayfa, whose encounter with Jesus on the lake and on the sacred mountain in Galilee became pivotal; Kayfa, who can be recovered with some certainty from the primitive tradition and with research using risk analysis; Kayfa the charismatic, one of Jesus' leading exorcist—the man who abandoned and rejected Jesus when captured and then returned into hiding to subsistence fishing, only at night; and who was protected by kin, to avoid detection and capture. It is, therefore, clear why his encounter was not only considered pivotal, but the basis on which the others were willing to risk all and join with him. Kayfa embraced immense perilous risk that only would be possible if the alternative would have been more catastrophic,[109] that is, denying what had encountered. But more, Kayfa's abandonment of subsistence existence for a return to the heightened perilous risk of itinerant exorcism and war on Satan was startling and absolute confirmation that he had an encounter with Jesus. Kayfa embraced the encounter as transformative and reengaged. With this context in place, we now turn to our risk assessment of the tradition.

---

108. They include a deadly curse, spirit and soul transportation, and destruction of the flesh by judgment of Paul!

109. Dr. Paul Slovic in a discussion Sept 21, 2015, has confirmed that with regard to research on human behavior in response to perilous risk and the *affect heuristic*: "If the risk option, by itself, would carry negative affect, then that risk in the context of a severe negative alternative would probably convey mixed feelings—better that the alternative, but still not good." In other words, the encounter with Jesus heightened perilous risk, but the alternative of denying the event would tacitly be a rejection of divine insertion into history personally experienced. For this reason, the heightened perilous risk, based on research on human behavior in response to peril, would be consistent with the response of the Kayfa. This response if perfectly reflected in Paul's own statement in his letter to the Corinthians (1 Cor 9:16) previously cited: "For when I preach the gospel, I cannot boast, for I am compelled to preach. Woe to me if I do not preach the gospel."

Luke 24:34 and Qualitative Risk Analysis

We can begin our risks analysis of the unit, employing first, qualitative risk. In this analysis, the encounter cannot be a countermeasure to the elite, but must heighten the perilous risk of the Galilean exorcists and the conflict with opponents.

To begin, the shocking news that Kayfa had encountered Jesus post-crucifixion[110] became the watershed event that convinced other Galilean exorcists to come out of hiding,[111] reengage battling satanic forces and hostile demons, and risk capture by deadly opponents. Consequently, it was this specific post-crucifixion event, one completely unexpected[112] that dramatically increased the perilous risk of not just Kayfa but also other exorcists who accepted its authenticity.[113] Kayfa's encounter ended the conviction that Jesus had been annihilated by being brutalized and crucified, as well as removed the terrifying fear of retaliation, that is, against those exorcists who had abandoned him. But the consequence of accepting Kayfa's report as valid meant embracing not only the risk of reengaging and satanic attack, but capture and execution by powerful enemies, the sympathizers of Rome, whose spies permeated the region. Despite not having a direct description

---

110. The first post-crucifixion event others considered unquestionable, valid, i.e., *ontos*.

111. Abandon their return to subsistence fishing at night, protected by kin; e.g., the basis of the original tradition behind John 21:3.

112. Based on risk analysis noted, the encounter on the lake and tradition recovered from (Matt 14:22–36; Mark 6:45–56; John 6:16–24)

113. Kayfa took up itinerancy, ultimately fleeing Palestine for Antioch. He and other ecstatics were not immediately attacked (i.e., when they returned to Jerusalem to assault satanic forces there) for fear they would unleash a retributive phantasm, the spirit of Jesus, on his assassins. They tolerated the exorcism of demons among the disenfranchised. However, when Stephanos, a Hellenistic "God-fearer" and charismatic possessed by the Spirit (trained by Jesus' exorcists and, through an ecstatic ritual, possessed by the Spirit), was cornered by spies and assassins of the Jerusalem elite (led by a brutal, violent Roman sympathizer, Saul—see Acts 8 and Gal 1:13), Stephanos called on the name of Jesus and entered into ecstatic trance. Crying out, he warned them that he saw Jesus coming, and doing so as the apocalyptic Son of Man coming to judge his executors. Fearing that Stephanos was trying to conjure Jesus' spirit to attack them, they quickly stoned him and threw his body out of the city into the dump (Acts 6–7, but it was recovered). Since Saul's encounter with Jesus was in 34–35 CE, this event would be dated to 33–34 CE, i.e., within a year of the first encounter with Kayfa. Stephanos' death led to violent persecutions. Other deaths followed, but we are not told the names of others, only that Saul violently seized others and "tried to annihilated the church." There is no question that the perilous risk of the followers of Jesus, including Kayfa, was dramatically heightened. With the ascension of Herod Agrippa 1 (44 CE), Yacob was captured and killed in Jerusalem, beheaded by sword, so as to mutilate his body, thereby preventing retaliation by this exorcist.

of the event, given the increased risk that was accepted, this event passes the test of qualitative risk analysis.[114]

Luke 24:34 and the Criteria of Dissimilarity and Embarrassment

In the test using the *criterion of dissimilarity*, encounters must differ from the needs and influence of the early church on the one hand and first-century Judaism in Palestine on the other.

The application of this test creates significant difficulties as to its historicity. The report of Kayfa's encounter with Jesus became the cornerstone of early Christianity's claim to the *euangelion* of the resurrected Lord and a returning future messiah.[115] Further, a contextual setting within Palestinian Judaism with complex analogies to messianic traditions of a retributive messianic figure soon to return, such as the Son of Man.[116] As such, this tradition, unless it is associated with the event on the lake, fails this test. However, with recourse to the risk tradition of Kayfa's lake encounter with Jesus—if it is allowed as the encounter referenced in this tradition—then this post-crucifixion event stands separate from the needs of the church

---

114. The reason why Kayfa's specific encounters are not described is clearly because they were problematic, likely similar to both the lake and mountain encounters. These were encounters with Jesus similar to an encounter with a phantasm. As such, they created significantly difficulties for the early church as the first encounters. This is why these two traditions were displaced as post-crucifixion encounters between Kayfa and Jesus, and were reset into the itinerant activity of Jesus.

115. 1 Cor 15:3–5; Paul is not ashamed of the gospel, Rom 1:16; Gal 5:17.

116. Perrin, *Modern Pilgrimage*, 84–93, and Morrison, *Turning Point*, 140–43. That is, *bar nasha*, the Aramaic circumlocution for oneself, or "I," or "me" translated "son of man"; later Jesus' use of this common circumlocution for I was understood in the early church as a christological title, the future Son of Man, but this is far from what is intended by Jesus during his activity. As Finkelstein shows, the literature included the writings the authors of Enoch (Finkelstein, *Pharisees*, 148) and Daniel, both of which include the explicit imagery of the divine Son of Man, who judges. Foerster (*From the Exile to Christ*, 98) notes that the conception of the messiah was already tied to the Son of Man in the century preceding Jesus' activity, arising from the influence of the book of Daniel. This influence was certainly influential earlier than its latter appearance in Rabbinic literature, and thus, must have been a prominent feature of the Pharisaic traditions, i.e., during the period of Jesus' ministry (Paul used the opposition of the Pharisees and Sadducees over resurrection of the dead as an opportunity to distract his opponents, see Acts 23:6; Psalms of Solomon are associated with the Pharisees by some, although it is apparent that apocalyptic literature, such as IV Ezra or I Enoch may also be associated with them). The Parables of Enoch, also with contemporaneous influence, include reference to the Son of Man, his protection of the righteous and the agony of those who oppose them. Todt also supports the predominant influence of Son of Man expectations on Palestinian Judaism during Jesus' lifetime (Todt, *Son of Man*, 53).

(i.e., the tradition was displaced as a resurrection encounter and inserted into the itinerant activity of Jesus due to its problematic nature as an encounter with a *phantasm*) and Palestinian Judaism. Only on this basis can the tradition pass the test of the criterion of dissimilarity. As such, because analysis confirms that the lake encounter was a post-crucifixion encounter with Kayfa, and it stands as distinctive from the context of Palestinian Judaism given contemporary sources, Luke 24:34 can be considered reliable.

Similarly, if Luke 24:34 references the lake encounter, analysis has established this event was displaced as a post-crucifixion experience because Jesus is perceived as a *phantasm*, a ghost, and was problematic—an embarrassment. The redactor/editor of Mark, followed by other redactors, retained this placement. Consequently, the tradition passes the *criterion of embarrassment*.

Summary of Risk Analysis

An analysis of Luke 24:34 has isolated compelling elements of the unit by employing the various criteria of risk analysis, assuming reference is to the lake encounter with Jesus. Based on this analysis, set on the basis of the lake event, the event should be considered reliable within its contemporary setting.

Luke 24:34 and the Contextual Tests

We now turn to contextual analyses. Here an event must be coherent with the sociological risk setting, including the subsistence struggle of the Galileans, the background from which they came to join Jesus' band of exorcists. Once again, the contextual risk tests previously established are as follows:

1. Encounters with original members of Jesus' band of Galilean exorcists, those who faced capture, death and social isolation and starvation, are given priority.

2. Encounters should be consistent with the ecstatic practices of Jesus that engendered the original perilous risk with his opponents. Specifically, encounters that encouraged the remaining exorcists to continue the ecstatic activity of Jesus and his war on Satan are preferred.

3. Encounters near or on the lake of Galilee, particularly related to subsistence fishing, and similar to the animistic control exhibited by Jesus, are preferential (i.e., the remaining exorcists escaped there).

4. Finally, encounters that may have led the Galileans to again abandon subsistence existence (i.e., to which they returned for survival post-crucifixion) are also preferred.

LUKE AND THE REFINEMENT OF POST-CRUCIFIXION TRADITION 167

In each of the foregoing tests, the original form of the unit recovered through risk analysis is evaluated.

With regard to the contextual analyses, Luke 24:34 in association with the lake encounter, passes all contextual tests. If this were the encounter, the event has the highest degree of reliability as a post-crucifixion encounter with Jesus.

Conclusions on the Veracity of Luke 24:34

Based on the risk and analytical criteria employed, combined with contextual analysis, the tradition reflected in Luke 23:34 should be considered an authentic post-crucifixion encounter with Jesus; but one where the tradition must be associated with the encounter with Jesus by Kayfa at night on the lake of Galilee. As such, in the context of human risk experience, this encounter with Jesus is a compelling in its contemporary context and setting. The redactor/editor of the Lucan community has reset the events at the Lake in Galilee to Jerusalem and wishes to relate the original event to the *sitz im leben* of the current community.

Luke 24:36–43: Why Was a "Closed Door" Event Reported?

Jesus suddenly appears in a locked room to the remaining exorcists hiding in Jerusalem, standing in their midst (he materializes among them). Jesus speaks: *erine humin*, "peace to you,"[117] in Hebrew, *Shalom*, although more than a greeting here—a conveyance of charismatic power to receive comfort. Those present are terrified (*tpoenthentes de kai emphoboi*) and think they see a *pnuema*,[118] a ghost, but Jesus shows his wounds and invites them to handle him (*pselaphesate*) to see he has "flesh and bones (*sarka kai ostea*)." There is no indication that they do. They disbelieve "for joy." Jesus eats in front of them. The disciples are instructed to "remain in Jerusalem" until they receive power "from on high."

---

117. A greeting used by Jesus in post-crucifixion appearances in John 20:19–21, 14:27; Paul, Rom 15:33, 1 Cor 1:3, 2 Cor 2:1.

118. Other ancient manuscript witnesses (e.g., *D*) use *phantasm*, which may be the more original wording, see Plummer, *Luke*, 559.

Luke 24:36–43, Risk Analysis and the Criteria of Dissimilarity and Embarrassment

The context of the Jerusalem encounter is a complex mix of post-crucifixion elements that reflect early traditions, as well as later Christian developments previously analyzed. To begin, the event is placed in Jerusalem, a fictitious location, as risk analysis has established that all of Jesus' exorcists (but Magdalene) abandoned and denied him, fleeing to Galilee after the crucifixion. The materialization of Jesus in a locked room as a *phantasm*, an event that terrorized those present, has parallels in Hellenistic literature previously cited.[119] However, such parallels can be contrasted with Jesus' invitation to those that disbelieve to handle him as flesh and blood. Expansion of the tradition to demonstrate that Jesus was fully physically present, i.e., in flesh and bones, was a later development, intended to prove that the encounters were not just *phantasm* encounters, a trance, docetic event (an illusory body associated with Gnosis), or simply a common ghost story—a need of the early church in conflict with what it considered unorthodox theology and communities.[120]

However, this expansion suggests that the original event in its contemporary setting *was* a *phantasm* experience, perhaps with some form of a material body attached to it.[121] It was this form of the tradition that was problematic and embarrassing to the community of Matthew's gospel (80 to 90 CE) due to contemporary competing theologies, such as emergent Docetism. As such, the original encounter must have been similar to other mass events with Jesus, such as those cited by Paul (54 CE) as matters of fact. Paul is the earliest witness to report group appearances similar to this; i.e., to the "the twelve," as well as with "all the apostles," and to "over five-hundred brethren" (1 Cor 15:5–8), many of whom he states were alive and available to attest to the encounter. Paul does not state that these were events with a material body present. Consequently, the materiality of the body of Jesus was not a pressing problem in primitive Christianity contemporary with

---

119. Ogden, *Magic*: "The Ghost of the Girl Philinnion Returns to Sleep with the Lodger," 140 CE (from an earlier tradition recorded by Phlegon of Tralles, Mirabella I), 150–52. This is an important ancient tradition in that the girl chooses to materialize based on her love, then dematerializes when handled (see Jesus encounter with Mary, John 20:17, where Jesus warns Mary not to handle him). Other traditions of what Ogden calls "revenants" require others to conjure them, e.g., 114–15.

120. For a discussion on docetism and its evidence in conflict with primitive churches toward later decades of the first century and within the Gospel of John, see Van Wahlde, *Gnosticism*, 61–82.

121. As noted, a form that has contemporary examples in Hellenistic literature.

Paul's authentic writings.¹²² Nonetheless, that the original form of the tradition was embarrassing to the Matthew's community and was expanded only goes to underscore its reliability—there was a post-crucifixion encounter with the some of Jesus' original exorcists, and not in Jerusalem, but in Galilee. The original form of the tradition, based on contextual and risk analysis would be as follows:

> Indeed, Jesus appeared standing among them [at the place they hid during the day]. They were terrified, thinking they saw a *phantasm* [retributive or malevolent spirit of the dead], but he spoke to them, "receive peace." "See, it is I, look at my hands and feet!" Do not doubt!

Consequently, embedded within the tradition, which relates Jesus' post-crucifixion encounter with his exorcists (an event similar to that reported by Paul in 1 Cor 15:5), is a more primitive oral traditional formula, similar to the one described by Paul, i.e., the "twelve."¹²³ Our contextual analysis must also take into account that all strata of tradition confirm that Jesus' exorcists returned to itinerant activity and the battle with demonic forces in preparation for the arrival of the kingdom of God after. It was this additional encounter, not just Kayfa's, which resulted in acceptance of increased perilous risk, including the risks of possession, betrayal, capture and death. Given that an original form of a phantasm encounter stands behind this tradition, the criteria of the contextual tests would be met.

Luke 24:36–43 and Contextual Analysis

The more primitive form of this tradition suggested by risk analysis would pass the contextual tests:

1. The encounters is with original members of Jesus' band of Galilean exorcists, those who faced capture, death and social isolation and starvation.

2. The encounter is consistent with the ecstatic practices of Jesus that engendered the original perilous risk with his opponents. Specifically,

---

122. The resurrected body was a *soma pneuma*, a spiritual body, not one of flesh and blood; 1 Cor 15:44.

123. This oral traditional formula repeated by Paul with its reference to Jesus' being seen by the "twelve" is problematic. There were only eleven left, as Judas was absent or dead. Can Paul mean that the encounter took place after Judas was replaced? If so, this would conflict with the traditions in the Synoptics and the Johannine traditions, as well as other noncanonical gospels. Consequently, the question arises as to Paul's understanding of Kayfa, the twelve and just to whom these encounters occurred.

the encounter encouraged the remaining exorcists to continue the ecstatic activity of Jesus and his war on Satan.

3. The encounter is near the lake of Galilee, and is particularly related to subsistence fishing (i.e., the remaining exorcists escaped there).
4. Finally, the encounter led the Galileans to again abandon subsistence existence (i.e., to which they returned for survival post-crucifixion).

Given that an earlier form of the tradition passes the contextual tests, we may turn to the veracity of Luke 24:36–39.

Conclusions on the Veracity of Luke 24:36–43

Based on the risk and analytical criteria employed, combined with contextual analysis, the tradition of an encounter between Jesus and some of his exorcists (a mass vision or trance) now embedded in Luke 24:36–39 may be considered a reliable post-crucifixion encounter with Jesus, likely at a group vision of a materialized Jesus post-crucifixion. As such, in the context of human risk experience, this encounter with Jesus is compelling within its original context and setting. Once again, the redactor/editor of the Lucan community has reset the events at the lake in Galilee to Jerusalem for theological purposes and wishes to relate the original event to the *sitz im leben* of the current community, including the need to demonstrate that Jesus rose in bodily form, to combat competing communities similar in theology to nascent docestism. The early tradition in Paul that Jesus appeared to "the twelve" is testimony to this event, and, as Paul notes, could be confirmed by those "still living," including Kayfa. Analysis will later show that Kayfa formed the "twelve" after his encounters, and included Magdalene and Cleopas, but named exorcists of Jesus who also privately encountered Jesus post-crucifixion.

Luke 24:50–53: Did the Early Church Create the Departure Event?

Jesus takes the followers to Bethany. They are blessed and then he "parted (*dieste ap auton*, withdrew) from them." The implication is that he dematerialized or ascended to heaven.

To begin, scholars almost universally see this event as the theological conclusion of the earthly ministry of Jesus devised by the redactor/editor (the end of Jesus' journey),[124] thereby setting the stage for the miraculous expansion of the gospel from Jerusalem to Rome. Koester has asserted that Luke 24:50–53, along with the Emmaus event, were later additions to help divide Luke-Acts, as the ascension is more appropriately set at the beginning of Acts.[125] The most compelling analysis suggests that the ascension ended speculation as to new claims of encounters with Jesus, bringing all legitimate encounters within the prevue of Acts ending with Paul.[126]

There are many problems with the risk and contextual setting in Luke 24:50–53, all of which point to a later origin for the unit. The event is located in Jerusalem, not Galilee. Those present are given a priestly blessing,[127] thereby eliminating perilous risk by suggesting victory over enemies and protection from Satan and demonic forces. There are no references to a return to subsistence existence or abandonment of that existence despite facing peril and death. The tradition cannot pass the test of the criterion of dissimilarity, as it serves the needs of the early church and the theological program of Luke-Acts, nor is there evidence of embarrassment.

Given these factors, no further risk analysis is required. This tradition fails the qualitative risk and contextual tests and cannot be considered an authentic encounter with Jesus, post-crucifixion.

---

124. Denaux, *Studies in the Gospel of Luke*, 305. See also Parsons, "Narrative Closure," 201–23.

125. Koester, *History*, 316.

126. Funk and Jesus Seminar, "Empty Tomb," 449–95. Also suggested by Plummer, *Luke*, 565.

127. E.g., Hendriksen, *Exposition of the Gospel according to St. Luke*, 43; Mekkattukunnel, "Priestly Blessing of the Risen Christ," 714.

10

Post-Crucifixion Encounters as Sign (*Semeion*) in John

Haunted Galilee, Magdalene's Visit to the Tomb, and the Exorcist Toma

Risk and contextual analysis now turns to the Johannine tradition, specifically, the Gospel of John. Like other gospels, community influences are evident (many of which reflect second or third generation needs), but also evident are what appear to be risk events that may date to the period of Jesus' war on Satan. These original forms are recovered using risk and contextual analysis, and then their veracity is assessed. Did the Johannine community consider these "signs" (*semeion*) of transformation from death to life—ones in which they can participate immediately upon hearing?[1] We begin with one recovery of an event that was never placed in the post-resurrection events found in John.

John 6:16–24 (also Mark 6:45–56 and Matt 14:22–36): Why Was a Phantasm Event Retained by John?

After a day of exorcism and the miraculous feeding five thousand on the "far side of Galilee," Jesus retreats to the mountains by himself. Remarkably, the exorcists' decide to leave Jesus behind, and do so at night. They row against heavy winds across Galilee to reach Capernaum. When they are three to

---

1. The Signs source may include sections of John 20 and John 21. Risk event as a "sign" of metamorphosis or transformation from death to life are evident. See the Jesus Seminar Forum, http://virtualreligion.net/forum/complete.html, and listing on that page, *Sign's Gospel*, http://www.earlygospels.net, *Early Christian Writings*.

four miles out, a figure appears and begins to approach the boat. It is Jesus, who is mistaken for a malevolent *phantasm* wandering atop the haunted waters of Galilee, one of the dreaded fears of fishermen.[2] The exorcists are terrified. Finally, Jesus is recognized, and as he is helped into the boat they suddenly appear at the shores of Capernaum. The sudden arrival suggests that this is an ecstatic experience, perhaps a dream or trance.[3] This has led to debate as to the original setting of the tradition. Recent analysis has suggested this was a post-crucifixion encounter with Kayfa, later transposed into Jesus' Galilean ministry.[4]

A *sitz im leben*, where Jesus orders the exorcists to cross the lake at night during his itinerant war on Satan, is a highly unlikely and problematic. Risk analysis has demonstrated that night was when evil roamed over Galilean lake waters. Jesus would not order his exorcists into this kind of danger, particularly while in conflict with the vicious demons of Satan. Only subsistence fishermen who were forced to work at night to meet crushing quotas would have been on the lake and taken such deadly risks. Certainly these fishermen expected to encounter a *phantasm*, having heard multiple reports of malevolent encounters—indeed, this tradition presumes such events were feared and well known. Demons were known to haunt the waters of Galilee, having been cast or expelled there by exorcists (including Jesus),[5] where they found refuge.[6]

The tradition of the lake encounter is multiply attested—Mark (6:45–56), Matthew (14:22–26) and John (6:16–24). It is one of the few traditions, other than the passion narrative that appear in all three of the four canonical gospels. Luke drops this tradition altogether due to the controversial nature of Jesus having been identified as a *phantasm*. If this were a post-crucifixion encounter, the nature of Jesus' appearances after the crucifixion as an apparition or spirit of the dead would lead to either a change in setting to the ministry of Jesus (so Mark, Matthew and John), or its omission (Luke).[7]

2. Mark 6:45–56.

3. This event is also found in Mark 6:45–56 and Matt 14:22–36. In Mark, Jesus is trying to pass by the disciples without notice about 3–6 a.m. as they fight the strong winds, but the exorcists see Jesus and think he is a *phantasm*. He joins them in the boat and the wind ceases. In Matthew, Jesus sees them in trouble and comes directly to assist. Again, they believe they also see a ghost. Kayfa tries to join Jesus on the water but begins to sink, only to be taken by Jesus' hand and rescued. The winds cease.

4. See the discussion by Patterson, *Beyond the Passion*, 113–14. Madden, "Jesus Walking on the Sea," 30–156.

5. Mark 5:1–17.

6. More discussion will be provided in sections on the waters of Galilee being the home of demons below.

7. Steve Patterson believes this was a resurrection event, but was pushed back

Given the perilous risks involved with night fishing, the most likely setting is a post-crucifixion encounter. The rising winds signaled demonic attack and risk of death.[8] As risk analysis has confirmed, Jesus' exorcists fled Jerusalem for Galilee, and returned to subsistence fishing at night to avoid detection, protected by kin from spies and those seeking to destroy all of Jesus' exorcists. These fishermen would only return to night fishing out of desperation to sustain a meager, dangerous subsistence existence and avoid capture. While they would have feared *phantasms* and demonic attack, starvation was not a viable alternative. They would not have expected to encounter Jesus, believing him annihilated on the cross under a divine curse.[9]

Consequently, the reaction of the exorcists is accurately portrayed. They are terrified, clearly expecting the *phantasm* to attack,[10] with demonic winds capable of driving their boat underneath the waters—i.e., where they would be taken under by demonic powers. The retention of this tradition confirms the social and cultural context of desperation, risk, and fear associated with the everyday life of agrarian farmers and fishermen as they faced malevolent forces that surrounded them. The tradition also accepts Galilee to be haunted. Fishermen were powerless against these forces, and must have incorporated specific practices and rites to mitigate such perilous risks.[11] That Kayfa is prominently mentioned in each version of the tradition, and Jesus' appearance is as a *phantasm*, the problematic nature suggests the original context to be a post-crucifixion setting.

---

into the ministry of Jesus because of the controversial nature of Jesus appearing as a *phantasm*.

8. Van der Toom et al., *Dictionary of Demons*, 236: "They held power during dangerous situations and times: Chiefly at night, during sleep, during a wind storm or an eclipse, or heat of mid-day, and especially in child birth."

9. Multigenerational families huddled in small rooms with a central small courtyard, cooking with a simple stone oven, primarily a bread, olive and fish diet. Dwellings were made of rough basalt stones, filled with mud and pebbles, covered with twig and mud roofs.

10. See examples from 300 BCE to 44 BCE in Hellenistic literature, such as Ogden, *Magic*, 152, 158, and 162–63, "Direction for the laying of an attacking ghost"

11. Hull, *Hellenistic Magic*, 104. That Jesus is accused of being possessed by Beelzebul and is able to control the fish for the benefit of subsistence fishermen (to deceive them according to his enemies) presents an interesting correlation between possession of the waters Galilee, under the control of Jesus, and the Red Sea, by Beelzebul's son. Jesus' enemies must have understood this connection, which to us is clearer and now probable.

John 6:16–24, Risk Analysis and the Criteria of Dissimilarity and Embarrassment

We can begin our risks analysis of the unit, employing first, qualitative risk. In this analysis, the encounter cannot be a countermeasure to the elite, but must heighten the perilous risk of the Galilean exorcists and the conflict with opponents.

This event could only have originated in Galilee and is reliable due to its controversial nature. The disciples encountered what they thought was a "ghost Jesus"; a *biaeothanati*, able to curse, punish and harm, even kill his murderers, as well as those that abandoned him.[12] The intense risk setting underscores both the desperate plight of the exorcists and the terrifying fear they had about retribution, having denied Jesus, and fled to Galilee. Based on qualitative risk analysis, the perilous risk of the Galilean is significantly heightened, and there is no evidence that the event can be understood in any way as a countermeasure to Jesus' original enemies.

Further, we can be certain that this event would not have been manufactured by the early church for a number of reasons, including the concern that opponents would claim Jesus' resurrection appearances were nothing more than a *phantasm* encounter. In addition, there are no contemporary parallels in Palestinian Judaism. Consequently, the tradition passed the criterion of dissimilarity.

Traditions identified as problematic to the early church (e.g., Jesus' baptism by John; his betrayal by one of the exorcists he had personally selected), represent embarrassment, and if retained and modified, have a claim to authenticity. The early community would never have manufactured such traditions due to the controversies they fostered.[13] The tradition was problematic as a resurrection event, as Jesus was identified as a *phantasm*, a ghost, reducing the experience as ethereal, subjective—a common ghost story. By placing the tradition back into the ministry of Jesus, concern that the resurrected Jesus was nothing more than a ghostly experience, perhaps

---

12. Ogden, *Magic*, 152–53; 158.

13. Another aspect of this tradition is the sudden appearance of the boat at the shore when Jesus enters the boat, where this immediate transportation suggests a trance-like experience, and not a physical encounter of any kind. This aspect of the tradition underscores its problematic nature as a resurrection appearance to the early church, but the retention of this aspect of the tradition can only be understood as strengthening the claim that this event was as a post-crucifixion encounter with Jesus.

in a trance, is eliminated.[14] Consequently, John 6:16–24 clearly represents such a tradition, and so meets the criterion of embarrassment.[15]

Having employed risk analysis, and the criteria of dissimilarity and embarrassment, the recovered tradition passes all risk tests.

John 6:16–24 and Contextual Analysis

The recovered form of this tradition suggested by risk analysis would pass the contextual tests as follows:

1. The encounters is with an original member of Jesus' band of Galilean exorcists, those who faced capture, death and social isolation and starvation.
2. The encounter is consistent with the ecstatic practices of Jesus that engendered the original perilous risk with his opponents. Specifically, the encounter encouraged the remaining exorcists reengage in the ecstatic activity of Jesus and his war on Satan.
3. The encounter is near the lake of Galilee, and is particularly related to subsistence fishing (i.e., the remaining exorcists escaped there).
4. Finally, the encounter led the Galileans to again abandon subsistence existence (i.e., to which they returned for survival post-crucifixion).

Given that an earlier form of the tradition passes the contextual and risk tests, we may turn to the veracity of John 6:16–24.

Conclusions on the Veracity of John 6:16–24

Based on the risk and analytical criteria employed, combined with contextual analysis, the tradition of an encounter between Jesus and Kayfa on the lake of Galilee, or a vision or trance of an encounter on the lake in Galilee, is a reliable post-crucifixion encounter with Jesus. The redactor/editor of the Johannine community (as in Mark and Matthew) has taken a post-crucifixion encounter and reset it into Jesus' itinerant activity.

---

14. The development of the tradition is also apparent. While Mark and Matthew use the word *phantasm*, Matthew expands the tradition with the inclusion of Kayfa, showing that Jesus was more than ghostly, he was material and extraordinarily powerful. John, eliminates *phantasm* altogether and has the boat arrive at its destination when Jesus boards. Mark's version is the earliest form.

15. Meier, *Marginal Jew*, 93.

John 20:11–18: Why Would Magdalene Risk Going to the Tomb at Night?

Jesus encounters Mary, the Magdalene, outside the empty tomb, she assuming he is the gardener until she hears his voice calling her name. She attempts to hold him, but he stops her, saying he has not yet "ascended."

John 20:11–18, Risk Analysis and the Criteria of Dissimilarity and Embarrassment

Mary, the Magdalene (which, as noted in Hebrew and Aramaic is translated "tower," the "fortress," or the "high one"),[16] is the identification that renders the proper understanding of Mary's position among her fellow exorcists and within the original risk context. As noted, the tradition of women conversing with Jesus, and Mary having equal standing with Kayfa, is rooted in early Christian literature and is multiply attested.[17] Recent studies have confirmed that women and men prayed, sang and conducted charismatic activity as part of the same community, particularly ascetic communities like the Theraputae,[18] a contemporaneous ecstatic community that, as we have seen, lived near water and whose disbursement included Palestine and Magdala. We cannot discount that this activity was patterned in Paul's *ecclesiae*, where men and women shared equal standing.[19]

This encounter is distinct from Matt 28:9–10. In Matt 28:9–10, Mary *the Magdalene* and "the other Mary" have the first ecstatic encounter with Jesus, post-crucifixion.[20] As noted earlier, they had gone to see the tomb the evening after the Sabbath "toward the dawn," which, from a risk perspective

---

16. As noted earlier, this is a very old tradition that was retained in early Christianity, even repeated by Jerome in 412 CE in his letter to Principia, recounting the life of Marcella: "and how specially Mary Magdalene—called *the Tower* the earnestness and *glow* of her faith [glow here can also infer ecstatic behavior]—was privileged to see the risen Christ first of all before the very apostles," Kraemer, *Maenads, Martyrs*, 181.

17. See the excellent analysis of sources and the *Gospel of Mary* by King, *Gospel of Mary*, 175–76; Mary is known as an apostle in various early Christian writings, from the *Dialogue of the Savior*, *Apocalypse of James*, and the confrontation with Kayfa is recorded also in the *Gospel of Thomas*, 114. The multiple attestation of Mary's role as an apostle and women as apostles is indisputable.

18. McDowell, *Prayers of Jewish Women*, 148–50.

19. Galatians ("there is neither male nor female"), Romans (Phoebe and Junia), and Corinthians (Prisca).

20. The problematic nature of a report coming from the witness of a Jewish women in first-century Palestine will be addressed below when applying the various risk criteria, including the criterion of dissimilarity.

makes their effort striking—not because it was dark, but it was exactly when malevolent ghosts, evil spirits and demons were believed to roam seeking victims, particularly near tombs and graveyards. Our risk and contextual analyses demonstrated why Magdalene would have taken such a perilous risk, particularly when the very demonic forces that had just succeeded in overwhelming and killing Jesus, the man they thought to be a powerful exorcist possessed by the "finger of God," would have been present. Qualitative risk and contextual analyses would suggest their visit to the tomb had a specific risk motivation and one that can be recovered.

Analysis has confirmed that Magdalene was most certainly an itinerant ecstatic and exorcist, just as were the male exorcists who had followed Jesus—a tradition that was undoubtedly later suppressed.[21] Unlike the male exorcists who fled, Mary made a conscious, perilous risk decision—she *chose* to remain, risk capture, *secretly* following (at a distance)[22] to see not only who took the brutalized body of Jesus, but more important, to see *where* it is taken.[23] They watch as it is *sealed* in a rock tomb, the entrance blocked by a heavy rolling stone. There are examples of sealing spirits and ghosts in stone tombs to trap them[24]—certainly the fear of those who sealed up Jesus' body. Finally, when alone and before guards arrive, they face or *sit over against* the tomb. The tomb is then guarded (as noted, by special priests, likely in white robes, not by soldiers).[25]

After the Sabbath ended, and at the most dangerous time of night, Magdalene returns. Mark and Luke include that it was to "anoint the body" (Mark 16:1–2 or Luke 24:1), adding also the names of other women present with them.[26] However, the editor/redactor of Matthew knew Palestine and

---

21. See the discussion below on the suppression of women in subsequent gospel traditions, particularly Kraemer, "Autonomy, Prophecy and Gender," 130–31; We know that Junia and Phoebe were likely itinerant ecstatics, as Junia is identified by Paul as an apostle of note among the others, and was known to be one long before he had his own encounter with Jesus, Rom 16:7. Paul is very clear about the qualities of true apostles like himself in 2 Cor 12:1–20.

22. Matt 27:55.

23. If these men were sympathizers of Jesus, the women would not have had to follow at a distance, or wait until their departure, and only then approach the tomb.

24. Ogden, *Magic*, for example: "A mage seals a friendly ghost into its tomb, to the dismay of its mother" (164–66).

25. Matt 27:61: Guarding the tomb was indicative of fear of retribution, i.e., to monitor it to ensure it remain still and inactive.

26. Other women are mentioned in Mark 16:1–2: Mary Magdalene, Mary the Mother of James and Salome; other gospels have different groups and interactions, but are unanimous that women found the empty tomb and tried to report it to Kayfa, only be told it was an "idle tale."

that anointing a decaying body would have been inconceivable and repugnant after three days;[27] and with the brutalized condition of Jesus' body, possibly further mutilated,[28] simply too horrible. Indeed, no anointing was needed. That Jesus' body had been dressed is certainly correct. However, based on the risk and contextual setting previously analyzed, Jesus' body was more likely covered with a concoction of magical herbs, amulets and written spells. This was done to ensure his ghost/spirit would remain at rest under a divine curse, his enemies fearing that, as a minion of Satan's demonic prince, Beelzebul, he would seek deadly retribution.[29]

Consequently, going to the tomb had nothing to do with anointing a decaying and mutilated body. Employing a contextual risk perspective within the original setting, Magdalene went to raise up, claim or communicate with Jesus' spirit, intending to seek his protection, or that of "the finger of God," the Spirit that possessed him. This presents the possibility that Magdalene was responsible for Jesus' post-crucifixion appearances, and the origin of primitive Christianity. Only these circumstances adequately address the actual risk context of Magdalene's ecstatic visit to the tomb.[30] Of course, when the ritual priests rolled back the tomb that morning, the body was gone, and this followed Mary's activity earlier that morning.

At the tomb, Magdalene has an ecstatic experience, likely entering a trance and vision (much like Kayfa's recovered early in this study).[31] She witnesses the descent of an angel, a tremendous earthquake, and then sees the rolling back (*kulio*) of the large stone that sealed the tomb to trap Jesus' body and spirit. An angel of God instructs the her to tell the exorcists that the tomb had been vacated. Jesus' body does not appear. It is presumed that the tomb was already empty, just as in the tradition of Phlegon previously noted in the account of a deceased girl, Philinnion.[32] The women rush to tell the other exorcists when they encounter Jesus. Whether this occurs in the vision or as a separate event on a road is uncertain,[33] but Jesus appears suddenly. They fall to their feet, wrap their arms around and worship him.

Turning to the tradition in John 20, Magdalene comes to the tomb *skotias eti ouses*, "while it is still dark," the time of malevolent and dangerous

27. The very point of John 11:39 within the canonical gospel tradition.

28. Ogden, *Magic*, 162.

29. Busse, *To Be Near the Fire*, 55–56.

30. See examples in Ogden, *Magic*, 64–65, 146–47, 149–52, 161–62, 164–65, on tombs and encounters with ghosts and spirits there.

31. As determined in our previous analysis of the metamorphosis of Jesus, or as in Act 10:10.

32. Phlegon of Tralles, *Mirabilia I*, in Ogden, *Magic*, 159–60.

33. If on a road, the tradition may have been created as an echo to Paul's Damascus experience. Were this the case, the encounter was during the trance.

evil activity. Despite the darkness, she sees the stone sealing the tomb rolled back. She finds Kayfa to tell him "they have taken away the master," *eron ton kurion*. Kayfa is then the first to enter the tomb, thereby making Kayfa prominent, i.e., as the first witness to empty tomb (and a male). However, it is clear that his entry is short and the meaning uncertain for Kayfa, while Magdalene's is revelatory, exactly the opposite. Interestingly, the tradition provides extraordinary detail about the arrangement of the burial linens, including the linen that wrapped the head that is witnessed by Kayfa. The historical veracity of such burial linens, with a separate wrapping for the head, was found in an excavation of an elitist Jerusalem tomb dated from 1 to 30 CE.[34] In 20:11 Magdalene is then said to be outside the tomb weeping, but "stoops down" and looks in (still being dark). Unlike Kayfa, she sees two *aggelous en leukos* sitting inside, one at the head of the stone bench and the other at the where the feet where the body had been laid.[35] Magdalene is not terrified, nor does she avoid contact.[36] Instead, she converses with the angels when they ask why she is crying. They do not answer her question, so she turns away and sees a man behind her. It is Jesus, but she fails to recognize him,[37] thinking he is the *kepouros*, gardener and likely keeper of the tombs. He asks why she is weeping. After explaining her desperation, he speaks her name, *Maria*. Magdalene recognizes the voice, calls him *rabboni*, "teacher." Jesus demands she not touch him for he had not ascended *pros ton patera* to the Father.

Magdalene's encounter in John 20:11–18 has been properly identified as an ecstatic trance and vision—a separate tradition from both her visit to the tomb to conjure the spirit of Jesus and the ecstatic vision she has of the descending angel.[38] Risk analysis has demonstrated that Kayfa is not in Jerusalem, he is in Galilee, and so the sequence of events is improbable, unless it were a separate a vision or trance. There is no reference to Jesus' body or to his corporality; only that Magdalene sees what she thinks as a gardener, but by voice reveals the presence of Jesus.

The importance of this event to the Johannine community stands out among the post-crucifixion encounters. Scholars that argue Magdalene is marginalized by the Gospel of John have to explain why this encounter is not only the first, but also private, stressing its importance and Magdalene

---

34. Discovery by Gibson and a team of archaeologists: Gibson, *Final Days*, 127–48.

35. Hachlili, *Jewish Funerary Customs*, 514–15.

36. This would support the event as ecstatic, a trance, i.e., an experience not unfamiliar to Magdalene and the other exorcists.

37. A common theme similar to the Emmaus encounter with the mysterious traveler, Luke 24:13–35.

38. Pagels, "Visions," 415–16.

as the primary witness.³⁹ If suppression were the editor's/redactors' intent, the tradition would not have been repeated and Mary's name would have been omitted. Clearly, it was impossible to suppress traditions about Mary the Magdalene because they were so prevalent. More, the two witnesses that are portrayed as having equal standing at the empty tomb, Magdalene and Kayfa, are Jesus' chief exorcists. Certainly this reflects competing traditions of preeminence of Kayfa or Mary that were active during John's composition (between 95 to 110 CE). In John 20:11–18, Magdalene's encounter is stressed as absolutely legitimate, vastly expanded over that of Kayfa's, and includes other divine presence and voices;⁴⁰ it ultimately culminates in the most intimate and personal encounter with Jesus in the New Testament. How does one reconcile Magdalene's encounter in Matthew (the ecstatic vision of the angel and encounter with Jesus) with this encounter?

Because of multiple-attestation,⁴¹ as well as risk and contextual analyses previously conducted, Magdalene's ecstatic activity at the tomb before dawn, when demonic powers ruled and perilous risk and danger were overwhelming, is certain.⁴² The encounter is a trance or vision. Employing specific practices used by Roman period exorcists to determine Jesus' fate, which include special herbs and incantations, Magdalene enters a trance and witnesses the angelic arrival and tomb's opening, confirming that Jesus has vacated it and is active. Matthew then has Magdalene encounter Jesus on the road and then grasp him. But in John, Jesus' forbids contact, which even more strongly suggests that Magdalene's encounter in John is an ecstatic trance and vision. As noted, contact immediately ended a vision.⁴³ A trance and vision are experiences familiar to Jesus' exorcists post-crucifixion, including Kayfa and Paul. Kayfa fell into a trance and had an ecstatic vision that included instructions from heavenly voices (speaking to him three times to ensure the instructions were understood).⁴⁴ Paul relates an analogous experience.⁴⁵ As such, both of Magdalene's encounters must have been similar trances, and both lead her to take extraordinary heightened risk; namely, returning to Galilee to find Kayfa and the other exorcists, hiding and in fear of retribution. Returning to Galilee was a perilous journey. It

---

39. Maccini, *Here Testimony Is True*, 218–33.

40. *Duo aggelous*, "two angels who speak," *gunai ti klaieis*, "woman, why are you lamenting?"

41. Synoptics, John and extra-canonical, *Gospel of Mary* (30–120 CE) and *Gospel of Peter* (150 CE)

42. See the previous risk analysis of Matt 28:16–20.

43. Ogden, *Magic*, 159–60.

44. Acts 10:1—11:18.

45. 2 Cor 12:2.

brought her back into a land filled with spies and assassins, including those hunting for followers of the crucified Jesus. Consequently, Magdalene's two ecstatic encounters are highly probably. The message she brought was clear: Jesus was active and available to his exorcists. These separate events underscore the multiplicity of post-resurrection encounters that richly populate the Synoptic, Johannine and extra-canonical sources. Visionary, trance and dream experiences were real in every sense to Magdalene and to the other exorcists in the context of first-century Palestine.

The *Gospel of Mary* and the *Gospel of Peter* also describe trances of Magdalene and Kayfa. Both are absolutely understood as personal, quite real within the fabric of the first- and second-century world.[46] In the *Gospel of Mary*, Magdalene asks Jesus while in a trance, "How does he who sees a vision see it?" The answer from Jesus is that it is a visionary experience in the mind—just as real and material to those receiving the encounter. While the *Gospel of Mary* is understood to be an esoteric or Gnostic text, it reflects similar experiences of visions as described here in John 20:11–18. None of Jesus' exorcists expected to have such an encounter, thinking Jesus had been annihilated. This experience was overwhelming, compelling and transformative.

Consequently, with regard to qualitative risk analysis, the encounter with Jesus in John 20:11–18 dramatically increased the perilous risk of Magdalene, confirming that Jesus was active and available to his exorcists. This resulted in a dangerous journey to Galilee, and a high-risk attempt to quietly find those hiding among subsistence night fishermen that had abandoned Jesus, convincing them that he had not been annihilated, and was not seeking revenge. Magdalene's ecstatic practices had been rewarded by this event, and likely a second revelatory trance. It was this experience that may have driven her to first find Kayfa, and the "disciple whom Jesus loved." Because perilous risk was dramatically increased for Magdalene, this event passes the test of qualitative risk analysis.

Applying the criterion of dissimilarity, this event, is consistent with troubling visionary trances related to encounter with Jesus post-crucifixion and at the empty tomb. Since is recast from its original form as a visionary trance, it would stand as dissimilar to the needs of the early church and passes this criterion. Accepting the current form of the tradition in John would not render it dissimilar. Magdalene is elevated and made equal with Kayfa, thereby reflecting the controversy over the importance of her role and its place within the Johannine community—she is honored and to be revered. In the current form, the vision serves to convince the hearer/reader of the gospel of the truth of these events and convert them to the community's form and practice of nascent Christianity, both men and women:

46. See Pagels, *Gnostic Gospels*, ch. 1.

> Jesus performed many other signs in the presence of his disciples, which are not recorded in this book. But these are written that you may believe that Jesus is the Messiah, the Son of God, and that by believing you may have life in his name.[47]

The tradition comes from "the beloved disciple" who is claimed to have been a witness to the events by the community and the editor of John.[48] Since our analysis has determined convincingly that Mary's role was devalued in John (also held by scholars),[49] the original vision that asserts the legitimacy of her experience and her important standing demonstrates that the recovered vision is dissimilar to the needs of the early church. More, there are no contemporary parallels in ancient Judaism to a trance and vision of Palestinian ecstatic and exorcist. Consequently, this tradition is also dissimilar to contemporary Palestinian Judaism, and so, passes the test of the criterion of dissimilarity.

With regard to the criterion of embarrassment, the tradition has been altered from a vision to an experience at the tomb, and has Mary meeting with Kayfa in Jerusalem, not Galilee. As such, the tradition has been altered from a visionary trance to a physical encounter, and placed in Jerusalem with Kayfa present. This suggests that the original event was considered an embarrassment to the early church because it was a vision or trance, including in the Johannine community, and had its *sitz im leben* altered. Mary was an important leader to this community and setting her on equal par (or better) with Kayfa was essential to it. Consequently, this tradition passes the criterion of embarrassment.

In sum with regard to overall risk analysis, the results point to a reliable experience in John 20:11–18. We now turn to contextual analysis

---

47. John 20:30–31.

48. John 21:24: This is clearly the assertion of John 21:24–25, as it is a paratextual statement to confirm the authenticity of its authorship and context as coming from the "beloved disciple." John 19:35 reflects the statement of John's editor that also confirms the tradition is from the "beloved disciple" and that his testimony is true. John is the only gospel to have such a statement See Jackson, "Ancient Self-Referential Conventions," (versus Kummel), and Bauckham, *Jesus and the Eyewitnesses*, as analyzed in Culpepper, "John 21:24–25." Culpepper falls short of this attestation by stating that John 21:24–25 is what he terms a "sphragis," or a "seal" of authenticity.

49. For a thorough discussion of this subject and excellent analysis, see D'Angelo, "Reconstructing 'Real' Women," 105–28. The *Gospel of Thomas*, saying 114, takes on the challenge of reaffirming the equality of women who embrace its traditions and practices, for they become complete beings, i.e., the male, which was thought to be a complete human being. This may appear to be a devaluation of women, but instead it confirms the elevation of women made possible by the *Gospel of Thomas* to equal status. See Ehrman, *Peter, Paul and Mary Magdalene*, 211.

John 20:11–18 and Contextual Analysis

The vision of Magdalene at the tomb, or while in Galilee, must be tested against the contextual challenges set forth in this study. The recovered form of this tradition suggested by risk analysis provides the following results:

1. The encounter is with an original member of Jesus' band of Galilean exorcists, those who faced capture, death and social isolation and starvation.

   > This test is met, as Magdalene was an original member of Jesus' exorcists and a leader within his charismatics and in his war on Satan. The vision dramatically increased her perilous risk, having employed techniques of exorcists at the tomb to communicate with Jesus.

2. The encounter is consistent with the ecstatic practices of Jesus that engendered the original perilous risk with his opponents. Specifically, the encounter encouraged the remaining exorcists reengage in the ecstatic activity of Jesus and his war on Satan.

   > This test is met. Magdalene employs charismatic techniques used by Jesus' exorcists, some of which led to her ecstatic experience and encounter via trance or vision with Jesus, therefore confirming Jesus had not been annihilated and was active and available to his exorcists.

3. The encounter is near the lake of Galilee, and is particularly related to subsistence fishing (i.e., the remaining exorcists escaped there).

   > This test is not met. It is not in Galilee, nor did Magdalene abandon subsistence existence.

4. Finally, the encounter led the Galileans to again abandon subsistence existence (i.e., to which they returned for survival post-crucifixion).

   > This test is not met. It is possible, as noted in the study, that Magdalene sought out Kayfa as a result of the trance, but the tradition has no direct confirmation that she took the perilous journey to find him in hiding among kin. This is most certainly what must have occurred, but this conclusion goes beyond evidence in this tradition.

In sum, only two of the four contextual tests are passed. This renders John 20:11–18 inconclusive as to the likely historicity of the tradition, in this case with regard to the contextual tests.

Conclusions on the Veracity of John 20:11–18

Based on the risk and analytical criteria employed, combined with contextual analysis, the tradition of an encounter between Jesus and Magdalene in a trance is rendered possible but inconclusive. As such, in the context of human risk experience, this encounter with Jesus cannot be confirmed as a post-crucifixion encounter in its historical context and setting.

Corollary Findings: The Nature of the Post-Crucifixion Encounters and the Agape

One important but ancillary observation can now be offered in relation to all the reliable post-crucifixion encounters, including John 20:11–18 (albeit inconclusive). Each encounter is remarkably personal, caring and instead of encouraging retribution, is a portrayal of *agape*. These encounters had to be shared. Jesus' use of name in this instance speaks to the intimate nature of these encounters and visions, i.e., between the exorcists and Jesus. This should be considered a reliable feature of these encounters, and more, characteristic of Jesus during his ecstatic encounters and exorcisms: Compassion, forgiveness and *agape* for the demon possessed, disenfranchised and suffering, including for the exorcists who abandoned and betrayed him to demonic forces and fled, as each encounter is remarkably dissimilar to virtually every contemporaneous encounter with the dead. The reflection of Jesus, indeed what was most characteristic of the nature of his itinerant activity and war on Satan, is made evident in each, founded on *agape* as well as a perilous and deadly commitment to release those from bondage who would embrace the emerging kingdom of God. Each of the recovered events demands *agape* concurrent with the demand to embrace perilous risk for the kingdom of God, or dissolve into the kingdom of Satan.

John 20:19–23: What's Different about John's "Closed Door" Encounter?

Jesus appears to the exorcists despite the doors being locked (for fear of the "Jews"). He shows his hands and side and is recognized and gladly received. While the appearance feigns materiality, there is no indication it is material. Jesus breathes the Holy Spirit, authorizing them to forgive sins or "retain" them, and they are sent out to do so. Not all the exorcists are present.

The tradition reflects several characteristics useful to a later generation of Christians in conflict with opponents, and so likely reflects the needs of a late first-century Johannine community (90 to 110 CE). The most telling is the conflict with Pharisaic Judaism.[50] For example, John 20:19 states that the "Jews (*ioudian*)" are "feared (*phobon*)," and by implication, the Jews (not the Jerusalem elite or Herodians who are tacitly Romans) are to be blamed for Jesus' death.[51] More telling, the Jews are to be associated with Satan, who is their father.[52] Evidently, the Gospel of John reflects a community in perilous conflict with Judaism—certainly a post–Second Temple conflict of the early church, and one that is also reflected in Matthew (85 CE). Indeed, there is no longer any evidence of Jesus' conflict with satanic forces that possessed the land, or demonic imperialism of the elite, that is, the risk characteristic of Jesus' war on Satan. The enemy has become the "Jews," which reflects a post-antebellum period and the *sitz im leben* where the community was in desperate and deadly confrontation with Pharisaic Judaism of the synagogue[53] and Diaspora.[54] Consequently, this event is artificial and to be used for polemic purposes by the community of the beloved disciple.

In this event, Jesus shows the wounds of crucifixion—his nail-pierced hands and spear-pierced side, rather gruesome[55]—to demonstrate the materiality of his body, and more important, that it is he, not a mysterious traveler (as in the Emmaus event, who is recognized and disappears) or a *phantasm*.[56] Our foregoing risk analysis has shown that these materiality traditions were intended to mute emergent docetic theology concerning Jesus' true divinity that denied his having a body[57] since he was truly divine,

---

50. See John 9. For a further discussion of John and the conflicts with Pharisaic Judaism after 70 CE see Brown, *Community of the Beloved Disciple*, 41.

51. Blame for Jewish rejection of Jesus is also recorded in John 7:45–52; 8:39–59; 10:22–42; 12:42.

52. John 8:37–39, 44–47.

53. John 9:22; 12:42; and expulsion from the synagogue and as described in Charlesworth, *Jews and Christians*, 76–96.

54. See Tomson, "Johannine 'Jews,'" 197–99.

55. The showing of few wounds described glosses over the horrific view of Jesus expected to be seen by first-century Palestinian peasants, that is, of his brutalized body. Jesus expected that the condition of the body at death, or with the arrival of the general resurrection, would be similar to the body that "entered life" (Mark 9:47; Matt 5:29; 18:9), however maimed or disfigured. This is consistent with the view of first-century peasants and the historical Jesus. Consequently, this event is inconsistent with these views, which provides further evidence that the tradition is not Palestinian and is later.

56. Or a *biaeothanati*; a ghost, able to curse, punish and harm, even kill his murderers, under the authority that empowered him—physically, politically and spiritually.

57. Despite Kasemann's view that the Gospel of John itself was a kind of naïve docetism. Kasemann, *Testament of Jesus*, 26.

like a god, and so above human flesh and mundane existence.⁵⁸ Paul, a generation before John's gospel, knows the rejection of Jesus based on the crucifixion, the "folly of the cross."⁵⁹ Docetic Christians rejected the bodily death of Jesus as a ridiculous belief; mere men could not execute a divine being, and certainly not the divine Word of God, i.e., divine wisdom. As such, the community of John encountered powerful alternative communities in the Hellenistic/Roman milieu that denied that Jesus suffered on a cross at all, being unnecessary (and impossible). Contextually, this supports the further conclusion that the use of this post-crucifixion event served the needs of the Johannine community as it faced the challenge of defending its legitimacy, and thus, was in peril. John's appeal to witnesses who could testify to the materiality of these events, and thus Jesus' humanity, only serves to confirm that the tradition is an apologetic for the community.

The "breathing" (*enephusesen*) of the Holy Spirit (*pneuma hagion*) on those present (i.e., those that witness the materiality of Jesus' presence among them, the founders of the Johannine community) is not only affirmation of "orthodoxy," it is the charismatic transfer of power and authority to them alone: to forgive sins (releasing the curse of death, 7:38–39), properly interpreting sayings and practices instituted by Jesus (John 16:7–14), awarding salvation (facilitate possession and "rebirth" by the Spirit, thereby assuring divine protection and "life," John 3:36, 6:33), or condemning those who reject the truth of their encounter with Jesus (the deceitful voice of Satan, John 8:44–45, 14:30).⁶⁰

This suggests that John 20:19–23 is a later tradition that served the needs of a Johannine community in conflict with communities that rejected their teachings as valid—charges that attempted to vacate their claim to legitimacy and, thus, salvation. Consequently, the Johannine community is in crisis, having unexpectedly lost its primary witness, and so, is facing perilous risk. The countermeasure is their attestation to have received authority from the risen Jesus, which is unimpeachable, and is something they still retain; indeed they received the Holy Spirit indicating union with God and

58. Von Wahlde, *Gnosticism, Docetism*, 61–67.

59. 1 Cor 1:17–25.

60. For analysis of the breathing of the Holy Spirit in John 20:22, which includes analysis of the unique us of *enephusesen*, see Bennema, "Giving of the Spirit." According to Bennema, the breathing of the Holy Spirit reinstates the disciples and recreates them by giving life-giving Spirit. This is a three-stage process in the theology of the Gospel of John. There is certainly a reinstatement taking place, just as there is for Kayfa in John 21. The concept of recreation is also contextually coherent with an encounter with Jesus, particularly where he imparts the Spirit, possessing them with its authority and power. But here, it serves the needs of the Johannine community, where it is imbued with authority to forgive or let curse or death prevail.

Jesus, and the authority that can only be bestowed by them, or declared valid by them. To deny this assertion is to risk condemnation, blaspheming the Holy Spirit, the "unforgivable sin," as mentioned in 1 John.[61]

Is there a core tradition embedded in John 20:19–23, that is, evidence of an original post-crucifixion visionary experience with Jesus? Can the criteria of risk and contextual analysis recover an earlier version of the tradition? It is to this analysis we now turn.

Risk Analysis of John 20:19–23 and Evidence of an Earlier Tradition

As it stands, the event in John 20:19–23 evidences none of the risk[62] or contextual factors[63] supporting conclusions as to its veracity. Instead, analysis suggests its *sitz im leben* is the community of the beloved disciple.[64] However, there are risk elements suggesting that an earlier report of an encounter with Jesus post-crucifixion may stand behind this heavily redacted tradition.

The original event must have occurred in Galilee.[65] Coherent with this risk context, Jesus' exorcists remain in hiding, living in fear and danger, and accepting the protection of kin by working at night among the demons of Galilee's waters so as to avoid identification by informants. During an encounter, Jesus reinstates one of the exorcists, Kayfa. Kayfa is reinstated through provision of the Holy Spirit, or in its original setting, "the finger of God" that possessed Jesus. Jesus breathes on him, conveying the spirit—certainly

---

61. 1 John 5:16.

62. In its present form, the tradition fails the tests of Qualitative Risk Analysis (it fails to evidence the acceptance of heightened perilous risk by the exorcists); the Criterion of Dissimilarity (the tradition is not dissimilar to the needs of the Johannine community in that it asserts that it is the only valid community of the risen Lord with the authority to bind and loose sins, having received the Holy Spirit); or the Criterion of Embarrassment (the physical nature of Jesus' appearance overcomes any embarrassment of an encounter with a *phantasm*).

63. While the exorcists are present, the tradition is not in Galilee and there is no indication of a return to subsistence existence, or abandonment of it. In essence, the tradition fails three of the four contextual tests.

64. John 20:19–23 also suggests the development of the Holy Spirit traditions for the original activity of Jesus.

65. Risk analysis has demonstrated that all reliable traditions occurred in Galilee following the exorcists' escape from Jerusalem; then protection of kin who provided a return to subsistence existence, but now in the perilously dangerous work of night fishing. This work was left for the criminals and least desired peasants, whose lives were considered expendable, or for those desperate and in hiding.

a practice of a first-century exorcist in bestowing the spirit.[66] Consequently, the original oral tradition was about the reinstatement of Jesus' chief exorcist, Kayfa, which is a theme repeated in other reliable post-crucifixion traditions previously discussed.

In this form, the tradition has risk credence since is negatively asserts the historicity of Kayfa's abandonment of Jesus when captured and then crucified. The reinstatement includes the authority to take control of demons and expel them. Since Kayfa and the exorcists fled Jerusalem after having abandoned and publicly denying Jesus, the event explains how he and the others, once overcome by Satan, receive *agape* and are empowered by the post-crucifixion Jesus to overcome Satan and aggressively engage his demonic forces. Indeed the authority to forgive or retain sins in John 20 reflects an original context in Jesus' itinerant war on Satan, i.e., where the exorcists are imbued with the authority to expel and bind demons or to curse as they willed. The implication of this form of the tradition is clear—Kayfa and the exorcists are to reengage in charismatic exorcism, and therefore, embrace heightened perilous risk. This form of the tradition would merit further evaluation.

It is this oral tradition, perhaps from Kayfa, that became the basis of the later community tradition found in John 20:19–23, but is now obscured or lost.

Conclusions on the Veracity of John 20:19–23

Based on the risk and analytical criteria employed, combined with contextual analysis, the tradition of an encounter between Jesus the exorcists in Jerusalem fails to pass all risk tests. However, behind this tradition is evidence of an earlier oral tradition of an encounter, likely between Kayfa and Jesus, where Kayfa is reinstated and receives authority to continue the war on Satan. As such, in the context of human risk experience, the original event and encounter with Jesus cannot be confirmed in a post-crucifixion context and setting. The redactor/editor of the Johannine community has reset the events and context once again.

---

66. In Acts 2:1–2, the blowing wind signifies the arrival of the Holy Spirit, which covers all of those gathered.

John 20:26–29: Would Toma Deny Jesus Was Active Post-Crucifixion?

Eight days after the foregoing appearance (i.e., John 20:19–23), Toma, one of Jesus' leading exorcists according to the Gospel of John[67] (mysteriously absent from the last event), suddenly seeks refuge among the former exorcists still in hiding.[68] He vehemently rejects their report that Jesus materialized and appeared to them (suggesting that if a *phantasm* or *biaeothanati* appeared, it was *not* Jesus).[69] Toma's rejection is striking. Because it is a "negative tradition" (why would such a startling rejection be created by the early church, even if a confession then followed, if not true?) and appears to meet the criterion of embarrassment, it has merit. As such, the risk context of the tradition must be evaluated to confirm this merit. More, was Toma's rejection even more startling given a recovered risk context?

To begin, as a chosen member of Jesus' band of exorcists, Toma had accepted and faced perilous risk, even encouraging his fellow exorcists to enter Jerusalem with Jesus and die if necessary.[70] Toma is consequently portrayed as a leader of the exorcists in John. It is he, not Kayfa,[71] who commits to die in a confrontation with the Jerusalem elite.[72] Most important, it is Toma who encourages the others to embrace *heightened perilous risk*.[73] It is within this risk context we can begin to evaluate Toma's reaction to the report of appearance.

First, the report comes to Toma from the very exorcists who, like he, had joined in Jesus' aggressive war on Satan and the demonic pollution of the land, yet he rejects it. Second, he had participated with them in expelling

---

67. John 11:16, 14:5. Thomas is named in all lists of apostles, e.g., Luke 6:15.

68. The setting in the Gospel of John is Jerusalem.

69. Toma may have not denied that there was an event, but refused to accept that it was Jesus. From a risk perspective, Jesus had been thought annihilated by all the exorcists, who fled to Galilee to escape capture and death. Toma would have expected to be attacked by demons and powerful forces with Jesus having been apparently overcome. It is no wonder he rejected that Jesus was active, assuming the exorcists has encountered something quite different to deceive them.

70. John 11:16.

71. *Gospel of Thomas*, saying 13, portrays Toma as more insightful than Kayfa or Mattay. Even though the *Gospel of Thomas* calls James the leader, it is Toma who understands Jesus esoteric sayings and their saving power. See saying 12.

72. Kayfa is not even mentioned.

73. Kayfa says he would die for Jesus in John 13:37, but later denies him. This contrast makes Toma's blatant willingness to risk everything, and encourage others to do the same in a concrete, decision oriented, historical setting, sets his demand as significant contextually.

demons and even raising the dead, albeit with varying degrees of success, but clearly now believes that Jesus had been annihilated by the power of Satan—the demons had won out. Third, Toma had embraced perilous risk, becoming an itinerant exorcist like Jesus who publicly criticized the Herodians and Jerusalem elite, meaning he was fearless, unafraid of risking capture and death; so accepting an appearance and announcing it, which brought on heightened perilous risk, would be something Toma would embrace—but for Toma this was not possible (again, Jesus had been annihilated). Fourth, Toma came to them *for refuge*, which clearly underscores his high degree of trust in them to find safety, but still he rejects their report about Jesus. Fifth, Toma was a significant member of Jesus' inner circle of trained exorcists. His name, Toma, the "twin," was the exorcist name awarded by Jesus to Judah, a Galilean subsistence worker, whom he trained. This charismatic name signified that Jesus held Toma's authority and ability to exorcise aggressive demons on par with his own. It was the highest compliment possible from Jesus. Toma was therefore a powerful exorcist who would have expected similar encounters, such as an encounter with the dead. But, he again rejects this as a possibility. Lastly, Toma's demand to see the crucifixion wounds to prove the materialized spirit was Jesus, only underscores that for him Jesus had been destroyed—his mutilated body was not the body that materialized. Consequently, Toma's rejection, while stunning, is coherent with risk analysis of one who would embrace heightened perilous risk, but could not be based on what he knew of the circumstances of Jesus' death. Jesus had been destroyed, body and soul, at his crucifixion.

Then in John 20:26–27, Jesus materializes within a room behind locked doors with Toma and other exorcists present (they are still in hiding). Jesus demands that Toma "bring his finger (*phere ton daktulon!*)" to his wounds (although it is unclear if he does). Toma acknowledges it is the wounded body of Jesus revived and identifies him as "my Lord and my God." Jesus tells Toma that those who believe without seeing (or "perceiving," i.e., that Jesus is active) are "happy," (or blessed). Here in John, Jesus is made equal with God. In the context of this event, Jesus' saying is the capstone of the encounter. As such, the saying should be separated from the foregoing encounter and analyzed to determine if it is a later construction, which meets the needs of the Johannine community.

Clearly, later generations of Johannine Christians are no longer encountering Jesus post-crucifixion the way the exorcists had. More, their primary witness—the witness who was presumed to live until Jesus' return—has died, throwing the community into perilous risk and turmoil.[74]

---

74. John 21:23.

Now, those who believe "without seeing" will be blessed, i.e., they will encounter the general resurrection if they believe that Jesus "is the Christ and Son of God." And there is no need for fear, for that belief already sets them within a sphere of safety, for they "will never die."[75] More, the Holy Spirit will both comfort and guide them into all truth (i.e., the community is the authority in interpreting practice and theology—an important motif further analyzed below). In the Johannine community, believing encompasses absolute acceptance of Jesus' bodily resurrection, the comfort and guidance of the Spirit, the formation of a community of like believers who practice *agape*; a charismatic community that now holds fast to both their salvific state and expectation of a future, coming resurrection and judgment, where they are protected and empowered to life by belief in Jesus as the Son of God. Consequently, the saying cannot be detached from the community and its needs. This leaves the rejection of Toma for further analysis.

This is truly a remarkable tradition.[76] As noted, from a risk perspective it negatively asserts that some of those closest to Jesus, in fact one of Jesus' most powerful exorcists, had not only abandoned and rejected him, but also refused to believe he was active after the crucifixion. Consequently, John 20:26–29 is a sobering admission for any risk analyst studying human response to perilous risk—and it rings true. Whether the tradition is to be specifically related to Toma or not, it reflects the rejection of heightened perilous risk that we have shown others remarkably accepted, having had a post-crucifixion encounter—including Paul. This contextual situation, where some exorcists reengaged and embraced heightened perilous risk based on a post-crucifixion encounter with Jesus while others rejected it, must be considered reliable based solely on the criteria of qualitative risk analysis. This aside, and more specifically as to this study, why does the Johannine community identify Toma as the example of this conflict, and more, why is it he who comes to accept a risen Jesus based only on a physical encounter with Jesus? Only in answering these questions can we ascertain if this specific event will pass the risk and contextual tests. Consequently, risk and contextual analysis must unravel this tradition to ascertain is dependability in its contemporary setting.

---

75. John 3:16.

76. We are spiritual beings and as such even a moment given in love can extend beyond that moment that ends, extending to infinity, and this was the encounter of the Johannine community that embraced faith in the death, burial and resurrection of Jesus.

Risk and Contextual Analysis of John 20:26–29

While John 20:26–29 has been identified as simply another event primarily intended to confirm the materiality of Jesus' body for later theological purposes (i.e., to meet the needs of a Christian community in conflict with those that rejected a bodily resurrection, such as Docetic, or nascent pre-Gnostic communities), it cannot escape us that the event is portrayed as having occurred in Syria-Palestine,[77] which suggests that there were communities in this same region who required proof that Jesus' appearances were not just visions, dreams, *phantasms*, or disappearing fellow travelers. In fact, it is has been convincingly demonstrated by Koester that competing communities utilized a similar sayings tradition trajectory within that region, but did so employing difference hermeneutics.[78] There were those who demanded that the encounter was a bodily, material manifestation—a tangible encounter that the general resurrection was either near, or was inbreaking *now*. Others appealed to the charismatic power in Jesus' sayings. Therefore, we may have evidence in the Johannine tradition that the encounter of Toma with Jesus was just such a conflict. What other contemporaneous oral or written traditions in the Syria-Palestinian region appealed to the authority of Toma, and can we determine may have been were conflict with the Johannine community? It is to this contextual analysis we turn.

The *Gospel of Thomas* (40 to 95 CE)[79] is a collection of esoteric wisdom sayings attributed to Jesus, i.e., a "sayings tradition," the source of which is Didymas Judas Thomas according to the ascription at the beginning of this gospel.[80] As Koester notes, "The basis of the *Gospel of Thomas* is a sayings collection which is more primitive than the canonical gospels, even though its basic principal is not related to the creed of the passion and resurrection."[81] The community of Thomas made no appeal to the bodily or material resurrection of Jesus, only the life-giving power of the "Living"

---

77. On the region of Syria-Palestine, see Malina and Robaugh, *Gospel of John*, 44–45.

78. Koester, *Ancient Christian Gospels*, 114, in particular the communities of John and Thomas: "John and Thomas interpret the same traditional sayings, albeit with the use of quite different hermeneutic principles."

79. The range of dates depends on the formation of Q. Some argue for a more primitive version of Q. See, e.g., Patterson, *Gospel of Thomas*, 245–46, 257, and "Paul and the Jesus Tradition," 23–41. As noted, Koester believes that 1 Cor 2:9 was from an early version of Q. See *Trajectories*, 158–204, and *Ancient Christian Gospels*, 58–59.

80. See the translation by Stephen Patterson and Marvin Meyer, http://gnosis.org/naghamm/gosthom.html.

81. Koester, *Trajectories*, 186.

Jesus' words:[82] "For the Gospel of Thomas, the significance of Jesus was that when he spoke, the reign of God became a present reality for those who heard and understood what he was saying . . . they criticized other early Christian interpretations of Jesus, which understood him within the context of apocalyptic eschatology."[83] Thomas has been studied thoroughly by groundbreaking scholars, including Koester, Robinson,[84] Kloppenburg,[85] and Patterson.[86] While this analysis will draw critical insights from these studies, its focus will be on examining the post-Easter Johannine tradition through the lens of qualitative risk analysis. At the core of this investigation is John 20:26–29, which intentionally portrays both Toma's vehement rejection of Jesus and his acceptance based on a material post-crucifixion experience. Is there a connection between the *Gospel of Thomas* and the exorcist Toma, other than the gospel's appeal to Toma's name, on which it derives its authority?

The *Gospel of Thomas* contains no resurrection event, but does evidence a reliance on a sayings tradition whose trajectory is shared by both John and Thomas.[87] In Thomas, the "secret" words of Jesus, the "Living One," once discovered (saying 1), imbue the Thomas Christians with escape from perilous risk of deception (leading to death), through what is a *charismatic gnosis*. Proper interpretation provides immediate access to eternal life and safety—"[the proper interpreters] will not taste death." This implies that *Thomas is a charismatic gospel*; one that has displaced Jesus' war on Satan and exorcisms in preparation for the kingdom of God with Jesus' words that exorcise deadly ignorance and deception (also evil that possess and "blinds" humans). This "gnosis" is in sharp contract with other communities, such as that of John, which made their authoritative appeal to the teaching of witnesses who encountered Jesus in a material form post-crucifixion, and announced a future expectation of his return that brought about the general resurrection and judgment. Belief in this provides immediate access to life, and Jesus words are confirmed as living through his resurrection. For the Thomas Christians, Jesus was either not present at the crucifixion or his spirit survived execution and the curse of the cross, proving that *his words*

---

82. *Gospel of Thomas*, saying 1, "Whoever finds the meaning of these words will not taste death"

83. Patterson et al., *Q Thomas Reader*, 119.

84. Koester and Robinson, *Trajectories*, the classic analysis of the Thomas and Q traditions and their trajectories in primitive Christianity.

85. Kloppenborg et al., *Q-Thomas Reader*; also Kloppenborg, *Formation of Q*.

86. Patterson, "Jesus Meets Plato," 181–205; also Patterson's recreation of the documents used by these groups; *Lost Way*, 195–215, 219–41.

87. Koester, *Ancient Christian Gospels*, 114.

carried divine authority to "awaken" the soul, free one from ignorance and evil, and give eternal life. To "preach the gospel" and to "receive" it was to attain immediate salvation for both John and the Thomas Christians. Consequently, to find the esoteric transformative meaning of the sayings and "awaken" in Thomas (which brings one into a blessed and protected union with the divine) was to attain life. As such, the authority of the Living One and his sayings negated the need for a bodily resurrection or future eschatological or apocalyptic events.

The *Gospel of Thomas* has been identified as "Gnostic," "proto-Gnostic," "nascent Docetic," or even "pre-Gnostic." But from a risk perspective in its contemporary context, Thomas is something much more—it is infectious, carrying salvific power that is given by both encountering Jesus' words, the one who is "Living" and beyond this material world in the divine realm. The encounter is not simply *gnosis* in the sense of transformative wisdom, i.e., as to how to live one's life and then later attain salvation. It is strikingly individual and personal, an awakening of one's true divine state. As such, none of these classifications adequately capture its overwhelming revelatory and transformative authority to lift one immediately from death to life. Indeed, perhaps none are valid labels when set within the risk context of Palestinian Judaism and the earliest stages of oral transmission of Jesus' sayings. That is, unless they are linked to the charismatic work of Jesus and his exorcisms—his freeing of the possessed and awakening of the "hardened of heart (those possessed and deceived by Satan)."[88] In both John and the Synoptic Gospels, Jesus' use of words of authority to drive demons away, or to command the spirits to abandon their victims, or employ parables and esoteric sayings to reveal the kingdom of God as present in his activity;[89] all of these carried transformative power and authority to free one from evil and death. This "awakening," tacitly a freeing from a satanic world and control, was most certainly a key feature of Jesus' itinerant activity in his war on Satan.[90] For the early Christian tradition to retain that "he taught as one with authority"[91] is consequential to our discussion, as it confirms that those who heard and followed Jesus received new understanding that carried charismatic authority—a connection with the divine that afforded safety and protection from Satan as well as access to eternal life—*now*.

88. Mark 8:17.

89. See Busse, *To Be Near the Fire*, 131–65. Jesus' use of *mashal* was as charismatic words to awaken and free his listeners from deception as to the kingdom of God present in his words; that is, they were possessed and under the authority of Satan.

90. Ibid., 89–130.

91. Mark 1:22.

Consequently, the *Gospel of Thomas* must be considered a *charismatic document* in its contemporary context. It brought transformation to the reader/listener, where words of the exorcists and Lord, now the Living One, Jesus, drive out ignorance and deception, even demonic possession, returning life and safety to the individual. Just as Jesus drove out Satan, now his words do so. Thomas is a charismatic document in the fullest sense of what charismatic activity was intending to provide—relief from perilous risk. The trajectories of the early Christian tradition, all trailing from Jesus, can be traced to his charismatic authority and activity—particularly evident in the *Gospel of Thomas*.

But herein lies a new problem in accepting the historicity of any portion of John 20:26–27. The Johannine community portrays a Toma that first vehemently rejects the bodily resurrection of Jesus, but then makes him the center of a confession in a bodily resurrection. Indeed, Toma is linked to three events in John: Toma's commitment to die with Jesus (in the body), John 11:16; Jesus' correction of Toma about who will lead followers into *gnosis* and all knowledge, John 14:5 (i.e., the Holy Spirit, not Jesus' words that Thomas secretly conveys); and lastly, Toma's encounter with the physically resurrected Jesus. All of these evidence a theological motif, where the community of John wishes to demonstrate that Toma, the apostle claimed as authoritative by other communities, was not only willing to die bodily with Jesus, but would never claim to have secret knowledge about his sayings, as he only became reinstated and active again as a result of his physical encounter with Jesus post-crucifixion. Consequently, these traditions in John about Toma are intended to contest an alternative community asserting immediate salvation that was found only in the secret words of Jesus given to Toma, e.g., a community whose reliance was on the *Gospel of Thomas*. Given this evidence, the traditions in John 20:26–27 fail to pass the tests of qualitative risk analysis, the Criterion of Dissimilarity and the Criterion of Embarrassment (embarrassment has been shifted to the competing community!).

Conclusions on the Veracity of John 20:26–29

Based on the risk and analytical criteria employed, combined with contextual analysis, the tradition of Toma's encounter with Jesus fails to pass all key tests. The redactor/editor of the Johannine community has taken a valid tradition related to the rejection of Jesus' appearances by some of Jesus' exorcists (indeed, there were only seven present according to John 21:1–23) and used it to establish that even Toma, one of Jesus' leading exorcists, later embraced the materiality of Jesus' resurrection. But more, the redactor/

editor employs the tradition as a countermeasure to the perilous risk of a competing Syria-Palestinian community and its theology (similar to that reflected in the esoteric tradition of the *Gospel of Thomas*), which claims exclusive rights to salvation and eternal life, centered on apprehending and "awakening" to life through understanding the secret sayings of Jesus. Consequently, a competing community has rejected the testimony of the community of John's witness to a resurrection of Jesus, along with its eschatology of future judgment. The tradition serves the needs of the Johannine community and, therefore, was likely formed for this purpose. However, as noted in our analysis, there is evidence that behind this tradition stands a core event related to the rejection and acceptance of post-crucifixion encounters that may be reliable in its contemporary setting. Indeed, the tradition of rejection of Jesus by his family, including by his brother James who later became the leader of the Jerusalem community (see Gal 2), stands as evidence for the compelling nature of such a tradition.

John 21:1–23: Why Retain a Breakfast Meal Encounter?

The longest and most detailed of the post-crucifixion encounters in the four canonical gospels,[92] John 21:1–23 has Jesus appearing at dawn along the shores of Galilee. He employs animistic powers once again, directing Galilean fish into specific seine nets, then cooks a charcoal breakfast, inviting Kayfa, Toma, Nathanael, Yecob and Yohannes, and two others[93] to eat—seven exorcists in all.[94] Kayfa is fishing with these seven overnight (recall that they are in hiding and only fish at night to avoid detection from informants seeking followers of the crucified Jesus; they have no choice to feed themselves, and are risking all by being on the lake at night, as they face attack from aggressive demons that inhabit the waters).[95] They catch nothing, failing to help kin meet the harsh, daily catch-quotas—a serious issue for subsistence "hand to mouth" existence, risking starvation. At dawn, Kayfa sees a figure suddenly standing on the shore[96] and answers a question

92. Perhaps an appendix to the gospel, however, all extant manuscripts, including the fragment P66, of John include this section, or what is now ch. 21.

93. The *Gospel of Peter* has a different list, and only five exorcists. The common disciple between this gospel and John's is Kayfa. See Brown, *John*, 1068.

94. Likely these are the only exorcists who regrouped after the crucifixion in Galilee to return, under the protection of kin, to subsistence fishing, but at night, but without much success to support themselves and meet rigorous quotas.

95. See also Brown on the return of the disciples of subsistence fishing, Brown, *Gospel*, 1068–69.

96. The figure appears on the shore, similar to the appearance among the exorcists.

shouted to them about their catch. Kayfa confirms they have caught nothing all night. They do not know it is Jesus. The figure orders them to move their nets to another spot; this was no small task, but was a familiar order given to them by another charismatic in the past—Jesus. (Still, to follow the command of a stranger is surprising.) The quantity of the catch is overwhelming, and very specific—exactly 153 fish.[97] "The disciple whom Jesus loved" (the witness of the Johannine community), identifies the figure as Jesus, despite his being over one hundred yards away and poor early morning light. Kayfa dives into the water after putting on his clothes. They meet the figure on shore. Curiously, Jesus is not necessarily recognized, just the actions that have taken place identify him, but "they dare not ask him, 'who are you.'" Interestingly, the section ends with this event being the "third" time Jesus was revealed. Obviously, the appearance to Magdalene was not counted.[98]

This special section of John is likely an appendix to the original gospel, and its function has shifted attention back to Galilee in an altogether awkward way. As Bultmann notes:

> A still weightier consideration is that in ch. 21 the tradition of the appearances of the Risen Lord in Galilee emerges, and while this is attested by Mk. and Mt. it is completely ignored in ch. 20; in ch. 21 it comes without any preparation, without for example any mention being mad of the journey of the disciples first from Jerusalem to Galilee. But more! The story in 20.19–29 is related in such a manner that not only are there no further appearances of the Risen Lord anticipated, but no more could be awaited. After the commissioning of the disciples in 20.22ff., it is more than surprising that the disciples, instead of bearing testimony, are found fishing in the Sea of Galilee, there to experience a new appearance which now has no real meaning at all.[99]

Why they do not recognize Jesus, even at a distance, is disconcerting. More, when they come to shore and are invited to eat, there is no indication of wounds, and the negative implication that they knew it to be the Lord (but did not ask) suggests that Jesus was appearing in a different form.

97. Commentators have suggested that in the context of first-century Palestine, this was the number of presumed nations of the world, thereby representing the scope of the apostles' mission once commissioned by Jesus to preach the word to the world: Ross, "One Hundred Fifty-Three Fishes," 357, or Grant, "One Hundred Fifty Three Fishes (John 21, 11)," 273–75.

98. E.g., see Josephus, *Antiquities*, 4:219.

99. Bultmann, *Gospel of John*, 701.

This awkward construction[100] and placement of the section after John 20 makes suspect any ability to recover an earlier form that is reliable. Instead it must be considered an addition of the Johannine community, one used to address perilous risk issues. For example, there are many difficulties with the continuity of John 21:1–14; Kayfa's placement in and out of the boat, the broiling fish, and the need to bring the catch when breakfast is ready. This loose combination of elements and juxtaposition of scenes suggests more a recount of a heavenly dream or vision than an experience on the actual shore of Galilee. More, the eating of food may be intended to make the event substantive and material, not revelatory or illusory. The fact that the figure is simply known to be Jesus, but there is no clear identification, is stunning given John 20 with its very specific description and the absolute certainty that it is a material Jesus, identified by his wounds, with them. For Bultmann, the confusion of elements reflects a written document with editorial changes by a later editor/redactor.[101] The later section, John 21:15–23 is focused on Kayfa and the Beloved Disciple. Kayfa is reinstated as leader of the community, and the Beloved Disciple, acknowledged by Kayfa as his equal, and who was thought to live until Jesus' return, has unexpectedly died. As such, the weight of evidence is on this section as addressing community issues and crises. The witness has died, but their testimony of a materially risen Lord is true, and has been confirmed by Kayfa, on whose authority and name the community now appeals.

From a risk perspective, it appears that the Johannine community is in crisis with the loss of its leader and witness. It reaches out to the community of Kayfa that also adheres to a future eschatological event, i.e., Jesus' return with the judgment. The tradition links the two leaders together, and so, links the communities as a source of risk mitigation in the face of a challenge from an esoteric non-eschatological community, such as that represented by the *Gospel of Thomas*. Indeed, once again, we find Toma in the list of exorcists who encounter a material Jesus. Not only has Toma seen, and perhaps touched Jesus' wounds, now he eats a meal with him on the shore of Galilee. Toma is thrust into the "orthodoxy" of the Johannine community, and now, into the community associated with Kayfa. The traditions collected in John 21 therefore address a community crisis, and are intended to mitigate the perilous risks facing that community, and as such, fails to pass all risk tests—qualitative risk, the Criterion of Dissimilarity and the Criterion of Embarrassment.

---

100. Bultmann establishes that the section is not a unity, but of made up of two separate sections that cannot have belonged together (ibid., 702).

101. Ibid., 703.

John 21 does include elements that appear to meet some of the contextual tests, which raises interesting questions and implications as to actual events behind the tradition, but unfortunately, nothing more. For example, the scene is in Galilee; a group of exorcists have fled there and returned to subsistence existence and night fishing; and the encounter with Jesus encourages a return to an itinerant mission (i.e., to abandon fishing). Indeed, the command to Kayfa to "feed my lambs" presupposes just this—at least seven of the exorcists seemingly did engage in itinerant activity, including Kayfa, as the tradition looks back on this as well known. While these elements echo actual events, and even support our foregoing risk analysis conclusions on what did happen in Galilee, these elements are drawn together to mitigate risk to a community seeking unification with a broader base, namely, the community of Kayfa in Syria-Palestine.

Conclusions as to the Veracity of John 21:1–23

John 21 is an appendix serving the needs of a community in crisis. While it reflects contextual elements pointing to actual events, they have become obscured and made subservient to the community's risk crisis. Consequently, recovery of an earlier form of the tradition is not possible. The event in John 21:1–14 may reflect a visionary dream or revelation, but recovery is also not possible. As such, John 21 fails to pass both the risk and contextual tests. The veracity of John 21 cannot be confirmed.

11

The Noncanonical Sources

Women as the Critical Witnesses to Post-Crucifixion Events

We now turn to the noncanonical gospels and traditions, applying risk and contextual texts to evaluate their veracity. The analysis begins with a brief note on the *Gospel of Mary*, which was evaluated earlier in conjunction with Matt 28:1–10, then turns to the *Gospel of Peter* and others in more detail.

The Gospel of Mary (GM, 30 to 50 CE)

In the foregoing analysis of Matt 28:1–10, the *Gospel of Mary* (*GM*) was found to include perilous risk and contextual elements supporting the historicity of Magdalene's post-resurrection encounter with Jesus. Indeed, *GM* includes several startling events: Magdalene's confrontation with Kayfa and other exorcists as to the legitimacy of her interaction with Jesus post-crucifixion; Kayfa's jealously and temper; and Levi's defense of Magdalene as not only equal to the male exorcists, but her becoming male: "But rather, let us praise his greatness, for he has prepared us and made us into men" (*GM* 5:3).[1] Her presence with Kayfa and the others at meals indicates that Magdalene was considered equal in authority to Kayfa. More, Magdalene reported to the disheartened exorcists, presumably in Galilee, that (1) Jesus was active, (2) that she had a vision at the tomb, and (3) then encountered

---

1. If she becomes like a "male," i.e., what was perceived in the ancient world as the complete human being reflected in male form. See Meyer, "Making Mary Male." For this she would have cut her hair and wore male closing. See below on the discussion of the *Gospel of Mary* and the analysis by Karen King.

Jesus, not as a ghost, but in a substantive form that was present.[2] It is Magdalene that convinces the Galileans to again abandon subsistence fishing and return to itinerant ministry. She is cited as the authoritative source of Jesus' words and the only exorcist who is fully accepted by Jesus post-crucifixion.

As such, risk and contextual analysis must count Magdalene as one of the Galilean exorcists whose perilous risk was heightened following her encounter with Jesus.[3] While there is no confirmation that Magdalene continued exorcising demons in the Synoptic tradition or in John, extra canonical traditions confirm that Mary was an active and influential member among the remaining exorcists in Galilee and provided instruction to them about her vision of Jesus and her continuing relationship with him. The tradition that best captures Magdalene's standing and influence in the early movement and among Jesus' exorcists is the *GM*. Despite *GM* being a fragment (the extant copy is second to fifth century),[4] risk analysis confirms that the traditions likely predate the canonical gospels.

In sum, a review of the *GM* tradition confirms that Magdalene was believed to have influenced the return to subsistence existence as exorcists and *apostoloi* of Jesus, post-crucifixion. As such, these traditions, as noted, pass the risk and contextual tests.

Gospel of Peter 37–41 (150 to 190 CE with Oral Traditions to 30 CE)

The "elders," a centurion named Petronius, and Petronius' soldiers guarding the tomb witness two figures coming from heaven. The two enter a tomb and then walk out supporting a third figure with a cross following behind. There is no speaking or identification of the figure, but it is presumed to be Jesus. It is important that these three witnesses are independent (two to three independent witnesses were required to confirm validity in Jewish courts).[5] The disciples are not aware of what has happened. They fled to Galilee to "return to their homes," and Kayfa returned to "his nets." Magdalene enters and tomb, encounters a young man, and is told Jesus is risen. She and the other women with her flee.

---

2. As noted, encounters with the active spirits of the dead included material activity and contact.

3. *GM* 5:2–7.

4. King argues for composition between 30–130 CE (*Gospel of Mary*, 148).

5. Deut 19:15–16.

Risk Analysis of the Gospel of Peter (EvP)

The Gospel of Peter (*EvP*) has divided scholarship as to the date of its composition. Some scholars consider it a late construction (but before 200 CE)[6] and reliant on the Synoptics and Gospel of John.[7] Others, including Koester and Crossan, have argued for a mid-first-century date of composition in Syria and its independence.[8] An earlier date would suggest familiarity with Palestine, although there is little evidence of such, including ignorance of Jewish religious customs and political tensions during the Second Temple period (i.e., before 70 CE).[9] Moreover, analysis of the Greek in *EvP* shows that it has some unique vocabulary, distinct from both the Synoptic and Johannine traditions, although it also has Hellenistic and Attic Greek, and sometimes reflects a reliance on Lucan language constructions.[10] There are several other elements that are problematic in establish a date of composition.

> There are numerous features in these accounts which are obviously secondary: Jesus is condemned and crucified by Herod, while Pilate is completely exonerated; the anti-Jewish polemic seems intensified; the story of Jesus' resurrection from the tomb is told elaborately . . . the cross that follows Jesus out of the tomb speaks. Parallels with the passion and resurrection accounts of all four canonical gospels are numerous. Therefore, the first assessment of the newly discovered document almost unanimously favored dependence of the EvP upon all four gospels of the New Testament canon and argued for relatively late date in order to explain the uncontrolled growth of legendary features.[11]

However, scholars also notice that lack of *EvP*'s citation of the Old Testament (i.e., to describe the suffering of Jesus and its fulfillment), which suggests that *EvP* was composed before the canonical gospels. Matthew, for example, relies heavily on references to support critical events as fulfillment of prophecy and the Torah.[12] In addition, Koester's detailed analysis, comparing *EvP* with canonical gospels, specifically the mocking of Jesus and the

---

6. Koester, *Ancient Christian Gospels*, 216, based on fragments from Oxyrhynchus and a citation from Eusebius, quoting Serapion's book.

7. Wright, *Historical Jesus*, 314–15.

8. Koester, *Introduction*, 2:162–63, 182–83; Crossan, *Cross That Spoke*, 6–9.

9. Wright, 314.

10. Ibid., 321–26.

11. Koester, *Ancient Christian Gospels*, 218.

12. Ibid.

"scapegoat" tradition (i.e., tradition relating Jesus' death as sacrifice, similar to Isaiah's scapegoat references, Isa 50:6; Zech 12:10)[13] reveals that *EvP* cannot be explained as a late and "random compilation of canonical passages."[14] While it may be an independent and early gospel composition, and dating is undetermined, there are elements that suggest an earlier oral tradition may stand behind *EvP*.

EvP ends with Mary Magdalene's entry into the tomb, an encounter with a mysterious angelic figure, and a report that Jesus has risen. Mary, terrified that she will be spotted and captured as they approached the tomb, flees, telling no one of the events. Finally, the narrator (Kayfa) reports that after the crucifixion, the fellow exorcists left Jerusalem among the crowds and returned to their homes in despair. Kayfa, Andrew and Alpheus return to subsistence fishing on Galilee. Here the fragment abruptly ends. While *EvP* has no resurrection encounter and cannot be evaluated using standard risk tests of this study, there are several perilous risk elements that merit careful analysis. Some are quite striking and corroborate earlier risk findings of this study. These include:

1. There were no post-crucifixion encounters with Jesus in Jerusalem.
2. Mary approaches the tomb in terror of being discovered and captured.
3. The exorcists go into hiding then disband, fleeing Jerusalem for the safety of Galilee.
4. They unquestionably believe that Jesus has been annihilated, body and soul, expecting nothing, and know of no death and resurrection predictions.
5. They do not know or care about the disposition of Jesus' body—they are in fear for their lives—and likely assume it had been thrown into the refuse dump of the city for the animals to consume—the common practice for executed criminals.
6. Jesus' body is guarded by special elders (not only a centurion and his soldiers), indicating that his body was entombed to protect themselves from retribution ("to do us evil," v. 8) or would be used by his followers, who were thought to be "evildoers" and dark magicians.
7. There is no command to remain in Jerusalem, or to wait for the Holy Spirit, or an instance of the conveyance of the Holy Spirit.

---

13. Ibid., 224–25.
14. Ibid., 227.

8. The elders are understood to be complicit with Pilate, tacitly Roman sympathizers, and a group that Pilate disdained.
9. The exorcists, led by Kayfa, return to subsistence fishing.

While *EvP* has no recommitment of the exorcists to the itinerant war on Satan resulting from an encounter with Jesus, and thus, no evidence of heightened perilous risks, several of its elements, particularly 2, 3, 4, 5, 6, and 9, betray a level of human fear and risk avoidance that would be expected given the devastating circumstances found in our study. More, these *EvP* risk elements are clearly undeveloped, particularly when compared with the Synoptic and Johannine passion and post-crucifixion traditions. As such, they represent both an early and independent tradition that "rings true" from a perilous risk perspective; indeed, they reflect exactly what a devastated group of exorcists whose leader has been murdered by the very evil forces he opposed would do—flee! Consequently, these perilous risk elements within *EvP* evidence the human impact and disaster resulting from Jesus' brutal death. The resulting perilous risks events therefore pass the test of qualitative risk analysis.

Several of these perilous risk events are also distinct from the needs of the early church, as well as represent embarrassing traditions. Many of these would never have been created if not well known outside the community. Consequently, the risk elements, particularly 2, 3, 4, 6 and 9, adequately pass the tests of the criteria of dissimilarity and embarrassment. If we adjust our risk analysis to these perilous risk events, the veracity of each is rendered probable.

Contextual Analysis of EvP

Turning to the contextual tests, the risk elements are evaluated (2, 3, 4, 6 and 9) in lieu of a post-crucifixion encounter. These must therefore be coherent with the sociological risk setting, including the subsistence struggle of the Galileans, the background from which they came to join Jesus' band of exorcists.

Evaluation of the contextual risk tests, adjusted to the identified perilous risk elements, is as follows:

1. Perilous risk elements related to original members of Jesus' band of Galilean exorcists, those who faced capture, death and social isolation and starvation, are given priority:

    The risk elements in *EvP* pass this test.

2. Perilous risk elements should be consistent with the ecstatic practices of Jesus that engendered the original perilous risk with his opponents.[15] Specifically, encounters that encouraged the remaining exorcists to continue the ecstatic activity of Jesus and his war on Satan are preferred:[16]

> The risk elements of *EvP* do not meet this test, but because *EvP* is a fragment, it is certain that the lost section of the gospel would have reported some form of an encounter and return to either ecstatic or charismatic practices. But what is striking about *EvP* is the clarity as to the devastating impact on the exorcists, and the admission of returning to fishing in Galilee with the absence of a post-crucifixion encounter in Jerusalem. As such, this suggests that the response of the exorcists to a post-crucifixion event would be even more striking, i.e., a stronger emphasis on the perilous risks accepted by the exorcists than what is evidenced in either the Synoptic and Johannine traditions. This would suggest that this test is met, but without the complete gospel we must render it inconclusive.

3. Events near or on the lake of Galilee, particularly related to subsistence fishing, and similar to the animistic control exhibited by Jesus, are preferential (i.e., the remaining exorcists escaped there):[17]

> This test is partially met, given the return of the exorcists to subsistence fishing on Galilee.

---

15. Koester, *From Jesus to the Gospels*, 231.

16. Koester, *Literature*, 84: "There is at least no doubt that whatever was experienced was not without relationship to a previous direct or indirect knowledge of or about Jesus."

17. Because of the nature of Jesus' activity there, combined with tradition that the men returned to Galilee to take up their subsistence existence, any activity on or around Galilee relative to how they became followers of Jesus, i.e., as exorcists having witnessed Jesus' ability to employ animistic control (see the previous discussion on how Jesus' charismatic activity assisted with survival in a subsistence existence), such activities should be given preference.

4. Finally, events that may have led the Galileans to again abandon subsistence existence (i.e., to which they returned for survival post-crucifixion)[18] are also preferred:[19]

This test is not met.

In sum, two of the four contextual tests are met. This renders the contextual tests of *EvP* as inconclusive. However, as the document is a fragment, evidence suggests that all four tests may have been met. As such, the likely historicity of the perilous risk events reported in *EvP* noted is strong and supported in an application of the contextual tests.

Conclusions on the Veracity of EvP

Based on the risk and analytical criteria employed, combined with contextual analyses, only the selected perilous risk events of *EvP* are considered reliable within their original setting and in the context of human risk experience.

Gospel of Nicodemus (Acts of Pilate) 10:20-21, Chapter 13 (350 to 375 CE)[20]

A priest named Phinees, a schoolmaster named Ada, and a Levite named Ageus report that they saw Jesus with his eleven disciples on the Mount of Olives (v. 18). Jesus is then seen ascending. Pilate also reports that the guards

---

18. There is ample evidence that the exorcists returned to subsistence fishing after the crucifixion of Jesus and their having fled to Galilee. Both John and the *Gospel of Peter* reference Kayfa's decision to return to Galilee and fishing. As Brown notes: "The verb 'to fish' has the form of an infinitive of purpose which is rare in John (iv. 7, xiv 2) and more frequent in Matthew and Luke; MTGS, 134–35, reports that this construction was becoming increasingly popular in Greek from ca. 150 B.C. on. McDowell, 430ff., argues that the present tend of the verb 'to go' expresses more than momentary intention: Peter is going back to his earlier way of life and will stay with it. The point of the story, then, is that Jesus caused Peter to change his mind, especially in vs. 15: 'Do you love me more than these [nets, boats, etc.]?'" Brown, *Gospel of John*, 1068–69. Brown believes that this may be dubious, but it is compelling in a perilous risk context, so we must accept the premise.

19. Slovic, *Science*, 280–85. A discussion with Professor Slovic confirms that the human response to perilous risk has not changed in millennia, only the context of that risk. For the Galileans to perceive risk and perilous, but accept it as necessary, is a clear test of historicity, when the historical context can be adequately recovered.

20. From James's translation, "Apocryphal New Testament," http://www.gnosis.org/library/gosnic.htm.

also saw the risen Jesus. None of these witnesses are disciples of Jesus. There are three witnesses, once again, indicating legal corroboration of an event.

Risk Analysis of the Gospel of Nicodemus / Acts of Pilate (GN/AP):

GN/AP provides embellished and new risk elements that merit analysis. To begin, Pilate questions the Jewish elite about their charges against Jesus. Jesus is identified as an "evildoer," but this is now clearly defined as *sorcery*, and his exorcisms of demons are derived from Beelzebul—that is, Satan controls Jesus.

> 1.1 Pilate said unto them: By what evil deeds? They say unto him: He is a sorcerer, and by Beelzebub the prince of the devils he cast out devils, and they are all subject unto him. Pilate said unto them: This is not to cast out devils by an unclean spirit, but by the god Asclepius.

What our earlier risk analysis had confirmed as reliable concerning the accusation brought before Pilate against Jesus is now confirmed. This heightened risk accusation merits attention, and suggests that some of *GN/AP*'s traditions come from earlier sources that are reliable. Indeed, this is the most specific description linking Jesus' charismatic activity to Beelzebul and the charge against him as an "evildoer." However, Pilate rejects this description and associates Jesus' authority with Asclepius, son of Apollo, and the Greek healing god (and god of medicine), whose sanitariums were famous and spread throughout the Hellenistic world, the Asclepium. In essence, Pilate counters an accepted, certainly positive and democratized view of Jesus' authority to heal as being given to him by the benevolent gods. This implies that Jesus was not understood by Pilate as a sorcerer, but possibly as a divine man empowered by the gods—exactly what a first-century Roman would not just understand, but would attribute to such healing miracles that other witnessed—but this is a benign and inaccurate view, and a whitewash of the risk Jesus was perceived as presenting to Pilate and the Jerusalem elite. Risk analysis employed in *Fire* suggests that Pilate was terrified of Jesus and his ability to curse and harm him and his wife, leading him, along with the elite, to annihilate him on a cross and thereby rendering his retributive powers void. Nonetheless, this is an interesting risk countermeasure to the accusations brought against Jesus.

> 2.1 Pilate: Said we not unto thee that he is a sorcerer? Behold, he has sent a vision of a dream unto my wife [terrifying her].

With regard to the witnesses to the post-crucifixion activity of Jesus, one Joseph reports what he saw:

> And Joseph said: On the preparation day about the tenth hour ye did shut me up, and I continued there the whole Sabbath. And at midnight as I stood and prayed the house wherein you shut me up was taken up by the four corners, and I saw as it were a flashing of light in my eyes, and being filled with fear I fell to the earth. And one took me by the hand and removed me from the place whereon I had fallen; and moisture of water was shed on me from my head unto my feet, and an odor of ointment came about my nostrils. And he wiped my face and kissed me and said unto me: Fear not, Joseph: open your eyes and see that it is that speaks with you. And I looked up and saw Jesus and I trembled, and supposed that it was a spirit; and I said the commandments; and he said them with me. And [as] you are not ignorant that a spirit, if it meet any man and hear the commandments, straightway flees. And when I perceived that he said them with me, I said unto him: Rabbi Elias? And he said unto me: I am not Elias. And I said unto him: Who art thou, Lord? And he said unto me: I am Jesus, whose body you did beg of Pilate, and did cloth me in clean linen and cover my face with a napkin, and lay me in thy new cave and roll a great stone upon the door of the cave. And I said to him that spoke with me: Show me the place where I laid thee. And he brought me and showed me the place where I laid him, and the linen cloth lay therein, and the napkin that was upon his face. And I knew that it was Jesus. And he took me by the hand and set me in the midst of mine house, the doors being shut, and laid me upon my bed and said unto me: Peace be unto thee. And he kissed me and said unto me: Until forty days be ended go not out of your house: for behold I go unto my brethren into Galilee.

This is a post-crucifixion revelatory ecstatic vision or trance, and one that also includes additional details of an encounter that is absent from other gospels. In this event, Joseph of Arimathea[21] has an encounter while locked behind closed doors. It is midnight, and he is in ecstatic prayer. In a trance,

---

21. The report recorded in the *Acts of Pilate* of Joseph of Arimathea, a supposed member of the Sanhedrin, and sympathizer of Jesus. By tradition in the gospels (Mark 15:43; Matt 27:57; John 19:38), Joseph asks for and receives the body of Jesus from Pilate. Risk analysis has shown that this tradition is an embellishment of actual facts. The Sanhedrin was made up of carefully chosen Roman sympathizers selected by the high priest. Jesus' body was taken and sealed in a tomb to ensure he had been annihilated and could not seek retribution against his enemies.

a light flashes and he is transported to a different place when touched. He is covered with ointment, as if purified when entering a sacred realm. The trance is so vivid he can smell the ointment. When he looks up he sees Jesus, but he is terrified, thinking instead he is tricked and is seeing a phantasm. To drive the phantasm away, he recites the "commandments," i.e., likely the Decalogue or sacred passages memorized and worn in an amulet for protection[22]—a practice that is most certainly ancient and used by Jews for protection from evil spirits and demons; particularly at midnight, the hour of evil and attack. Recitation would drive the evil away, i.e., it would "flee." But the spirit recites the words of protection with him. Again, he is transported to the tomb by Jesus to prove it is he, active and capable of charismatic powers. Once again, he is transported back to his locked room, placed in bed and told to remain indoors for forty days. Joseph is told that Jesus is leaving to meet his followers in Galilee. This is purported then to be an encounter in Jerusalem before Jesus interacts with his exorcists in Galilee.

This encounter with Joseph reflects a later tradition, when the work of the Roman sympathizing Sanhedrin participated in the capture and entombment of Jesus to ensure he could not retaliate. With the destruction of Jerusalem and the end of the Sanhedrin and Joseph, gospel editors and redactors attempted to smooth over the tradition of why Jesus was entombed at all; namely, a sympathizer and member of the ruling class who was a "secret disciple" wished to honor Jesus. Risk analysis has demonstrated just the opposite. This indicates that *GN/AP* is highly reliant on other gospels, particularly Luke.[23] It therefore cannot be seen as independent of earlier traditions.

Veracity of the Gospel of Nicodemus / Acts of Pilate (GN/AP):

Most striking, Jesus is again emphasized as an evildoer, sorcerer, able to inflict damage to others in dreams, inciting terror among his enemies and one who must be annihilated. During Joseph's trance, we learn more about amulets and protection from evil spirits, soul transportation, and encounters made solely for the reason to prove Jesus has not been annihilated, but is active and still retains charismatic power and authority. Yet, the fact that it is Joseph who receives the encounter and is in Jerusalem is incoherent with earlier findings. Consequently, these passages cannot pass the risk tests,

---

22. Phylacteries, or sacred amulets worn by Jews, included Hebrew text, Exod 13:1–10, 11–16; Deut 6:4–9; 11:13–21. They kept the law before the adherent, as well a provided protection from evil.

23. E.g., Luke 3:1.

particularly the criteria of dissimilarity or embarrassment. Nor can these pass the contextual tests. Nonetheless, they are additive to our understanding of contemporaneous risk perceptions related to dark magicians and fear of their powers, and that they were threatening to the Roman elite.

This concludes the risk analysis of noncanonical gospels and passages. The veracity of these encounters will be evaluated and prioritized following risk analysis of Paul of Tarsus.

12

The Perilous Risk Context of Paul's Encounter

Encounter a Risk Event: "I Am Compelled" and "Woe on Me"

Having evaluated the post-crucifixion encounters with Jesus in the gospel and noncanonical traditions, analysis can now turn to the New Testament's most direct witness to encounters with Jesus, Paul of Tarsus. Paul is accessible. There are seven undisputed charismatic correspondences to the communities he founded, some of which describe his post-crucifixion experiences with Jesus in detail. Risk analysis is able to evaluate the ecstatic experiences of this once young, violent, and ambitious Pharisee; a Hebrew from the tribe of Benjamin, who was originally a paid and commissioned "hit man" of the Jerusalem elite.[1] Paul (then known as Saul) was authorized and did commit atrocities specifically against Jesus' sympathizers and followers, including participation in murder. Saul was a name that brought terror to his enemies.[2]

Saul had a radical transformation, his world turned upside down, following a traumatic and life-threatening ecstatic experience.[3] He changed his name to Paul. Scholars universally agree that in the years following that experience, Paul then provides the earliest firsthand written witness to encounters with Jesus, post-crucifixion. In fact, he describes multiple

---

1. The high priestly families, scribes, the Herodian aristocracy and rich elite aligned with Rome were *de facto* Roman patrons. There are multiple attestations to this view of the elite in Josephus, pagan historians and New Testament sources that will be cited in forthcoming discussions. See also Hanson and Oakman, "Social Impact," 146–54.

2. Gal 1:23.

3. 1 Cor 9:1; Gal 1:16.

encounters of various types, and also acknowledges that he was not the first; several others had preceded him based on a chronological, extensive list of witnesses he provides in 1 Cor 15:1–8.[4] Since Paul had various forms of encounters, he never insists that materiality was the only legitimate form. Several of Paul's letters, usually engendered by a risk response to opponents infiltrating and trying to disband his *ecclesiae* (including "spies" sent from James, the brother of Jesus!), described these experiences. Remarkably, and in addition to these, Paul engages in spirit[5] and soul[6] transportation, Spirit possession,[7] affliction by demons of Satan,[8] exorcisms,[9] and ecstatic outbursts of spiritual/heavenly prophetic language.[10] Paul was a charismatic Jew *par excellence*. Even his letters carried charismatic authority and power, as well as curses and blessings when read aloud, all of which became immediately effective.

Paul's reaction to his encounters with this resurrected being, which he depicts as having personally seen—specifically, *not* in a vision, a séance or trance familiar to his world,[11] nor in an encounter with a *Bi(ai)othanatori*,[12] but with his own eyes (*ophthe*) as a physical presence; that is, a real and visible manifestation with material substance,[13] are striking. He acknowledges that these radical events created for him heightened perilous risk, so dramatic, that he tossed aside his Hebrew name, devalued his religious heritage and legal training (calling it "refuse"),[14] and became the itinerant messenger of a crucified Jewish criminal he proclaimed the risen Lord. Often starving, hunted, beaten and wandering town to town in danger, he was an *apos-*

---

4. Koester, *Introduction*, 84.

5. 1 Cor 5:4.

6. 2 Cor 2:12; Paul describes his being lifted up to the place of redeemed humans in "heaven."

7. 1 Cor 14:1–25.

8. 2 Cor 12:7.

9. Acts 16:18; 19:13.

10. 1 Cor 14:8.

11. For the historical context and variety of ecstatic expressions, see Smith, *Jesus the Magician*, 75–80; also see Lewis for a broader definition of "trance" in *Ecstatic Religion*, 29–31, and then descriptions that correspond to Hellenistic and Roman settings such as in 39–57.

12. A ghost, "those dead by violence." Ogden, *Magic*, 146, 149–52.

13. The word "appeared" (*ophthe*) literally means that "he was seen" not as an apparition *but was literally seen as a person in historical time*, i.e., the same Jesus of Nazareth that was personally known to Cephas and had been buried for three days was "seen" as a living person again. For discussion, see Conzelmann, *1 Corinthians*, 256–57, esp. 257n74.

14. Phil 3:8.

tolos; the *slave* of that resurrected being that was "in him," i.e., possessed him.[15] This ecstatic event, in a world filled with gods, ghosts, angels, demons and spirits, and a religious law that Saul once embraced but now claimed condemned one to death,[16] defined for Paul the radical countermeasure to evil and Satanic control that once infected him—indeed the only "way"[17] to achieve freedom from death and eternal life—the Gospel.[18]

While Saul attempted to annihilate the followers of Jesus,[19] *Paul* called Jesus "Lord" and emulated Jesus' battle against Satan and his deceptive forces. He too was once Satan's victim of deception and was doomed.[20] Ultimately, Paul came to radically reject the Jerusalem elite like Jesus, which eventually included some of the leaders of the Jesus movement, indeed one of the "pillars" of the Jerusalem *ecclesia* who came to oppose him—Yecob, the brother of Jesus. He declared that Satan and his demons possessed and controlled some of these elite.[21] His "apology" letter to the Galatian *ecclesiae*, reviling the infiltration of James (whose spies attempted to disband his assemblies, calling his "gospel" *anathema*),[22] has been correctly categorized as a "magical letter":[23] Depending on whether the Galatians accepted or rejected Paul and his "gospel," they received a blessing of safety or were infected with a death-curse (i.e., including annihilation of the soul). There is no doubt that Paul placed this deadly curse on Yecob, which was an ecstatic practice he employed against enemies of Jesus. Paul uses a curse again in 1 Cor 5:3, "I have already judged . . . and give him over to Satan for the destruction of the flesh." Paul's "giving the man over to Satan" was the "blackest of magic" in the ancient world; the gospel writers minimize Jesus' use of such actions.[24]

---

15. 2 Cor 11:23–27.

16. 1 Cor 15:56.

17. Rom 7:6.

18. Jesus died on the cross under the deadly curse imposed by the Law, but was raised and made the Son of God, and so, "that at the name of Jesus every knee should bow, of those who are in heaven and on the earth and under the earth" (Phil 2:10).

19. Gal 1:13; also Acts 8:3.

20. Rom 8:37–39.

21. Gal 6:13–15; Schweitzer asserts that Paul's accusation of possession and curse is leveled against Cephas, James and John, who were the "Super Apostles." Schweitzer, *Mysticism of Paul*, 156–57.

22. Paul's response to the attack is a countermeasure of equal force to the charges leveled against him—he "curses" in response to the curse received in Gal 1:8–9.

23. See Betz, "Letter to the Galatians."

24. Smith, *Magic*, 110.

THE PERILOUS RISK CONTEXT OF PAUL'S ENCOUNTER 215

The deadly conflict embraced by Paul against Satan is a direct continuation of Jesus' war. Both Jesus and Paul were attacked by Satan,[25] yet both risked all, putting their lives at perilous risk, embracing annihilation, the curse of death for both body and soul, for the sake of the most powerful permeating substance ever encountered, the *euangelion*, "gospel" or "good news" of God. Once received by being united with God, whether in the charismatic rite of baptism in water, by *pistis* (charismatic faith in a risen Lord), or by baptism and possession of Spirit, or all of these, a material change began in that person's being, and with it, the kingdom was made present—Satan was overcome. The practice of *agape*, love, kept Satan at bay and confirmed one remained safe from death, even if the universe collapsed around them. A new person began to emerge, like a dead seed planted, watered and beginning to sprout anew.[26] It was a charismatic transformation engendered by God.

Jesus announced the charismatic force from God, the *euangelion*, i.e., Gospel, which saved victims of Satan from his possession and death. Similarly for Paul, new existence and rebirth was made immediately possible in *Gospel*; a word not as we may understand it today, that is, as a noun, but as a *powerful supernatural verb*,[27] saturated with life-giving power that overwhelmed body and soul, and supplanted one's risk of death and the capricious control of evil beings in that contextual world—a world completely "alien" to our own. Gospel literally altered the possibility of one's physical nature, from death to life, made impotent all evil powers,[28] all beginning with the return of Jesus from Satan's attempt to annihilate him—he became the "first fruits" of overcoming death.[29]

Like the small band of Palestinian exorcists selected and trained by Jesus, Paul's encounter with Gospel was an event that was shattering, irreversible and undeniably risky to reject.[30] It created a cataclysmic shift in what perilous risk now represented to each.[31] This terrifying risk of rejecting Gospel for Paul, having seen proof of Jesus presence (and regardless if it came as the result of the crucifixion of an accused sorcerer and magician under Roman law), brought on such a weighty curse, one's complete and ul-

---

25. Paul, 2 Cor 12:6–9; Jesus, Luke 4:9, and other ecstatic experiences in the desert wilderness of Judea.
26. 1 Cor 15:37.
27. Rom 1:16–17.
28. Rom 8:38.
29. 1 Cor 15:20.
30. 1 Cor 15:31.
31. Rom 7:24.

timate being was immediately to be considered void, useless, at an end, and was blanketed with death and consumed by evil.[32] Paul echoes this terror and fear of it when he says, "Woe on me if I do not proclaim Gospel!"[33]

It was this perilous risk that led this young Jewish zealot,[34] one who not only publicly participated in, but also led others to murder Jesus' fellow exorcists, and violently arrested and attacked sympathizers, to publicly announce he was both "in" (one with), as well as possessed by the Spirit of Jesus. More remarkable, he even invoked the powerful name of Jesus for protection or in condemnation.[35] Paul's transformation acknowledged that Beelzebul, the prince of demons, did not possess Jesus (as he, Saul, had most certainly had claimed in concert with the Jerusalem elite),[36] but instead announced that the Spirit of God did![37] Only a transformative encounter with Jesus post-crucifixion can explain acceptance of heightened perilous risk. Consequently, assessing Paul's encounters from a risk perspective is made possible.

There are at least four types of post-crucifixion encounters noted by Paul. Paul stated that he had seen Jesus with his own eyes, i.e., a material manifestation of Jesus in a new *soma*, which is then described.[38] Paul encounters Jesus in dreams,[39] where he receives instructions of the Lord,[40] commands and sayings.[41] He describes visions and revelations given by the Lord or the Spirit,[42] which include ecstatic transportation to heaven.[43]

32. 1 Cor 15:8.
33. 1 Cor 9:16.
34. Gal 1:14.
35. 1 Cor 5:4.
36. Mark 3:22; Morton Smith states: "Take that away, and all that remains is a collection of unrelated complaints, most of them not very serious; introduce it, and then these complaints can be seen as component elements of a comprehensive structure" (*Jesus the Magician*, 31–32).
37. The contrast between two kinds of spirits, Beelzebul and the Holy Spirit that possesses Jesus, is clear in Mark, particularly implicit in Mark 3:20. See Robinson, *Problem of History in Mark*, 36. As Robinson points out, "The rarity of this identification in Mark [i.e., the Holy Spirit as empowering Jesus' actions] show the importance the present issue has for him."
38. 1 Cor 9:1, 15:8.
39. Acts 16:9, 18:9. These were the most common of interactions described by Ogden in *Magic* form contemporary sources, noted previously in our study.
40. 1 Cor 7 (in response to questions, where Paul cites his and the Lord's instructions).
41. 1 Cor 11:23.
42. Gal 1:12; 1 Cor 2:2–12; also perhaps 11:23, and certainly 15:51; 2 Cor 12:1–10; 1 Thess 4:15–17; Rom 1:17; 16:25.
43. 2 Cor 12:2–4.

Finally, Paul states that he can enter into Spirit possession, evoking ecstatic prophetic language, and interpretations take place.[44] Paul can call on the powerful name of Jesus to curse or bless those he wills because of his relationship with Jesus, post-crucifixion.[45] All of these are set in the context of heightened perilous risk.[46] Fundamental to all of these was his encounter with the *soma* of Jesus and the danger that arose and brought deadly risk to Paul daily,[47] beginning with a narrow escape.[48]

To begin, Paul is certain that he will experience the "day of the Lord Jesus" during his lifetime, and this immanent charismatic and cataclysmic[49] event in history characterizes the tension between the current order of the world that is soon to collapse and the presence of the Lord and the general resurrection "at his coming [for] those who belong to Christ,"[50] meaning both those "who have fallen asleep" (death is not possible for those "in Christ"[51] through the Gospel), as well as those still alive; this is then followed by the period of subjection of all powers and delivery of the kingdom to God "by his son." It is Paul's expectation that the living believers he addresses will soon be changed, indeed, many of those hearing Paul's letter will experience a transformation of their body, *the soma*, and see it with their own eyes: "Lo! I tell you a mystery. We shall not all sleep, but we shall all be changed, in a moment, in the twinkling of an eye at the last trumpet.... For this perishable nature must put on the imperishable, and this mortal nature must put on immortal."[52] What is "sown as a body (*soma*) natural and [is] raised a body (*soma*) spiritual."[53]

---

44. Gal 4:6, Rom 8:15; for *glossolalia*, see 1 Cor 14:8.
45. 1 Cor 5:4; Phil 2:10; and then democratized to all in Rom 10:13.
46. 2 Cor 11:16–33.
47. 1 Cor 15:31.
48. 2 Cor 11:32.
49. 1 Cor 15:23–28: "But each in his own order; Christ, the first-fruits, then at his coming those who belong to Christ. Then comes the end, when he delivers the kingdom to God the Father after destroying every rule and every authority and power. For he must reign until he has put all his enemies under his feet. The last enemy to be destroyed is death. (For God has put all things in subjection under his feet). But when it says, (all things are put in subjection under him), it is plain that he is expected who put all things all under him. When all things are subjected to him, then the Son himself will also be subjected to him who put all things under him, that God may be everything to everyone."
50. 1 Cor 15:13.
51. 1 Thess 4:14–17.
52. 1 Cor 15:51–52a, 53.
53. 1 Cor 15:44b.

Paul's description of the resurrected (or transformed) body as "spiritual" has led to much controversy, but when set in the context of first-century primitive Christianity, evidence is contrary. Paul is a Jew and Pharisee, and in verses too numerous to cite, Paul speaks of the body as the *soma*, which is a term for the body that a Pharisee understands *as the physical body*. He consistently alludes to the body in this way[54] and is also consistent in his statements as to the physical, holy (i.e., temple of the Holy Spirit) and sinful nature of the body from the perspective of a Pharisee. Further, the Pharisees were also insistent as to the physical resurrection of the *soma* at the end of the age.[55] His analogy of the seed dying to produce a more glorious body, and the body as a type of seed that must die to become "imperishable," as well as his description of the many types of plant, animal and material "*soma*" God has chosen and made, all refer to realities.[56]

Soma is then a substantive reality. For Paul, the resurrected body is a "spiritual *soma* (*soma pneumatikon*)," just as the food and drink that the Jews ate in the wilderness with Moses was "spiritual food and drink," i.e., substantive food and drink, but given by God's miracle, thus making it spiritual.[57] So it is with what is raised as "imperishable," meaning it is a spiritual *soma* whose characteristics are given by the miracle of God; but it is substantive resurrected *soma*, not just ethereal spirit, and unlike anything known up to that time with the exception of the risen Jesus. And as Paul says, "Christ was the first fruits,"[58] so the resurrected *soma* Paul is describing is similar to that he saw of Jesus, which Paul has seen with his own eyes in its full glory. In other words, what Paul has seen, he is describing—the new *soma* of Jesus. As noted, visions and traces in the ancient world were considered "real" experiences, where what was "seen" with one's eyes and felt as presence were considered substantive. Again, this is not the only type of encounter Paul has with Jesus post-crucifixion, but for him, it is pivotal. If Paul were to have intended to teach only transformation into an ethereal spirit at the resurrection day he would have been clear that this was "out of the body (*soma*)," just as he did when he recounted his experience being "caught away" to the "third heaven" (not "caught up" as in some translations; caught away is consistent with the ancient Jewish belief of the highest heaven being somewhere other than up or above): "I know a man in Christ

---

54. 1 Cor refers to the *soma* 35 times, more than any other New Testament work.

55. This continued into the rabbinical period and is still one of thirteen fundamental tenets of current rabbinic Judaism.

56. 1 Cor 15:37–42.

57. 1 Cor 10:1–5.

58. 1 Cor 15:23.

who fourteen years ago was caught up to the third heaven—whether in the body or out of the body, I do not know, God knows."[59] Paul knows and could explain the difference firsthand.

Paul was able to articulate the transformation, calling those who reject it as deceived by Satan—those "superlative apostles." He introduces the question: "But someone asks, 'How are the dead raised? With what kind of body do they come?'"[60] Phantasms, ghosts, retributive spirits, and angels of demons were all associated with activities of the dead. However, some encounters were substantive, and as noted in this study, the dead could materialize, attack, appear in distant places, and even pass through stone and out of tombs, leaving behind physical evidence of their presence. This question is instead addressing Paul's assertion that the substantive encounter of the dead is similar to the *soma*, which his enemies reject as possible. "You foolish one!" Paul *never* addresses the believers as "foolish (i.e., *aphron*)." He employs a play on words; *a* = "without," and *phren* = "understanding," or "foolish," clearly a reference to the opponents. Paul is not simply calling them "fools," he is accusing them again of being "without understanding" about the *eschatos*, meaning they are deceived and in perilous danger.

Paul then begins to describe examples of physical transformation from death to life that are observable in nature, all of which provide irrefutable proof that resurrection is the ultimate miracle in God's creative design. He begins with the simplest analogy, the seed: "What you sow does not come to life unless it dies."[61] Paul states what is an observable fact to both the believers and opponents. How can the opponents be so ignorant as to not to notice what happens in nature when a seed is buried and "dies," but is then transformed into a new "body," becoming more glorious and full than its last form? Paul provides more specific examples, but first clarifies that what is sown at death is not the final body. Just as the seed that dies, one's true and full being is only realized following the death of the body and resurrection to full and new life given solely the miracle of God. Faith is the agent of life, the transformative power of God, who responds in love for the sake of his son. Again using examples from nature, Paul cites "bare grain" perhaps of "wheat" or "some other kind. . . . God gives to it a body as he wished and to each of the seeds their own body."[62] Paul's remarkable analogy is witnessed and commonplace, but still is a miracle. This same analogy is found in the Talmudic literature, where Rabbi Meier also uses the transformation of a

---

59. 2 Cor 12:2–3.
60. 1 Cor 15:35.
61. 1 Cor 15:36.
62. 1 Cor 15:37.

seed as evidence for the physical resurrection of the body—a miracle: "If a kernel of wheat is buried naked and will sprout forth in many robes, how much more so the righteous."[63] This type of analogy of seed to plant and transformation would also explain Paul's use of Jesus of Nazareth's resurrection as the "first fruits," that is the first transformation to the substance of new resurrected body, just like evidenced in nature, particularly that of the seed. This new body is the "spiritual body," it has substance and form and physical reality that is as God designed it to be, first revealed in the encounter with the resurrected Jesus. The resurrected body, the "spiritual *soma*," has yet to be obtained by the opponents, and so quite obviously, they have not attained yet the true resurrection because the general resurrection when this miracle is present has yet to occur. Even more, the fact that those who have "fallen asleep" have yet to have made the transformation, evidenced in the eschatological order of Paul's apocalypse in 1 Thessalonians or 1 Corinthians, presses his point that only at the returned presence of the Lord does the general resurrection occur and that those who have not fallen asleep and those who are still alive will also be transformed: "We shall not all fall asleep, all we shall be changed, in a moment, in a glance [twinkling] of an eye at the last trumpet (*salpiggi*); for a trumpet will sound and the dead will be raised incorruptible, and we shall be changed."[64] Thus, the miracle of the resurrection is not given solely to the dead, but at the *Parousia* to those alive, just as Paul expects for himself.

Paul then presents a new and radical eschatological expansion of the nature of death for the believer "in Christ," one that not only matches the claims of the opponents (i.e., there is immediate transformation, yes, but through faith, not gnosis), it is more wondrous. It redefines the intermittent state of death as a part of the unfolding of God's loving plan and transformative care for the believer—eternal life is now inbreaking. Since the resurrection has already begun, those believers who die only "sleep" in the body, but are raised to be with the Lord, whether "in the spirit or body, I do not know, only God knows."[65] Thus, during the interim between bodily death and the *Parousia*, the believer is immediately taken to the "third heaven" to be with the risen Christ, remaining with him until the *general resurrection*:

> Therefore, being always of good courage, and knowing that while we are at home in the body we are absent from the Lord—for we walk by faith, not by sight—we are of good courage, I say,

---

63. See, *b. Sanhedrin* 90b.
64. 1 Cor 15:51–52.
65. 2 Cor 12:2.

and prefer rather to be absent from the body and to be at home with the Lord.⁶⁶

Accepting this perilous risk, understanding that doing so paradoxically gains assurance of life, Paul says:

> For to me, to live is Christ and to die is gain. But if I am to live on in the flesh, this will mean fruitful labor for me; and I do not know which to choose. But I am hard-pressed from both directions, having the desire to depart and be with Christ, for that is very much better; yet to remain on in the flesh is more necessary for your sake.⁶⁷

This statement fits the heightened risk context evident in the eschatology of Paul's letter to the Corinthians; that at the general resurrection, after the kingdom is delivered to God and death has been abolished (the "last enemy" to be destroyed), the prophetic saying will be realized. It is on this basis that Paul makes the emotional and joyous statement to the believers: "But thanks be to God, who gives us the victory through our Lord Jesus Christ!"⁶⁸

Paul asserts a spiritual *soma* of substance, something he has seen with his own eyes. The perilous risk of abandoning the transformative gospel and not proclaiming what he has seen with his own eyes, Jesus in his spiritual substantive *soma*, would lead to curse and annihilation. Consequently, Paul's encounter with Jesus forced him to abandon his violent subsistent existence and affiliation with the Jerusalem elite and become an itinerant exorcist and *apostolos*, doomed and hated, but serving the most powerful figure of his time, Jesus. His new life was fraught with heightened perilous risk. Jesus communicates and interacts with Paul in every form validated in our earlier study. But more, Paul is the witness who insists that the encounter was much more than any common experience with a *phantasm*, or a vision, séance or trance. Jesus could command any and all forms. This is what the essence the spiritual *soma* was able to do in its glory. Thus, Paul asserts that there has never been this kind of being before. Post-crucifixion, Jesus commands the long promise and glorified spiritual *soma* for the first time. He is the first fruits, the only one to have this power after death. All who have *pistis* and practice *agape*, accepting this powerful *euangelion*, can attain the same, and soon, even in the "twinkling of and eye."

---

66. 2 Cor 5:6–8.
67. Phil 1:21–24.
68. 1 Cor 15:57.

Summary—Paul of Tarsus

Paul is a direct witness to the multiplicity of post-crucifixion encounters with Jesus that were experienced by the exorcists and followers of Jesus, particularly those known as *apostolos*, including the individuals and groups listed in 1 Cor 15:1–8. These experiences must be included as authentic, meeting the heightened perilous risk test of the qualitative risk analysis. Paul was an outcast, rejected by Yecob, brother of Jesus, thought to be a charlatan by his opponents and the recipient of attack from all forces, human and demonic. As such, it is impossible to ascribe these events to an "orthodoxy" of belief in the early church. Paul experienced Jesus in all forms familiar to the ancient world of post-death encounters, but now also in the form of a spiritual *soma*. Paul asserts something completely different that what was expected by his contemporaries, and was reviled for it.

Consequently, all of Paul's encounters pass the test of the criteria of dissimilarity and embarrassment. While the contextual setting is not in Galilee, Paul's escape from Palestine and Damascus, then his subsequent arrest after returning to the temple of Jerusalem, is not dissimilar to the exorcists' escape to Galilee and then reengagement by returning to itinerancy and war on Satan. Therefore, the itinerancy of Paul meets the contextual tests.

13

Risk Analysis and the Recovery of Reliable Events in their Contemporary Setting

The foregoing analyses have employed risk and contextual tests to ascertain the veracity of post-crucifixion encounters with Jesus, and recovered the most original form and context of these traditions. It is now possible to summarize the findings, categorizing them according to a priority and context that is based on a recovery of the risk content that survives these testing filters. First, the results are presented in order by each source analyzed, followed then by a second presentation ordering them by veracity and placed within a sequential context.

Summarizing the Recovered Events, Forms and Contents: Determining Veracity

Based on a rigorous and consistent application of perilous risk analysis and the four contextual tests to canonical and noncanonical sources, the veracity of findings can be summarized. Critical to these findings is the fundamental tenet of acceptance of heightened perilous risks. The Galilean exorcists would not have embraced significantly heightened and life-threatening perilous risk unless encounters with Jesus, post-crucifixion, had occurred. The chart below presents the findings of the comprehensive risk analysis within the contextual setting of first-century Palestine. The source, the scope of the recovery effort to ascertain the original form of the tradition, the type of encounter recovered, what test results showed, and conclusions on veracity are presented in detail.

Source	Adjustment a	Encounter b	Risk Tests c	Results d	Veracity e
Mk 16:9–20	Significant	Vision	Pass All	3 Neutral	Probable
Mk 9:2–8	Significant	Trance	Pass All	Pass All	Certain
MT 28:1–10	Significant	T/Substance	Pass All	Pass All	Certain
MT 28:16–20	Moderate	Vision	Fail D/E	Fail All	Low
Lk 24:13–35	Significant	V/Substance	Neutral	Pass All	Probable
Lk 24:34	Intact	V/Substance	Pass All	Pass All	Certain
Lk 24:36–43	Significant	T/Substance	Pass All	Pass All	Certain
Lk 24:50–53	Intact	V/Substance	Fail All	None	Fail All
Jn 6:16–24	Moderate	Vision	Pass All	Pass All	Certain
Jn 20:11–18	Significant	Trance	Neutral	3, 4 Fail	Low
Jn 20:19–23	Intact	V/Substance	Fail All	Fail All	None
Jn 21:1–23	Moderate	Substance	Fail All	Fail All	None
G Peter	Intact	Dialogue	Md Pass All	Md Pass All	Probable
G Mary	Intact	Other	Md Pass All	Md Pass All	Probable
G Nicod/AP	Intact	Other	Md Pass All	Md Fail QR	Low

a. Adjustment Required: In each case, the original source(s) or document is reevaluated through rigorous analysis of contemporary risk context and setting (i.e., its *sitz im leben*), and appropriate elements or forms are recovered for application into the risk and contextual test filters. The categories are: Significant (extensive reconstruction has been required); Moderate (the original setting and form has had recovered through association with context and setting); Intact (the passage or source is taken virtually verbatim with contextual context discussed); and Unrecoverable (the original form is not recoverable).

b. Encounters: The event encounter categories are Trance (an ecstatic event where the recipient is transported or enters into a spiritual state while conscious with other worldly events, entities or beings); Vision (similar to trance, but can occur in dream and unconsciousness); and Substantial (a manifestation of a phantasm or spirit with material substance attached—either encounter or seen with the eyes, felt, touched while not thought to be in a Trance or Vision). As such, Substance encounters may be thought to have been experienced also in a Trance or Vision (V-Substance, T-Substance).

c. Risk Tests: Qualitative Risk Analysis, where heightened perilous risk is confirmed; the Criteria of Dissimilarity (D) and Embarrassment (E). Md = if modified, pass all.

d. Contextual Tests: There are four noted. Ones not passed are identified by numbered. They are: (1) Encounters with original members of Jesus' band of Galilean exorcists, those who faced capture, death and social isolation and starvation, are given priority; (2) Encounters should be consistent with the ecstatic practices of Jesus that engendered the original perilous risk with his opponents. Specifically, encounters that encouraged the remaining exorcists to continue the ecstatic activity of Jesus and his war on Satan are preferred; (3) Encounters near or on the lake of Galilee, particularly related to subsistence fishing, and similar to the animistic control exhibited by Jesus, are preferential (i.e., the remaining exorcists escaped there); (4) Finally, encounters that may have led the Galileans to again abandon subsistence existence (i.e., to which they returned for survival post-crucifixion) are also preferred.

e. Veracity: Certain (the event is reliable within the risk context and setting recovered); Probable (while not certain, the risk context and setting recovered render the event highly likely in a similar form to that reported); Low (the predominant characteristics and test can recover elements that may fit the contemporary risk context, but cannot be confirmed); Inconclusive (the tests are inconclusive and no conclusion of veracity can be made); None (the risk tests render the recovered source or its elements unrecoverable and most likely the product of the early church or a specific community).

The outcomes as to veracity of each encounter, based on a comprehensive application of contextual risk analysis, is striking. Of the fifteen traditions (two recovered from the pre-crucifixion accounts reattributed to Jesus' itinerant war on Satan due to their problematic nature: Mark 9:2–8 [the metamorphosis], John 6:16–24 [the lake encounter]), five were rendered "certain" when their original forms were recovered. Recovering three of these certain events required "extensive" or "significant" risk and contextual analysis to arrive at the most original form of the tradition—the metamorphosis on the sacred mountain, the materialization behind closed doors with doubt, and Magdalene's encounter at the tomb and road to Galilee. Only one tradition was found to be intact as is, Luke 24:34, the report of Kayfa. Four "probable" events were isolated, two of which come from noncanonical gospels. The remainder could not be recovered, or were found to be the products of the communities they served with neutral or no perilous risk content.

Those events recovered from their original sources not only provide new insights into the original risk form of the events, but significant contextual revision to an understanding of the formation of primitive Christianity in its original setting, including specific techniques and locations of exorcisms; the various exorcisms each of Jesus' band could perform; the nature of a trance, vision and substance; the significant role of Magdalene; the role of Kayfa as exorcist and leader; the radical transformation of Saul to Paul and many others. In each, risk analysis has provided such clarity and transparency into the original event and its perilous risk context that is often disturbing; thus, the need for the community to soften or alter it to a more acceptable form or community eschatology or theology. In some cases the event is used as a risk defense to attack from competing communities, or to explain the loss of its founding witness. The risk history of each event is rich and revealing, both as a human story of interaction with forces that saturated that alien world, but the courage to embrace perilous risks in the face of torture, starvation and even death. The human response to perilous risk, and even to embrace heightened perilous risk, can be recovered and evaluated in its original contextual setting to render insight and transformative meaning today.

The recovered events can now be ordered in a proposed chronological sequence to stress the import of events and their impact in the formation of primitive Christianity:

Source	Adjustment	Encounter	Risk Tests	Results	Veracity
MT 28:1–10	Extensive	T/Substance	Pass All	Pass All	Certain
Jn 6:16–24	Moderate	Vision	Pass All	Pass All	Certain
G Mary	Intact	Other	Md Pass All	Md Pass All	Probable
Mk 9:2–8	Significant	Trance	Pass All	Pass All	Certain
Lk 24:13–35	Extensive	V/Substance	Neutral	Pass All	Probable
Lk 24:34	Intact	V/Substance	Pass All	Pass All	Certain
Mk 16:9–20	Significant	Vision	Pass All	Neutral	Probable
G Peter	Intact	Dialogue	Md Pass All	Md Pass All	Probable
Lk 24:36–43	Significant	T/Substance	Pass All	Pass All	Certain

RISK ANALYSIS AND THE RECOVERY OF RELIABLE EVENTS 227

Elements within the following contribute to the understanding of risk and context:

Jn 20:11–18	Significant	Trance	Neutral	3, 4 Fail	Low
G Nicod	Intact	Other	Md Pass QR	Md Fail All	Low
MT 28:16–20	Moderate	Vision	Fail D/E	Fail All	Low

The recreation of events may be described as follows employing the risk and contextual tests as follows:

Risk Context and Order of Post-Resurrection Events

Countermeasure to Perilous Risk—Annihilating the "dark magician," Jesus Ritual Capture:

An informant and assassin of the Jerusalem elite infiltrated Jesus' exorcists, Yehuda from Galilee (not Judea). Jesus recognized Yehuda was an enemy, possessed by Satan, but thought to have exorcised his demon(s), at least temporarily. Yehuda was then trained as an exorcist, likely on the sacred mountain in Galilee with the others. Once trained, Yehuda was given his exorcist's name, *Iscariot*, the "strangler," an exorcist employing strangulation to drive out demons, usually through immersion in sacred water where the demon was expelled and captured, but in some cases the adherent may have perished. Under this practice, which may have been the same he employed as an informant on John the Baptist, Yehuda likely feigned the expulsion of demons. As a paid informant and assassin, he waited until Jesus was within reach of the elite near Jerusalem. Jesus' common practice was to find refuge from demonic retribution and attack at night when demons were most active. Safety could be found in a large cave were an olive press was present. Olive oil was used by exorcists to expel demons, and so this cave Jesus thought was secure from attack. Yehuda entered Gethsemane with special priests and guards armed with brass swords, amulets and other spells to control evil spirits and demonic attack by phantasms, which they believed Jesus controlled through Beelzebul, prince of demons, who possessed and empowered him. Yehuda found and approached Jesus, the kiss being an attack by passing on a spell to disarm and neutralize Jesus' power. Jesus was vulnerable for capture and attack. Jesus' exorcists fled, terrified at Yehuda's success, as well as fearing attack by aggressive and deadly demons they had expelled.

Ritual Annihilation and Entombment

Once captured, Jesus was ritually destroyed so the perilous risks he presented to his enemies as dark magician were neutralized. Following the brutalization and mutilation of Jesus' body to ensure as a *phantasm* he could not attack his enemies as one of the untimely dead, he is crucified. Crucifixion was demanded by his enemies and approved by Pilate. Crucifixion annihilated Jesus, body and soul, under Jewish law and its divine curse of being hung on a tree. The perilous risk Jesus posed to his enemies as an "evildoer," that is, a dark magician, required this form of death. What remained of his body was wrapped in a concoction to ensure that if his spirit did survive, it would be trapped. The body was covered with written scroll spells, special herbs and magical amulets to contain the spirit in case it was not destroyed, which would be feared from one who had practiced the darkest of magic, necromancy. There may have been additional body mutilation, including armpitting or dismemberment. To complete containment, the body was then sealed in a rock or stone tomb, likely one empty so it could not possess the spirits of others in the tomb and escape. The body was to remain at rest without activity for at least three days to ensure it had been destroyed; that it had not escaped to seek retribution. Ritual priests wearing white robes guarded the tomb, armed with powerful weapons that repelled demonic attack, including spells and brass swords. The fear that Jesus' exorcists might take his body was a real concern, because it could imply he was active (a countermeasure) or his body could be used against the elite for retribution (necromancy, i.e., to manipulate the body and communicate with the dead Jesus, then attack enemies). Daily, at dawn, or certainly on the third day, the ritual priests would roll back the stone sealing the tomb to ensure the body (and the spirit) had not escaped and was active. When done on the third morning, the body was already absent, terrorizing the elite. Jesus could seek retribution as a *biaeothanati*, able to curse, punish and harm, even kill his murderers, under the authority that empowered him.[1] This danger, they believed, was of Beelzebul, prince of the demons of Satan.[2]

Risk Response of Kayfa and Other Exorcists to Jesus' Arrest

The Galilean male exorcists immediately fled Jerusalem with Jesus' capture. They were terrified by the threat of vicious attacks from demons (Jesus' authority had been vacated, they had no protection), as well as the assassins

---

1. Ogden, *Magic*, 152–53; 158; and as disputed by Tertullian in 200 CE, 149–50.
2. Busse, *To Be Near the Fire*, 54–58.

sent out by the elite the very night Jesus was taken. Reaching Galilee, their kin hid them. Barely able to survive themselves under harsh agrarian quotas imposed by their licensed overseers, these kin accepted the perilous risk of detection, capture and brutalization for hiding the "evildoers." Starving, the exorcists were forced to return to subsistence fishing, but at night, when demons and phantasms, including *biaeothanati*, roamed the lake waters of a haunted Galilee seeking victims and retribution. They clearly knew Jesus had been killed and crucified, but likely assumed his body had been either thrown in the town dump for the animals to consume, or burned in the dump; possibly that he had been ritually entombed to ensure he had been annihilated. It is clear that they not only had abandoned and publicly denied Jesus, but also the exorcists believed that Satan and demonic imperialism had overcome Jesus. There was no safety; no power to offset the pollution of the land; and certainly little to be gained from continuing their war on Satan. Jesus' band of exorcists had disbursed, just as other Galilean rebellious groups when their leader was captured and destroyed.

Risk Response of Maria, the Magdalene, to Jesus' Execution

Risk analysis of Matt 28:1–10 resulted in the recovery of the original, and first, post-crucifixion encounter with Jesus, coherent with the perilous risk context and contemporary setting of first-century Palestine under Roman domination. This original form has been found to be "certain" based on a rigorous and consistent application of multiple risk and contextual tests. It is this event that led a small sequence of authentic encounters.

Maria, a Galilean charismatic (and likely a Theraputae), renamed by Jesus *the Magdalene*[3] or "the Fortress,"[4] was a powerful ecstatic and exorcist, and an itinerant serving in Jesus' war on Satan; she was an exorcist disliked as well as feared by some of the male exorcists among Jesus' closest followers—all traditions that were later suppressed or altered.[5]

---

3. As noted, a practice Jesus employed for all of his trained and empowered exorcists: Kayfa, Toma, Boanerges are just some of the examples. Magdalene (Greek form from the Aramaic) was such an exorcist's name assigned to Maria of Galilee.

4. Aramaic, *Magdala*; not the village, but the exorcist name given to Maria (Luke 8:2), "the fortress," she was one who had taken multiple demons into her, a common practice among exorcists (discussed previously in our study, and known in contemporary times by the research of I. M. Lewis and others), thus, the fortress against demonic attack, or fortress holding demons.

5. See the discussion below on the suppression of women in subsequent gospel traditions, particularly Kraemer, "Autonomy, Prophecy and Gender," 130–13. Paul is very clear about the qualities of true apostles like himself in 2 Cor 12.

Unlike virtually all Jesus' exorcists who immediately abandoned and fled to Galilee upon his arrest (including Kayfa, a leader among Jesus' exorcists), Magdalene chose to not only remain after Jesus' arrest, but to discover the fate of his soul and spirit, thereby embracing heightened perilous risk. She made this perilous decision, risking detection and capture,[6] so as to secretly follow (at a careful distance)[7] and learn who had the brutalized body of Jesus (Jesus' deadly enemies, led by a member of the Sanhedrin, who was no sympathizer),[8] but more important, *where* it was taken and *how* the body was contained or destroyed.[9] Magdalene sought to determine if Jesus had indeed been annihilated or if his spirit could be rescued and engaged.

The area near Jerusalem where the body was taken must have been adjacent to the city's dump (where the body of crucified criminals were often thrown) or the *nekropolis*. Maria witnessed the body intentionally set into a rock-hewn tomb, whose entrance was temporarily blocked by a heavy rolling stone and sealed. When alone and before ritual priests arrive to further stigmatize the body of Jesus,[10] Magdalene sits over against the tomb, in an attempt to try and ascertain if Jesus had been destroyed—whether by trance, dream, or encounter with his phantasm—but with no success.

The ritual priests arrive, dressed in white robes, fully armed with powerful amulets, magical herbs, spells written on scrolls, and brass swords[11] to trap any spirit remaining and protect them from demonic or phantasm attacks. They wrap the body with huge amounts of these herbs[12] filled with

---

6. Her appearance set her apart. As noted, she became a "male," shortening her hair, wearing the ritual garb of an exorcist, and there may have been tattoos or other distinguishing marks.

7. Matt 27:55.

8. The legend of Joseph was added again later to mute the embarrassment of Jesus' body being thrown into a tomb to guard against his emergence as a retributive phantasm that would kill his murders.

9. If these men were sympathizers of Jesus, the women would not have had to follow at a distance, or wait until their departure, and only then approach the tomb.

10. In about 37 BCE, Marc Antony beheaded *and* crucified the Hasmonean king Matitiyahu Antigonus. A beheading prevented the spirit of those executed from seeking retribution, just as Herod's beheading of John the Baptist.

11. See previous analysis of the burial of Jesus, the use of special amulets to ward off evil, herbs and scroll spells, as well as brass swords that were thought to control demons. Felton, *Haunted Greece and Rome*, XIII, 12, 33, and describes controlling ghosts using swords.

12. According to John 19:38–42, the body had been covered with unusually large amounts of burial spices; over one hundred pounds of myrrh and aloes, while only forty pounds were used for the highly respected and revered Rabbi Gamaliel, Josephus, *Antiquities*, 17:8.3. Jesus' body was more likely covered with a concoction of magical herbs, amulets and written spells. This was done to ensure his ghost/spirit would

amulets and spell scrolls to prevent escape of his retributive spirit.[13] Jesus' body is likely further mutilated.[14] Nails used to crucify him may have been placed in the tomb as well, as these were considered powerful protective amulets.[15] The tomb's stone is rolled into place by the priests and sealed, further covered with amulets. They set a watch. If discovered, Magdalene's presence at the tomb meant her death. There are numerous contemporary accounts of brutal attacks on men and women, even innocent bystanders, whether by Pilate, the elite or their informants[16] that were recorded by Josephus and others.[17] Indeed, the actions to secure the body by Jesus' enemies and ensure they had crushed the "evildoer," the dark magician, protecting against retribution fits the contemporary risk context of this alien world (and so are most assuredly authentic), but is on par with Magdalene's own risk of capture.[18] Both were acting to either ensure or determine if Jesus has been destroyed. While Magdalene's first attempt (leaning on the tomb) failed, she returned, embracing heightened perilous risk.

After the Sabbath ended, and at the most dangerous time of night when evil and demons roamed seeking victims, Magdalene returns with an assistant, both trained exorcists of Jesus. Mark and Luke report that it was to "anoint the body" (Mark 16:1-2; Luke 24:1), adding also the names of other female exorcists present with them.[19] However, the editor/redactor of Matthew knew Palestine and that anointing a decaying body would have

---

remain at rest under a divine curse, his enemies fearing that, as a minion of Satan's demonic prince, Beelzebul, he would seek deadly retribution. The fear would explain the extra large quantity of materials used and why the body was quickly bound in linens.

13. For a detailed discussion of these practices, see the aforementioned analysis of this event in our study of Matt 28:1-10.

14. Matt 27:61: Guarding the tomb was indicative of fear of retribution, i.e., to monitor it to ensure it remain still and inactive.

15. Crucifixion nails have been found in various tombs, including the tomb of Caiaphas in 1990 and reported in 1992: Greenhut "'Caiaphas' Tomb"; the Mishna records that nails were used as amulets, *Mishna Shabbat* 6.10; *J. Talmud Shabbat* 6:9, 7c-d, *B. Talmud Shabbat*, 67a.

16. Including Saul of Tarsus by his own admission in Galatians as noted.

17. See Horsley and Hanson, *Bandits, Prophets and Messiahs*, 29-32, 41-42; Josephus, *Antiquities*, 8:60-62, 18:3.3, 18:85-89; Philo, *Embassy*, 302; see also Busse, *To Be Near the Fire*, 20-27; Saul, originally an agent and spy of the Jerusalem elite, brutalized both men and women who followed Jesus.

18. Mark 14:70; Luke 22:58; Matt 26:73; John 18:17.

19. Other women are mentioned in Mark 16:1-2: Mary Magdalene, Mary the Mother of James and Salome; other gospels have different groups and interactions, but are unanimous that women found the empty tomb and tried to report it to Kayfa, only be told it was an "idle tale."

been inconceivable and repugnant;[20] and with the brutalized condition of Jesus' body, impossible, and so it was dropped. Carrying heavy spices at that time of night (let alone purchasing them while in hiding) would also have been very difficult, if not impossible, and since the tomb was guarded and ritually sealed,[21] any approach would have led to their being attacked by the guards (i.e., not knowing if they were spirits, ghosts or exorcists of Jesus) with special protective weapons, e.g., the bronze swords or casting (throwing) deadly curses.[22]

Consequently, going to the tomb had nothing to do with anointing a decaying and mutilated body. Employing a contextual risk perspective within the contemporary setting, these exorcists went to raise up, claim or communicate with Jesus' spirit, intending to seek his protection, or that of "the finger of God," the Spirit that possessed him. They may have brought esoteric herbs and spices used by exorcists to carry out ecstatic prayer near the tomb, either to burn or ingest, with the intent of having an ecstatic vision, that is, to determine if Jesus' spirit had been annihilated, or if he could be contacted. To accomplish this, ancient ecstatics, exorcists and *goetes* went to the tomb of the victim, particularly during predawn hours. This presents the possibility that these women were responsible for activating Jesus' post-crucifixion appearances—the origin of primitive Christianity. Only these circumstances adequately address the actual and original risk context of the two Marys visitation to the tomb.[23]

Accordingly, the women then have an ecstatic experience, when in a trance or vision (later like that of Kayfa),[24] but at the site of the tomb. They witnessed the descent of an angel, felt a tremendous earthquake, and then the rolling back (*kulio*) of the large stone that sealed the tomb.[25] An angel

20. The very point of John 11:39 within the canonical gospel tradition.

21. To keep the body of Jesus and his spirit trapped, preventing retributive attack on enemies as was expected by the "untimely dead."

22. Pre-Tamidic literature speaks of Solomon's sword, transformed into the magic sword of Moses (Pesik 140a, Pesik R15, Testament of Solomon), where the sword is able to ward off evil at night, certainly including ghosts and spirits. Jesus' body was taken by his enemies to ensure he had been annihilated, both body (they brutalized and mutilated it as a first precaution) and spirit (killing him under a divine curse, being "hung on a tree"). It was then sealed in the tomb and guarded by special priests ordered to monitor the body, rolling back the stone at dawn each day to verify it remained still, i.e., to ensure his spirit was not "restless" to seek retribution as one of the untimely dead.

23. See examples in Ogden, *Magic*, 64–65, 146–47, 149–52, 161–62, 164–65, on tombs and encounters with ghosts and spirits there.

24. As determined in our previous analysis of the metamorphosis of Jesus, or as in Act 10:10.

25. Recall, our study has shown other examples in antiquity where there was no

of God instructs the women to tell the eleven exorcists the tomb had been vacated. Jesus' body did not appear; the tomb was already empty, just as in the tradition of Phlegon previously noted in the account of a deceased girl, Philinnion.[26]

The tradition then has the women instructed to rush to the eleven exorcists, who were either in hiding or already in the process of fleeing to Galilee. Magdalene then encounters Jesus. Whether this occurs in the vision or on a road as they seek to find the exorcists is uncertain,[27] but it is likely in the same vision. Jesus appears suddenly and is experienced in a substantive form. She and her assistant fall to their feet and wrap their arms around and worship Jesus. He commands the women to tell the exorcists, "Go to Galilee where they will see me." These instructions are contrary to those reported in Luke (i.e., they are to remain in Jerusalem, see Luke 24:49), and so certainly reflect the earlier tradition of Jesus' first encounters (aside from these exorcists) with the exorcists in Galilee. It is Magdalene that first encounters Jesus, and it is due to her activity at the tomb on Jesus' behalf. She confirms he is active and is to report the good news to the others if she can find them in hiding there.

This event underscores the remarkable perilous risk embraced by Magdalene. Indeed, this explains why the traditions of Magdalene having equal standing with Kayfa is rooted in early Christian literature and is multiply attested. Consequently, the tradition that "the Lord is risen indeed and has appeared to Peter (Kayfa)" should not be understood as proof the women were ignored, perhaps for days or weeks—it is not a reflection that they were simply women and their report could not stand as an "idle tale," which devalues their report. Instead, until Kayfa had a post-resurrection encounter, the exorcists who fled to Galilee and had denied Jesus were uncertain if they would be subject to Jesus' retribution. They had been vacated of all authority, and were hunted by spies of the elite on orders of Herod or Pilate. These exorcists believed that Jesus had been annihilated, that they had failed; they had publicly rejected and abandoned him. Any report of a post-crucifixion encounter (so Thomas, John 20:25) was *leros*, i.e., nonsense—that is until the encounter with Kayfa. Paul, like the other exorcists that had denied Jesus, al listed in 1 Cor 15:1–8, traced their charismatic authority to Kayfa's encounter as confirmation of inclusiveness as an *apostolos*. Consequently, until the encounter with Kayfa, primitive Christianity was

---

need for a stone to be rolled away to free a body and spirit—as noted, bodies and spirits could materialize even if entombed. Thus, this is a vision or trance-like experience.

26. Ogden, *Magic*, 159–60.

27. If on a road, the tradition may have been created as an echo to Paul's Damascus experience. Were this the case, the encounter was during the trance.

strictly associated with Mary Magdalene and other female *apostoloi*, thus explaining the primacy of Junia in Paul's greetings and ascription to her as an *apostlos* in Rom 16.

This allows a contextual reconstruction of *the Magdalene*, the fortress and leader of the women exorcists of Jesus; indeed, the woman who may have facilitated the first activity of Jesus, post-crucifixion, at the tomb. Mary had embraced the perilous risk of joining in Jesus' war on Satan. Magdalene, the fortress, was the leader of Jesus' female exorcists, undoubtedly trained and empowered by Jesus, and who facilitated the first post-crucifixion encounters and ecstatic experiences. In the earliest tradition, now lost to history, Magdalene was undoubtedly the leader of the remaining exorcists, until Kayfa had his own post-crucifixion encounter with Jesus. With the passing of time and male domination of leadership in the second and third centuries, traditions of Mary the Magdalene were either no longer needed or were problematic, and so were not retained in oral tradition, other than in the noncanonical gospels, including Thomas. But as Luke 8:1–3 shows, before this occurred, Magdalene's authority over demons was feared and respected, and her relationship with Jesus was revered as equal with that of Kayfa.[28]

Magdalene, therefore, encountered Jesus near the tomb in a trance and material or substantial manifestation, then set off for Galilee as instructed by Jesus. An application of risk analysis renders this event "certain." Kayfa and the other exorcists are in hiding in Galilee, protected by kin. Starving, they have returned to subsistence life and fishing, but at night to avoid detection, when demons seek victims and malevolent *phantasms* look for revenge. Kayfa, and the other exorcists, face the terror of aggressive confrontation.

Risk Response of Kayfa to a Lake Encounter

The original tradition in John 6:16–24 (also Mark 6:45–56; Matt 14:22–36) has Jesus walking across the Sea of Galilee at night. Jesus' exorcists enter a boat and row against heavy winds toward Capernaum, leaving Jesus off in the mountains. When they are about three or four miles out they see a figure. Jesus approaches the boat, but the exorcists assume it is a malevolent *phantasm* coming to assault them, i.e., exactly the fear of Galilean fishermen. When Jesus is recognized, he is helped into the boat. Suddenly they find themselves on the shore of Capernaum.[29]

28. *Gospel of Thomas*, 114.

29. This event is also found in Mark 6:45–56 and Matt 14:22–36. In Mark, Jesus is trying to pass by the disciples without notice about 3–6 a.m. as they fight the strong

Risk analysis has shown that this event was a post-crucifixion encounter with Kayfa, later transposed back into Jesus' Galilean ministry.[30] As a post-crucifixion encounter, the tradition was problematic. Jesus was at first identified as malevolent *phantasm*, e.g., a *biaeothanati*, able to curse, punish and harm, or seek his murderers (perhaps even those that had abandoned him).[31] By placing the event back into the itinerant mission of Jesus, concern that the resurrected Jesus was simply a *phantasm*, a common ghost, was eliminated, as was the devastating embarrassment to the community. Certainly these fishermen-turned-exorcists, including Kayfa and others that fled Jerusalem, knew the danger, but they had no choice in order to survive. While terrifying, they accepted it was likely they would encounter a *phantasm*, having heard multiple reports—in fact, this tradition presumes such events were feared and well known. Indeed, demons were presumed to haunt the waters of Galilee, having been cast or expelled there by exorcists (including Jesus),[32] where they found refuge.[33] The tradition is multiply-attested—recorded in the Synoptic and Johannine traditions, Mark (6:45–56), Matthew (14:22–26) and John (6:16–24). It is one of the few accounts found in the Synoptic gospels to also appear in the Johannine tradition. The editor/author of Luke drops this tradition altogether due its controversial nature, i.e., to ensure that his appearances post-crucifixion were not confused with apparitions, demons or spirits of the dead in the Hellenistic/Roman world.[34]

Given the perilous risks involved with night fishing, the only possible setting is Galilee, post-crucifixion and an encounter with Jesus, either on the lake at night, or in a dream/vision or, most likely a trance of Kayfa,[35] who was engaged in that perilous endeavor daily while in hiding. Rising winds signaled demonic attack and risk of death, whether on the lake or in a vision. A Galilean fisherman-turned-exorcist would have been terrified, clearly expecting a *phantasm* or demonic appearance, with winds and an

---

winds, but the exorcists see Jesus and think he is a *phantasm*. He joins them in the boat and the wind ceases. In Matthew, Jesus sees them in trouble and comes directly to assist. Again, they believe they also see a ghost. Kayfa tries to join Jesus on the water but begins to sink, only to be taken by Jesus' hand and rescued. The winds cease.

30. See the discussion by Patterson, *Beyond the Passion*, 113–14; Madden, "Jesus Walking on the Sea," 79–86.

31. Ogden, *Magic*, 152–53.

32. Mark 5:1–17.

33. More discussion will be provided in sections on the waters of Galilee being the home of demons below.

34. Patterson believes this was a resurrection event, but was pushed back into the ministry of Jesus because of the controversial nature of Jesus appearing as a *phantasm*.

35. Similar to his trance, Acts 10:9–16.

attack capable of driving a boat underneath the waters, where victim(s) and their souls would be overcome.

That Kayfa is prominently mentioned in each version of the tradition, and Jesus' appears as a floating or water-walking phantasm that consistently interacts with Kayfa, suggests this is a post-crucifixion encounter with Kayfa. The intense risk setting underscores both the desperate plight of the exorcists, including Kayfa, and the terrifying fear he had for retribution, having abandoned and denied Jesus and fled to Galilee. The early community would never have manufactured such traditions due to the controversies such a rejection ultimately fostered for generations and in oral lore before bringing them into the written gospels.[36]

In sum, based on the risk and analytical criteria employed, combined with contextual analysis, this tradition is rendered "certain." It reports the first encounter between Jesus and Kayfa, but in a dream/vision or in a trance, set on the lake in Galilee, where Kayfa is reinstated by Jesus, being set safely on the shore of Capernaum. Kayfa finds the other exorcists also in hiding and reports the event. Specifically, it is this tradition that is reported by Kayfa to other exorcists in hiding, followed by the report that spread among other exorcists: "It is true! The Lord has risen and has appeared to Kayfa" (Luke 24:34). They will not receive retribution and attack, but acceptance.

While Kayfa has been reinstated and is appointed the first witness of the Galilean exorcists that denied and rejected Jesus, they must reengage in the war on Satan, thereby embracing perilous risk. As such, in the context of human risk experience, this encounter with Jesus is an authentic in a post-crucifixion context and setting, and occurred within days of Magdalene's encounter, but before she located Kayfa and the other exorcists.

Magdalene Arrives in Galilee— Risk Reaction of Kayfa and the Galilean Exorcists

In the foregoing risk analysis of Matt 28:1–10, the *Gospel of Mary* (*GM*) was found to include perilous risk and contextual elements supporting the historicity of Magdalene's post-resurrection encounter with Jesus. Magdalene found the exorcists hiding in Emmaus of Galilee (see the analysis below of Luke 24:13–35). Magdalene's arrival and report is met with skepticism and

36. Another aspect of this tradition is the sudden appearance of the boat at the shore when Jesus enters the boat, where this immediate transportation suggests a trance-like experience, and not a physical encounter of any kind. This aspect of the tradition underscores its problematic nature as a resurrection appearance to the early church, but the retention of this aspect of the tradition can only be understood as strengthening the claim that this event was as a post-crucifixion encounter with Jesus.

vehement doubt; even by Kayfa, who is still coming to terms with the meaning of his encounter on the lake and his reinstatement. Indeed, *GM* includes several startling events: Magdalene's confrontation with Kayfa and other exorcists as to the legitimacy of her interaction with Jesus post-crucifixion; Kayfa's jealously and temper, and Levi's defense of Magdalene as not only equal to the male exorcists, but her becoming male: "But rather, let us praise His greatness, for He has prepared us and made us into *Men*" (*GM* 5:3).

Her presence with Kayfa and the others at meal indicates that Magdalene was considered equal in authority to Kayfa. More, Magdalene reported to the disheartened exorcists that (1) Jesus was active, not annihilated, (2) that she had a vision at the tomb, and (3) then encountered Jesus, not as a ghost, but in a substantive form.[37] It is then that Magdalene convinces the Galileans to consider abandoning subsistence fishing and return to itinerant ministry. She is cited as the authoritative source of Jesus' words and the only exorcist who is fully accepted by Jesus post-crucifixion. Kayfa's role is diminished significantly, and Magdalene's is elevated to leader.

The results of risk and contextual analysis must count Magdalene as one of the Galilean exorcists whose perilous risk was heightened following her encounter with Jesus.[38] While there is no confirmation that Magdalene continued exorcising demons in the Synoptic tradition or in John, extra canonical traditions confirm that Magdalene was an active and influential member among the remaining exorcists in Galilee and provided instruction to them about her vision of Jesus and her continuing relationship with him. The tradition of that best captures Magdalene's standing and influence is the *Gospel of Mary*. Despite *GM* being a fragmented document, the extant copy of which is second to fifth century,[39] risk analysis confirms that its traditions predate the canonical gospels.

It is this encounter that most likely results in the reinstatement of the ecstatic meal and hope of an event with Jesus at this meal. *GM* confirms that Magdalene's arrival and interaction with her fellow exorcists is rendered "probable." Kayfa returns to the Galilean mountain to seek an encounter with Jesus and further instructions. It was on this mountain that they has been empowered and trained as exorcists by Jesus.

---

37. As noted, encounters with the active spirits of the dead included substantive, even material activity and contact.

38. *GM* 5:2–7.

39. King argues for composition between 30–130 CE (*Gospel of Mary*, 148).

Kayfa's Mountain Encounter and Risk Response

Mark 9:2–8 originally presents an ecstatic experience of three exorcists, Simeon (i.e., Kayfa), Yecob and Yohannes (Boanerges) on a Galilean mountain, known as *the transfiguration*, but is better described, as it is in the Greek, as the *metamorphosis* of Jesus before Kayfa,[40] where Jesus is transformed into his heavenly state. Risk analysis in this study has confirmed this was a post-crucifixion event and encounter with Jesus, reinserted into the itinerant war period of Jesus' activity. Evidence is abundant: The literary unit begins, "After six days," and is set in Galilee, which is consistent with the aforementioned risk context with the exorcists fleeing Jerusalem.[41] The nature of this ecstatic experience in Galilee is markedly different than other post-crucifixion encounters said to have occurred in Jerusalem. As it is an ecstatic trance, its placement as a resurrection event was problematic in the oral tradition and to the Marcan community. In its original setting, it likely follows the arrival of Magdalene and her report, and Kayfa's lake encounter. He goes to the mountain in Galilee to confront the perilous risks now present.

This setting and placement can be confirmed. The Marcan unit begins, "after six days," and is set on the sacred mountain in Galilee. The count of days stands out,[42] as "six days" is the most specific description of passing time found in the Gospel of Mark aside from the predictions of the passion, a perilous risk event. The designation of days demands a relationship with a perilous risk event, namely the crucifixion, consistent with the Marcan editor's use of days elsewhere, which reference that event.[43] Consequently, Mark 9:2–8 is a post-crucifixion encounter with Jesus that has been reset back into the days of Jesus' itinerant mission.[44] The location is consistent with the aforementioned risk context of the exorcists fleeing Jerusalem for the safety of Galilee. According to Matthew and Mark,[45] the mountain in

---

40. This does not preclude that Kayfa, after his trance about the lake encounter, took others with him to the sacred mountain in Galilee.

41. Mark 16:7.

42. Lunn, *Original Ending*, 359; Lunn also mentions the six days that Moses was on the mountain before the voice of God called him from the cloud. While this may be an important parallel, the location and temporal reference when combined are more significant. Six days would allow the exorcists to return to Galilee after the crucifixion and be hidden by kin among night fishermen.

43. Not a reference back to a theological point. Perrin, "Towards an Interpretation of the Gospel of Mark," 8–9, 27–28.

44. Stein, "Is the Transfiguration," 79–96.

45. Matt 28:7; Mark 16:7.

Galilee was familiar to the exorcists[46] and to Jesus,[47] and so must have been a specific location where he sought ecstatic prayer,[48] solitude and encounters with the divine. Jesus' history with ecstatic mountain experiences began with his confrontation with Satan (Matt 4:8). It ends with his metamorphosis in Galilee at the "appointed" mountain.

This event is most certainly a spiritual journey via an ecstatic trance, where Jesus reveals his true heavenly self—his glory.[49] While there is some evidence this was a shared séance or spiritual journey among the three exorcists, guided by an encounter with Jesus and then interrupted by Kayfa's question leading to the end of the trance, this is uncertain.[50] Shamans are able to produce group visions, but usually through rhythmic music and dancing, however, there is no evidence this is a shamanic experience.[51] What is certain is that Kayfa was present and that Kayfa would seek another encounter to confirm Jesus was not simply a phantasm.

The nature of this ecstatic experience to Kayfa in Galilee stands out from other post-crucifixion encounters reported in other canonical gospels. As it clearly an *ecstatic trance*, its placement as a resurrection event was considered troubling.[52] Consistent with a trance, Kayfa suddenly awakes and finds he is alone with Jesus, i.e., he "looked around" (v. 8) and saw no one else.[53] The trance abruptly ends. With the experience being ethereal and otherworldly, reliant on itinerant Jewish exorcists—men who were reputed by their opponents to follow a divinely cursed, dark magician possessed by Beelzebul—a new setting was required. Kayfa's experience is to witness to Jesus' metamorphosis personally while in the third heaven. Like Paul then, God revealed his son to Kayfa—remarkably similar experiences. Jesus is now seen as enthroned with God in the third heaven. This encounter then extends Mary's, where Jesus was clearly active and available but "not yet ascended," to his acceptance to the place with God. This difference set Kayfa's encounter as significant and different from Mary's, and ultimately

46. Mark 3:13–19.
47. Matt 8:1, 14:23; Luke 5:16, 6:12; also see Mark 1:35.
48. Mark 6:46.
49. Smith, *Magician*, 120–22.
50. Ibid., 122.
51. Lewis, *Ecstatic Religion*, 53.

52. The disappearance of Apollonius of Tyana from a temple led to presumptions he was taken to paradise. The subsequent appearance of Apollonius in a dream to a follower, attempting to convince him of eternal life, is a good example of the contemporary appearance of the dead in a dream.

53. The experience is characterized as puzzling and ethereal, and so is less tangible than seeing Jesus with the marks of crucifixion evident on his body.

took precedence over Mary's in the primitive Christian tradition, and as reflected by Paul in 1 Cor 15:1–5.

The recovered core risk tradition of this encounter is as follows: There are two possibilities that fit the risk context of this event. First, late at night, or in heavy sleep,[54] there is a second ecstatic transportation of Kayfa by trance or vision,[55] this time to the sacred mountain in Galilee, a place familiar to Kayfa and the exorcists,[56] and then to paradise itself (e.g., similar to 2 Cor 12). A second, and more likely, risk setting has Kayfa on the sacred mountain seeking confirmation of Jesus' glory, having gone there (at great risk) shortly after the lake trance, where he was reinstated by Jesus. Kayfa enters the trance.[57] The metamorphosis of Jesus is witnessed revealing Jesus now in a glorified state (the change in appearance, dazzling clothing, and shining face);[58] angelic figures appear (to confirm presence in paradise), ensuring that Jesus is active and blessed; Kayfa is terrified (*ekphoboi*) and inappropriately speaks, bringing the vision to a close; there is covering by a sacred cloud (the sign of divine presence). Kayfa now has confirmation that Jesus resides in the third heaven with God and the angels, even with Moses and Elijah (added to the event later). There is a pronouncement: God speaks and identifies Jesus as "my son." Kayfa awakens alone on the mountaintop and reports the event to others. Based on risk and contextual analysis, this recovered form of the risk event is rendered certain.

Kayfa now knows that he, along with the other exorcists who will join him, must embrace heightened perilous risk and reengage Satan in an aggressive war to continue Jesus' mission to inaugurate the kingdom of God. They are led and empowered by the glorified Son who was revealed to Kayfa; they are to "listen to him." Kayfa awaits another encounter and specific instructions on how this charismatic engagement is to be executed. This will also determine who is to be included in that war.

Kayfa reports to the other exorcists his encounter. Soon thereafter, the exorcist Cleopas arrives in Emmaus in Galilee (see analysis below), and

---

54. Luke 9:32.

55. Pilcher, "Transfiguration of Jesus," 57–60; Scharlemann, "Transfiguration," 886–88.

56. Shillington, *Jesus and Paul Before Christianity*, 42. As noted, the mountain in Galilee (likely modern day Mt. Tabor) was sacred to Jesus; it is where he escaped to have ecstatic encounters and pray (Mark 6:46), sometimes for days; where he selected and trained his exorcists (Mark 3:13–19; Busse, *To Be Near the Fire*, 76), and contested with Satan (not necessarily a mountain in the Judean desert).

57. Just as he did in Acts 10:10 while praying, i.e., deep spiritual breathing and meditation.

58. Luke 9:29, while praying, Jesus' face begins to change. This tradition portrays the metamorphosis more accurately.

during and ecstatic meal, one like that instituted by Jesus before his death, has an encounter that is reported to the other exorcists who arrive.

The Risk Response of Cleopas—Encounters Multiply in Galilee

The event in Luke 24:13–35 is peculiar to Luke alone, other than a reference to a similar tradition from the oral tradition condensed in Mark 16:12 (see below). Here, two followers of Jesus, one named Cleopas, are heading to a village called Emmaus when they meet a stranger, a "lonely sojourner from Jerusalem," on the road. He joins them and reveals the secret meaning of events that occurred the same day in Jerusalem concerning Jesus of Nazareth (primarily the meaning of crucifixion and the empty tomb). They ultimately recognize the stranger as Jesus when at an evening meal he blesses and breaks bread; upon recognition, he vanishes or disappears (*aphantos*) out of their sight.

There is evidence that an earlier tradition stands behind the Emmaus encounter, as there is a close parallel in Graeco-Roman literature.[59] Most interesting, and as established by risk analysis, Josephus identifies an Emmaus, "Ammathus," as a village *on the shore of Galilee*,[60] the very area of Jesus' ecstatic activity (i.e., where he freed villages and their synagogues from demonic possession)[61] and where his exorcists escaped immediately after the crucifixion (only 16 km, or 10 miles from Capernaum).

The location on the western shore of Galilee and proximity to other followers of Jesus would explain why Kayfa's encounters were quickly shared with other exorcists.[62] Emmaus was a village where Jesus' followers may have both *lived and practiced* and was considered safe from satanic attack *and* demonic imperialism. Josephus mentions the powers of the warm waters of Emmaus. As noted, springs and waters in Galilee were considered possessed by spirits and demons, i.e., that the waters were under their control and even cursed. Waters in Emmaus were more than just warm springs that aided in health, they were considered powerful, able to pull out and absorb demons and spirits by the work of angels.[63] Exorcists and ecstatics such as Jesus would have frequented these sites, employing charismatic authority to

---

59. Plutarch describes how Romulus met with a friend on a road after his death, then vanished after revealing he was now the god Quirinus: *Parallel Lives of Plutarch*, vol. 1, 28:1–4.

60. Josephus, 18.36.3, near Tiberias with warm baths.

61. Busse, *To Be Near the Fire*, 79–80.

62. The first encounter while subsistence fishing at night (being hidden by kin), and then his visit to the sacred mountain to communicate with Jesus.

63. A similar tradition is reflected in John 5:4.

call on these same angels to assist in freeing the possessed and trapping their demons in the waters. Extensive evidence was presented that confirms Jesus expelled demons into various waters in Palestine.

Consequently, the "healing waters" of Emmaus that absorbed demons would certainly have been a location where Jesus and his follow exorcists would have been active, and a village he would have liberated. As such, Galilean Emmaus would have been a village to which his followers would have fled post-crucifixion, and been in hiding, having vacated both Jerusalem and Capernaum for fear of spies and capture.

In this context, the name Cleopas, meaning "glory of the father," must have been an exorcist name given by Jesus, i.e., such as *Kayfa, Boanerges, Toma*, and *Magdalene*—each given to the exorcist he trained and accepted into his circle. Indeed, this would explain why this name continued to be attached to the tradition, i.e., if this were one of Jesus' recognized exorcists in the primitive community. This form of the recovered tradition of the Emmaus appearance is thus set within a context of perilous risk.

With regard to the risk context of the encounter in Emmaus, the event leading to the recognition of Jesus by the exorcist Cleopas is the blessing (*eulogesen*) and breaking (*klasas*) of bread by the traveler (*paroikeis*) at the evening common meal. It was an *eschatological meal* celebrating the presence, but still future arrival of the kingdom. It was, therefore, an ecstatic experience of the kingdom emerging around them, in "their midst," and in which they participate as a community.

This ecstatic prayer that began the evening meal followed a solemn, liturgical pattern,[64] similar to contemporary Jewish prayers,[65] but more urgent, as taught by Jesus. The petition cries out from the context of perilous risk.[66] Paul confirms that Jesus spoke it at the common meal.[67] It was uttered, perhaps even sung,[68] over the meal, while holding the bread to imbue it with divine power, not to just give sustenance, but to act as the communal nourishment against Satan's forces that night and for the next day's battle. It was said by either the leading (i.e., most powerful) exorcist (such as Cleopas, the Magdalene or Kayfa) or by all present in unison.[69] The prayer was to affirm and plea for their protection from Satan, as well as request for

---

64. Jeremias, *Lord's Prayer*, 15.

65. Such as the *Qaddish* and *Shema*; Jeremias, *Prayers*, 77–78; but transformed into a charismatic, urgent plea and invocation for protection and power in the face of perilous risk and danger.

66. Jeremias, *Lord's Prayer*, 22.

67. 1 Cor 11.

68. Chase, "Lord's Prayer," 147–51.

69. Luke 11:1–13; see also the *Didache*, 9:2–4.

continued success in bringing the kingdom's presence and inbreaking into the land. But more, it was a call to be possessed and protected by the Spirit given to Jesus by *Abba*.[70] The final petition recovered in our analysis of the ecstatic prayer was abrupt, pressing, and an affirmation of their source of protection from the "evil one," Satan.[71]

In Emmaus, Jesus, post-crucifixion, materializes, or is recognized by the traveler during the meal, i.e., when the bread is broken and the call on protection and plea for the kingdom's full arrival and victory is made. He is seen, or better recognized, and is present with Cleopas. As such, the Emmaus event confirmed that Jesus was not only active, but was present and still part of the inbreaking kingdom, but now as its risen Lord of the exorcists. The Emmaus event was retained in the oral tradition for this very reason, i.e., because it was the watershed event that redefined the meaning of the original ecstatic meal, linking it with Jesus' death and the post-crucifixion experience with him as active master over the exorcists and children of God. He was available,[72] his name carried power,[73] and he continued to direct the war on Satan—the kingdom was still inbreaking led by Jesus, the Spirit and Abba.[74] Ultimately, the story of the passion was linked to the meal, becoming the community sacrament of union with the risen Lord, the Eucharist, as found in Paul's letter to the Corinthians. But all this began with the Emmaus event.

Heightened Perilous Risk: The Signs of Legitimate Charismatics and Kayfa's Encounter

Embedded in this Marcan unit are very striking post-crucifixion instructions of Jesus addressed to exorcists and charismatics that create significant, heightened perilous risk. Those that reengage in the war on Satan that are legitimate exorcists will evidence specific "signs." Overall, these instructions of the post-crucifixion Jesus raise important qualitative risk issues, as the instructions not only echo but demand the continuation of the same charismatic activities that brought Jesus into deadly confrontation with his opponents, thereby creating continued perilous risk for Jesus' followers. The encounter is either with Kayfa, his third (reaffirming his leadership), or Magdalene (in concert with

---

70. Jeremias, *Lord's Prayer*, 20–21; Paul, as noted, confirms: "When we cry out '*Abba*' it is the Spirit bearing witness," Rom 8:16, also Gal. 4:6, meaning the Spirit has entered the believer.

71. Jeremias, *Prayers*, 106.

72. Matt 18:20.

73. 1 Cor 5:4.

74. Gal 4:6.

her encouragement of reengaging in the war on Satan). This event is either in a vision, trance or substantial encounter. It is also possible that the event included other exorcists, even "the eleven," which must have included Magdalene and Cleopas based on our foregoing risk analysis of those present in Galilee. According to Mark 16:17–18, Jesus commands the following:

> *In my name* to cast out demons, they will speak in new tongues [or in heavenly language, *glossais*, in ecstasy], the will pick up serpents [*opheis*], and if they drink any deadly thing, it will not harm them; they will lay their hands on the sick and they will recover.[75]

The expectation of "speaking in new tongues (*glossais*)" has been often cited as the principal evidence that this section is a conflation of later practices.[76] Jesus is never explicitly tied to speaking in tongues in the synoptic or Johannine traditions, however, the multiple interactions with demons, identifying and silencing them, his groaning in spirit and prayer,[77] must be assumed to have included understanding and speaking in angelic and demonic language.[78] Indeed, when Jesus' exorcists fail to expel the demon of a young boy, they ask why, to which Jesus replies that only prayer (implying special type of prayer) and fasting could succeed.[79] That this expectation immediately follows the command to exorcise is additional evidence that this charismatic power is associated with communication with demons, spirits and the reception of heavenly instruction as well, as well as commands to exorcise demons. Curses and the ability to mute opponents were often written in secret language, or on hidden tablets.[80] Jesus and his exorcists were able to release victims from such demonic curses,[81] understanding and affecting exorcisms

---

75. Mark 16:17–18.

76. See Hull, *Mark*, 673–74.

77. John 11:33, or Mark 7:34, and the use of specific words that are interpreted by the gospel editors, but whose original use may have parallels with un-intelligible words (Morton), such as his words in Mark 5:41, "talitha, koum."

78. For further discussion on the use of special language in Jesus' exorcisms, see Smith, *Magic*, 95. "Talitha, koum" was also circulated without translation as a magical formula.

79. Smith believes this was "secret" prayer, but the implication are for prayers that may be said ecstatically and under the influence of the Spirit, and so, in heavenly language. That fasting is associated with this prayer implies that a special state of ecstatic experience and language is possible. See Smith, *Magic*, 95.

80. Ogden, *Magic*, 211, "A legal, tongue-binding, lead curse tablet from Selinus"; also see 215.

81. See discussion above on the deaf and mute man of Bethsaida, whom Jesus commands not to reenter his village, as he likely had been cursed by someone there, i.e.,

that neutralized them. Consequently, this practice is contextually coherent with the others in Mark 16:17–18, and is to be associated with the continued itinerant activity of the exorcists as they encounter and communicate with demons, neutralize curses and evil spirits that they must control and expel.

Jesus also commands charismatics/exorcists to raise up (*arousan*) serpents (*opheis*). In the ancient world, particularly in Judaism, snakes were often the personification of Satan, evil, and capable of possession or engendering dangerous, and sometimes fatal deception.[82] Consequently, this is a charismatic directive of Jesus and appears to imply that the exorcists held animistic powers over snakes as creatures of Satan, i.e., they could take control, just as they controlled demons, and render them harmless, or even destroy them.[83] If to destroy them, this raises interesting and contemporary parallels where serpents are killed by "blasting." Blasting was a well-recognized charismatic power, albeit considered sometimes a dark power (conducted by incantation, or often by those who practiced manipulation of the dead, i.e., necromancy). In the Hellenistic world, this authority was associated with powerful sorcerers or magicians, often foreigners, such as Chaldeans, Babylonians, Assyrians or Egyptians.[84] The charismatic, using animistic powers, would communicate with the snake(s), collect or call them together by command, then destroy them, in many cases by breathing on them with fire—i.e., blasting[85]—or would trap them in tombs. Jesus gave his charismatics a similar authority to destroy creatures that were thought to be controlled by Satan, or by his demons, particularly snakes and scorpions in Luke 10:19: "I have given you authority to trample (*pantein*) on snakes and scorpions and to overcome all the power of the enemy; nothing will harm you." This power is the equivalent of crushing serpents and scorpions, and so, the original intent of this saying was to "take away" or blast the serpent, and hold it up showing it destroyed, exorcised.[86] Satan would then be shown powerless, as even the creatures of evil that attacked could be an-

---

a person who would repeat the process.

82. See Rev 12:9 and Gen 3:14; also see Paul, 2 Cor 11:3 for a comparison of Eve and the serpent and the deception of the Corinthian believers. Jesus equates the Jerusalem religious elite with vipers and serpents in Matt 23:33, again because these creatures were controlled and possessed by Satan and demons and used to hamper or kill enemies.

83. Jesus was known to have animistic powers; the directives on catch of fishes, the coin in the fish's mouth and others previously described, see Mark 1:16–20; Matt 4:18–22; Luke 5:2–11; John 21:6; Matt 17:27.

84. See Ogden, "Chaldeans and Syrians," in *Magic*, 49–50.

85. Ibid., 50.

86. Ogden, referencing Lucian in *Pharsalia* (6.413–587), *Philopseudes* (11–3) and Ovid, *Amores* (2.1.23–8), in *Magic*, 49–50, 121–24, 238.

nihilated when encountered by Jesus' command and authority. Ultimately, the use of Jesus' name alone was able to neutralize serpents, including their venom, among Jews.[87]

The next command, drinking poison unharmed, is without parallel in the New Testament, with only a single reference found in Eusebius.[88] The reference to "poisons" again should not be thought of as toxic chemicals that immediately kill, but instead, are the result of witchcraft and evil potions and concoctions intended to harm the recipient in multiple ways, even driving one insane.[89] Poisons were slipped into water, wine or other drinks, or added to foods, and depending on their intent, could be deadly to soul or body, or were sometimes even intended to engender love or eroticism.[90] Such poisons were also combined with spells and curse tablets often hidden in the walls or floors of homes by enemies, which caused illness to accelerate, or bring on death. Poisons had wide application and were placed in contact with the victim for malevolent intent, many times secretly. For the Galilean charismatics, opponents would seize every opportunity, including the use of magic and witchcraft (even hiring famous witches if needed), to kill them, a common practice in the Roman world.[91] Consequently, this charismatic expectation comes with reassurance and protection from magic, curses and dark spells, and so, Jesus' exorcists are to not fear any poison, as they will remain unharmed if ingested. This risk context of this saying is clearly to be set in the post-crucifixion itinerant ministry of the exorcists and the mission to drive Satan from the land.

In this final expectation, Jesus commits his exorcists to the *laying on of hands* (*keiris epithesousin*), as required to drive out demons of illness,[92] i.e., another very specific form of exorcism, since illness was associated with demonic possession or evil, whether undeserved, or more commonly, resulting from a curse or contamination arising from evil actions or wrongs against

---

87. This was said by Jews about 120 CE, see Hull, *Hellenistic Magic*, 71.

88. Eusebius, *Ecclesiastical History*, 3:39.9.

89. Ogden, *Magic*, 115: "Canidia and Sagana perform necromancy and erotic magic," as reported about 30 BCE, Horace, *Satirea* 1.8; "so much as the women who try to twist about human minds with spells and poisons (*venena*)."

90. Ibid., 117–18, a love potion considered a type of "poison."

91. So with Germanicus. To counter the poisons and spells, Germanicus' wife hired a woman "renowned for poisoning/witchcraft (*veneficia*) in that province (Syria)" to counter the poisons, curses and spells found.

92. Mark 6:5, 7:32, Luke 4:40. It is important to note that Jesus charismatic activity in Nazareth, the Galilean town where he was raised, was limited to laying on of hands to drive out illness, i.e., direct contact to convey power to drive out demons. As such, Jesus' practice use of touch, or the laying on of hands, to drive out demons of illness was passed to his exorcists, and so references to this practice have the highest claim to authenticity.

RISK ANALYSIS AND THE RECOVERY OF RELIABLE EVENTS 247

a deity (e.g., the presumption of "sins," willful acts of defiance, committed by the victim or members of the victim's family).[93] Jesus used this practice of exorcism only after all other methods had failed in Nazareth.[94] Touching with hands was not just a soothing element, but a powerful charismatic act to drive off evil that required special technique and knowledge.[95] There are multiple examples to be found in ancient sources, both Hellenistic and Jewish.[96] Jesus affected several cures with the use of his hands, either in terms of touching the affected victim or in creating substances for application to the areas infected with evil. For example, in Mark 7:32–35, Jesus is asked to lay on his hands to a man possessed with a demon causing deafness and confused language. Jesus takes the man aside, privately, because the exorcism may not succeed. We are then provided one of the most thorough descriptions of a charismatic exorcism in ancient literature. Jesus first places his fingers in the man's ears. He then uses spittle, a substance previously described as a powerful healing substance of magicians and charismatics. Jesus spits on his fingers and touches the man's tongue. Then he goes into a trance, blows out his mouth in a "deep sigh," likely to release power and blast the demon, followed by pronouncement of command, "*ephphatha*," or "be opened." The man is freed. This remarkable account of "laying on of hands" provides descriptive evidence that specific practices taught by Jesus to the exorcists stood behind this command, most of which are now lost. There must have been multiple techniques employed by Jesus, evidenced by Luke 4:40. John 9:6 mentions Jesus making an application of mud and saliva. Another example is Mark 8:22–26. Here Jesus is specifically asked to lay his hands on a blind man who appears to have been cursed and attacked by a demon. Taking him out of the village of Bethsaida, perhaps to avoid those affecting the curse on the man, Jesus spits on his eyes. The cure is incomplete. Jesus then rubs his eyes with his hands and the man is able to see. He then orders the man to go to his home and avoid the village, indicating that Jesus was concerned that the cure would either be temporary, or that there was a risk of return of the demon if the man was cursed again by his

---

93. See John 9:3.

94. Mark 6:5, dealing with only a few and likely in private.

95. Also to pass along charismatic power and authority: See Acts 9:17, also Acts 8:17–18, the baptized received the gift of the Holy Spirit, the dominant of all Spirits and so the most powerful available to charismatics and others who take on the risk of following the crucified man, the accused "evildoer" of Galilee. Other references include Heb 6:2.

96. E.g., Apollonius who is said to have learned this from the priests of Asclepius in Aegae; Eshel, "Jesus the Exorcist," 183–85.

attacker in the village, i.e., the attack would be repeated. Jesus would have trained his exorcists with these methods.[97]

The "laying on of hands" was common to Jesus' practice of exorcism-healings, driving out demons and releasing the afflicted from curse or possession. As such, this final command to the exorcists, i.e., the expectation of laying on of hands and the special techniques employed, is coherent with the forgoing list of charismatic practices to be embraced by Jesus' exorcists.

In sum, these instructions, embedded within the Marcan appendix, are very early, and must come from a period in time when those who were Jesus' most intimate followers—the exorcists of Galilee—decided to continue the perilous mission of Jesus based on this encounter. Kayfa had encountered Jesus on the lake and was reinstated. He then sought Jesus on the sacred mountain, entering an ecstatic trance where he was transported to the third heaven. The event confirmed Jesus' glorious state and authority. Kayfa was told to listen to Jesus. In each of these events, the perilous risk of Kayfa, Magdalene, and now all legitimate exorcists of the risen Lord were significantly heightened. Kayfa, Magdalene and perhaps other exorcists, received specific instructions from the risen Lord as to the charismatic practices to be employed in reengaging in the war on Satan. These practices become the "sign" and evidence of a legitimate exorcist of Jesus. When set in this context, the instructions to exorcists provided in Mark 16:17–18 must be rendered "probable," matching the risk context of a post-resurrection encounter.

Confirmation of Perilous Risk
(Gospels of Peter, Nicodemus, Various Fragments)

The *Gospel of Peter* (*EvP*) has no resurrection encounter. As such, it cannot be evaluated using standard risk tests of this study. However, *EvP* does contain several perilous risk elements that merit careful analysis, and some are quite striking.

1. There were no post-crucifixion encounters with Jesus in Jerusalem.
2. Mary approaches the tomb in terror of being discovered and captured.
3. The exorcists go into hiding then disband, fleeing Jerusalem for the safety of Galilee.

---

97. As implied by Luke 10:9, i.e., Jesus' sending of the exorcists into the towns and villages to drive Satan and demonic pollution out. They are to "heal" the sick, or employ the laying on of hands and the techniques taught by Jesus to drive demons out and away. They also were effective by employing Jesus' name in exorcising demons.

RISK ANALYSIS AND THE RECOVERY OF RELIABLE EVENTS 249

4. They unquestionably believe that Jesus has been annihilated, body and soul, expecting nothing, and know of no death and resurrection predictions.

5. They do not know or care about the disposition of Jesus' body—they are in fear for their lives—and likely assume it had been thrown into the refuse dump of the city for the animals to consume—the common practice for executed criminals.

6. Jesus' body is guarded by special elders (not only a centurion and his soldiers), indicating that his body was entombed to protect themselves from retribution ("to do us evil," v. 8), or would be used by his followers, who were thought to be "evildoers" and dark magicians.

7. There is no command to remain in Jerusalem, or to wait for the Holy Spirit, or and instance of the conveyance of the Holy Spirit.

8. The elders are understood to be complicit with Pilate, tacitly Roman sympathizers, and a group that Pilate disdained.

9. The exorcists, led by Kayfa, return to subsistence fishing.

While *EvP* has no recommitment of the exorcists to the itinerant war on Satan resulting from an encounter with Jesus, and thus, no evidence of heightened perilous risks, several of its elements, particularly 2, 3, 4, 5, 6, and 9, betray a level human fear and risk avoidance that would be expected devastating historical circumstances. More, these *EvP* risk elements are clearly undeveloped, particularly when compared with the Synoptic and Johannine passion and post-crucifixion traditions. As such, they represent both an early and independent tradition that "rings true" from a perilous risk perspective; indeed, they reflect exactly what a devastated group of exorcists whose leader has been murdered by the very evil forces he opposed would do—flee! Consequently, these perilous risk elements within *EvP* evidence the human impact and disaster resulting from Jesus' brutal death. The resulting perilous risk elements support both "certain" and "probable" risk findings.

Similar elements of risk confirmation can be found in the *Gospel of Nicodemus* (Jesus as a dark magician), John 20:11–18 (Magdalene's encounter at the tomb) and Matt 28:16–20 (the great commission) in our earlier study. These elements go to confirm other risk findings of the "certain" and "probable" events. No further analysis of these elements is provided given they are contributory or risk findings described.

The Confirming Event—Encounter with "the Twelve"

As noted, Jesus suddenly appears in a locked room to the remaining exorcists hiding in Jerusalem, standing in their midst (he materializes among them). Jesus speaks: *erine humin*, "peace to you,"[98] in Hebrew, *Shalom*, although more than a greeting here—a conveyance of charismatic power to receive comfort. Those present are terrified (*tpoenthentes de kai emphoboi*) and think they see a *pnuema*,[99] a ghost, but Jesus shows his wounds and invites them to handle him (*pselaphesate*) to see he has "flesh and bones (*sarka kai ostea*)." There is no indication that they do. They disbelieve "for joy." Jesus eats in front of them. The disciples are instructed to "remain in Jerusalem" until they receive power "from on high."

Risk analysis has shown that the context of the Jerusalem encounter is a complex mix of post-crucifixion elements that reflect earlier traditions, as well as later Christian developments previously analyzed. However, this expansion suggests that the original event in its contemporary setting *was* a *phantasm* experience, perhaps with some form of a substantial body attached to it.[100] It was this form of the tradition that was problematic and embarrassing to the community of Matthew's gospel (80 to 90 CE) due to contemporary competing theologies, such as emergent Docetism. As such, the original encounter must have been similar to other mass events with Jesus, such as those cited by Paul (54 CE) as matters of fact. Paul is the earliest witness to report group appearances similar to this; i.e., to the "the twelve," as well as with "all the apostles," and to "over five-hundred brethren" (1 Cor 15:5–8), many of whom he states were alive and available to attest to the encounter. Paul does not state that these were events with a material body present.

Consequently, the materiality of the body of Jesus was not a pressing problem in primitive Christianity contemporary with Paul's authentic writings.[101] Nonetheless, that the original form of the tradition was embarrassing to the Matthew's community and was expanded only goes to underscore its reliability—there was a post-crucifixion encounter with the some of Jesus' original exorcists, and not in Jerusalem, but in Galilee. The original form of the tradition, based on contextual and risk analysis would be as follows:

---

98. A greeting used by Jesus in post–crucifixion appearances in John 20:19–21; 14:27; Paul, Rom 15:33; 1 Cor 1:3; 2 Cor 2:1.

99. Other ancient manuscript witnesses (e.g., D) use *phantasm*, which may be the more original wording; Plummer, *Luke*, 559.

100. As noted, a form that has contemporary examples in Hellenistic literature.

101. The resurrected body was a *soma pneuma*, a spiritual body, not one of flesh and blood; 1 Cor 15:44.

> Indeed, Jesus appeared standing among them [at the place they hid during the day]. They were terrified, thinking they saw a *phantasm* [retributive or malevolent spirit of the dead], but he spoke to them, "receive peace." "See, it is I, look at my hands and feet!" Do not doubt!

Thus, embedded within the tradition, which relates Jesus' post-crucifixion encounter with his exorcists (an event similar to that reported by Paul in 1 Cor 15:5) is a more primitive oral traditional formula, similar to the one described by Paul. Our contextual analysis must also take into account that all strata of tradition confirm that Jesus' exorcists returned to itinerant activity and the battle with demonic forces in preparation for the arrival of the kingdom of God after. It was this additional encounter, not just those of Kayfa, Magdalene and Cleopas, which resulted in acceptance of increased perilous risk, including the risks of possession, betrayal, capture and death by the larger group of exorcists, formed again by Kayfa to constitute the "twelve."

Based on risk and contextual analysis, the tradition of an encounter between Jesus and several exorcists embedded in Luke 24:36–39 may be considered a reliable post-crucifixion encounter with Jesus, likely at a group vision of a materialized Jesus post-crucifixion, similar to those reported in the Hellenistic/Roman world. As such, in the context of human risk experience, this encounter with Jesus is reliable in its contemporary post-crucifixion context and setting. The early tradition in Paul (1 Cor 15) that Jesus appeared to "the twelve" is testimony to this event, and, as Paul notes, could be confirmed by those "still living," including Kayfa, who is mentioned as alive, an itinerant exorcist traveling with this wife. Analysis will later show that Kayfa formed the "twelve" after his encounters, and that this collection of exorcists included Magdalene and Cleopas, both named exorcists of Jesus who also privately encountered Jesus post-crucifixion.

These then compose the certain and probable encounters with the risen Jesus.

14

Other Risk Implications
The Messianic Secret and House Churches

This prioritization of recovered risk events is remarkable in that it clearly lays out the "certain" and "probable" events in a chronological sequence that is compelling, and which renders startling clarity as to the return of the Galilean exorcists to the war on Satan, as well as why they would have accepted dramatically heightened perilous risk. In the context of human risk response, the sequence of events recovered using risk and contextual analysis affords us a view into an alien world that explains the emergence and the rise of primitive Christianity. It is a risk track that moves from the charismatic practices of Galilean exorcists at war with Satan, those who disbanded in terror when their Jesus was captured, brutalized and thought annihilated on a cross, to a reconstituted collection of hesitant, but emboldened exorcists following various ecstatic encounters with Jesus post-crucifixion.

Risk and contextual analysis have provided new tools that have helped to isolate and recover the original form of nine "certain" or "probable" risk events from a world alien to our own. These tools are based on human risk response to perilous risk, and remarkably, human acceptance of heightened perilous risk. Risk analysis has recovered reliable events that demonstrate that Jesus was active post-crucifixion with his exorcists in a variety of forms, whether visions, dreams, trance or forms of material presence. These recovered events fostered the emergence of a new, dynamic sect of charismatic Jews in first-century Galilee. Men and women, all exorcists, aggressively sought the overthrow of Satan and demonic imperialism, and recapture of a possessed land.

Their acceptance of heightened risk initiated the intervention of God. The kingdom was both inbreaking through their actions and still fully at hand, as Satan's failure to annihilate Jesus was the sign that he was "falling like lightening." All hope was now in the hands and under the authority of Jesus' reconstituted exorcists of Galilee. Encountering Jesus post-crucifixion defined the practices and signs that were to be employed in the continued battle to overthrow demonic forces until the kingdom vanquished his power. All was at risk, and the peril of failure meant dark victory of evil, annihilation and death. These represent the recovered encounters with Jesus in their original setting as recovered by risk and contextual analysis. These were Jesus, Resurrected.

The final implications of this study reveal the origins of the long debated Messianic Secret controversy, where William Wrede[1] and subsequent scholars debated why Jesus ordered his followers, as well as those he exorcised, to remain silent.[2] Jesus was performing what amounted to dark magic, and post-crucifixion encounters with Jesus were considered communication with a demonized dark magician who was thought destroyed. Mark's gospel in particular expresses the suppression of Jesus' activity as a dark magician. The Messianic Secret was the reflection of this suppression and fear of retribution by authorities and other enemies. The crisis that led to the production of Mark (the Jewish revolt and destruction of Jerusalem) did not need to provide appearances. All that was needed in Mark was an empty tomb—everyone in the ancient world knew what that meant. Jesus would seek retribution as one of the untimely dead. The Son of Man traditions fit perfectly with the retributive Jesus against his enemies and what they had brought on themselves. This ultimately provided the bridge between Jesus' activity as a dark magician and his retributive role as the Son of Man, a messianic figure who would return and also bring the kingdom of God. The refusal of Jesus to admit his messianic role was transposed back to his orders to keep his illegal activity silent.

Paul's attempt to annihilate the church of God, found in house churches, is also now explained.[3] The followers of Jesus associated with an executed dark magician, a criminal, and at first never publicly admitted or announced their association or encounters. Their experiences were limited to cultic meals, where his body and blood provided protection, since he remained active and powerful after death. This body and blood, and his

---

1. Wrede, *Messianic Secret*; this theory has been criticized, but has never been satisfactorily dismissed as invalid; see *The Gospel of Mark*, vol. 2, by Donahue and Harrington (28–29), for example.

2. See Mark 1:43–45, 4:11, 8:29–30.

3. E.g., Paul's own reference to greeting those in the house church in Rom 16:5.

name, was used to continue what was considered illegal, dark magic and charismatic activity. They met secretly in the homes of fellow exorcists and charismatics, relating the experiences of Jesus with demons, ghosts and evil spirits; retelling his words and parables spoken at exorcisms and in confrontations with his enemies; but most importantly, they interpreted his brutal death. He was hobbled and ritually executed, only to survive beyond death. Only God could have allowed this to occur, Jesus having been ritually executed under a divine curse. Visions and trancelike experiences of Jesus in the third heaven[4] confirmed for these charismatic men and women that they must continue with his mission to drive away Satan and bring about the kingdom to God.

There are other implications, from Jesus' saying about bringing the "sword"[5] (the brass and iron sword was thought to drive away and expel demons in his violent war with Satan—one was carried by Kayfa), to the baptism of John in water, the place where demons and evil spirits were captured. Consequently, these findings paint a detailed and valid picture of the origins of Christianity, proving that Jesus was considered to have practiced dark magic, was executed for doing so, and was encountered again unexpectedly, forcing a redefinition of his activity, words and meaning by his remaining exorcists. To deny these unexpected encounters was to deny divine intervention and an active Jesus. This demanded a rejection of everything expected, engendering the gospel and extension of charismatic practices in homes until his retributive return to bring justice.

---

4. See analysis of these ecstatic experiences above, and also Mark 9:2–13 and 2 Corinthians 12:2 for a description, particularly Paul's.

5. Luke 12:51; Matt 10:34.

Bibliography

Adna, Jostein. "The Encounter of Jesus with the Gerasene Demoniac." In *Authenticating the Actions of Jesus*, edited by Bruce Chilton et al., 279–301. Leiden: Brill, 1999.
Allegro, John. *The Dead Sea Scrolls*. New York: Penguin, 1956.
Anderson, Charles C. *The Historical Jesus: A Continuing Quest*. Grand Rapids: Eerdmans, 1972.
Aune, David. *Prophecy in Ancient Christianity and in the Mediterranean World*. Grand Rapids: Eerdmans, 1991.
Avioz, M. *Josephus' Interpretation of the Books of Samuel*. London: T. & T. Clark, 2015.
Avshalom-Govi, Dina, and Arafan Najar. "Migdal." In *Hadashot Arkheologiyot: Excavations and Surveys in Israel* 125 (2013) 121–23.
Bar-Ilan, Meir. "Exorcism by Rabbis: Talmud Sages and Their Magic." Translated by Rachelle Isserow and Saul Isserow. https://faculty.biu.ac.il/~barilm/exorcism.html.
———. "Exorcism of Demons by Rabbis: On the Involvement of Talmudic Sages." *Journal for the Study of Judaism* 16 (1985) 45–92.
Bar-Ilan, T. Canaan. "Haunted Springs and Water Demons in Palestine." *Journal of the Palestine Oriental Society* 1 (1920–21) 153–70.
Barr, James. "Abba Isn't Daddy." *Journal of Theological Studies* 39 (1988) 28–47.
Bauer, Walter. *The Greek English Lexicon of the New Testament and Early Christian Literature*. Chicago: University of Chicago Press, 1979.
Bennema, Cornelius. "The Giving of the Spirit in John 19, 20." In *The Spirit and Christ in New Testament and Christian Theology*, edited by I. Howard Marshall et al., 93–99. Grand Rapids: Eerdmans, 2012.
Berstein, Peter L. *Against the Gods: The Remarkable Story of Risk*. New York: Wiley, 1996.
Betz, Hans Dieter. *Galatians: A Commentary on Paul's Letter to the Churches in Galatia*. Philadelphia: Fortress, 1979.
———. "The Letter to the Galatians." In *The Interpreter's Dictionary of the Bible*, edited by Keith Crim et al., supplementary vol., 352–53. Nashville: Abingdon, 1976.
Boobyer, G. H. *St. Mark and the Transfiguration Story*. Edinburgh: T. & T. Clark, 1942.

Bolt, Peter. "Life, Death and Afterlife in the Greco-Roman World." Chapter 3 of *Life in the Face of Death: The Resurrection Message of the New Testament*, edited by Richard Longenecker. Grand Rapids: Eerdmans, 1998.

Borg, Marcus. *The Lost Gospel of Q: The Original Sayings of Jesus*. Berkley: Ulysses, 1996.

Bornkamm, Gunther. *Jesus of Nazareth*. Translated by James M. Robinson. London: Hodder and Stoughton, 1960.

Bousset, Wilhelm. *Kyrios Christos: A History of Belief in Christ from the Beginnings of Christianity to Irenaeus*. Nashville: Abingdon, 1970.

Bovon, François. *Luke*. Hermeneia. Minneapolis: Fortress, 2002.

Bowker, John. *Jesus and the Pharisees*. London: Cambridge University Press, 1973.

Boxer, B. M. "Wonder-Working and the Rabbinic Tradition: The Case of Hanina ben Dosa." *Journal for the Study of Judaism* 16 (1985) 42–92.

Brooten, Bernadette. *Women Leaders in the Ancient Synagogue*. Brown Judaic Studies 36. Atlanta: Scholars, 1982.

Brown, Raymond. *The Community of the Beloved Disciple*. Mahwah, NJ: Paulist, 1979.

———. "Roles of Women in the Fourth Gospel." *Theological Studies* 36 (1975) 688–99.

Bultmann, Rudolf. *Form Criticism*. Translated by Frederick Grant. New York: Harper, 1962.

———. *The Gospel of John: A Commentary*. Translated by G. R. Beasley-Murray et al. Philadelphia: Westminster, 1971.

———. *History of the Synoptic Tradition*. Translated by John Marsh. Oxford: Blackwell, 1972.

———. *Jesus and the Word*. Translated by Louise Pettibone Smith and Erminie Huntress Laterno. New York: Scribner, 1958.

———. *Primitive Christianity in Its Contemporary Setting*. Translated by R. H. Fuller. New York: Meridian, 1956.

———. *Theology of the New Testament*. Edited by Kendrik Grobel. New York: Scribner, 1955.

Burton, Dan, et al. *Magic, Mystery and Science: The Occult in Western Civilization*. Bloomington: Indian University Press, 2004.

Burton, Ian. *The Perception of Risk*. New York: Taylor and Francis, 2000.

Busse, Roger S. *The Essentials of Commercial Lending*. Portland, OR: WKB, 1995.

———. "The Son of Man in the Synoptic Tradition." BA thesis, Reed College, 1978.

———. *To Be Near the Fire*. Eugene, OR: Wipf & Stock, 2014.

Cameron, Ron. *The Other Gospels: Non-Canonical Gospel Text*. Philadelphia: Westminster, 1982.

Canaan, T. "Haunted Springs and Water Demons in Palestine." *Journal of the Palestine Oriental Society* 1 (1920–21) 153–70.

Castelli, Elizabeth. "Virginity and Its Meaning for Women's Sexuality in Early Christianity." *Journal of Feminist Studies in Religions* 2 (1986) 61–88.

Charlesworth, James H. *Apocalyptic Literature and Testaments*. Vol. 1 of *The Old Testament Pseudepigrapha*. Garden City, NY: Doubleday, 1983.

———. *James, Jesus and Archaeology*. Grand Rapids: Eerdmans, 2006.

———, ed. *Jews and Christians: Exploring the Past, Present and Future*. New York: Crossroad, 1990.

Chase, Frederic. "The Lord's Prayer in the Early Church." In *Texts and Studies: Contributions to Biblical and Patristic Studies*, edited by J. Robinson, vol. 1, no. 3. 1891. Repr., Eugene, OR: Wipf & Stock, 2004.

Chazon, Esther G. "Hymns and Prayers in the Dead Sea Scrolls." In *The Dead Sea Scrolls after Fifty Years*, edited by Peter W. Flint and James C. VanderKam, 244–70. Brill Academic, 1999.

Chestnutt, Randall D. "The Dead Sea Scrolls and the Meal Formula." In *The Dead Sea Scrolls and the Bible: Scripture and the Scrolls*, edited by James Charlesworth, 1:397–401. Waco, TX: Baylor University Press, 2006.

Chijoke Iwe, John. *Jesus in the Synagogue of Capernaum: The Pericope and Its Programmatic*. Rome: Gregorian University Press, 1999.

Cohen, Shaye. *From the Maccabees to the Mishna*. Louisville: John Knox, 2006.

Conzelmann, Hans. *1 Corinthians*. Translated by James W. Leitch. Edited by George MacRae. Philadelphia: Fortress, 1975.

———. *An Outline of the Theology of the New Testament*. Translated by John Bowden. New York: Harper, 1968.

———. *The Theology of St. Luke*. Translated by Geoffrey Buswell. New York: Harper, 1961.

Corcoran, Thomas H. "The Roman Fishing Industry of the Late Republic and Early Empire." PhD diss., Northwestern University, 1957.

Costa, Tony. "Exorcisms and Healings of Jesus within Classical Culture." In *Christian Origins and Greco-Roman Culture*, edited by Andrew Pitts and Stanley Porter, 125–45. Netherlands: Brill, 2013.

Craffert, Peiter. *The Life of a Galilean Shaman: Jesus of Nazareth in Anthropological-Historical Perspective*. Eugene, OR: Cascade, 2008.

Crossan, John Dominick. *The Cross That Spoke: The Origins of the Passion Narrative*. San Francisco: Harper, 1988.

———. *In Fragments: The Aphorisms of Jesus*. New York: Harper, 1983.

———. *The Historical Jesus*. San Francisco: San Francisco: HarperCollins, 1992.

———. *In Parables: The Challenge of the Historical Jesus*. New York: Harper and Row, 1973.

———. *Sayings Parallels: A Workbook for the Jesus Tradition*. Philadelphia: Fortress, 1986.

Cullmann, Oscar. *The Christology of the New Testament*. Translated by Shirley C. Guthrie and Charles A. M. Hall. Philadelphia: Westminster, 1963.

Culpepper, R. Alan. "John 21:24–25: The Johannine Sphragis." In *John, Jesus and History*, edited by Paul N. Anderson et al., 2:349–64. Williston, VT: Society of Biblical Literature, 2009.

D'Angelo, Mary. "Reconstructing 'Real' Women in Gospel Literature: The Case of Mary Magdalene." In *Women and Christian Origins*, edited by Ross Kraemer and Mary D'Angelo, 105–28. New York: Oxford University Press, 1999.

Daube, David. "Jesus and the Samaritan Women." *Journal of Biblical Literature* 69 (1950) 137–47.

Davies, Stevan. *The Gospel of Thomas and Christian Wisdom*. Califorina: Bardic, 2005.

Davies, W. D. *The Setting of the Sermon on the Mount*. London: Cambridge University Press, 1964.

Denaux, Adelbert. *Studies in the Gospel of Luke: Structure, Language, Theology*. Berlin: Lit, 2010.

Dickie, Matthew. *Magic and Magicians in the Greco-Roman World*. London: Routledge, 2001.

Dimant, Devorah, and Uriel Rappaport. *The Dead Sea Scrolls: Forty Years of Research*. Studies on the Texts of the Desert of Judah 10. Jerusalem: Magness, 1992.

Dodd, C. H. *Apostolic Preaching and Its Development*. New York: Harper, 1964.

———. *Parables of the Kingdom*. New York: Scribner, 1961.

Drabek, Tomas E. *Human Systems and Response to Disaster: An Inventory of Sociological Findings*. New York: Springer, 1986.

Ehrman, Bart D. *The New Testament*. Oxford: Oxford University Press, 2004.

———. *Peter, Paul and Mary Magdalene*. Oxford: Oxford University Press, 2006.

Eisenman, Robert. *The Dead Sea Scrolls and the First Christians*. Edison, NJ: Cascade, 1996.

———. *James the Brother of Jesus*. New York: Viking, 1997.

Eshel, Esther. "Jesus the Exorcist in Light of Epigraphic Sources." In *Jesus and Archaeology*, edited by James Charlesworth, 183–85. Grand Rapids: Eerdmans, 2006.

Evans, Craig A. "Jesus and the Jewish Miracle Stories." In *Jesus and His Contemporaries*, 214–43. New York: Brill, 1995.

———. "Jesus and Psalm 91 in Light of the Exorcism Scrolls." In *Celebrating the Dead Sea Scrolls: A Canadian Contribution*, edited by Peter W. Flint et al., 541–55. Atlanta: Society of Biblical Literature, 2011.

Farmer, William. *The Synoptic Problem: A Critical Analysis*. London: Macmillan, 1976.

Felton, D. *Haunted Greece and Rome: Ghost Stories from Classical Antiquity*. University of Texas Press, 1999.

Finkelstein, Louis. *The Pharisees: The Sociological Background of Their Faith*. Vols. 1 and 2. Philadelphia: Jewish Publication Society of America, 1946.

Fishoff, Baruch, et al. *Acceptable Risk*. London: Cambridge University Press, 1984.

Fitzmyer, Joseph A. *The Dead Sea Scrolls and Christian Origins*. Grand Rapids: Eerdmans, 2000.

———. *Gospel according to Luke X–XXV*. New York: Doubleday, 2007.

Foerster, Werner. *From the Exile to Christ: A Historical Introduction to Palestinian Judaism*. Translated by Gordon E. Harris. Philadelphia: Fortress, 1964.

Fortuna, Robert. *The Fourth Gospel and Its Predecessor*. Philadelphia: Fortress, 2007.

Frayer-Griggs, Daniel. "Spittle, Clay and Creation in John 9:6 and Some of the Dead Sea Scrolls." *Journal of Biblical Literature* 132 (2013) 659–70.

Freyne, Sean. "The Charismatic." In *Ideal Figures in Ancient Judaism-Profiles and Paradigms*, edited by G. W. E. Nickelsburg and J. J. Collins, 223–58. Chico, CA: Society of Biblical Literature, 1980.

———. *Galilee, Jesus and the Gospels*. Philadelphia: Fortress, 1988.

———. "The Geography, Politics, and Economics of Galilee and the Quest for the Historical Jesus." In *Studying the Historical Jesus: Evaluations of the State of Current Research*, edited by Bruce Chilton and Craig A. Evans, 75–121. Leiden: Brill, 1995.

———. "Herodian Economics in Galilee." In *Modeling Early Christianity*, edited by Phillip Esler, 23–46. New York: Routledge, 1995.

———. *Jesus, a Jewish Galilean: A New Reading of the Jesus Story*. New York: T. & T. Clark, 2004.

———. "Jewish Immersion and Christian Baptism: Continuity on the Margins?" In *Ablution, Initiation and Baptism: Late Antiquity*, edited by David Hellholm, 1:221–53. Grand Rapids: Eerdmans, 2009.

———. "Urban-Rural Relations in First-Century Galilee: Some Suggestions from the Literary Sources." In *The Galilee in Late Antiquity*, edited by Lee I. Levine, 75–91. New York: Jewish Theological Seminary of America, 1992.

Funk, Robert W., and the Jesus Seminar. *The Acts of Jesus: The Search for the Authentic Deeds of Jesus*. San Francisco: Harper, 1998.

Furnish, Victor Paul. *2 Corinthians*. Garden City, NY: Doubleday, 1984.

———. *The Love Command in the New Testament*. New York: Abingdon, 1972.

Gager, John. "The Social Practice of Magic in the Ancient Greco-Roman World." In *Philadelphia Seminar on Christian Origins*, vol. 14, set 1 minutes, October 5, 1976.

Gerhardsson, Birger. "Memory and Manuscript: Oral Tradition and Written Transmission in Rabbinic Judaism and Early Christianity." PhD diss., Uppsala, 1961.

———. *The Origins of the Gospel Traditions*. Philadelphia: Fortress, 1979.

Georgi, Dieter. "Forms of Religious Propaganda." In *Jesus in His Time*, edited by Hans Schultz, translated by Brian Watchorn, 123–31. Philadelphia: Fortress, 1971.

Gibson, Shimon. *The Final Days of Jesus: The Archaeological Evidence*. New York: Harper, 2009.

Goldberg, Gary. "The Coincidences of the Emmaus Narrative of Luke and the *Testimonium* of Josephus." *Journal for the Study of the Pseudepigrapha* 13 (1995) 59–77.

Grant, R. M. "One Hundred Fifty Three Fishes (John 21,11)." *Harvard Theological Review* 49 (1949) 273–75.

Graves-Brown, Carolyn. *Dancing for Hathor: Women in Ancient Egypt*. Auklund, New Zealand: MPG, 2010.

Greenhut, Zvi, "The 'Caiaphas' Tomb in North Talpiyot, Jerusalem." In *Ancient Jerusalem Revealed*, edited by H. Geva, 63–71. Jerusalem: Israel Exploration Society, 1994.

Hachlili, Rachel. *Jewish Funerary Customs, Practices and Rites in the Second Temple Period*. Boston: Brill, 2005.

Hanson, K. C. "The Galilean Fishing Economy and the Jesus Tradition." *Biblical Theology Bulletin* 27 (1997) 99–111. Available at http://www.kchanson.com/ARTICLES/fishing.html.

Hanson, K. C., and David C. Oakman. *Palestine in the Time of Jesus: Social Structures and Social Conflicts*. 2nd ed. Minneapolis: Fortress, 2008.

———. "The Social Impact and Implications of Herod's Temple, Temple and Elite." In *Palestine in the Time of Jesus*, 146–51.

Hartvigsen, Kirsten Marie. "Matthew 28:16–20 and Mark 16:9–20: Different Ways of Relating Baptism to the Joint Mission of God, John the Baptism, Jesus, and Their Adherents." In *Ablution, Initiation and Baptism: Late Antiquity, Early Judaism*, edited by David Hellholm et al., 657–709. Berlin: de Gruyter, 2011.

Hengel, Martin. *Crucifixion*. Philadelphia: Fortress, 1977.

———. *The Four Gospels and the One Gospel of Jesus Christ: An Investigation of the Collection and Origin of the Canonical Gospels*. Harrisburg, PA: Trinity, 2000.

———. *The Son of God: The Origin of Christology and the History of Jewish Hellenistic Religion*. Philadelphia: Fortress, 1976.

Hock, Ronald F. *The Social Context of Paul's Ministry: Tentmaking and Apostleship.* Philadelphia, Fortress, 1980.
Horsley, Richard. *Archaeology, History and Society in Galilee.* Valley Forge, PA: Trinity, 1996.
———. "High Priests and the Politics of Roman Palestine." *Journal for the Study of Judaism in the Persian, Hellenistic and Roman Period* 17 (1986) 23–55.
———. *Jesus and the Spiral of Violence.* San Francisco: Harper, 1987.
———. *The Message and the Kingdom.* Minneapolis: Fortress: 1997.
Horsley, Richard, and John Hanson. *Bandits, Prophets and Messiahs.* San Francisco: Harper, 1985.
Hull, John M. *Hellenistic Magic and the Synoptic Tradition.* Studies in Biblical Theology, 2nd ser. London: SCM, 1974.
Hyman, Aaron. *Sefer Toledot Tannaim we-Amoraim* [The history of the Tannaim and Amoraim]. 3 vols. Jerusalem, 1964.
Isaac, E. "(Ethiopic Apocalypse of) Enoch (Second Century B.C.-First Century A.D.)." In Charlesworth, *Apocalyptic Literature and Testaments*, 5–89.
Jackson, H. M. "Ancient Self-Referential Conventions." *JTS* 50 (1999) 1–34.
Janowitz, Naomi. *Magic in the Roman World.* London: Routledge, 2001.
Jenott, Lance. *The Gospel of Judas.* Studien un Texte zu Antike und Christentum. Tubigen: Seibek, 2011.
Jeremias, Joachim. *Abba.* Gottingen: Vandenhoeck & Ruprecht, 1966.
———. *The Central Message of the New Testament.* Philadelphia, Fortress, 1965.
———. *The Eucharistic Words of Jesus.* London: SCM, 1966.
———. *Jerusalem in the Time of Jesus.* Philadelphia: Fortress, 1967.
———. *Jesus' Promise to the Nations.* London: SCM, 1956.
———. *New Testament Theology: The Proclamation of Jesus.* NewYork: Scribner, 1971.
———. *The Parables of Jesus.* New York: Scribner, 1972.
———. *The Prayers of Jesus.* London: SCM, 1967.
———. *The Problem of the Historical Jesus.* Philadelphia: Fortress, 1964.
———. *Rediscovering the Parables of Jesus.* New York: Scribner, 1966.
Johnson, Maxwell. *The Rites of Christian Initiation: Their Evolution and Interpretation.* Minneapolis: Order of St. Benedict College, 2007.
Kasemann, E. *Testament of Jesus: Study of the Gospel of John in the Light of Chapter 17.* Translated by G. Krodel. Philadelphia: Fortress, 1978.
Kee, H. C. *The Origins of Christianity: Sources and Documents.* Englewood Cliffs, NJ: Prentice Hall, 1973.
———. "Testament of the Twelve Patriarchs." In Charlesworth, *Apocalyptic Literature and Testaments*, 775–828.
———. "The Transfiguration in Mark." In *Understanding the Sacred Text*, edited by John Reumann, 85–94. Valley Forge, PA: Judson Press, 1972.
Kahneman, Daniel, et al. *Judgment Under Uncertainty: Heuristics and Biases.* Cambridge: Cambridge University Press, 1982.
Kelber, Werner H. *The Oral and the Written Gospel: The Hermeneutics of Speaking and Writing in the Synoptic Tradition, Mark, Paul and Q.* Philadelphia: Fortress, 1983.
King, Karen. *The Gospel of Mary: The First Woman Apostle.* Santa Rosa, CA: Polebridge, 2003.
Kloppenborg, John. *Excavating Q: The History and Setting of the Sayings Gospel.* Minneapolis: Augsburg, 2000.

———. *The Formation of Q*. Philadelphia: Fortress, 1989.
Kloppenborg, John, et al. *Q-Thomas Reader*. Sonoma, CA: Polebridge, 1990.
Klutz, Todd. *The Exorcism Stories in Luke-Acts: A Sociostylistic Reading*. Society for New Testament Studies Monograph Series 120. Cambridge: Cambridge University Press, 2004.
Koch, Klaus. *The Growth of the Biblical Tradition: The Form-Critical Method*. Translated by S. M. Cupitt. New York: Scribner, 1969.
Koester, Helmut. *Ancient Christian Gospels: Their History and Development*. Philadelphia: Trinity, 1992.
———. *From Jesus to the Gospels*. Philadelphia: Fortress, 2007.
———. "GNOMAI DIAPHOROI: The Origin and Nature of Diversification in the History of Early Christianity." In *Trajectories through Early Christianity*, edited by H. Koester and J. M. Robinson, 114–57. Philadelphia: Fortress, 1971.
———. "The Historical Jesus: Some Comments and Thoughts on Norman Perrin's Rediscovering the Teachings of Jesus." In *Christology and a Modern Pilgrimage: A Discussion with Norman Perrin*, edited by Hans Deiter Betz. Missoula: Scholars, 1974.
———. *Introduction to the New Testament: History and Literature of Early Christianity*. Vol. 2. Philadelphia: Fortress, 1984.
———. "The Memory of Jesus' Death and the Worship of the Risen Lord." *Harvard Theological Review* 91 (1998) 335–50.
———. "One Jesus and Four Primitive Gospels." In *Trajectories through Early Christianity*, edited by H. Koester and J. M. Robinson, 158–204. Philadelphia: Fortress, 1971.
———. "The Structure and Criteria of Early Christian Beliefs." In *Trajectories through Early Christianity*, edited by H. Koester and J. M. Robinson, 205–31. Philadelphia: Fortress, 1971.
Kraemer, Ross. *Her Share of the Blessings: Women's Religions among Pagans, Jews, and Christians in the Greco-Roman World*. Oxford: Oxford University Press, 1992.
———. *Maenads, Martyrs, Matrons, Monastics: A Sourcebook on Women's Religions in the Graeco-Roman World*. Philadelphia: Fortress, 1988.
Kummel, Werner Georg. *Introduction to the New Testament*. Translated by H. C. Keen. Nashville: Abingdon, 1975.
Lauterbach, Jacob. *Rabbinic Essays*. New York: Ktav, 1973.
Layton, Bentley. *The Gnostic Scriptures: A New Translation with Annotations and Introductions by Bentley Layton*. Garden City, NY: Doubleday, 1987.
Lewis, I. M. *Ecstatic Religion: An Anthropological Study of Spirit Possession and Shamanism*. Middlesex, UK: Penguin, 1971.
Lichtenberger, Herman. "Demonology in the Dead Sea Scrolls and the New Testament." In *Text, Thought, and Practice in Qumran and Early Christianity*, edited by Ruth A. Clements and Daniel R. Schwartz, 267–80. Studies on the Texts of the Desert of Judah 84. Leiden: Brill, 2009. Abstract available at http://orion.mscc.huji.ac.il/symposiums/9th/papers/LichtenbergerAbstract.html.
Litwa, M. David. *Iesus Deus: The Early Christian Depiction of Jesus as a Mediterranean God*. Philadelphia: Fortress, 2014.
Longenecker, Richard N. *Biblical Exegesis in the Apostolic Period*. Grand Rapids: Eerdmans, 1975.

Lohse, Eduard. *Colossians and Philemon*. Edited by Helmut Koester. Translated by William R. Poehlmann and Robert J. Karris. Philadelphia: Fortress, 1971.

Luedemann, Gerd. *The Resurrection of Jesus*. Philadelphia: Fortress, 1994.

Luijendijk, Annemarie. *Forbidden Oracles? The Gospel of the Lots of Mary*. Studien und Texte zu Antike und Christentum 89. Tubingen: Seibeck, 2014.

Lunn, Nicholas P. *The Original Ending of Mark: A New Case for the Authenticity of Mark 16:9–20*. Eugene, OR: Pickwick, 2014.

Maccini, Robert. *Here Testimony Is True: Women as Witnesses in the Gospel of John*. Sheffield, UK: Sheffield Academic, 1996.

Madden, Patrick J. "Jesus Walking on the Sea: An Investigation of the Origin of the Narrative Account." *Beihefte zur Zeitschrift fuer die neutestamentliche Wissenschaft* 81 (1997) 30–156.

Malina, Bruce, and Richard Robaugh. *Social Science Commentary on the Gospel of John*. Philadelphia: Fortress, 1998.

Marshall, I. Howard. *New Testament Interpretation*. Grand Rapids:Eerdmans, 1977.

———. *The Origins of New Testament Christology*. Downers Grove: InterVarsity, 1976.

Marxsen, Willi. *The Resurrection of Jesus of Nazareth*. Philadelphia: Fortress, 1971.

McCrae, George. "The Jewish Background of the Gnostic Sophia Myth." *Novum Testamentum* 12 (1970) 81–101.

McDowell, Marcus. *Prayers of Jewish Women: Studies of Patterns of Prayer in the Second Temple*. Tubigen: Seibeck, 2006.

Meeks, Wayne A. *The First Urban Christians: The Social World of the Apostle Paul*. New Haven: Yale University Press, 1983.

Meier, John. *A Marginal Jew: Rethinking the Historical Jesus*. Vol. 1. New York: Doubleday, 1991.

Mekkattukunnel, A. "The Priestly Blessing of the Risen Christ: An Exegetico-Theological Analysis of Luke 24:50–53." *European University Studies* 23 (2001) 711–14.

Metzger, Bruce M. "The Fourth Book of Ezra." In Charlesworth, *Apocalyptic Literature and Testaments*, 517–60.

———. *Lexical Aids for Students of New Testament Greek*. Self published, Princeton, 1946.

———. *The Text of the New Testament: Its Transmission, Corruption and Restoration*. Oxford: Oxford University Press, 1968.

Meyer, Marvin. "Making Mary Male: The Categories 'Male' and 'Female' in the Gospel of Thomas." *New Testament Studies* 31 (1985) 554–70.

Morrison, Gregg. *The Turning Point in Mark*. Eugene, OR: Pickwick, 2014.

Neyrey, Jerome. "The Loss of Wealth, the Loss of Family, the Loss of Honor: A Cultural Interpretation of the Original Four Makarisms." In *Modelling Early Christianity: Social-Scientific Studies of the New Testament in Its Context*, edited by Phillip Esler, 139–49. New York: Routledge, 1995.

Nickelsburg, George. *Jewish Literature between the Bible and the Mishnah: A Historical and Literary Introduction*. Philadelphia: Fortress, 1981.

Nickelsburg, George, and J. J. Collins, eds. *Ideal Figures in Ancient Judaism-Profiles and Paradigms*. Chico, CA: Scholars, 1980.

Nun, Mendel. "Cast Your Net upon the Waters: Fish and Fishermen in Jesus' Time." *Biblical Archaeology Review* 19 (1993) 46–56, 70.

———. "Let Down Your Nets." *Jerusalem Perspective* 24 (1990) 11–13.

———. "Ports of Galilee." *Biblical Archaeology Review* 25 (1999) 19–31.

———. *The Sea of Galilee and Its Fishermen in the New Testament.* Ein Gev, Isreal: Kinnereth, 1989.

Oakman, Douglas E. "The Archaeology of First-Century Galilee and the Social Interpretation of the Historical Jesus." In *Society of Biblical Literature 1994 Seminar Papers*, edited by E. H. Lovering Jr., 220–51. Atlanta: Scholars, 1994.

———. *Jesus and the Economic Questions of His Day.* Studies in the Bible and Early Christianity 8. Lewiston, NY: Mellen, 1989.

Ogden, Daniel. *Magic, Witchcraft and Ghosts in the Greek and Roman World.* Oxford: Oxford University Press, 2009.

Pagels, E. *The Gnostic Gospels.* New York: Random House, 1979.

———. "Visions, Appearances and Apostolic Authority: Gnostic and Orthodox Traditions." In *Gnosis*, edited by U. Bianchi et al. Gottengen: Vandenhoeck and Ruprecht, 1978.

Parásso, G. M. "A Lease of Fishing Rights." *Aegyptus* 67 (1987) 89–93.

Parsons, Mikeal. "Narrative Closure and Openness in the Plot of the Third Gospel: The Sense of Ending in Luke 24:50–53." In *Society of Biblical Literature 1986 Seminar Papers*, edited by Kent H. Richards, 203–22. Atlanta: Scholars, 1986.

Patterson, Stephen J. *Beyond the Passion: Rethinking the Death and Life of Jesus.* Minneapolis: Fortress, 2004.

———. *The God of Jesus.* Harrisburg, PA: Trinity, 1998.

———. *The Gospel of Thomas and Christian Origins.* Boston: Brill, 2013.

———. *The Gospel of Thomas and Jesus.* Sonoma, CA: Polebridge, 1993.

———. "Jesus Meets Plato: The Theology of the Gospel of Thomas and Middle Platonism." In *Das Thomasevangelium: Entstehung.* Berlin: de Gruyter, 2008.

———. *The Lost Way.* New York: Harper, 2014.

———. "Paul and the Jesus Tradition: It's Time for Another Look." *HTR* 84 (1991) 23–41.

Pearson, Birger A. *Gnosticism, Judaism and Egyptian Christianity.* Philadelphia: Fortress, 1990.

———. *The Pneumatikos-Psychikos Terminology in 1 Corinthians: A Study in the Theology of the Corinthian Opponents of Paul and Its Relation to Gnosticism.* Missoula, MT: SBL, for the Nag Hammadi Seminar, 1973.

Penny, D. L. "By the Power of Beelzebub: An Aramaic Incantation Formula from Qumran." *Journal of Biblical Literature* 114 (1994) 620–50.

Perrin, Norman. *Christology and a Modern Pilgrimage: A Discussion with Norma Perrin.* Edited by Hans Deiter Betz. Missoula, MT: SBL/Scholars, 1974.

———. "The Composition of Mark IX, 1." *Novum Testamentum* 11 (1969) 67–70.

———. *Introduction to the New Testament.* New York: Harcourt, Brace, Jovanovich, 1974.

———. *Jesus and the Language of the Kingdom.* Philadelphia: Fortress, 1976.

———. *Rediscovering the Teachings of Jesus.* New York: Harper, 1976.

———. *The Resurrection according to Matthew, Mark, and Luke.* Philadelphia: Fortress, 1977.

———. "Towards an Interpretation of the Gospel of Mark." In Perrin, *Christology and a Modern Pilgrimage*, 1–78.

Philostratus. *The Life of Apollonius of Tyana.* Translated by F. C. Conybeare. Loeb Classical Library. Cambridge: Harvard University Press, 1969.

Pidgeon, Nick, et al. *The Social Amplification of Risk*. Cambridge: Cambridge University Press, 2003.

Pilcher, John. "The Transfiguration of Jesus: An Experience in Alternate Reality." In *Modelling Early Christianity: Social-Scientific Studies of the New Testament in its Context*, edited by Philip Esler, 47–61. London: Routledge, 1995.

Plessis, Paul du. *Borkowski's Textbook on Roman Law*. London: Oxford University Press, 2005.

Plummer, Alfred. *The Gospel according to S. Luke*. Edinburgh: T. & T. Clark, 1975.

Raban, Avner. "The Boat from Migdal Nunia and the Anchorages of the Sea of Galilee from the Time of Jesus." *International Journal of Nautical Archaeology and Underwater Exploration* 17 (1988) 311–29.

Reed, Jonathan. *The Population of Capernaum*. Occasional Papers, Institute for Antiquity and Christianity 24. Claremont, CA: Institute for Antiquity and Christianity, 1992.

Renan, Ernst. *Vie de Jesus*. France: Calmann-Levy, 1960.

Reynolds, Benjamin. *The Apocalyptic Son of Man in the Gospel of John*. Tubingen: Siebeck, 2008.

Robinson, James M. "Jesus: From Easter to Valentinus (Or to the Apostle's Creed)." *Journal of Biblical Literature* 101 (1982) 3–5.

———. *The Nag Hammadi Library in English*. Leiden: Brill, 1988.

———. *A New Quest for the Historical Jesus*. New York: Macmillan, 1968.

———. "On the Gattung of Mark (and John)." In *Jesus and Man's Hope*, edited by David Buttrick, 1:116–18. Pittsburg: Pittsburg Theological Seminary, 1970.

———. *The Problem of History in Mark*. London: SCM, 1957.

Ross, M. "One Hundred and Fifty Three Fishes." *Expository Times* 100 (1988) 374–45.

Rothschild, Clare C. *Baptist Traditions and Q*. Wissenshaftliche Untersuchungen zum Neuen Testament 190. Tubingen: Mohr Sieback, 2005.

Rousseau, John. "Exorcism." In *Jesus and His World: An Archaeological and Cultural Dictionary*, edited by John Rousseau and Rami Arav, 178–79. Minneapolis: Augsburg, 1995.

Sanders, E. P. *The Historical Figure of Jesus*. London: Penguin, 1993.

———. *Paul and Palestinian Judaism: A Comparison of Patterns of Religion*. London: SCM, 1977.

Sanders, Jack T. *The New Testament Christological Hymns: Their Historical Religious Background*. Edited by Matthew Black. Cambridge: Cambridge University Press, 1971.

Sandmel, Samuel. *A Jewish Understanding of the New Testament*. New York: University Publishers, 1956.

Scharlemann, M. S. "Transfiguration." In *The International Bible Encyclopedia*, edited by Geoffrey Bromiley, 4:886–88. Grand Rapids: Eerdmans, 1988.

Schmithals, Walter. *Gnosticism in Corinth: An Investigation of the Letters to the Corinthians*. Translated by John E. Steely. New York: Abingdon, 1971.

Schweitzer, Albert. *The Mysticism of Paul the Apostle*. New York: Seabury, 1968.

———. *The Quest of the Historical Jesus*. Translated by F. C. Burkitt. Baltimore: Johns Hopkins University Press, 1998.

Shillington, George. *Jesus and Paul Before Christianity: Their World and Work in Retrospect*. Eugene, OR: Cascade, 2011.

Sim, David C. *Apocalyptic Eschatology in the Gospel of Matthew*. Cambridge: Cambridge University Press, 1996.

Slovic, Paul. "Perception of Risk." *Science* 236 (1987) 280–85.

Slovic, Paul, et al. "Risk as Analysis and Risk as Feeling: Some Thoughts about Risk as Affect, Reason, Risk, and Rationality." *Risk Analysis* 24 (2004) 311–22.

———. "Trust, Emotion, Sex, Politics, and Science: Surveying the Risk Assessment Battlefield." *Risk Analysis* 19 (1999) 689–700.

Smith, David. *"Hand This Man Over to Satan": Curse Exclusion and Salvation in 1 Corinthians 5*. London: T. & T. Clark, 2008.

Smith, Morton. *Clement of Alexandria and a Secret Gospel of Mark*. Cambridge: Harvard University Press, 1973.

———. *Jesus the Magician*. San Francisco: Harper, 1978.

Snapp, James, Jr. *Authentic: The Case for Mark 16:9–20*. Self-published, 2011. Kindle edition.

Stein, Robert H. "Is the Transfiguration (Mark 9:2–8) a Misplaced Resurrection Account." *Journal of Biblical Literature* 95 (1976) 88–89.

Stern, Ephraim, ed. *The New Encyclopedia of Archaeological Excavations in the Holy Land*. Vol. 3. Jerusalem: Israel Exploration Society, 1993.

Strauss, David Friedrich. *The Life of Jesus Critically Examined*. Edited by Peter C. Hodgson. Translated by George Eliot. Philadelphia: Fortress, 1972.

Streeter, B. H. *The Four Gospels*. London: McMillan, 1951.

Strugnell, John. "A Plea for a Conjectural Emendation in the New Testament with a Coda on 1 Corinthians 4:6." *Catholic Bible Quarterly* 36 (1974) 555–58.

Suggs, M. Jack. *Wisdom, Christology, and Law in Matthew's Gospel*. Cambridge: Harvard University Press, 1970.

Taylor, Joan. "The Name Iskarioth." *Journal of Biblical Literature* 129 (2010) 369–85.

Thatcher, Tom. "I Have Conquered the World." In *Empire in the New Testament*, edited by Stanley Porter et al., 140–63. Eugene, OR: Pickwick, 2011.

Theissen, Gerd. *The Social Setting of Pauline Christianity: Essays on Corinth*. Edited and translated by John H. Schutz. Philadelphia: Fortress, 1982.

Throckmorton, Burton, Jr., ed. *Gospel Parallels: A Synopsis of the First Three Gospels*. New York: Nelson, 1957.

Todt, H. E. *The Son of Man in the Synoptic Tradition*. Translated by Dorothea M. Barton. London: SCM, 1963.

Tomson, Peter. "The Johannine 'Jews.'" In *Anti-Judaism in the Fourth Gospel*, edited by Reimund Bieringer, 197–99. Louisville: Westminster John Knox, 2001.

Van der Toom, Karel, et al. *Dictionary of Demons and Deities in the Bible*. Boston: Brill, 1999.

Van Wahlde, Urban. *Gnosticism, Docetism and Judaisms in the First Century*. London: T. & T. Clark, 2015.

Vermes, Geza. *The Changing Faces of Jesus*. New York: Viking, 2001.

———. "Hanina ben Dosa." In *Post Biblical Jewish Studies*, 178–214. Studies in Judaism in Late Antiquity 8. Leiden: Brill, 1975.

———. *Jesus the Jew: A Historian's Reading of the Gospels*. London: Collins, 1977.

———. *Post-Biblical Jewish Studies*. Leiden: Brill, 1975.

Wachsmann, Shelley. *The Sea of Galilee Boat: A 2000 Year Old Discovery from the Sea of Legends*. Cambridge, MA: Perseus, 2000.

Wassertein, Abraham, ed. *Flavius Josephus: Selections from His Works*. New York: Viking, 1974.

Weeden, T. J. "The Heresy That Necessitated Mark's Gospel." *Zeitschrift fur die neutestamentliche Wissenshaft* 59 (1968) 145–48.

Wells, George. *The Historical Evidence for Jesus*. Amherst, NY: Prometheus, 1982.

Willis, Wendell Lee. *Idol Meat in Corinth: The Pauline Argument in 1 Corinthians 8 and 10*. Eugene, OR: Wipf & Stock, 2004.

Wrede, William. *The Messianic Secret*. Translated by James C. G. Grieg. Cambridge: James, 1971.

Wright, David F. *The Historical Jesus*. Edited by Craig Evans. London: Routledge, 2004.

Wuellner, Wilhelm H. *The Meaning of "Fishers of Men."* New Testament Library. Philadelphia: Westminster, 1967.

www.ingramcontent.com/pod-product-compliance
Lightning Source LLC
Chambersburg PA
CBHW050434240426
43661CB00055B/2382